MONETARY THEORY AND POLICY

MILTON H. MARQUIS
Florida State University

WEST PUBLISHING COMPANY

Minneapolis/Saint Paul   New York   Los Angeles   San Francisco

To my parents, Harold and Ina Marquis

PRODUCTION CREDITS
Copyediting: Emily McNamara
Text Design: John Edeen
Illustration: Visual Graphics Systems
Composition: Parkwood Composition, Inc.

Production, Prepress, Printing and Binding by West Publishing Company.

WEST'S COMMITMENT TO THE ENVIRONMENT
In 1906, West Publishing Company began recycling materials left over from the production of books. This began a tradition of efficient and responsible use of resources. Today, 100% of our legal bound volumes are printed on acid-free, recycled paper consisting of 50% new paper pulp and 50% paper that has undergone a de-inking process. We also use vegetable-based inks to print all of our books. West recycles nearly 22,650,000 pounds of scrap paper annually—the equivalent of 187,500 trees. Since the 1960s, West has devised ways to capture and recycle waste inks, solvents, oils, and vapors created in the printing process. We also recycle plastics of all kinds, wood, glass, corrugated cardboard, and batteries, and have eliminated the use of polystyrene book packaging. We at West are proud of the longevity and the scope of our commitment to the environment.

West pocket parts and advance sheets are printed on recyclable paper and can be collected and recycled with newspapers. Staples do not have to be removed. Bound volumes can be recycled after removing the cover.

♻ PRINTED ON 10% POST CONSUMER RECYCLED PAPER   Printed with **Printwise** Environmentally Advanced Water Washable Ink   ∞

British Library Cataloguing-in-Publication Data. A catalogue record for this book is available from the British Library.

Library of Congress Cataloging-in-Publication Data
Marquis, Milton H., 1948—
    Monetary theory and policy / Milton Marquis.
        p.   cm.
    Includes index.
    ISBN 0-314-06923-2 (hardcover : alk. paper)
        1. Monetary policy. 2. Money. 3. Monetary policy—United States—History—20th century. 4. Board of Governors of the Federal Reserve System (U.S.) I. Title.
HG230.3.M356 1996
332.4—dc20   95-42064
                                                              CIP

CONTENTS

PART III EQUILIBRIUM ANALYSIS 169

9 "FULL EMPLOYMENT" AND MONETARY POLICY NEUTRALITY 170

10 ECONOMIC FLUCTUATIONS AND MONETARY ACCOMMODATION 199

11 STABILIZATION POLICY WHEN FIRMS SET PRICES IN ADVANCE 219

12 STABILIZATION POLICY IN THE PRESENCE OF LONG-TERM NOMINAL WAGE CONTRACTS 244

PART IV DESCRIPTIVE DYNAMICS AND INFLATION 275

13 A CRITIQUE OF STABILIZATION POLICY 276

14 MONETARY RULES 294

15   INFLATION AND SEIGNIORAGE: WHAT IS OPTIMAL?   310

PART V   THE MECHANICS OF POLICY AND POLICY-MAKING   323

16   OPTIMAL TARGETING AND THE RESPONSE OF FINANCIAL MARKETS   324

17   DESK OPERATIONS AND THE REPO MARKET FOR TREASURIES   348

18   TIME INCONSISTENCY AND THE CREDIBILITY OF MONETARY POLICY   362

PREFACE

The material in this book was assembled in large measure from lecture notes for an upper division undergraduate course in monetary economics that I taught for eight of the past 10 years at Florida State University. During the remaining two of those 10 years, when much of the manuscript for the book was prepared, I worked as an economist in the Monetary Affairs Division of the Board of Governors of the Federal Reserve System. The latter experience illuminated for me the tension between the many practical problems involved in policy making and the fundamental issues that are the principal focus of contemporary research in monetary economics. That tension is reflected somewhat in this book, where an attempt has been made to remain true to the modern general equilibrium paradigm in which current research is conducted while recognizing, wherever possible, the important institutional factors and the inherent economic uncertainty that render monetary policy decision making something other than the practice of pure science.

I wanted the book to be generally "self-contained" in terms of coverage of the various topics in monetary economics. As a result, much of the material normally covered in a generic money and banking course (to the extent that one exists) is included in addition to more advanced topics, although the treatment is often at a slightly higher intermediate level. The book therefore may be suitable for a money and banking course if that course is sequenced after the intermediate macroeconomic theory course in the student's curriculum.

Part I provides the basics for the subsequent development of issues in monetary theory and policy. Chapter 1 describes monetary versus barter economies within a strictly nonmathematical general equilibrium context to emphasize the role of money in solving the basic trading frictions that naturally arise in decentralized markets. It provides a background for many of the subsequent discussions ranging from optimal monetary policy to the endogenous development of financial institutions to monetary policy effectiveness. Chapter 2 shifts from an abstract economy to the Federal Reserve's definitions of money. The primary focus is why certain aggregates were selected and how they have evolved over time. Chapter 3 then gives theoretical background on money demand and velocity and portrays the historic behavior of velocity for the aggregates described in the preceding chapter. Chapter 4 introduces capital asset valuation formulas and the theory of the term structure of interest rates.

Part II pertains to institutions. Chapter 5 examines the various market frictions associated with intertemporal trading, that is, those involving credit, with reference to the general equilibrium environment of Chapter 1. Chapter 6 then describes how an array of financial institutions has emerged to fill the market niches created by the basic trading frictions. Chapter 7 is a relatively standard discussion of the money multiplier process associated with an open market operation, although it includes some additional institutional information beyond what is normally found in standard money and banking texts. Chapter 8 briefly describes the evolution of the Federal Reserve as the nation's monetary authority with a policy-making mandate.

Parts III and IV of the text give an intermediate-level treatment of many of the important topics in monetary theory and policy. The "core" theory chapters are in Part III. The basic theoretical model is a graphic depiction of a representative agent economy. The model is assembled in Chapter 9 and the "classical" result of "policy neutrality" is established. The model is used as a frame of reference for much of the subsequent discussion of macroeconomic fluctuations and the consequences of monetary policy actions. In Chapter 10, the responses of the economy to permanent productivity shocks and to transitory preference shocks are described and a policy of monetary accommodation is discussed in the context of stabilization objectives. Chapter 11 reexamines the model when prices are set in advance, which raises the possibility of a constructive "stabilization policy" role for the central bank with respect to the real economy. Examples are given of policy mistakes caused by a "signal extraction problem," which is created by transitory preference shocks and which the monetary authority must confront. Chapter 12 introduces Keynesian-like rigidities in the labor market, as well as long-lived preference shocks that eventually die out. The consequences for monetary policy are then examined.

Part IV addresses major issues that have been perennial sources of debate over the proper conduct of monetary policy. In Chapter 13, the monetarist criticism of stabilization policy is described with a focus on the very practical problems facing a monetary authority that attempts it. Chapter 14 examines monetary rules versus discretion. In Chapter 15, many views on what the "optimal" inflation rate ought to be are offered, including a description of seigniorage as a source of government revenue.

Part V addresses additional aspects of policy making. Chapter 16 begins the discussion of the mechanics of monetary policy with an analysis of optimal targeting and the historical targeting regimes selected by the Federal Reserve in recent years. Targeting is described within the context of choices of policy instruments (etc.), and subsequent discussion examines how efficient financial markets respond to policy announcements and/or policy actions and to other policy-related "news." Added to this discussion is an overview of the recent literature on "base drift." Chapter 17 explores open market operations in more detail. It includes descriptions of the RP market for government securities, its relation to the federal funds market, and the (implementation) decisions made by the Desk about the optimal mix and timing of RPs, MSPs, and outright purchases. Chapter 18 explains the time inconsistency problem of optimal monetary policy, which is then related to the issues of credibility and the inflation bias in monetary policy. The chapter closes with a discussion of the provisions in the optimal contract that would induce a monetary authority to eliminate its inflation bias while continuing to operate within a discretionary policy regime.

The book has benefited greatly from the suggestions of individuals who reviewed all or selected chapters or commented on the overall project. I particularly thank Randall Holcombe, Barry Hirsch, George Macesich, Kislaya Prasad, and Allen Lynch (Florida State University), Kevin Reffett (Arizona State University), David VanHoose (University of Alabama), Fred Thum (University of Texas), Benjamin Kim (University of Nebraska), Charles Hultman (University of Kentucky), Jose C. Blanco (Utah State University), Ronnie J. Phillips (Colorado State University), Clinton Greene (University of Missouri–St. Louis), Michael E. DePrano (University of Southern California), Radha S. Bhattacharya (California State University, Fullerton), Joseph M. Phillips, Jr. (Creighton University), Frank G. Steindl (Oklahoma State University), George A. Selgin (University of Georgia), William R. Dougan (Clemson University), and Sherry Edwards and Jim Clouse (Board of Governors of the Federal Reserve System). I express a special thanks to Joe Coyne (Board of Governors of the Federal Reserve System), who shared with me his wealth of knowledge on the Federal Reserve System as an institution. Nothing in this book should be construed as reflecting opinions of any of the persons mentioned, as I am sure that not all would endorse the methods employed and/or the emphasis given to many of the theoretical issues. The views in this book do not necessarily reflect those of the Board of Governors of the Federal Reserve System or its staff.

FUNDAMENTALS OF MONETARY THEORY

CHAPTER 1

CURRENCY IN AN ISLAND ECONOMY

Why do rational people willingly give up tangible real assets in exchange for the intrinsically worthless pieces of paper known as currency? They do so with the understanding that other people, whom they may never have met and perhaps may see only once in their lives, will also accept currency without question in exchange for goods and services that they in turn possess. But where is the assurance that other people will value currency when there is no real asset for which it ultimately can be redeemed?

Currency-for-goods transactions appear to be a confidence game. They provide opportunities for fraud and the participants may incur large risks. Yet virtually all economies around the world engage in such currency transactions, which dwarf pure barter exchanges (goods-for-goods transactions) in volume. Clearly, currency-for-goods transactions must afford substantial benefits to an economy. We can examine these benefits systematically by constructing an artificial economy that is initially producing at a point of autarky—that is, everyone is producing only for their own consumption—and examining how it passes by stages through a bilateral exchange economy to a monetary economy. First, however, some preliminary discussion of the nature of exchange is necessary.

1.1 MONEY AND BARTER

Monetary theory can be defined as the study of monetary economies, in which goods are reallocated via monetary transactions rather than by barter as in pure exchange economies. However, for this definition to be useful, we must differentiate monetary transactions from barter. We begin by generalizing the notion of a currency-for-goods transaction. A monetary transaction is an exchange of money for goods and goods for money, whereas barter is an exchange of goods for goods. Our task is to determine exactly what it is in the economy that distinguishes "money" from "goods." A useful approach is to identify items in the economy that satisfy the following condition: *Money can be exchanged for any good, and any good can be exchanged for money, but a good cannot be exchanged for all other goods.*[1]

As an example, consider a small island economy having three types of individuals, differentiated by preferences as A, B, and C, and four types of commodities: pineapples, papayas, fish, and corn. Type A individuals detest fish but like each of the other commodities, Type B individuals like all four commodities, and Type C individuals loathe papayas but like pineapples, fish, and corn. The problem is that these preferences are not matched by endowments. Type A individuals possess all of the island's pineapples, Type B individuals own the economy's papayas, Type C individuals have all of the economy's fish, and all individuals possess some corn. Initially, assume that all individuals are averse to acquiring any additional amounts of corn. What exchanges are possible? That is, what is the feasible set of trades?

The smallest feasible set of trades would result if the trades were restricted to be bilateral exchanges in which *both* participating individuals acquire commodities they desire. In this case, Type A individuals can trade their pineapples for Type B individuals' papayas; however, Type C individuals can trade with neither Type A nor Type B. Of course, each individual can also trade with others of the same type. Feasible trades are shown in Figure 1.1a. The reason for this pattern is that Cs possess nothing desired by As, who despise fish, and Bs possess nothing desired by Cs, who hate papayas. This basic "trading friction" in economies is known as the "lack of double coincidence of wants." It plays a fundamental role in creating a demand by individuals in an economy for "money" to serve as a common medium of exchange.

To continue the example, suppose all individuals are now willing to acquire additional quantities of corn in trade. In this case, in addition to the trade between the As and Bs already described, the As can trade pineapples with the Cs for corn and the Bs can trade corn with the Cs for fish. Note also that the trade between the As and the Bs can consist of a Type A individual trading corn with a Type B for papayas and a Type B individual trading corn with a Type A for pineapples. Thus, the feasible set of trades is expanded to that shown in Figure 1.1b. According to the preceding definition of money and goods, corn is money and pineapples, papayas, and fish are goods.

■1.2 METHOD OF ANALYSIS

To examine how and why benefits are derived from the introduction of fiat money into an economy as a common medium of exchange, a measure of those

---

[1]This distinction was first made by Clower (1967). He illustrated it with the example that follows in the text, which implies that the medium-of-exchange property is what makes money unique. In actual economies, clearly identifying the objects that serve as money is difficult. This issue is discussed at length in Chapter 2.

Figure 1.1

Feasible Trades in a Four-Commodity, Three-Person Economy

Figure 1.1a
The feasible trades when there are no trades involving corn are marked by an "x" in the table. Note that this is not a monetary economy.

	PINEAPPLES	PAPAYAS	FISH	CORN
Pineapples	x	x		
Papayas	x	x		
Fish			x	
Corn				x

Figure 1.1b
The feasible trades when trading in corn does occur are marked by an "x" in the table. Note that only corn can be traded for any of the other goods, because fish cannot be traded for either pineapples or papayas. Therefore, corn is "money" and pineapples, papayas, and fish are "goods."

	PINEAPPLES	PAPAYAS	FISH	CORN
Pineapples	x	x		x
Papayas	x	x		x
Fish			x	x
Corn	x	x	x	x

benefits and a systematic method of analysis are necessary. Economists rely on the fundamental microeconomic notion that the individual household (1) maximizes utility, given (2) the technology available to it, (3) the resources it possesses, and (4) the trading environment it faces.[2]

As a basis for analysis, (1) household preferences, in the form of a utility function, (2) technology, in the form a production function, and (3) resources, in the form of factors of production, must be fully specified. The analysis then consists of altering (4) the trading environment as the economy evolves from autarky to barter to systems of monetary exchange, and examining how the household, by employing its available technology, will reallocate its given resources to maximize utility, which is based on a given set of preferences. "Benefits" (or losses) to the economy can then be measured as the utility gains (or losses) that result from the more (or less) efficient allocations of the economy's resources.

---

[2]The term "trading environment" is intended to include not only the set of rules that govern the nature of exchange in the economy, which is the focus of this chapter, but also any set of government regulations and policies and any naturally occurring phenomena, such as the "frictions" that lead to adjustment costs, etc., or random elements in the economy such as productivity shocks, that affect optimal resource allocations. Many of these factors are studied in subsequent chapters.

1.3 AN ISLAND ECONOMY

Again consider an isolated island economy, but one that consists of a large number of households (imagine 1000 or 10,000) and produces a wide variety of goods (numbering in the thousands). Now define a period to be a standard interval of time, which could be thought of as a week or a month. In each period, every household engages in the home production of a subset of the economy's K goods, and each household owns the means, or factors, of production for its home goods. Those factors include both physical capital, denoted k, and human capital, denoted h, here the latter is a measure of the household's skill level in production. The household also has a limited amount of time available each period, denoted T. Time is a real economic resource that the household must allocate among competing uses. Some of the time is devoted to production and is denoted n. Some households on the island produce flour, some catch fish, others grow crops, and so on. However, because their production decisions all pertain to resource allocations, an individual "representative household" can be used to examine those decisions. Refer to this household as household i and designate quantities associated with it by the subscript i.

The production technology of household i has two factor inputs. One is the stock of physical capital, k_i, which is assumed to be task specific in that it can be used only in the production of designated goods. The other is the stock of human capital, h_i, that is combined with hours of labor, n_i, to yield skill-weighted or effective hours of labor, $(h_i n_i)$. The technology for transforming factor inputs into output goods can be represented by the household's production function as $f_i[k_i,(h_i n_i)]$. For simplicity, assume the stocks of physical and human capital are held constant over time.[3] This limits the production decision to a determination of the amount of time devoted to production, n_i, which is the sole remaining variable in the production function. Therefore, the production function can be rewritten as $f_i(n_i)$. This function has the property of diminishing marginal returns to labor, implying that a small increase in labor yields a lesser increase in output at high levels of production than at low levels of production. (See Mathematical Appendix 1.1 for the mathematical representation of the household's technology and resource constraints.)

The wide variety of goods produced in the economy is represented pictorially in Figure 1.2 by the set K. This set can be partitioned into a set of perishable goods, G, and a set of durable investment goods, X. The distinction is that perishable goods cannot be stored and therefore must be consumed within the period, whereas durable investment goods add to the household's stock of physical capital and are storable, but depreciate over time.[4] Now further imagine

---

[3]These stocks will be allowed to vary when investment decisions are examined in subsequent chapters.

[4]Investment goods include both intermediate and capital goods. No distinction is made between them because it is their similarities that are important here. That is, both are durable goods and both are used up in production.

Figure 1.2
Commodity (Goods)
Space

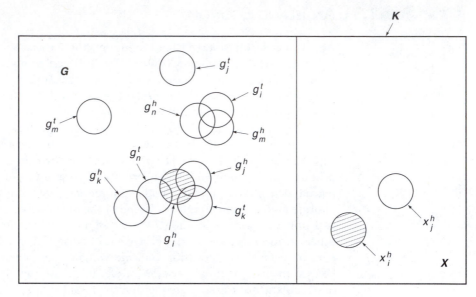

G = set of perishable goods produced in the economy

X = set of durable goods produced in the economy

g_i^h = set of (home) perishable goods produced by household i

g_i^t = set of perishable goods not produced by household i,
    but from which household i derives utility in consumption

x_i^h = set of (home) durable goods produced by household i

that households can sustain life by consuming only from their own home production. For household i, this production consists of the set of goods that includes the subsets g_i^h (where the superscript stands for goods produced at home)
and x_i^h of the sets G and X, respectively. Note, however, that the sets of home-
produced goods across households are not all disjoint. For example, household
j produces the subset of perishable goods g_j^h, which includes some but not all of
the goods in g_i^h in addition to goods that are not produced by household i. In
addition, household j's home production of durable investment goods, x_j^h, does
not (in this case) intersect x_i^h.

To specify preferences, we assume that households derive utility not only
from leisure, denoted l_i, and from each of their home-produced consumption
goods, g_i^h, but also from a subset of the other perishable consumption goods
produced elsewhere on the island. For household i, the latter goods are contained in subset g_i^t (where the superscript stands for goods acquired through
trade).[5] The preferences can then be expressed by the utility function

---

[5]Note that several other households, such as m and n, engage in the home production of
various goods (elements) in g_i^t. (That is, the sets represented by the intersections of g_i^t
with g_m^h and g_n^h, respectively, are not empty.) To avoid the situation of having monopoly
producers in the economy, we will assume that the number of producers of any one
good (element) in G is large.

$U_i(g_i^b, g_i^t, l_i)$. This function includes the property of diminishing marginal utility associated with increased consumption of goods and of leisure. The implication is that at very low levels of consumption of a good, the marginal utility associated with a unit of consumption of that good is very high. (See Mathematical Appendix 1.2 for a mathematical representation of the household's preferences.)

Each household in the economy is making production and consumption decisions similar to those of representative household i. Consequently, the resource allocations and consumption levels of household i can be taken as representative of the economy as a whole. The level of utility attained by household i will rise and fall with the economywide average or aggregate per capita utility level. This average is a standard measure of welfare and is the basis for determining whether the economy is made better off or worse off by changes in the fundamental rules and environment that govern trade. The essential question asked throughout this chapter, then, is: For a given amount of resources, can the trading environment be altered to allocate those resources more efficiently and thus raise the economy's overall level of welfare?[6]

1.4 AUTARKY

In the early stages of development of the island economy, each household produces goods only for its own consumption. This state of the economy is known as autarky. The level of utility received each period by the representative household is determined by its decisions about the quantity of its home-produced goods to consume and the amount of leisure time to take. That is, because $g_i^t = 0$, the level of utility is $U_i(g_i^b, 0, l_i)$. These decisions will be made jointly by the utility-maximizing household. Refer to Figure 1.3. In this case, the production of durable investment goods in each period is just sufficient to offset the rate at which the durable goods depreciate, thus maintaining a fixed stock of physical capital over time.[7] The decisions therefore reduce to how the household should optimally allocate its time, T, between labor, n_i, and leisure l_i. Because of diminishing marginal utility in consumption and diminishing marginal returns to labor in production, the household will choose to allocate its time optimally in such a way that the marginal utility derived from the last unit of leisure taken is just equal to the marginal utility derived from the consumption of the additional units of g_i^b produced from the last unit of time allocated to labor. If the household were to increase the time allocated to leisure beyond this optimal level, it

---

[6]Note that this chapter is concerned only with issues of economic efficiency. Distinctions between households, although not of concern here, would be necessary to address equity issues.

[7]Note that the household could increase production of perishable goods by reducing leisure time and by cutting production of durable goods. This would enable it to increase the allocation of time to the production of perishable goods in the current period. However, because investment goods add to the economy's capital stock, this decision would adversely affect output and therefore utility in future periods.

Figure 1.3
Production and
Resource Allocation
Decisions Under
Autarky (No Trades)

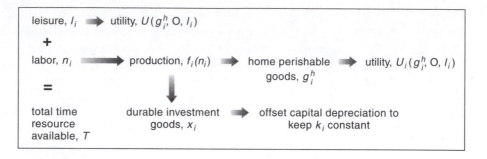

would derive additional utility from leisure. However, because its total time resource is constrained, it can do so only by reducing its labor time, which in turn would lower the production of g_i^h. Because of diminishing marginal utility (and diminishing marginal returns in production), utility losses from lower consumption would exceed the utility gains from increased leisure.

By treating household i as representative of the economy as a whole, we can characterize aggregate per capita resource allocations, aggregate per capita consumption levels, and aggregate per capita utility as in Figure 1.4. The per capita allocations of time devoted to the production of perishable and durable goods and to leisure each period under autarky is represented by the histogram in the middle panel of Figure 1.4 for the exchange environment denoted "a." In the bottom panel, a bar chart indicates the aggregate per capita quantities of the output and consumption of perishable goods for the economy under autarkic production. Note that all of the output is consumed. The implication is that the production of perishable goods is just equal to the quantity of perishable goods that households want to consume, and therefore none are wasted.

Finally, the top panel of Figure 1.4 is a graph of the aggregate per capital level of utility received by households in the economy. As previously stated, this average level of utility that households receive each period can be taken as an overall measure of welfare on the island. It varies with changes in the average levels of perishable goods consumed and leisure time taken. Its autarkic value is indicated by U_a. We will use this level of welfare as a baseline for comparison of alternative trading arrangements.

1.5   BARTER UNDER BILATERAL EXCHANGE WITH NO INTERMEDIATE TRADES

Suppose that at some point in the island's history, while the economy is still producing at autarky, households on the island decide to consider a very limited form of trade with one another. Only bilateral exchanges of perishable goods that involve no intermediate trades would be permitted. That is, a household could exchange a perishable home good only for a perishable market good that it plans to consume. (The reason for imposing this constraint on trade is to highlight the effect of specific trading frictions on production and consumption decisions, and ultimately on welfare.) Two questions must be answered. Is there

Figure 1.4
Per Capita Levels of
Utility (or Welfare),
Consumption, and
Output and the
Allocation of Time

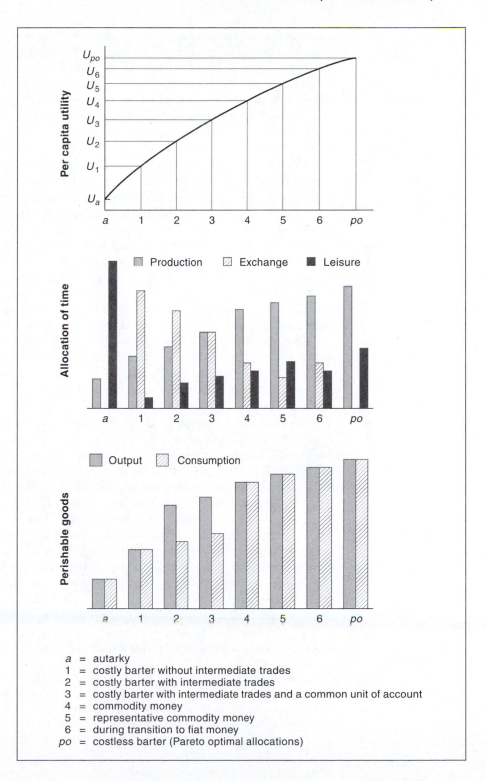

a = autarky
1 = costly barter without intermediate trades
2 = costly barter with intermediate trades
3 = costly barter with intermediate trades and a common unit of account
4 = commodity money
5 = representative commodity money
6 = during transition to fiat money
po = costless barter (Pareto optimal allocations)

an incentive for households to trade, and are there any feasible trades of the type described? The answer to both of these questions is yes.

From Figure 1.2, we see that households such as i, j, k, m, and n could receive utility from goods they do not produce at home that are produced at other homesites around the island; that is, the sets g_i^t, g_j^t, g_k^t, g_m^t, and g_n^t are non-empty. Furthermore, trade is feasible between, for example, household i and household n. Household i produces some perishable goods that household n does not produce but would like to consume; that is, the intersection of g_i^h and g_n^t is non-empty. In addition, household n produces some perishable goods that household i does not produce but would like to consume; that is, the intersection of g_n^h and g_i^t is non-empty. Therefore, a "double coincidence of wants" is present between households i and n, which is a necessary condition for barter to take place between them. Some bilateral trades cannot occur, however. For example, household i cannot trade with household k because there is no double coincidence of wants between them. Referring again to Figure 1.2, we see that the intersection of g_i^h and g_k^t is non-empty, implying that household i produces goods that household k would like to consume; however, the intersection of g_i^t and g_k^h is empty, indicating that household k produces no goods that household i demands. Therefore, household k has nothing with which to make the trade.

Because only (perishable) "goods" are being traded, that is, commodities for which households have positive demands, a set of relative prices for the goods can be determined by the relative strength of the demands as expressed by the households' utility functions. For simplicity, assume trade takes place once each period, say at the end of each week, and prior to trading, individual households are canvassed to determine the supply of their home goods that they want to trade and how much they would be willing to exchange for other commodities. This information is compiled and the set of relative prices that would just clear the markets is determined and distributed to the households. Informing households of the market-clearing price of each good in terms of every other good is the function of the Walrasian auctioneer.[8] The set of relative prices represents the terms of trade to which everyone agrees.

In the first week of trade, the household increase their home production of perishable goods in anticipation of future exchange. This action implies that the quantity of leisure time taken is reduced.[9] Were markets to clear at the prices announced by the Walrasian auctioneer, the perishable goods produced throughout the island would reach the households that demanded them and in just the right quantities. As in autarkic production, nothing would be wasted and all the marginal (utility) conditions for optimality would be met. The amount of time per capita allocated to the production of perishable goods, as

---

[8]The "Walrasian auctioneer" is a fictitious person created by the nineteenth-century economist Leon Walras to describe how markets process information and arrive at market-clearing prices. It was the auctioneer's job to match up supplies with demand such that all trades occurred at the single equilibrium price.

[9]Note that the production of durable goods may increase in anticipation of higher future production of g_i^h, thus enabling this production to be more (physical) capital intensive so as not to require as much foregone leisure.

well as the aggregate per capita consumption of perishable goods, is represented in Figure 1.4 for the exchange environment labeled "po." The aggregate per capita level of utility for the economy, denoted U_{po}, is also plotted on the graph. It represents the Pareto optimal allocations of resources and levels of production, and puts an upper limit on the highest attainable level of utility for the island economy. (We are assuming immobility of the factors of production.) That is, it represents an economy in which trade is unrestricted and frictionless (costless).[10]

Assume that during this first week of trade, there is no market organization other than the Walrasian auctioneer's distribution of the table of relative prices, which are universally adopted as the terms of trade. Households therefore must pack up their home-produced perishable goods and travel from homesite to homesite in search of someone who has the perishable goods they want to acquire and who demands the goods they are offering. When they happen upon someone with whom they can trade—when they discover a double coincidence of wants—they pull out the price table and identify the relative price, the exchange is made, and the search goes on.

At the end of this first week of trading, the Walrasian auctioneer performs a second canvass of households to determine the relative prices for the next trading period. He discovers that although the relative prices have not changed much, the total volume of goods to be exchanged is much smaller than the volume in the previous week. When he asks why this reduction occurred (although that is clearly not his job!), he discovers that households spent so much of their time conducting trades that they had less time available to allocate among competing uses, that is, for production of perishable and durable goods and for leisure. As we can see in Figure 1.5, the economic "pie" became smaller because of the high transaction costs associated with trade.

Moreover, not all desired trades took place. There were no markets for some exchanges simply because the cost of "making" those markets was too

Figure 1.5
Production and Resource Allocation Decisions with Markets for Trade in Non-Home-Produced Perishable Goods

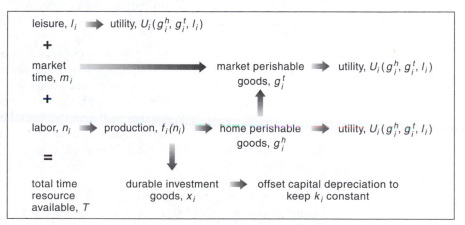

---

[10]Townsend (1983) discusses U_a and U_{po} as the lower and upper limits on aggregate per capita utility in an economy with infinite and zero trading costs, respectively.

high. In such cases, many households were left with an oversupply of their own home-produced perishable goods. Those goods did not literally go to waste, in that all of the households did derive utility from consuming them, but the levels of consumption of these home-produced perishables were suboptimal. Given the limited number of desired trades that the households were able to complete, their consumption bundles consisted of too many home-produced perishables and too few market perishables, and they had too little leisure time. (Note that some households may have completed all of the trades in some, but not in all, of the market perishable goods to attain the Pareto optimal levels of consumption in those few goods.)

Figure 1.4 indicates the aggregate per capita allocation of time to the production of perishable goods and to the market trading activities during the previous week. Note that more time was being devoted to the production of perishable goods than was the case under autarky. This observation suggests that despite the high transaction costs and the missing markets, the overall level of utility rose. Consequently, households are still interested in conducting trade. This situation is plotted on the graph in Figure 1.4 and denoted U_1. Clearly, if transaction costs were sufficiently high, households would prefer and choose autarky.

1.6   Barter under Bilateral Exchange with Intermediate Trades

The first week of trade on the island was very chaotic. It essentially consisted of households randomly searching for homesites where bilateral exchanges could be made, all of which had to satisfy the double coincidence of wants of the trading partners. With trades restricted to bilateral exchanges at the terms of trade established by the Walrasian auctioneer, the high transaction costs provided a strong incentive for households to seek a more efficient method of barter.

Suppose the initial innovation that takes place in subsequent periods is the introduction of intermediate trades. That is, when the double coincidence of wants problem occurs, households can accept some goods in exchange that they do not want to consume. They do so with the knowledge that if they devote enough of their time to trade, they will eventually find an individual who demands those goods. From that individual they can either acquire the goods they want to consume or acquire an additional set of goods that can eventually be traded for the desired goods. The question that must be asked is whether or not any such trades are feasible.

One such trade can be described with reference to Figure 1.2. Because the intersection of g_i^h and g_k^t is non-empty, household k has a positive demand for a subset of the perishable goods produced by household i.However, the converse is not true, as the intersection of g_k^h and g_i^t is the null set. To solve this lack of a double coincidence of wants, a third household, n, could mediate the exchange. Note that the intersections of the sets g_i^t and g_n^h, g_i^h and g_n^t, g_i^h and

g_k^t, and g_k^b and g_n^t are all non-empty. Hence, household n could trade goods contained in the intersection of g_i^t and g_n^b with household i to acquire not only the goods that it wants to consume (those contained in the intersection of g_i^b and g_n^t), but also the goods produced by household i that are in demand by household k (those contained in the intersection of g_i^b and g_k^t). It could offer the latter goods to household k in exchange for the goods produced by household k that it desires, which are contained in the intersection of g_k^b and g_n^t.

When the next trading period begins, the island households once again set out with the price table and their home goods to visit the homesites. This time they are willing to make the intermediate trades, knowing that if all of the markets clear at the correct relative prices, they will have successfully exchanged their home goods for the market goods they desire.

After a few weeks of trading, the Walrasian auctioneer again surveys the households to construct the price table for the upcoming trading period. He learns that not all desired trades were made, and that many households ended each period with goods they did not want to consume. These unwanted perishable goods went to waste. Nonetheless, he discovers that households had come closer to achieving the desired consumption levels, which implied that the number of missing markets had been reduced. He also discovers that less time was used up in the search for the right sequence of trades. (Note that there is not a unique sequence of bilateral trades that would clear the markets; this complicates the search process.) The freeing of time enabled households to increase the quantity of goods they produced for exchange and the amount of leisure time they took. This reallocation of time from exchange or market time to production and to leisure is represented by the bar graph in Figure 1.4 for the exchange environment labeled 2. Because of the greater utilization of time in production, the innovation in trading (the intermediate trades) allowed output to rise. By increasing output and reducing the number of incomplete markets, the trading innovation allowed consumption to rise, even though some output was "wasted." In the bottom panel in Figure 1.4, the higher levels of output and consumption are outcomes of the reduction in the transaction costs associated with trading. The "waste" is indicated by the fact that output exceeds consumption. Nonetheless, with the reduction of transaction costs by the introduction of intermediate trades, the level of aggregate per capita utility rises to U_2. In comparison with the idealized exchange economy of costless barter, where transaction costs are zero, the output, consumption, and utility levels are all lower.[11]

I.7   EXCHANGE WITH COMMODITY MONEY

The auctioneer learns during his canvass that the table of relative prices had become very cumbersome when intermediate trades were introduced. For ex-

---

[11]Starr (1972) and Ostroy and Starr (1976) discuss how minimizing transaction costs leads to welfare improvements, and how the introduction of a common medium of exchange can achieve significant reductions by decentralizing trades.

ample, households that wanted to exchange flour for fish, but first had to exchange flour for dates that could be traded for fish, had to worry with both the flour price of dates and the dates price of fish when their real interest was the flour price of fish.

Before distributing the price list for the next trading period, the auctioneer simplifies the table by quoting prices of all commodities in terms of a single common good. He decides to choose a good that has relatively little week-to-week variation in quality, and settles on flour. This innovation, the adoption of a standard unit of account, simplifies the trading in the next period. Upon canvassing households to determine the flour price schedule for the following period, the auctioneer discovers that there were fewer missing markets and that even less time was used up in the search process. These modest improvements are reflected in Figure 1.4 for the exchange environment labeled 3 as increases in consumption, output, and utility (to U_3) and as a decline in the difference between output and consumption, the amount of output wasted as a result of missing markets.[12]

However, problems with trading persisted. Transaction costs that used up the economic resource of time remained high, so the total production of goods over the island seemed much too low. In addition, missing markets persisted because all trades were conducted at Walrasian prices that would be market-clearing only when markets were complete. Households still were left with unwanted goods. Because those goods were perishable, a significant portion of output was wasted.

Another innovation was ultimately introduced into the economy in an effort to eliminate the waste of output. The problem was that households were acquiring unwanted goods in what they hoped would be intermediate trades, but were failing to consummate all of the final trades for the desired goods. Many households would return home with, for example, unwanted flour, which could not be stored on the island because of the weather. If flour could be stored it could be taken to the market during the next trading period and thus not lost to waste. (Note that only perishable goods are being exchanged, as no household has a positive demand for durable goods other than the ones it produces.)

To rectify this problem, the auctioneer notes that the millers produce flour from the corn they grow at their own homesites. Because corn is easily stored, he reasons that the millers would be just as willing to buy corn from others in exchange for the flour they produce as they would be to grow their own corn.[13] The implication is that corn has an intrinsic value due to the millers' positive demand for corn as a commodity. Like the perishable goods that were being traded, corn could be acquired in intermediate trades as households sought to

---

[12]Brunner and Meltzer (1971) discuss the information value of a good medium of exchange, which includes its role as the economy's standard unit of account.

[13]This could lead to aggregate utility (or welfare) gains from specialization in production, but here we are interested only in gains resulting from the adoption of a common medium of exchange.

attain their optimal consumption bundles through a sequence of bilateral exchanges. Unlike perishable goods, however, corn is durable, so households acquiring it would have no need to fear that it may subsequently go to waste. A household could simply exchange the home goods it brought to the market for corn, and then seek other households that were offering the goods it wanted. If it found such households, it could exchange the corn for the desired goods. Other households would be willing to accept the corn because they know of its intrinsic worth. If no other households were offering the desired goods, the household could return home with a stock of corn that it could take to the market during the next period. Thus, intermediate trades could become intertemporal as well.

Over the next few trading periods, the auctioneer promoted this trading arrangement. He discovered that intermediate trades in perishable goods had ceased and nearly all transactions had become corn-for-goods exchanges. Only in the few cases of a double coincidence of wants between trading partners did any bilateral goods-for-goods transactions not involving corn continue to take place. Moreover, because of the ability to conduct intertemporal, intermediate trades, specialization of market activities was possible within the household. As shown in Figure 1.6, one member could take the home-produced goods to market to exchange for corn, using m_i^m units of the household's time, and another member could take the household's stock of corn to market to exchange for the non-home-produced goods desired, using m_i^t units of time. This arrangement significantly reduced the time used in transacting each period, and thereby freed time for production and leisure.[14] The market had become perfectly decentralized; all transactions were corn-for-goods and goods-for-corn exchanges, and the problem of missing markets had been eliminated.[15]

The result of this innovation is shown in Figure 1.4 in the exchange environment labeled 4. As shown in the middle panel, the time allocated to trading fell; and a portion of that time was reallocated to labor activities, thereby raising output, and the remainder allowed leisure time to be increased. Moreover, because the missing intraperiod markets were replaced by completed intertemporal markets, all perishable goods that were produced were consumed and waste was eliminated.[16] These two features of the new trading arrangement raised aggregate per capita utility to U_4 through increases in both the variety and the level of consumption of desired goods and an increase in leisure time. In response to the success of this new trading environment the Walrasian price

---

[14]Search models of money, as described by Kiyotaki and Wright (1989, 1993) and Boldrin, Kiyotaki, and Wright (1993), emphasize the ability of money to reduce search costs when there is uncertainty about whether the desired good can be found.

[15]From a minimum transaction cost perspective, Lucas (1980) makes clear that "money" can perfectly decentralize markets by replacing the intraperiod sequence of trades involving intermediate trades with a series of bilateral exchanges that involve only one intermediate, albeit interperiod, trade to acquire each desired good.

[16]Because credit markets have not yet appeared in this economy, they could be thought of as "missing markets." The set of trading frictions that cause these markets to be missing is emphasized by Townsend (1983, 1987).

Figure 1.6
Production and
Resource Allocation
Decisions with
Markets for Trade in
Non-Home-Produced
Perishable Goods and
with Specialization in
Market Activities

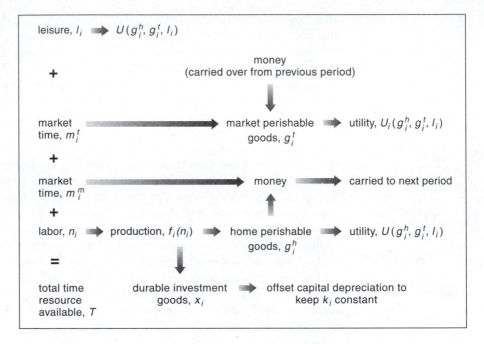

list was changed from flour prices to corn prices. The island economy had become a monetary economy. Its money was corn.

Because corn had an intrinsic worth and was durable, it was a good store of value. That fact was known by all households in the economy. Therefore, when considering an intermediate trade, an individual household was willing to make goods-for-corn transactions, knowing that all others in the economy also would be willing to make such exchanges. Previously only a few households (the millers) had demanded corn as a commodity, but now all households demanded it as a common medium of exchange. It therefore had come to serve a dual purpose in the island economy as a commodity money. Like most monies, it had the properties of unit of account, store of value, and medium of exchange.[17]

Kitchen Utensils and the Russian Ruble.   The inefficiencies of barter in contrast to monetary exchange were starkly illustrated in Russia after the collapse of the Soviet Union. The currency of the former Soviet Union had been the ruble, which had virtually no value outside the Soviet Union as it was not convertible into any other currency. Once the Soviet Union collapsed, it was not clear how many of the newly created republics would continue to use the ruble, nor was there any confidence that the Russian central bank could avoid rapidly

---

[17]Hoover (1990) stresses the fact that the medium-of-exchange and store-of-value properties of "money" are not separable. That is, money is a store of value only because it is the common medium of exchange, and it would not be the common medium of exchange if it were not a store of value.

debasing the currency through overproduction, thereby leading to escalating inflation. Consequently, confidence in the ruble fell dramatically, and even state-owned Russian enterprises began to refuse payment in rubles.

In one case, a Siberian aircraft manufacturing facility that had begun converting from military to civilian production in the aftermath of the cold war found that it could no longer acquire intermediate goods, such as machine tools, in monetary transactions involving the ruble. It had no way to barter with suppliers because its only product was aircraft, and a firm that produced drill bits, for example, would not be able to meet the terms of trade. (How many drill bits would be required in exchange for one civilian aircraft?!) The Siberian firm responded by converting a warehouse into a stamping plant that produced kitchen utensils. Those products were used to barter with small equipment suppliers for intermediate goods whenever the terms of trade were feasible. (How many knives, forks, or spoons is a drill bit worth?) Of course, the small equipment suppliers then had to find a market for the kitchen utensils!

1.8   EXCHANGE WITH REPRESENTATIVE COMMODITY MONEY

Although the transaction costs associated with trading on the island were significantly reduced by the introduction of commodity money, one drawback to the new arrangement began to emerge over the next several trading periods. When making his weekly canvasses, the auctioneer heard persistent complaints that corn was a very cumbersome medium of exchange. Households had to transport not only goods, but also sacks of corn, to and from the market. To alleviate this problem, the auctioneer came upon the idea of households issuing IOUs for the corn they possessed. The IOUs could be redeemed for corn in the future by whoever possessed them and wanted to exchange them for corn. He discovered, however, that households would be unwilling to accept IOUs written by one household as payment for goods unless they believed others that had goods they wanted would also accept the IOUs. In goods-for-IOU trades, the seller of the good might not know and perhaps would never meet the issuer of the IOU, and therefore would have no way to verify the integrity of the IOU. Obviously, if this system of circulating IOUs was to replace the commodity money system, it would have to be supplemented with some procedure for verifying the authenticity of the IOUs.

One procedure conceived by the auctioneer was simply to perform audits himself each week to ensure that no household was issuing IOUs in excess of its corn holdings.[18] However, he quickly discarded that procedure as being much

---

[18]Such monitoring costs would render the payments system of economies with multiple currencies inefficient. See Meltzer (1987) for a discussion. However, the costs associated with this inefficiency may be relatively small in modern monetary economies. Conceivably, competitive pressures to preserve the "name brand" of the issuers of private monies would ensure the integrity of the monies that would remain in circulation over time.

too costly.[19] Instead, he promoted the idea of relying on a single issuer of IOUs so that verification would be a much simpler process. This approach met with resistance. Verifying how much corn was in stock in a single location would be easy, but determining how many IOUs were in circulation throughout the economy would not. However, the auctioneer pointed out that a mechanism could be established whereby the IOUs could always be redeemed for their stated value in terms of corn, and over the next few trading periods this innovation gained acceptance.[20]

To implement the new trading arrangement, it was agreed that the auctioneer would become the issuer of IOUs. The quantity of IOUs that he would issue initially would be determined by the amount of corn currently held by households in the economy strictly for the purpose of transacting. The auctioneer therefore bought up all of the households' corn holdings, other than those the millers would use for producing flour, with the IOUs. The corn was placed in a central location for storage. Any household in possession of IOUs could acquire the corn from the auctioneer on demand in the amount stated on the IOUs. The IOUs could now freely circulate on the island as the economy's representative commodity money. They retained the features of unit of account and store of value, but in addition they were superior to corn as a medium of exchange because of their greater portability.

The effect of the innovation on the economy after several trading periods is shown in Figure 1.4 for the exchange environment labeled 5. Again, time that previously had been used in transactions was freed to be reallocated to production and leisure. Output and consumption rose, and aggregate per capita utility (or welfare) also rose to U_5.

Over the next several periods, the island began to undergo a steady population growth for the first time. This growth increased the volume of trading proportionately, and consequently raised the demand for IOUs needed to conduct the trades. The auctioneer had to decide how fast to expand the quantity of IOUs in circulation. He thus became the economy's monetary authority who regulated the supply of money. He quickly discovered that the simplest way to keep up with growth was to make the IOU-corn exchange operation work both ways. That is, he would not only redeem IOUs for corn at a fixed exchange rate, but would also supply IOUs on demand in exchange for corn at that same fixed

---

[19]This monitoring activity is in effect one function performed by financial intermediaries in their supply of "inside money." Inside money is usually associated with monetary assets with transaction privileges that are issued by banks, such as checkable deposit accounts. See Pesek and Saving (1967) and King and Plosser (1984). However, monetary assets are not strictly necessary here; the simple provision of accounting services by banks could perform the same function. Black (1970) discussed this point in his futuristic paper, "World Without Money." For less futuristic (although abstract) discussions of the costly nature of these services, see Marquis and Reffett (1992, 1994) and Ireland (1994).

[20]This mechanism is analogous to the "gold window" operated by the Federal Reserve from 1948 to 1971, whereby the dollar was fixed in value with respect to a given quantity of gold. Access to the "gold window" was restricted to foreign governments, however.

exchange rate. This procedure allowed the market to regulate the island's money supply while maintaining a constant relative price of corn in terms of IOUs. What made this mechanism work was the millers' willingness to exchange IOUs for corn. Whenever a miller was willing to pay more than the auctioneer, households found that they could arbitrage the two prices for profit by exchanging their IOUs for corn from the auctioneer and then selling the corn to the miller for a higher price in IOUs. This process would continue until the miller lowered the price that he was willing to pay for the corn to the price paid by the auctioneer. The result of such a process would be a decrease in the quantity of IOUs in circulation, and a corresponding decrease in the corn holdings of the auctioneer. An increase in the quantity of IOUs would result from the opposite set of arbitrage conditions.

1.9   Exchange with Fiat Money

The households were generally satisfied with the new trading arrangement, but they could still recognize that it was costly to support. One of the costs was the stock of corn used to back the IOUs. Corn is a real economic resource of the island that has alternative uses both as seed corn and as an intermediate good in the production of flour. The idling of this resource induced opportunity costs in an amount equal to the utility value of forgone consumption goods produced from the corn.[21] It was clear that those costs could be lowered by simply reducing the stockpile of corn held by the auctioneer.

The auctioneer/monetary authority noticed that the volume of his corn-for-IOUs transactions in each period was small in relation to his total stock of corn. He reasoned that he could increase the supply of IOUs each period without acquiring additional corn in exchange. To achieve this monetary injection of IOUs into the economy, he simply completed his regular canvass each period, determined the volume of trading that was to take place, and calculated the quantity of money needed to support those trades so that the IOU-corn price was fixed. The additional money would then be distributed uniformly to households in equal proportions. Any mistakes in his calculations would be taken care of by the IOU-corn exchange operations. If he oversupplied IOUs, households would simply exchange them for corn, and vice versa. Over time, the amount of real resources of corn needed to support the transaction arrangements, or the economy's payment system, would become smaller on a per capita basis; output and consumption would rise and again per capita utility levels also would increase.

As time passed, confidence in the integrity of the IOUs, and therefore in the auctioneer in his capacity as the economy's monetary authority, became virtually complete.[22] The auctioneer could be counted on to maintain a fixed IOU price of

---

[21]Friedman (1966) discusses the resources costs of commodity monies with particular reference to the gold standard.

[22]This scenario is hypothetical and intended only to make a point about the efficiency of a payment system. There are many reasons why government agencies with discretionary authority to regulate the money supply cannot be entrusted to maintain price stability, even when that is their explicitly stated mandate.

corn by issuing IOUs in the proper amount each period, and without backing of any kind. The households unanimously agreed that he could do away with the corn stockpile by gradually redistributing that wealth uniformly across households until it was ultimately depleted. The auctioneer carried out this mandate of the households while continuing to supply IOUs in an amount that maintained the IOU price of corn as before. The additional resources again raised consumption, output, and per capita utility to higher levels until all of this wealth had been consumed. These periods are represented on Figure 1.4 for the exchange environment labeled 6, with utility at U_6. Afterward, per capita consumption, output, and utility returned to their previous levels, with utility at U_5.

The economy had clearly benefited by consuming the idle corn resources. Once the stockpile had been depleted, however, it was only the personal integrity and competence of the auctioneer/monetary authority that could ensure IOU price stability. That is, the economy had evolved into a monetary economy relying strictly on fiat money, the intrinsic value of which is zero. The term IOU had become a misnomer.

1.10 SUMMARY

Fiat money is one of the more common types of money in use in economies around the world. Given the potential problems associated with maintaining its value as a common medium of exchange, it must afford significant benefits. However, many of the benefits typically attributed to money do not require fiat money, or even representative commodity money, to be realized.

In the island economy just described, we see that whenever households' endowments and production possibility frontiers do not coincide with their preferences, autarkic production and consumption can be improved upon by trade. However, transaction costs are associated with trade. Many of the transaction costs can be reduced by allowing intermediate trades to take place. Associated with such trades is the expense of wasted output resulting from the introduction of incomplete consumption goods markets into the economy. The waste can be reduced by increasing the efficiency of the markets by relying on a standard unit of account and adopting a common medium of exchange. The latter requires durability, which enables trade to become intertemporal, and thereby completely decentralizes the markets. All of these welfare gains can be achieved by commodity money.

Representative commodity money (IOUs) produces an additional efficiency gain over commodity money due to greater portability. However, it introduces the possibility of fraud and counterfeiting, which implies high monitoring costs. To reduce monitoring costs, a single currency in the form of a representative commodity money could emerge. A passive monetary authority would be needed to ensure the integrity of the currency, essentially by managing a mechanism for exchange between the currency and the commodity it represents to maintain a fixed relative price between the two.

What is the additional benefit of fiat money over representative commodity money? The stockpile of real economic resources used as backing for the currency has been withdrawn from productive use. It represents a form of wealth that could be redistributed to the economy. Its redistribution would have the effect of raising output and freeing time for leisure, both of which would raise utility and thereby generate additional welfare gains. However, a major problem may be introduced into the growing economy. The rate of growth of the currency supply must now be determined by a centralized monetary authority. The issues of how that decision ought to be made and the consequences of poor decisions are addressed in much of the material covered in the remainder of the book.

■ REVIEW QUESTIONS

1. Consider the small island economy described in the text, which consists of three types of individuals: As (who detest fish), Bs (who like all of the foodstuffs on the island), and Cs (who hate papayas). Alter their initial endowments by restricting those of the papaya-haters, the Cs, to fish; assume the As initially own all of the pineapples and some corn, and the Bs initially own all of the papayas and some corn.
   (a) What is the feasible set of trades that satisfy the double coincidence of wants? Is there any money is this economy?
   (b) Now allow trades to become intertemporal, so that intermediate trades are permitted. After two periods, or rounds, of trading, what is the feasible set of trades? Is there any money in this economy?
   (c) Describe the properties of the commodities (one or more) that make intertemporal trades possible.

2. In reference to the characteristics of "money," describe what is meant by greater portability, durability, and divisibility. How do these characteristics affect the desirability of an asset that acts as money in terms of its economic functions of medium of exchange, store of value, and unit of account?

3. For the following pairs of trading environments, explain how the resources in the island economy are allocated more efficiently in the environment that yields the higher level of welfare.
   (a) Representative commodity money versus costly barter with intermediate trades.
   (b) Autarky versus costly barter with intermediate trades and a common unit of account.
   (c) Commodity money versus costly barter without intermediate trades.
   (d) Costless barter versus autarky.

*4. In the island economy, the welfare gains achieved by replacing representative commodity money with fiat money were contingent on a faithful execution of monetary control by the Walrasian auctioneer/monetary authority who provided price stability. In actual economies that rely on fiat money, inflation, and *not* price stability, is the norm. Discuss why this is true and alternative ways of structuring the decision-making process that could better achieve price stability. Have such approaches been tried?

*5. Compare the monetary system in the fictional island economy operating under the corn exchange with the U.S. monetary system under the classical gold standard of the 1920s. Compare it with the U.S. monetary system under the Bretton Woods Agreements after World War II.

1.1 MATHEMATICAL APPENDIX

Technology and Resource Constraints Facing Households

Households are maximizing utility as described in Appendix 1.2. However, they do not have unlimited resources. To produce perishable goods, g_i^b, households must make use of their physical and human capital, k_i and h_i, respectively, and their total time, T. Therefore, the sum of perishable consumption goods, g_i^b, and durable investment goods, x_i, cannot exceed total household production expressed as a function of the two factor inputs, physical capital and quality-adjusted labor. The latter is given by the amount of time devoted to production, n_i, scaled up by the level of human capital, h_i. Mathematically, this constraint is

$$g_i^b + x_i \leq F[k_i,\, h_i n_i]$$

where the household production functions, $F[k_i, h_i n_i]$, describes the technology available to the household. There are diminishing marginal returns to increased factor usage, implying that although the first partial derivatives of the production function are both positive, the second partial derivatives are negative.

The stock of physical capital available at the beginning of period $t + 1$, $k_i(t + 1)$, can be increased by producing more investment goods in period t, $x_i(t)$, at the expense of fewer consumption goods, g_i^h. Given that capital depreciates each period at a rate δ, the constraint on capital accumulation is given by

$$k_i(t + 1) = (1 - \delta)k_i(t) + x_i(t).$$

Any investment in excess of depreciation (that is, whenever $x_i(t) - \delta k_i(t)$ is positive) therefore will expand the production possibilities frontier in the future. Also, the total amount of time each period, T, must be allocated among its competing uses in production, n_i, leisure, l_i, and market activity associated with conducting transactions, m_i. Therefore,

$$n_i + l_i + m_i = T.$$

In general, human capital accumulation may result from the allocation of time to education.

In the special case considered in this chapter, the level of investment is assumed always to be just sufficient to offset depreciation, or

$$x_i(t) = \delta k_i(t).$$

This assumption implies that the capital stock is fixed over time, as $k(t + 1) = k(t)$. If it is further assumed that the stock of human capital is fixed, the production function can be written in terms of a single variable n_i, and the production constraint can be rewritten as

$$g_i^b \leq f_i(n_i) = F[\overline{k}_i, \overline{h}_i n_i] - \overline{x}_i$$

where the bars over k_i, h_i, and x_i indicate that they are constants. Therefore, once the amount of nonleisure time devoted to production is determined, the quantity of the home-produced perishable good is also determined.

■ 1.2   MATHEMATICAL APPENDIX

Household Preferences (the Utility Function)

Household i derives utility from (1) the consumption of perishable goods produced at home, g_i^h, (2) the consumption of perishable goods acquired through, trade g_i^t, and (3) leisure, l_i. The level of utility each period is determined by how strong these preferences are and by the quantities of consumption of each of the goods and the amount of leisure time taken. This information is summarized by the utility function,

$$U_i = U_i[g_i^h, g_i^t, l_i].$$

This function is monotonically increasing in each of its arguments, but at a decreasing rate; that is, diminishing marginal utility is associated with higher consumption levels of any one good or leisure. Mathematically, the first partial derivatives are all positive and the second partial derivatives are all negative. For illustration, this function is plotted below in $U_i - g_i^t$ space (for fixed g_i^h and l_i), in $U_i - g_i^h$ space (for fixed g_i^t and l_i), and in $U_i - l_i$ space (for fixed g_i^t and g_i^h). Note that the level of utility associated with zero consumption of g_i^t is zero, whereas the level of utility associated with zero consumption of g_i^h and with zero leisure is negative infinity. This is a mathematically consistent way of allowing for autarky to be feasible. That is, it requires utility-maximizing households to consume positive amounts of home-produced consumption goods, g_i^h, and leisure, l_i, while allowing them to avoid consumption of market-produced goods, g_i^t. Under autarky, the cost of making transactions markets across homesites is assumed to be infinite, so those markets are missing.

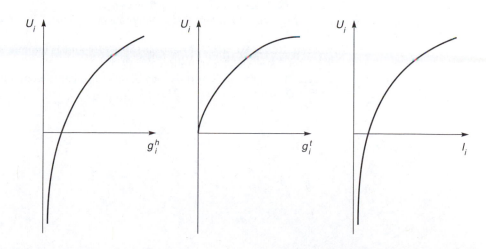

▓ REFERENCES

Black, Fischer. 1970. "Banking and Interest Rates in a World Without Money: The Effects of Uncontrolled Banking." *Journal of Banking Research* 1 (Autumn): 9–20.

Boldrin, Michele, Nobuhiro Kiyotaki, and Randall Wright. 1993. "A Dynamic Equilibrium Model of Search, Production, and Exchange." *Journal of Economic Dynamics and Control* 17 (September): 723–59.

Brunner, Karl, and Allan H. Meltzer. 1971. "The Origin and Uses of Money: Money in the Theory of Exchange." *American Economic Review* 61 (December): 784–805.

Clower, Robert. 1967. "A Reconsideration of the Microfoundations of Monetary Theory." *Western Economic Journal* 6 (December): 1–8.

Friedman, Milton. 1966. *Essays in Positive Economics.* Chicago: University of Chicago Press.

Hoover, Kevin D. 1990. *The New Classical Macroeconomics: A Skeptical Inquiry.* Cambridge, MA: Oxford Press.

Ireland, Peter. 1994. "Economic Growth, Financial Innovation, and the Long Run Behavior of Velocity." *Journal of Economic Dynamics and Control* 18 (May/July): 815–48.

King, Robert A., and Charles I. Plosser. 1984. "Money, Credit, and Prices in a Real Business Cycle Economy." *American Economic Review* 74 (March): 363–80.

Kiyotaki, Nobuhiro, and Randall Wright. 1989. "On Money as a Medium of Exchange." *Journal of Political Economy* 97 (August): 927–54.

———and ———1993. "A Search-Theoretic Approach to Monetary Economics." *American Economic Review* 83 (March): 63–77.

Lucas, Robert E. 1980. "Equilibrium in a Pure Currency Economy." *Economic Inquiry* 18 (April): 203–20.

Marquis, Milton H., and Kevin L. Reffett. 1992. "Capital in the Payment System." *Economica* 37 (August): 351–64.

———and ———1994. "New Technology Spillovers into the Payment System." *Economic Journal* 104 (September): 1123–38.

Meltzer, Allan H. 1987. "Monetary Reform in an Uncertain Environment." In *The Search for Stable Money,* ed. James A. Dorn and Anna J. Schwartz. Chicago and London: University of Chicago Press.

Ostroy, Joseph M. and Ross M. Starr. 1976. "Money and the Decentralization of Exchange." *Econometrica* 42 (6): 1093–1113.

Pesek, Boris P., and Thomas R. Saving. 1967. *Money, Wealth, and Economic Theory.* New York: Macmillan Publishing Company.

Starr, R. M. 1972. "Decentralized Nonmonetary Trade." *Econometrica* 22, No. 5: 1087–99.

Townsend, Robert M. 1983. "Financial Structure and Economic Activity." *American Economic Review* 73 (December): 895–911.

———. 1987. "Asset Return Anomalies in a Monetary Economy." *Journal of Economic Theory* 41 (February): 219–47.

CHAPTER 2

THE MONIES OF A MODERN ECONOMY

What is money? In Chapter 1 it is distinguished from goods by the criterion: "Money can be exchanged for (all) goods, and (any) goods for money, but goods cannot be exchanged for (all) goods."[1] This definition suggests that what makes money unique is its role in the economy as a common medium of exchange. In addition, as noted in the artificial economy described in Chapter 1, money has the properties of unit of account and store of value. Corn, the commodity money, also had those properties, but it was seen to be inferior to representative commodity money and fiat money as a medium of exchange because of its relative lack of portability. Efficiency arguments then led to the adoption of a single money for the island's economy.

In actual modern economies, these distinctions are not as clear (which is why economists study artificial economies). In particular, multiple media of exchange coexist in modern economies. Government-issued currency is normally the unit of account, but many media of exchange have the property of store of value, and some are better stores of value than others. The latter property clearly affects the demand for these media of exchange because it alters their asset values. In addition, debt instruments such as credit cards often are used to conduct transactions. Reliance on this form of exchange is affected by one's ability and willingness to incur debt, and by the convenience of credit cards for certain transactions. Some transactions in modern economies are conducted through an intermediary, such as a commercial bank, and involve neither the idling of wealth in the form of monetary assets (such as holding currency in advance of a purchase) nor the acquisition of debt. They are called cash management services and take many forms such as zero balance accounts for firms and overdraft privileges on checking accounts for households. Such

---

[1]This is Clower's (1967) definition.

sophistication of financial markets complicates the problem of identifying what it is in the economy that serves as money. In this chapter, the various forms of money are discussed with particular emphasis on the definitions of money that have been constructed by and are monitored by the Federal Reserve to assist in the conduct of monetary policy.

2.1   THE MONETARY AGGREGATES

A distinction can be drawn between monetary assets and capital market assets in terms of maturity. In general, financial assets with a maturity of one year or less are considered monetary assets and those with maturities in excess of one year are considered capital market assets.[2] Using this distinction, the Federal Reserve identifies all of the monetary assets in the economy and groups them into monetary aggregates on the basis of their demand substitutability with one another. For example, if households want to raise their currency holdings, they are more likely to draw down their checking account balances than to cash in a certificate of deposit (CD). Hence, currency and checking account balances are stronger substitutes than currency and CDs.

The Federal Reserve monitors the total dollar volume of each of the aggregates over time and attempts to identify its behavior. It examines how changes in the dollar values of the aggregates are associated with changes in other variables that track the state of the economy over time, such as interest rates, the real gross domestic product (GDP), and a measure of the price level such as the consumer price index (CPI). These relationships, which are based on the demand for "money" by households and firms, are discussed in detail in Chapter 3.

The supply of the monetary aggregates, measured in nominal (or current dollar) terms, can be strongly influenced by the Federal Reserve because of its regulatory authority over the banking system and its monopoly control over the currency supply. To the extent that changes in the supply of the monetary aggregates induce changes in the real sector of the economy (output, consumption, investment, employment, etc.), the Federal Reserve may be able to influence the real economy. The decisions on how to regulate the supply of one or another of the aggregates are the monetary policy decisions of the Federal Reserve. Much of this book is devoted to analyzing the effects and consequences of those decisions. First, however, it is important to understand the composition of the monetary aggregates and the logic behind their construction.

2.2   M1

The demand substitutability of monetary assets is determined largely by their asset properties of return, risk, and liquidity. Return is the interest rate paid to

---

[2]In the Federal Reserve's monetary aggregates, the exceptions are some CDs with maturities up to five years and U.S. government savings bonds with maturities up to 20 years.

owners of the assets.[3] Risk is the probability that the asset will lose some or all of its value over some time interval. In general, there is a tradeoff between these two properties: the higher the perceived risk, the higher the expected return the asset holder demands. The liquidity of an asset is defined by the relative ease and cost with which it can be converted into an investment or consumption good or into another asset. If the monetary asset is viewed as a form of wealth (which it is), liquidity can be thought of as the relative ease and cost of converting that form of wealth into consumption or into another form of wealth.

Monetary assets that serve as an economy's common media of exchange have very high liquidity by definition. The M1 monetary aggregate consists of nearly all of the U.S. economy's assets that serve as its media of exchange. As listed in Table 2.1, they consist of currency, demand deposits, traveler's checks, and other checkable deposits. Figure 2.1 shows the growth in nominal (current-dollar) terms of the total stock of M1. The relative magnitudes of its components (as a percentage of the total stock of M1) are plotted in Figure 2.2.

Currency's share of the total stock of M1 has remained relatively stable since 1959, growing modestly from about 21 to approximately 29 percent by 1994. Currency consists of coins, which are minted by the Treasury Department, and Federal Reserve notes (or paper money), which are issued by the Federal Reserve. Note that coins are commodity monies because they have an intrinsic worth in terms of their copper, tin, and/or silver content. Paper money is fiat money with virtually no intrinsic worth. However, as Federal Reserve notes constitute more than 90 percent of the total dollar volume of currency in the hands of the public, for all practical purposes U.S. currency can be thought of as government-issued fiat money.[4] This was not always the case. From the end of World War II until 1971, the U.S. dollar was on the gold standard as part of the international monetary accords known as the Bretton Woods Agreements. Under those agreements, foreign governments that held Federal Reserve notes could exchange them at the "gold window" for claims to gold held by the U.S. government in its vaults at Fort Knox, Kentucky. The exchange rate was fixed at $35 per fine ounce for most of that period.[5] Therefore, while the Bretton Woods Agreements were in effect, the U.S. dollar was a representative commodity money. The story of the collapse of the gold standard in 1971 and how that event was precipitated by an incompatible monetary policy is recounted in Chapter 8.

Demand deposits are a second major component of M1. From Figure 2.2, we see that they accounted for more than three quarters of the total stock of

---

[3]Asset returns are priced as nominal interest rates. The demand for assets is based on real interest rates, the return after inflation is taken into account.

[4]The term "public" actually refers to non-U.S. government and government agency holdings. Although the exact figure is unknown, 50 to 75 percent of U.S. currency is believed to be held abroad.

[5]Because of an increase in the U.S. inflation rate in the late 1960s, the official gold exchange value of the U.S. dollar was adjusted to 42.22 per fine ounce, which remains the official valuation of gold by the Treasury and the Federal Reserve.

Table 2.1   Components of the Monetary Aggregates (as of April 1995)

	DOLLARS (in billions)	PERCENT
M1		
Currency	365.7	31.8
Demand deposits	381.2	33.2
Traveler's checks	9.2	.8
Other checkable deposits	393.6	34.2
Total	1149.7	100.0
M2		
M1	1149.7	31.6
Small time deposits	896.8	24.6
Savings and MMDAs	1082.5	29.7
MMMFs (retail)	396.0	10.9
Overnight repurchase agreements	84.6	2.3
Overnight Eurodollar deposits	30.1	.8
Total	3642.8	100.0
M3		
M2	3642.8	83.2
Large time deposits	378.7	8.6
MMMFs (institutions only)	192.9	4.4
Term repurchase agreements	115.6	2.6
Term Eurodollar deposits	62.2	1.4
Total	4380.1	100.0
L		
M3	4380.1	80.3
Short-term Treasury securities	406.8	7.5
Commercial paper	475.2	8.7
U.S. savings bonds	180.9	3.3
Bankers' acceptances	10.3	.2
Total	5453.4	100.0

M1 in 1959. They declined sharply in 1980 and had fallen to approximately 34 percent by 1994. Demand deposits are essentially non-interest-bearing checking account balances. Such accounts compete with interest-bearing checking accounts, such as negotiable orders of withdrawal (NOWs), which are grouped under the heading "Other Checkable Deposits." Note from Figure 2.2 that those deposits were almost nonexistent prior to 1980, and by 1990 accounted for roughly 37 percent of M1.

The reason for the shift in the holdings of interest-bearing and non-interest-bearing checking accounts was a change in government regulations that accompanied the Depository Institutions Deregulation and Monetary Control Act (DIDMCA) of 1980 and the subsequent Garn–St. Germaine Amendment in 1982. That legislation allowed depository institutions other than commercial

Figure 2.1   The Monetary Aggregates

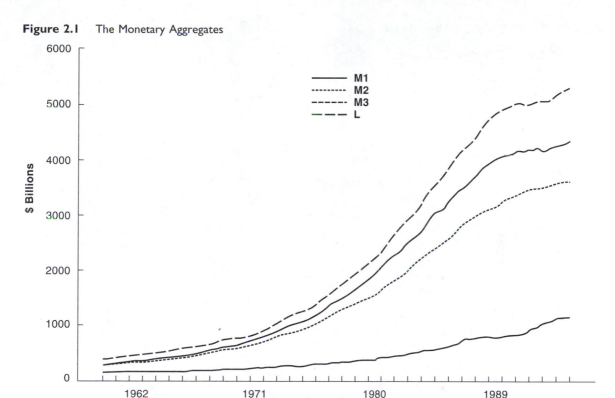

banks, such as savings and loans, credit unions, and mutual savings banks, to offer checking accounts to their customers. Moreover, it lifted the prohibition on interest payments on checkable deposit accounts that had been in effect since the Banking Act of 1933. Financial institutions began offering two types of checking accounts. One was interest bearing, but required that a service charge be paid for checks drawn on the account, and in many cases also required that a minimum balance be maintained in the account to receive interest. The second type of checking account did not pay interest on the deposit balance, but did not assess a service fee for checks drawn on the account. Obviously, households that wrote numerous checks each month could benefit by the latter (demand deposit) account, whereas those that wrote few checks could benefit by the former (other checkable deposit) account that paid interest on their deposit balance.

One regulation that was not eliminated by either the DIDMCA of 1980 or the Garn–St. Germaine Amendment of 1982 was the prohibition against interest payments on nonpersonal checking accounts. Checking accounts of businesses, termed commercial accounts, are required by law to be non-interest-bearing. The rationale for maintaining this regulation was to prevent commercial banks from competing with each other for large corporate deposits by offering higher interest rates. The belief was that such competition could cause instability in the banking system due to the rapid movement of deposit funds from one bank to another in response to small changes in deposit rates. The resultant volatility in bank deposits would increase the banks' risks of being short of the liquid assets necessary to meet withdrawal demands.

Figure 2.2   MI Components as a Percentage of MI

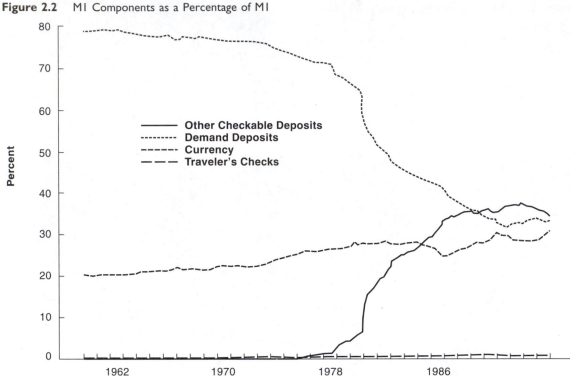

In practice, banks and their major corporate clients have found ways around this prohibition. One arrangement is the zero balance account. It is essentially a demand deposit account against which firms can write checks and in which firms maintain, as the name implies, a zero balance. As checks written against the account arrive at the bank, they are held until a certain predetermined time during the day. Then the bank totals them up and reports the amount to the firm's corporate cash manager, who shifts funds from an interest-bearing asset, usually another account at the same bank, into the zero balance account to clear the checks. Because the holding time for these funds in the non-interest-bearing demand deposit account is zero, the forgone interest income is also zero. Firms pay the commercial banks a fee for providing this service.

An alternative arrangement that became very popular during the 1970s and is an integral part of modern corporate cash management practices today is the use of "earnings credits." Businesses maintain positive balances in non-interest-bearing commercial accounts, which are merely demand deposit accounts with checking privileges. The bank keeps track of the average daily deposit balances and calculates the interest income that the firm would have received on the deposits had the bank been able to pay interest to the firm. The interest rate used in these calculations is usually tied to the prime rate (the interest rate banks charge their major corporate clients for short-term loans) or to a Treasury bill rate. This foregone interest income becomes earnings credits that the firm accrues. The bank then performs services for the firm, such as processing some of the firm's accounts receivable, and determines the total cost to the firm of those services. The firm uses its earnings credits as payment to the bank for the services rendered. Thus, despite regulation prohibiting banks from paying explicit interest on firms' account balances, arrangements between banks and firms enable banks to make implicit payments to firms for the use of their deposits.

The smallest component of M1 is traveler's checks. As shown in Figure 2.2, they constitute less than 1 percent. Traveler's checks can be thought of as privately issued fiat monies that maintain a fixed exchange rate with the U.S. dollar. They differ from government-issued money in that an individual who "purchases" traveler's checks is buying insurance against the possibility of loss or theft. However, they are similar to Federal Reserve notes in that they are backed only by the good name of the issuing company (for example, American Express and Citicorp), which has been sufficient to circulate as a medium of exchange. Their acceptance suggests that competitive pressures to maintain "brand name capital" could possibly allow multiple currencies to circulate successfully in an economy, eliminating the need for the federal government's monopoly control over the economy's money supply.[6]

2.3 M2

The M2 monetary aggregate is a "broader" measure of the money supply than M1. As shown in Table 2.1, it includes all of the components of M1, that is, all of the assets that represent the economy's media of exchange, and several highly liquid, short-term interest-bearing assets: small time deposits (CDs), savings and money market deposit accounts (MMDAs), some money market mutual funds (MMMFs), overnight repurchase agreements issued by banks, and overnight Eurodollar deposits at commercial banks. From Figure 2.1, we see that the total dollar volume of M2 is approximately four times that of M1. The relative contributions of the components of M2 are given in percentage terms in Figure 2.3. The striking change in these percentages between 1960 and 1990 was due to two factors, the market response to the high inflation rates of the 1970s and the deregulation of the banking system principally associated with the DIDMCA of 1980 and the Garn–St. Germaine Amendment in 1982.

In 1960, the U.S. dollar was on the gold standard under the Bretton Woods Agreements and the economy was in a period of general price stability. The inflation rate for that year was essentially zero. However, the banking system was heavily regulated. It was still governed by the Depression-era banking laws of the 1930s. The principal financial products that commercial banks were permitted to offer to attract funds were demand deposit accounts, passbook savings, and small denomination (non-negotiable) certificates of deposit.[7]

---

[6]Privately issued fiat currencies were in use during the nineteenth century in the United States and Scotland. A significant amount of research has been devoted to assessing the merits of these monetary arrangements. See, for example, Rolnick and Weber (1986).

[7]Savings and loans (and the much smaller mutual savings banks and credit unions) were not authorized to offer checking accounts of any kind.

Figure 2.3   Non-M1 Components of M2 as a Percentage of M2

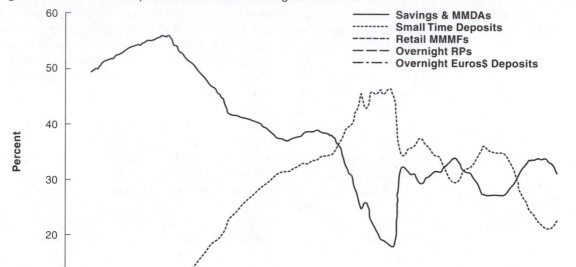

Moreover, interest rate ceilings on passbook savings were set at 5 percent for commercial banks and 5.25 percent for savings and loans. Because the inflation rate was so low, these ceilings were not binding. The passbook savings rate was therefore determined by the market, and for many years was about 3 percent. Passbook savings accounts were a principal vehicle for household savings during the 1950s and 1960s. As Figure 2.3 indicates, they made nearly 50 percent of M2 in 1960 (MMDAs did not exist).

The certificates of deposit available to households in 1960 were also limited in scope. They were issued in denominations up to $10,000 and for maturities ranging from three months to five years. Higher interest rates could be paid on CDs if the household was willing to tie up its money for longer periods of time.[8] However, the liquidity of these assets was low because they carried a penalty for early withdrawal and were non-negotiable. CDs are liabilities of the issuing bank. They are promises to pay their owners a fixed amount at some future

---

[8]The interest received on long-term assets has not always exceeded that received on short-term assets of comparable risk. A graph of the relationship between short-term and long-term interest rates at any point in time, or the yield curve, reflects market expectations of future economic activity and future inflation rates. A theory of the "term structure of interest rates" that explains the shape of the yield curve is described in Chapter 4.

date. Because they are non-negotiable, their owners cannot sell these claims on the bank to a third party at whatever price the third party would be willing to pay. This lack of negotiability (low liquidity) increased the interest rate that banks had to pay on CDs to entice buyers.

During the 1970s, the inflation rate in the United States rose sharply, and by 1980 it had reached 14 percent. Therefore, a nominal interest rate of at least 14 percent would have been necessary on households' savings to prevent a decline in the purchasing power of those assets. Interest rate ceilings on passbook savings were imposed by law. In addition, the prohibition of interest payments on demand deposits made it more costly for households and firms to use checks to conduct transactions. Consequently, households and firms began to pay more attention to the management of their portfolios of short-term assets, and began to seek alternatives to the financial product offerings of commercial banks and S&Ls.

In the late 1970s, numerous private financial firms began to offer services to assist households and nonfinancial firms in coping with this cash management problem. Among these offerings were retail money market mutual funds (MMMFs), such as those offered by Merrill Lynch, Prudential Bache, Goldman Sachs, and other firms. They filled a market niche by acquiring funds that were intended by their owners to be held in highly liquid, short-term assets and placing those funds directly in short-term investments that paid a market rate of interest. Many such investments had been unavailable to most small savers because of the high minimum denomination of the issues. For example, the smallest Treasury bill that one can purchase is $10,000. Table 2.2 is a typical portfolio of assets in (taxable) MMMFs. Many of these assets are included in the monetary aggregates M3 and L (discussed in section 2.4).

Money market mutual funds were very successful in attracting savers during the late 1970s. The growth of retail MMMFs during that period is shown on Figure 2.3. Note that retail MMMFs as a percentage of M2 rose from virtually zero in 1960 to about 10 percent by 1980. The reason for their success was the combination of the Federal Reserve's high inflation policy and low interest rate ceilings on bank deposits. As an example, in 1979 a household could withdraw funds from a passbook savings account that were earning the legal

Table 2.2 Representative Portfolio of MMMFs

	PERCENTAGE OF PORTFOLIO
Commercial paper	35.4
Large CDs	6.8
Bankers' acceptances	.7
Repurchase agreements	15.9
Treasury securities	15.1
Other U.S. securities	14.5
Other	11.6
Total	100.0

maximum of 5.25 percent, place them on deposit with an MMMF, and begin receiving 20 percent interest on the same funds! The high market interest rates (reflecting the high inflation rates of the period) caused households and firms (which invest primarily in institution-only MMMFs, discussed below) to reduce their demand deposit balances by more closely managing their short-term assets. As a result, the supply of funds to the banking system was drying up.

The flight of funds from the banking system created a problem known as disintermediation whereby households were no longer relying on banks and S&Ls to perform the function of a financial intermediary that brings together lenders (and their small deposits) and borrowers (who request large-denomination loans).[9] The disintermediation of the late 1970s not only created problems for the Federal Reserve in conducting monetary policy, but also substantially weakened the banking system and laid the foundation for much of the S&L industry's subsequent difficulty during the 1980s.

The disintermediation problem finally induced Congress in the early 1980s to enact the first major pieces of banking legislation since the Depression-era laws of the 1930s.[10] Some of the provisions of the DIDMCA of 1980 and the Garn–St. Germaine Amendment of 1982 are cited in section 2.2. Beginning in 1980, the prohibition of interest payments on checking accounts (other than commercial accounts) was phased out.[11] In addition, the commercial banks' monopoly over the supply of checking accounts was lifted.[12] S&Ls could now compete with commercial banks in this arena.

One additional regulatory change (part of the Garn-St. Germaine Amendment of 1982) that was very important in solving the disintermediation problem was the legalization of money market deposit accounts (MMDAs). It effectively allowed the regulated depository institutions (principally the commercial banks and the S&Ls) to offer financial products that were competitive with MMMFs. Such products were an overnight success.[13] MMDAs as a per-

---

[9]The theory of financial intermediation is the subject of Chapter 5. Many of the various types of U.S. financial institutions that are important to the money markets and therefore to monetary policy are described in Chapter 6.

[10]The Bank Holding Company Act of 1956 can be seen as equally important from a historical point of view.

[11]This provision in the law was known as Regulation Q. Legal restrictions on interest payments on checking accounts were not completely eliminated until April 1986.

[12]Because of loopholes in the laws and the desire of the Federal Reserve as one of the chief regulators of the banking system to see Regulation Q lifted, some commercial banks in the New England states, in addition to credit unions around the country, offered interest-bearing checkable deposit accounts. The presence of these accounts prior to their nationwide legalization in 1980 can be noted in Figure 2.3.

[13]This success is attributable partly to aggressive initial pricing of MMDAs by depository institutions. They offered above-market interest rates for several months after these accounts were introduced.

centage of M2 rose dramatically from zero to 8 percent in just two months after their initial offerings in December 1982, and by 1990 they represented 25 percent of M2. In dollar terms, the numbers were impressive. Just three months after the initial offerings, more than $300 billion had been invested in MMDAs—an amount roughly equivalent to the dollar volume of all U.S. currency in circulation and more than one-third of the dollar volume of M1. Funds were flowing back into the banking system.

The success of MMMFs and MMDAs created problems for the Federal Reserve in its effort to measure and monitor the nation's money supply. Prior to 1980, the monetary aggregates that the Federal Reserve had defined as its empirical measures of the money supply did not include MMMFs. However, MMMFs had become an important repository for the short-term assets of households and firms. Moreover, the success of MMMFs caused erratic movements in the dollar volume of the (earlier) monetary aggregates that the Federal Reserve could not explain. The definitions of the money supply became less useful in conducting monetary policy because the Federal Reserve was less certain about how fast the aggregates should be allowed to grow. This problem was rectified in 1980 when the Federal Reserve completely redefined the monetary aggregates to take into account the changes that had occurred in the financial markets, as well as the regulatory changes that had already taken place and those anticipated in the near future.[14]

One issue was where to include the new money market instruments, such as retail MMMFs, in the new monetary aggregates. The degree of demand substitutability between the assets was the principal factor in these decisions. For example, when deciding on where to place retail MMMFs in the monetary aggregates, the Federal Reserve recognized that the large quantity of funds flowing into retail MMMFs was flowing out of passbook savings and small time deposits (CDs). The latter two assets were part of M2, so the Federal Reserve was logically led to include MMMFs as a component of M2.[15] A similar problem arose in 1982 when MMDAs were legalized. Again, the Federal Reserve conducted studies to determine where the enormous flow of funds into MMDAs originated.[16] The evidence indicated three primary sources: small retail CDs, retail MMMFs, and passbook savings. Hence, the Federal Reserve included MMDAs in M2. Authorizing the regulated depository institutions to issue MMDAs did reverse some of the disintermediation of the previous decade, but

---

[14]The previous monetary aggregates had explicitly recognized the distinction between commercial banks and other regulated financial institutions. From a legal standpoint, this distinction has largely, although not completely, vanished.

[15]As seen in Table 2.1, some of the funds in MMMFs are in fact investments in other components of M2, such as small CDs. To avoid double counting, they are subtracted from the total volume of CDs outstanding in calculation of the total value of M2.

[16]See Tatom (1983) for an analysis of the flow of funds just after the introduction of MMDAs.

most of the funds that were flowing into MMDAs were coming at the expense of other financial product offerings of the banks and S&Ls.[17]

Retail MMMFs, which are comprised of money funds with less than $100,000 per account have found a permanent market niche because they provide three advantages not found elsewhere. First, they enable households to enter investment markets that once were closed to small investors. Second, they offer diversification in money market instruments, enabling households to invest a portion of their funds in some risky assets and thus receive a higher expected rate of return on their investment. This advantage is reflected in the positive spread between the interest rates received on retail MMMFs and MMDAs.[18] The third advantage is that MMMFs complement stock and bond mutual funds, which have grown dramatically. As households have turned in large numbers to mutual fund investing, money market mutual funds have helped to diversify the households' overall investment portfolios and have been a convenient short-term repository for funds that are moving into and out of the capital markets. In recent years, commercial banks have developed in-house mutual fund operations, including stock and bond mutual funds as well as MMMFs, as the popularity of this form of investment has continued to grow. In 1994, commercial banks had only a small share of the mutual fund business, but their share is expected to grow rapidly in the future.

A legacy of the high inflation rates of the 1970s is a much more efficient allocation of liquid assets in the U.S. economy. It has been reflected in the growth in money market mutual funds and businesses' closer control of their cash management practices. Two assets that are important to both mutual fund managers and individual corporate cash managers, and therefore have become larger markets since the mid-1970s, are overnight repurchase agreements issued by commercial banks and overnight Eurodollar deposits at commercial banks. They are the two remaining components of M2 listed in Table 2.1.[19] Overnight

---

[17]One of the mysteries of the late 1970s and early 1980s was why passbook savings accounts remained in demand by households. The interest differential between passbook accounts and retail MMMFs exceeded 10 percentage points, and the limited checking privileges on retail MMMFs suggested that those funds offered greater liquidity. Passbook deposits did decline through the period, but slowly. Even more difficult to understand is how well passbook accounts withstood the introduction of MMDAs. Not only were those assets paying roughly three percentage points more in interest at the time, but they were issued by the same institutions and had virtually the same liquidity. Minimum balance requirements on retail MMMFs and MMDAs could explain some of this behavior, but certainly not all.

[18]Whereas all investments in MMDAs are federally insured up to $100,000, only the portion of the investment portfolio of MMMFs that is issued by commercial banks and S&Ls is insured. The primary uninsured asset in MMMFs is commercial paper. However, very little risk is associated with that asset.

[19]To avoid double-counting, the overnight bank RPs and Eurodollar deposits at commercial banks that are reported as separate components of M2 exclude those held by MMMFs.

repurchase agreements, also known as repos or RPs, are essentially contracts for overnight collaterized loans whereby the lender agrees to repurchase the funds the following day at a price that is reduced by the amount of interest that would have accrued on the funds overnight. One of the principal sources of RP collateral is U.S. Treasury securities.[20] The lender of the funds takes possession of the securities during the term of the agreement, (overnight), then returns them to the borrower when the loan is paid off. Overnight Eurodollar deposits at commercial banks are similar financial arrangements. The source of funds is deposit accounts at banks outside the United States. The non–U.S. banks lend money overnight to U.S. banks, which return them with interest the following day. Bank RPs and Eurodollar deposits at commercial banks are included in the monetary aggregates because they represent sources of funds to domestic banks that are alternatives to traditional deposit accounts. Although these assets are not a large part of M2, as Figure 2.3 indicates, they are a major source of volatility in M2 on a weekly basis.

2.4 M3 AND L

The remaining monetary aggregates constructed by the Federal Reserve are M3 and L. Historically they have been much less important in monetary policy than M1 and M2, but they continue to be closely monitored. Their components are listed in Table 2.1.

In aggregating up to M3 and to L, the Federal Reserve adds to M2 certain sets of assets typically used by large investors, usually firms. Such assets are not as substitutable for M1 assets as the non-M1 components of M2. For M3, they consist of large time deposits, generally large denomination (jumbo) CDs, institution-only (IO) MMMFs, term bank RPs, and term Eurodollars at commercial banks. To obtain the aggregate L, the Federal Reserve adds Treasury bills, commercial paper, U.S. savings bonds, and banker's acceptances to M3. Figures 2.4 and 2.5 show the dollar volumes of these assets as percentages of M3 and L, respectively.

Large CDs typically have a minimum denomination of $100,000 and a maturity in excess of three years. However, their liquidity is generally enhanced by negotiability. They can be sold to a third party through a secondary market and are often used in individual corporate cash management portfolios. The value of CDs included in this separate M3 listing excludes CDs that make up a portion of the portfolios of MMMFs. Even so, more than $300 billion is invested in these CDs and they comprise approximately 12 percent of M3.

Large investors such as large corporations, bank trusts, and some pension funds that have more than $100,000 to invest in short-term money market instruments often choose MMMFs for convenience and diversification. Because

---

[20]The repo market for Treasuries plays a vital role in the actual implementation of monetary policy decisions through open-market operations. It is discussed at length in Chapter 17.

Figure 2.4   Non-M2 Components of M3 as a Percentage of M3

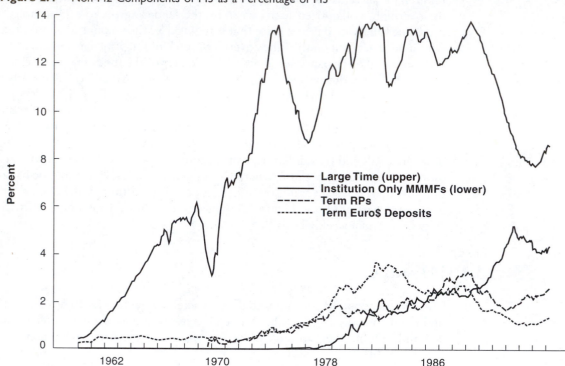

these large investors in MMMFs manage their asset portfolios much more closely than small investors in MMMFs, their investments tend to be much more interest sensitive and are close substitutes for large time deposits. They are therefore listed separately as IO MMMFs and are included in the M3 monetary aggregate.

Bank term repurchase agreements and term Eurodollar deposits at commercial banks are identical to their overnight counterparts, but their maturities exceed 24 hours. Together they represent only about 1.5 percent of M3. Commercial paper is often characterized as a "corporate IOU." In practice it is a mechanism by which large, very creditworthy corporations such as IBM can raise funds to cover short-term expenses without borrowing against their credit lines with commercial banks. In some cases, it is cheaper for the firms to borrow directly in the credit markets than to go through a financial intermediary. The maturity of commercial paper generally ranges from six months to one year.

Banker's acceptances are very old and specialized financial instruments. They are used primarily to finance the purchase of internationally traded goods while the goods are in transit. (See the Appendix 2.1.) Banker's acceptances are highly liquid assets because they are actively traded in the secondary market. In addition, they are essentially riskless in that they are backed by the commercial banks. They therefore carry a lower interest rate than commercial paper. The percentages of both commercial paper and banker's acceptances reported in Figure 2.3 exclude the share in MMMFs, which for commercial paper is a substantial fraction of the total.

Figure 2.5   Non-M3 Components of L as a Percentage of L

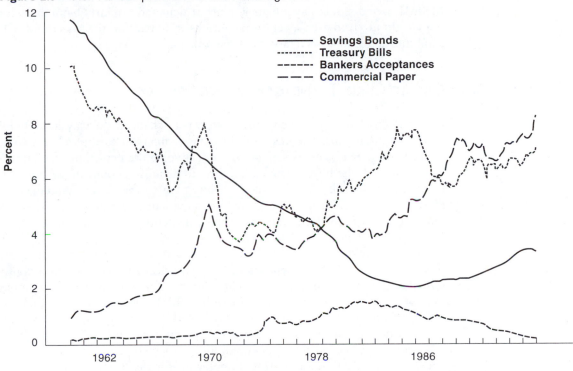

2.5 UNITS OF MONEY

The discussion in subsequent chapters relies heavily on the abstraction of an aggregate money market. Money demand and money supply are discussed as though "money" were a homogenous asset, which of course it is not. Therefore, for this concept of "money" to be useful, a unit of money must be defined in a meaningful way. The most sensible definition is one based on the relative quantities of various money market instruments in the economy. A portfolio of those assets can be constructed with weight given to each asset in proportion to its actual share in the economy. A unit of money can then be defined as one dollar's worth of the portfolio. For example, the portfolio could consist of all of the economy's monetary instruments with medium-of-exchange properties, or M1. A unit of money would then consist of 29 cents in currency, 34 cents in demand deposits, 37 cents in other checkable deposits, and a penny in traveler's checks. When we consider the demand for money, the asset properties of this portfolio would be very high liquidity (as all of the assets are media of exchange), very low risk (as they are all directly or indirectly backed by the government[21]), and a low return (in this case, .37 times the interest rate paid on other checkable deposit accounts). A similar definition could be developed in terms of M2. In

---

[21]Although FDIC insurance on bank deposits is limited to $100,000 per account.

that case, money would be less liquid and slightly riskier (because of retail MMMFs), and would pay a higher return, calculated similarly by multiplying the weight given to each asset by the interest rate paid on that asset and then summing across all assets. (See the Appendix 2.2.)

2.6 CREDIT CARD TRANSACTIONS AND MONEY

Over the past 20 years, credit cards have vastly changed the way households conduct transactions. The medium of exchange in credit card purchases is the credit card system. The exchange does not involve the depletion of a buyer's assets. Instead, the buyer incurs a liability. In acquiring goods or services, the buyer assumes a debt. An individual's ability to incur this debt is limited, either directly by the credit card issuer or by the individual's own prudence. The debt must be repaid in the future, necessitating a depletion of assets, some of which comprise the monetary aggregates.

For example, credit card bills are normally paid by check. The household therefore must have bank deposits sufficient to clear the check when it is presented to the bank. Thus, the credit card purchase ultimately involves a money market asset, the demand deposit (or other checkable deposit) account. The management of such deposit accounts and other monetary assets may have changed because of the increased usage of credit cards. Households may now hold more or less currency or maintain higher or lower checking account balances than they did in the past. It is important for the Federal Reserve to discover exactly how credit card transactions may have affected the overall demand for the monetary aggregates, because it is the supply of one or more of those aggregates that the Federal Reserve is attempting to control. It needs to know how fast the aggregates can be allowed to expand without inducing either a "credit crunch" (when they are expanded too slowly) or inflation (when they are expanded too rapidly). How the Federal Reserve approaches this issue is the subject of the next chapter.

2.7 SUMMARY

The Federal Reserve constructs monetary aggregates to assist in its conduct of monetary policy. To that end, it seeks to identify monetary aggregates whose dollar value bears a stable relationship to the macroeconomic variables, such as real GDP and the CPI, that are used to define the goals of monetary policy. By influencing the rate of expansion of the aggregates (which is the subject of Chapter 7), the Federal Reserve is able to affect the macroeconomy in a way that is consistent with its goals.

The monetary aggregates are alternative groupings of the various monetary assets in the economy and are based on the relative demand substitutability between those assets. The narrowest definition of money is the M1 aggregate, which includes all of the economy's media of exchange. Over time, the relationship between M1 and the macroeconomy changes, not only in response to regulatory changes, but also as the payment system evolves. For example, the current trend toward greater reliance on credit and debit cards and the increasing use of electronic funds transfers may mitigate the need for large holdings of monetary assets that have medium-of-exchange features. To the Federal Reserve, what is important about these changes is that they are not always predictable.

Less liquid short-term assets are successively added to the list of M1 assets to arrive at the broader definitions of money, M2 and M3. The demand for those aggregates has been less influenced by the evolution of the economy's payment system than the demand for M1. However, other institutional factors, such as the rapid growth of bond and stock mutual funds, have affected the demand for M2 and M3. Obviously, the Federal Reserve must understand how these and other regulatory, institutional, and technological factors affect the demand for the monetary aggregates if the aggregates are to remain useful in policy deliberations. For that reason, the study of the demand for money—which is the topic of the next chapter—is an ongoing process at the Federal Reserve, and at its center are the monetary aggregates.

◼ REVIEW QUESTIONS

1. More than 50% of the U.S. currency is estimated to be held abroad.
   (a) Discuss this phenomenon in terms of the functions of money in an economy as a medium of exchange, store of value, and unit of account.
   (b) Under what conditions could this phenomenon create a problem for the Federal Reserve in interpreting the behavior of the M1 aggregate for policy purposes? Under what conditions does it not create a problem?

2. Demand deposit accounts and other checkable deposits are types of checking accounts.
   (a) Which institutions are legally able to offer such accounts? This group of institutions has changed over time. When and why was there a change?
   (b) How do the accounts differ?
   (c) Who holds demand deposit accounts and why?

3. Compare the following assets in terms of risk, return, and liquidity.
   (a) Retail MMMFs and small time deposits.
   (b) NOW accounts and passbook savings.
   (c) Commercial paper and MMDAs
   (d) Banker's acceptances and Treasury bills
   (e) Large time deposits and demand deposit accounts

*4. Since the mid-1970s, retail money market mutual funds have become extremely popular with the public, and institution-only (IO) money market mutual funds have become equally popular with large investors. By definition, these two categories of MMMFs differ only in investment size, consisting of investments smaller than $100,000 and investments larger than $100,000, respectively.

(a) Examine the components of the M2 and M3 aggregates and speculate on why retail MMMFs were included in M2 whereas IO MMMFs were included in M3.

(b) The interest rate paid on shares in MMMFs is determined as a weighted average of the individual returns on the assets in a fund's portfolio of holdings. Because these assets are all of relatively short maturity, MMMF managers generally hold them until maturity. As a result, there is a lagged response in the adjustment of MMMF rates to changes in market rates on the underlying assets that make up the funds' portfolios. Explain how and why you would expect the total volume of funds in MMMFs to change in response to a rise in short-term market interest rates. Speculate on whether this response is likely to be greater in retail MMMFs or in IO MMMFs and why.

*5. The term "retail bank deposits" is often used to refer to demand deposits, other checkable deposits, passbook savings, MMDAs, and small time deposits. When short-term market interest rates are rising in the economy, the demand for total retail bank deposits falls. However, the various types of deposits do not respond identically; small time deposit rates generally rise more rapidly than other retail deposit interest rates.

(a) From the bank's point of view, speculate on why deposit rates behave in this way.

(b) In the case of rising short-term market interest rates, how would you anticipate the growth in these various retail deposits to vary?

(c) Is there likely to be more variation in the growth of the individual types of retail deposits than in their sum? What does this difference imply about the M2 aggregate?

2.1 APPENDIX

Banker's Acceptances: Their Role in Financing Internationally Traded Goods

Banker's acceptances can be illustrated best by way of example. The second largest internationally traded commodity (after oil) is coffee. For discussion, suppose a U.S. coffee importer wants to purchase a large volume of coffee from a Brazilian exporter, which the importer could then sell to a U.S. coffee processor. The problem is that the coffee processor is unwilling to pay for the coffee until it has been delivered, and the coffee exporter is unwilling to ship the coffee before being paid. However, it may take a week for the coffee to travel by sea from Brazil to the United States. The U.S. importer therefore must borrow the funds needed to pay the exporter for the length of time it takes to ship the coffee to the United States and sell it to the processor. To arrange for this financing, the importer can request that a commercial bank issue a banker's acceptance (BA) in the amount of the purchase price. The banker's acceptance is essentially a promise by the bank to pay its owner its face value on a predetermined date.

In this case, the date could be one week after the BA is issued. The exporter can then take the banker's acceptance to the secondary market and sell it to obtain the funds needed to purchase the coffee. The purchaser of the BA could be an MMMF manager who is looking for a short-term, highly liquid, relatively riskless asset to balance out the portfolio. Note that the MMMF manager, and not the bank, is actually making the loan to the importer. Once the importer has sold the BA, the funds can be sent to the exporter as payment for the coffee, which in turn is shipped to the United States. In one week the coffee arrives in the United States and the importer sells it to the processor, then takes the proceeds from the sale (less the profit from the transaction) to the bank in time for the bank to redeem the banker's acceptance when it matures. The bank receives a fee for this service.

2.2   APPENDIX

Calculating the Return on M1 Money and M2 Money

The return on money is defined as the interest rate received on a portfolio of the assets that make up a monetary aggregate. Weights are given to the assets of the portfolio in proportion to their shares in the aggregate.

For an assumed set of interest rates, the following returns on M1 and M2 are calculated by using the weights from Table 2.1. Notice that the higher return on M2 is due to the fact that a dollar of M2 is both less liquid and more risky than a dollar of M1.

COMPONENTS OF M1	WEIGHTS	INTEREST RATE (%)	RETURN (%)
Currency	.318	—	—
Demand deposits	.332	—	—
Other checkable deposits	.342	2.00	.68
Traveler's checks	.008	—	—
Total return on M1			.68

COMPONENTS OF M2	WEIGHTS	INTEREST RATE (%)	RETURN (%)
M1	.316	.68	.21
Small time deposits	.246	3.25	.80
Savings & MMDAs	.297	3.00	.89
MMMFs (broker/dealer)	.108	3.25	.35
Overnight RPs	.023	3.25	.07
Overnight Eurodollars	.008	3.25	.03
Total return on M2			2.36

2.3 APPENDIX

Total Nonfinancial Domestic Debt: An Aggregate Measure of Domestic Credit

Because the Federal Reserve can influence the rate at which overall credit in the economy is expanding, it has been suggested that it should attempt to regulate credit exclusively and not be concerned with the monetary aggregates. The Federal Reserve monitors a measure of aggregate credit in the economy called domestic nonfinancial debt, which consists primarily of U.S. government and U.S. government agency securities, corporate and foreign bonds, mortgages, consumer credit, and commercial paper. This credit aggregate has not proven to be as useful for policy decisions as the monetary aggregates because its relationship to the real economy is much weaker. (The relationships between the monetary aggregates and the real economy are discussed at length in Chapter 3.) However, the Federal Reserve continues to monitor this aggregate as it may provide some information on indebtedness that cannot be easily obtained elsewhere.

REFERENCES

Clower, Robert. 1967. "A Reconsideration of the Microfoundations of Monetary Theory." *Western Economic Journal* 6 (December): 1–8.

Rolnick, A. J., and Warren E. Weber. 1986. "Inherent Instability in Banking: The Free Banking Experience." *Cato Journal* 5 (Winter): 877–90.

Tatom, John A. 1983. "Money Market Deposit Accounts, Super-NOWs, and Monetary Policy." *Review*. Federal Reserve Bank of St. Louis (March).

CHAPTER 3

THE DEMAND FOR MONEY

In Chapter 2, money is defined as a portfolio of short-term financial assets. The definition of money can be changed by altering the composition of the portfolio. Moreover, because portfolios have different liquidity, risk, and return characteristics, the definition of money differs accordingly. Those characteristics represent the asset properties of money on which households' and firms' demands for money are based.

This chapter presents a theory of the demand for money that applies to both households and firms. The theory is narrowly focused and is often called a partial equilibrium model because it abstracts from the household's important economic decisions that determine the general equilibrium resource allocations for the entire economy. Those decisions include the allocation of income/wealth between consumption and savings, the allocation of time between leisure and labor (or nonleisure activities),[1] and the portfolio allocation of the household's wealth. In this chapter, discussion of the theory is confined to only one aspect of the portfolio allocation problem: how the household should optimally manage its short-term financial asset holdings, one of which is money.[2] The value of the theory is that it yields a "positive" prediction that certain (behavioral) relationships between money, income, interest rates, and prices exist.[3] Those predictions are examined for M1 and M2.

---

[1] The time allocation decision is the central feature of Chapter 1.

[2] An alternative partial equilibrium model of money demand is described in Chapter 14, which does not highlight the economic function that money performs in the economy as a medium of exchange, but concentrates instead on the store-of-value property of money. As noted in Chapter 1, fiat money is a store of value only because it is a commonly accepted medium of exchange and vice versa.

[3] A positive prediction implies that there is a testable aspect to the theory. The classic statement of the value of positive theories—that is, those with testable implications—is given by Friedman (1953).

3.1   A HOUSEHOLD'S TRANSACTIONS DEMAND FOR MONEY

Households have certain liquidity needs associated with consumption. They must be able to convert their income, which is a net addition to their wealth, into consumption purchases. Liquidity needs therefore depend on monetary assets that have the medium-of-exchange property. The greater the liquidity of the asset, the lower is the return. Hence, liquidity comes at cost, which implies that households have an incentive to manage their wealth portfolio to balance their liquidity needs against the loss of interest income.[4]

To examine the tradeoff between liquidity and interest income, we can think through how an individual household carries out its consumption plans once those plans are established.[5] Individual households normally receive income at regular intervals, such as once each week or every other week. Those intervals are called payments periods. A fraction of the income is consumed and the remainder is saved or added to the household's wealth. The fraction of income consumed is called the average propensity to consume, or apc.[6] For a given apc, an increase in income leads to a proportional increase in the level of planned consumption.

Once a household has made its consumption decision, it faces a cash management problem of how to implement its consumption plans optimally. The problem has two aspects. First, income is received in a lump sum at the beginning of each payments period, but the household generally wants to spread its consumption over the payments period, consuming some amount each day. Therefore, the income that has been set aside for consumption throughout the payments period must be stored in some form while it is gradually being drawn down for consumption purchases. Second, to purchase consumption goods, the household must have liquid assets that are media of exchange because a consumption purchase is an exchange of money for goods. To convert its stored income into consumption, the household must convert it into money, which can then be exchanged for goods. The cash management problem is to determine for each payments period the least costly way of retaining the stored income while fulfilling the consumption plans.

One option available to the household, call it plan A, is to convert all of the stored income that is to be consumed during the payments period into money at the beginning of the period. If the household consumes the same amount each day, the money balance will be drawn down uniformly until it is completely exhausted at the end of the payments period, as shown in Figure 3.1. It could

---

[4]This model was first developed by Baumol (1952) and Tobin (1956).

[5]How these plans are selected in a general equilibrium context is described at length in subsequent chapters.

[6]In the United States this fraction is approximately 97 percent, whereas in Japan it is approximately 80 percent. It reflects the notoriously low U.S. savings rate of 3 percent and the notoriously high Japanese savings rate of 20 percent.

Figure 3.1
Household Money
Balances over the
Payments Period
under Alternative
Cash Management
Plans

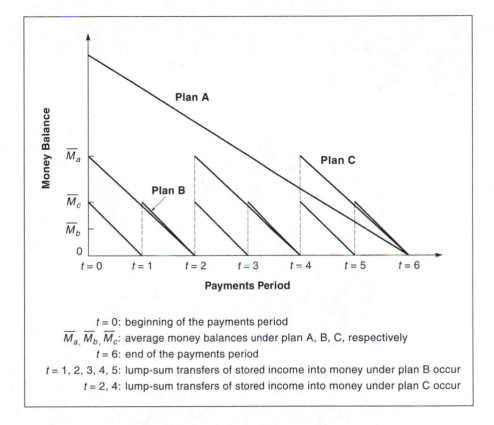

$t = 0$: beginning of the payments period
$\overline{M}_a, \overline{M}_b, \overline{M}_c$: average money balances under plan A, B, C, respectively
$t = 6$: end of the payments period
$t = 1, 2, 3, 4, 5$: lump-sum transfers of stored income into money under plan B occur
$t = 2, 4$: lump-sum transfers of stored income into money under plan C occur

then be replenished from next period's income. However, the interest rate received on money balances is generally very low because their liquidity is very high. An opportunity cost therefore is associated with money balances. It is determined by the interest income that could have been earned had the household chosen to place the stored income in a less liquid asset paying a higher interest rate. The interest income forgone is equal to the average money balance over the payments period, shown in Figure 3.1 as $\overline{M}_a$, times the spread between the interest rate paid on the less liquid asset, r_s, and the rate of return on money, r_m. The total interest income forgone is then equal to $(r_s - r_m)\overline{M}_a$. This cost is plotted on Figure 3.2 as TC_a.

A second option available to the household, call it plan B, is to place nearly all of the stored income in a less liquid asset at the beginning of the payments period, and then make frequent conversions into money whenever consumption purchases are to be made. Plan B is also represented in Figure 3.1. Note that it substantially reduces the average money balance for the period, denoted $\overline{M}_b$. Hence, the opportunity cost of money holdings is also much less under plan B than under plan A because they have been reduced by an amount equal to $(r_s - r_m)(\overline{M}_a - \overline{M}_b)$ dollars. A transaction cost is associated with the conversions, however. For example, the household may have to pay service charges for ATM usage as well as incur the cost of its time in making trips to the ATM machine. If each conversion has a fixed cost that is valued by the household at B_b dollars,

Figure 3.2
Total Cost of Cash
Management over the
Payments Period
under Alternative
Plans

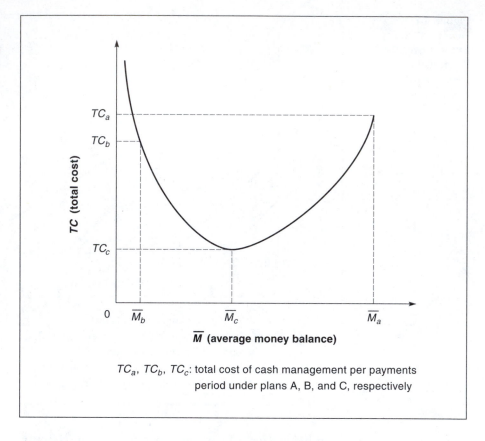

TC_a, TC_b, TC_c: total cost of cash management per payments
period under plans A, B, and C, respectively

and if the household makes n_b conversions during the payments period, then under plan B the household incurs the transaction cost of $B_b n_b$ dollars. When that cost is added to the interest income forgone for plan B, we see in Figure 3.2 that the total cost of cash management, TC_b, which equals $(r_s - r_m)\overline{M}_b + B_b n_b$ dollars, is very high. Note that $\overline{M}_b$ and n_b cannot be chosen separately. Choosing the average money balance for the period to be $\overline{M}_b$ necessitates n_b conversions. We can easily see how transaction costs could outweigh the additional interest income earned by maintaining lower money balances. The household therefore has an incentive to minimize the number of such conversions.

The optimal cash management plan is one that minimizes the sum of these two costs, such as plan C in Figure 3.1. Under this plan the household maintains a sufficient amount of liquidity (measured by $\overline{M}_c$) to carry out its consumption plans while avoiding both the excessive loss of interest income associated with high average money balances as in plan A and the large transaction costs associated with frequent conversions of its stored income from a less liquid asset into money as in plan B. The total costs of cash management, TC_c, are thereby minimized under this plan as shown in Figure 3.2. (See the Mathematical Appendix 3.1 for the optimization problem.)

3.2 A HOUSEHOLD'S PRECAUTIONARY DEMAND FOR MONEY

Typically, households cannot perfectly plan the timing or even the magnitude of their consumption expenditures. Moreover, their income stream cannot be completely predicted. Even if they know precisely what their nominal income is, price changes can alter the purchasing power of that income. To guard against unexpected expenditures or shortfalls of income, households generally hold a precautionary "buffer stock" of money. It represents the amount of money over and above the amount they plan to spend within the period, as reflected by the fact that, in general, households do not fully deplete their money balances. Buffer stocks tend to rise during times of increased uncertainty about real income.

3.3 THE DEMAND FOR MONEY BY FIRMS

The theory of the transaction demand for money was developed for an individual household, but it applies equally well to firms. Compare the pattern of lump sum income and continuous expenditures shown in Figure 3.1 for the household with the pattern of continuous receipts (from sales) and lump sum payments (or dispursements) shown in Figure 3.3 for firms.

Firms have different cash management problems than households in terms of the interest income forgone. As discussed in Chapter 2, the prohibition against interest payments on commercial accounts tends to raise the opportunity cost of holding money for firms. However, firms may choose among a different and generally larger set of assets when seeking to store the portion of their receipts (income) that is ultimately dedicated to payments (expenditures) within a period. In addition, firms confront a different set of costs of converting the stored income into money. Such costs typically involve capital and labor expenses as well as the costs associated with a "cash-out," a complete depletion of money balances.[7] In an uncertain environment, where both receipts and expenditures can fluctuate, the likelihood of a "cash-out" increases and firms optimally choose larger money balances for precautionary reasons.[8] Minimizing the total costs of cash management is the task of the modern corporate cash manager, who in general faces the same qualitative tradeoff as households in

---

[7]The latter costs are grouped under the heading of "illiquidity costs" and include reputation losses associated with missed payments and lost discounts on purchases of intermediate goods when payment is not timely (within 30 days). See Miller and Orr (1966), Whalen (1966), and Tsiang (1969) for discussions of these costs.

[8]With the close control that firms exercise today over their cash positions, it is likely that after the compensating balances held at commercial banks, and associated with "earnings credits" are deducted, the bulk of M1 assets held by firms, unlike those held by households, is held for precautionary reasons.

Figure 3.3
Firm's Money Balances over the Payments Period

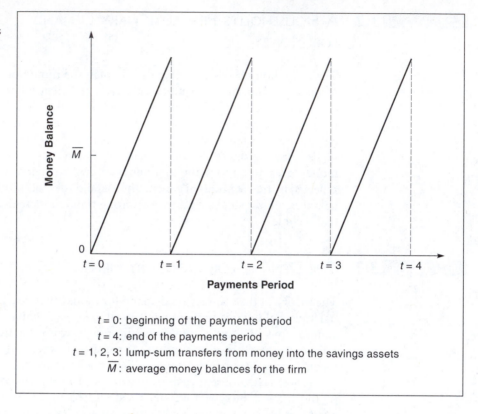

t = 0: beginning of the payments period
t = 4: end of the payments period
t = 1, 2, 3: lump-sum transfers from money into the savings assets
$\overline{M}$: average money balances for the firm

maintaining sufficient liquidity while avoiding an excessive loss of interest income.

3.4 AN AGGREGATE MONEY DEMAND FUNCTION

According to the theory just presented, the average money balances that households and firms choose to maintain are determined by several factors. One factor is the scale of overall monetary expenditures during the payments period, which is determined by the volume of real expenditures and the price per item or unit price of expenditures. For households, with a given *apc*, the volume of real expenditures is the level of consumption purchases, which is proportional to their real income, denoted y_h. For firms, the volume of real expenditures is equal to the real wage payments and the dollar volume of intermediate goods used in production.[9] In general, these expenditures can be assumed to be

---

[9]There are also rental payments on capital and interest payments to bondholders and other creditors of the firm. They are ignored here because the frequency of those lump-sum payments is much lower than the hypothetical "payments period," so their effects on the firm's demand for money are minimal.

roughly proportional to the firm's output, denoted y_f. The unit prices of all expenditures tend to rise and fall with a general inflation or deflation in the economy. To account for changes in the demand for money that are induced by inflation, a general price index must be computed that is a weighted average of the prices of monetary expenditures. For households, this price index would be similar to the consumer price index (CPI), which measures the price of an average market basket of consumption goods. Denote this price level by P_h. A similar price index could be constructed for firms that would weight the prices of labor and raw material inputs utilized by the firm. Denote this index P_f.

A second factor determining average money balances is the opportunity cost of holding money. On a per-dollar basis, this cost is the interest income forgone, which is equal to the spread between the interest rate of the less liquid asset and the interest rate of money. Denote this spread as $r = r_s - r_m$. Because of the differences in the opportunities available to households and firms for storing income short-term, and the differences in the media of exchange available to households and firms (primarily due to the prohibition on interest payments on commercial accounts discussed in Chapter 2), the opportunity cost may differ for households and firms. Therefore, denote the spread as r_h for households and as r_f for firms.

The third factor is the cost to households and firms of conversions of stored income into money, B. This cost is a reflection of the technology of the economy's payment system. As the technology improves, the conversions become less costly and B falls.[10] Again, this cost differs between households and firms because they employ different technologies. Denote such costs as B_h and B_f, respectively. Finally, the level of uncertainty about income and expenditures will affect the levels of precautionary money balances held by households and firms. Denote these levels of uncertainty by σ_h for households and by σ_f for firms (σ is the Greek letter "sigma").

The demand for money by households and firms can be expressed as functions of the three factors. The household's money demand function is

$$\overline{M}_h = f_h(\overset{+}{B_h}, \overset{-}{r_h}, \overset{+}{y_h}, \overset{+}{P_h}, \overset{+}{\sigma_h}) \tag{3.1}$$

where the signs above the factors indicate how the demand for money by households responds to increases in those factors. Similarly, the firm's money demand function is

$$\overline{M}_f = f_f(\overset{+}{B_f}, \overset{-}{r_f}, \overset{+}{y_f}, \overset{+}{P_f}, \overset{+}{\sigma_f}) \ . \tag{3.2}$$

---

[10]The rate of technological change in the payment system is a function of capital investment in the payment system. This is an endogenous choice made by firms that either provide the payment system for others, such as commercial banks, or utilize capital in their own cash management practices. The investment decision is influenced by distortionary monetary policies and banking regulations. See Marquis and Cunningham (1990) and Ireland (1994a).

The question now is: How can these theoretical money demand functions for individual households and firms be made useful? The answer to this question lies in our ability to generalize the functions, which is the process macroeconomists call aggregation. One generalization, or level of aggregation, could be to assume that a single money demand function similar to f_h can be applied to all households and that a single money demand function similar to f_f can be applied to all firms. We would then be able to estimate these functions statistically.

A still higher level of aggregation may be possible. As previously indicated, the factors in the money demand functions for households and firms differ but are obviously related. Improvements in information and telecommunications technology would be likely to lower both B_h and B_f and reduce the demand for money in both the household and firm sectors. Similarly, interest rates (for assets of like maturity and risk) tend to move together in such a way that the opportunity costs of holding money in the two sectors, measured by r_h and r_f, would tend to rise and fall together with qualitatively similar effects on the demands for money. Real personal income, y_h, and real output, y_f, for the economy are also related, as are the levels of uncertainty about that income and output, σ_h and σ_f. A general inflation throughout the economy would raise all prices, and therefore all price indices, including P_h and P_f, would tend to move together. Hence, it may be possible to estimate a single aggregate money demand function for the economy as a whole. It would take the following form.

$$M^d = \overset{+\ -\ +\ +\ +}{F(B, r, y, P, \sigma)} \qquad (3.3)$$

M^d is the aggregate demand for money, B is an average cost associated with conversion of stored income into money and is determined by the overall level of technology of the economy's payment system, r is the opportunity cost of holding one dollar of money versus holding that dollar in a "representative," less liquid asset, P is an aggregate price index such as the CPI, and y and σ are measures of overall economic activity, such as real gross domestic product (GDP), and the level of uncertainty associated with that level of economic activity due, for example, to business cycle fluctuations.

3.5   ESTIMATING THE DEMAND FOR MONEY

The aggregation process is simply a way to approximate the behavior of a large number of individuals from the predicted behavior of one individual. That is, real world counterparts to the factors in the functions discussed above could be selected; then, for a given definition of money from among those described in Chapter 2, estimates of quantitative responses of desired money holdings to changes in those factors could be made for all households, all firms, or the entire economy. For example, by estimating the function f_h, we could determine approximately how much households would increase their collective demand for money if their average income rose by a certain amount, say by 1 percent. Similarly, estimates of the function F could indicate approximately how much the demand for money in the economy as a whole would rise with an increase of, say, 1 percent in real GDP.

If the approximations are good, the aggregations can be a useful way to determine approximately how much money individuals want to hold or the quantity of money that is in demand by the entire economy. Obviously, the Federal Reserve must have such information when it decides how much money to supply. If the approximations are not good, the aggregations are not only not useful, but could actually be misleading to the Federal Reserve; in continuing to rely on them, it could mistakenly over- or undersupply money to the economy. Such mistakes can have consequences for the economy in the short run in terms of recessions and booms, and may also adversely affect the long-run growth potential of the economy. Because of the importance of these statistical relationships for the proper conduct of monetary policy, the Federal Reserve spends a significant amount of its resources on monitoring them and attempting to identify any changes in them that could cause its policy decisions to be incorrect.

To estimate the money demand functions, we must first choose a particular form for the functions. Both theory (see Mathematical Appendix 3.1) and experience indicate that useful approximations can be obtained with a log-linear model. For the aggregate money demand function, F, in equation (3.3), it would take the following form.

$$\log M^d = \alpha_0 \log B - \alpha_1 \log r + \alpha_2 \log y + \alpha_3 \log P + \alpha_4 \log \sigma \quad (3.4)$$

In principle, statistical estimates can be made of the values of α_0, α_1, α_2, α_3, and α_4. These so-called "coefficient estimates" have a useful interpretation. They are, in fact, elasticities. For example, α_3 is the price elasticity of the aggregate demand for money and its numerical value therefore has the following interpretation: an increase in the price level, P, of 1 percent raises the demand for money by α_3 percent when there are no changes in any of the other factors. Similar interpretations can be given to α_0, the transaction cost elasticity of money demand; $(-\alpha_1)$, the interest rate elasticity of money demand; α_2, the real GDP or real income elasticity of money demand; and α_4, the output or real income uncertainty elasticity of money demand.

In practice, good proxies for the average costs of converting stored income into money, B, and for the degree of uncertainty about the level of economic activity, σ, do not exist. Therefore, an additional approximation is commonly made by estimating the sum $(\alpha_0 \log B + \alpha_4 \log \sigma)$ as a single number, α.[11] Making this substitution into the log-linear model of aggregate money demand gives the following equation.

$$\log M^d = \alpha - \alpha_1 \log r + \alpha_2 \log y + \alpha_3 \log P \quad (3.5)$$

Similar log-linear models of the demands for money by households and firms can also be constructed and estimated.

---

[11]However, see Marquis and Witte (1989) for an attempt to estimate α_4 separately.

3.6 THE DEMAND FOR REAL MONEY BALANCES

Again, the models are simple representations of the fairly complicated behavioral relationships that are described in general terms by theory. Theory is very useful for identifying the primary factors that determine the quantity of money demanded by the economy, and whether the elasticities associated with those factors should be positive or negative. Unfortunately, theory is less helpful in predicting what the numerical value of the elasticities ought to be. The Federal Reserve therefore must rely on statistical estimates of the elasticities from equations such as those in the preceding section.

The statistical problem is that the behavioral relationships can and do change over time, and whenever they do, the elasticities in the money demand functions also change. Many factors have contributed to these changes in the past, such as the interaction of inflation, regulation, and financial innovations described in Chapter 2, the introduction of credit and debit cards as alternative media of exchange, and the growing use of ATMs as a cash management tool. However, some features of the money demand functions have remained relatively unchanged in the United States since the 1940s. They are referred to here as "empirical facts."

The first empirical fact is that the price elasticity of money demand is essentially one, regardless of the measure of money being used (M1, M2, or M3). This fact is consistent with the intuition that the demand for money is based on the *real* purchasing power of money. For example, if prices rise by 1 percent, the quantity of money required to purchase a given consumption bundle would rise by 1 percent. Setting α_3 in equation (3.5) equal to one yields the following expression (after a little algebra).[12]

$$\log(M^d/P) = \alpha - \alpha_1 \log r + \alpha_2 \log y \qquad (3.6)$$

This is the log-linear model of the aggregate demand for *real money balances,* (M^d/P). The equation expresses an important relationship, and a version of it is used to represent the demand side of the money market in the model of the macroeconomy developed in Chapter 9, as well as throughout much of Part II. Finally, note that similar expressions can be estimated for the household and firm sector demands for real money balances.

3.7 VELOCITY

Over time, the real demands for the various measures of money can exhibit long-run trends due to two fundamental causes. One is economic growth. As the economy expands, households increase the volume of their consumption purchases and firms increase their expenditures on labor and material inputs to production. Consequently, the aggregate demand for money rises. The other is

---

[12]Recall the mathematical relationships: $\log x + \log y = \log(xy)$ and $\log x - \log y = \log(x/y)$.

technology. The technology of the payment system evolves over time, enabling households and firms to conduct their monetary transactions more efficiently. Consequently, the demand for transaction assets, such as currency and checkable deposit accounts, falls. However, changes in the regulation of financial institutions or in the conduct of monetary policy (as described in Chapter 2) can cause the trends to change. Such changes are known as secular (or long-run) changes in the demand for money. It is essential for the Federal Reserve to identify secular changes in the demand for money to avoid systematically over- or undersupplying money to the economy.

The most common way to monitor trends in money demand is to rely on a statistical measure that allows the two principal causes of trends, economic growth and technology, to be separated. This measure is called the current income velocity of money or simply the velocity of money and is denoted V. It is defined as the ratio of real GDP, y, to the stock of real money balances in the economy, denoted M^s/P, where M^s is the nominal supply of money in the economy.

$$V = y/(M^s/P) \tag{3.7}$$

Taking the logarithm of both sides of equation (3.7) gives the following expression.

$$\log V = \log y - \log(M^s/P) \tag{3.8}$$

To identify the major factors that determine velocity, note first that when the money market is in equilibrium, the (log of) the supply of real money balances is just equal to the (log of) the demand for real money balances, and the latter is given by the aggregate money demand function in equation (3.4). With this information and the empirical fact that α_3 is essentially one, a little algebra reveals that the log-linear expression for the velocity of money can be written in the following form.

$$\log V = - \alpha_0 \log B + \alpha_1 \log r + (1 - \alpha_2) \log y - \alpha_4 \log \sigma \tag{3.8}$$

This equation can be simplified by using a second empirical fact: for most measures of money, the real income elasticity of the demand for money, α_2, is close to one.[13] Substitution of this number into (3.8) produces an equation that specifies the major factors that determine the behavior of velocity.

$$\log V = - \alpha_0 \log B + \alpha_1 \log r - \alpha_4 \log \sigma \tag{3.9}$$

Note that this equation is simply an alternative way to characterize the aggregate demand for money. It states that as the technology of the payment system improves, such that the transaction cost of converting liquid assets into money declines (that is, as B falls), the demand for money is also declining and velocity is therefore rising. As the opportunity cost of holding money falls, or as

---

[13]This is true for the firm-sector holdings of M1, but α_2 may be slightly less than one for the household sector. See Marquis and Witte (1989). Estimates of α_2 for the aggregate demand for M2 are all close to one. See, for example, Mehra (1992).

r decreases, the demand for money rises and velocity falls. Finally, as the level of income uncertainty rises, such that σ increases, precautionary balances rise and velocity falls.

Why is velocity useful for identifying secular changes in the aggregate demand for real money balances? To answer this question, recall that the two fundamental causes of trends in money demand are a growing economy and improved technology. From the preceding expression, we see that changes in real income due to long-run economic growth do not affect velocity. The reason is the empirical fact that the real income elasticity of real money balances is one, which implies that the percentage growth rate of the demand for real money balances is equal to the percentage growth rate in real income. Therefore, the only source of trend in velocity must be technology. As technology improves, the demand for transaction assets can be expected to decrease, which could lead to a secular rise in velocity. Note that there is no long-run trend in either the opportunity cost of holding money, *r*, or the level of uncertainty about real income, σ. This is reasonable, because *r* generally rises and falls with interest rate levels, which do not rise or fall indefinitely, and changes in σ tend to be mostly associated with business cycle swings with no tendency to rise or fall in the long run.

Clearly, a graph of velocity over time could be useful in identifying secular changes in the demand for real money balances. If no secular changes were occurring, the graph should show a pattern of fluctuations around some straight line, the slope of which is determined by the long-run effect of changes in the technology of the payment system.[14]

Figures 3.4 through 3.9 are graphs of velocity for six measures of money: M1, M2, M3, L, currency, and currency plus demand deposits. The focus of the following discussion is the velocity of M1 (Figure 3.4) and the velocity of M2 (Figure 3.5). Knowledge of the material covered in Chapter 2 is assumed. Historically, M1 and M2 have been the more important definitions of money in terms of the actual conduct of monetary policy in the United States since World War II. Section 3.10 provides some observations on the velocity of the other measures of money (Figures 3.6 through 3.9).

3.8 SECULAR CHANGES IN THE DEMAND FOR M1

The graph of the velocity of M1 in Figure 3.4 represents three distinct periods. The first (period 1) spans the years 1959 to 1973, during which the U.S. dollar was pegged to gold under the international monetary arrangements known as the Bretton Woods Agreements adopted after World War II. This monetary system is discussed in detail in Chapter 8. What is important to note here about this system is that it provided a "rule" under which monetary policy had to be conducted, and the rule effectively prohibited the Federal Reserve from adopt-

---

[14]This assumes a linear trend, suggesting that the rate of technological improvements in the payment system induces a constant rate of change in the demand for money over time.

Figure 3.4   Income Velocity of MI

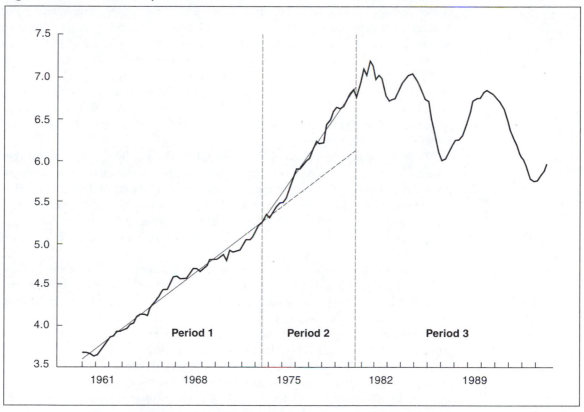

ing a high inflation policy for any protracted period of time. In fact, the average inflation rate from the beginning of period 1 until 1966 was nearly zero.[15] General price stability prevailed.[16]

During period 1, M1 consisted of currency and non-interest-bearing demand deposit accounts. Payment of interest on checking accounts was prohibited by a federal regulation termed Regulation Q. Therefore, M1 contained all of the economy's transaction assets, none of which had any savings properties. Because the inflation rate was effectively zero, these assets were not losing value over time. However, because they were non-interest-bearing, they were not earning any return. Households and firms therefore had an incentive to economize on their M1 balances. The result was a continual, gradual improvement in the efficiency of the payment system throughout the period. It generally took

---

[15]As described in more detail in Chapter 8, the advent of inflation in the late 1960s led to the collapse of the Bretton Woods Agreements. The process of collapse stretched over two years, from 1971 to 1973, and eventually led to the floating rate system for the U.S. dollar.

[16]Whether or not a zero inflation rate is optimal is discussed at length in Chapter 15.

the form of more efficient check-clearing systems developed by commercial banks and the Federal Reserve, as well as the development of innovative cash management practices by firms, such as lock-box collection systems. This improvement was reflected in a trend rate of growth of the velocity of M1 of approximately 3.5 percent per year over the 14-year period. In Figure 3.4 the trend is sketched as a straight line through the data. Notice that velocity fluctuated in a very tight band around the trend. The implication is that the velocity of M1, and hence the aggregate demand for M1, was very predictable during period 1. M1 therefore could have been taken as a useful definition of money for monetary policy purposes.[17]

Period 2 spans the years 1973 to 1980. It is framed by the collapse of the Bretton Woods Agreements in 1973 and the passage of the Depository Institutions Deregulations and Monetary Control Act (DIDMCA) of 1980. Once the gold standard had been lifted from the dollar, monetary policy became discretionary and the Federal Reserve, in its efforts to achieve low unemployment, subsequently adopted successively higher inflation policies that culminated in the double-digit inflation of the late 1970s.

What did those policies mean for the aggregate demand for money? In Figure 3.4, the period 1 trend line for velocity that is extended with a dashed line in period 2 lies below the actual velocity. That is, the slope of a straight line drawn through the period 2 data for velocity is steeper than the slope for velocity during period 1. Velocity increased at an annual rate of approximately 4 percent during period 2. This observation indicates that a secular change took place around 1973 and the demand for real money balances grew more slowly during period 2. The principal cause of the secular change in money demand was the fact that incentives for households and firms to economize on their money balances were altered by high inflation policies of the Federal Reserve. High inflation produced correspondingly high nominal interest rates on assets that could be held in lieu of M1 assets. To avoid the high opportunity cost of holding M1 assets, households and firms (in particular) began to find alternative ways to alter their cash management practices to reduce idle money balances. Many technological improvements to the economy's payment system resulted, including numerous financial innovations, many of which are described in Chapter 2. The secular growth in the demand for money fell and velocity grew more rapidly than in period 1, when the inflation rate was roughly zero.[18] Notice, however, that the fluctuations in velocity continued to be confined to a relatively tight band around the trend line during period 2. This pattern suggests that once the Federal Reserve understood that a secular change had occurred and could identify the new trend, the demand for M1 was still relatively predictable and M1 remained a good definition of money for the purpose of conducting monetary policy.

---

[17]Criteria for selecting a monetary aggregate as a primary target for monetary policy is discussed in more detail in Chapter 16.

[18]Evidence of these changes is cited by Marquis and Witte (1989) and Ireland (1994b). Also see Hester (1980) for a discussion of the interaction between inflation and regulation, and how it affected the cash management decision.

Period 3 spans the years 1980 to 1994. As is evident in Figure 3.4, the velocity of M1 underwent a very profound change in 1980. Overall, velocity fell during the period, although the new trend is difficult to identify because of the dramatic increase in the volatility of velocity. The period began with the passage of DIDMCA of 1980 and included the phasing out of interest rate ceilings on deposit accounts (other than commercial accounts), which was completed in April 1986. Many of the details of the new accounts introduced during this period are discussed in Chapter 2. However, a principal factor contributing to the decline in the velocity of M1 was the legalization of the interest-bearing checkable deposit accounts. That action drastically reduced the opportunity cost of holding M1, because a unit of M1 could receive interest income and act to some extent as a savings asset. The dramatic increase in demand for M1 caused a corresponding decline in velocity.

The volatility during the early part of period 3 had several causes. One was the gradual phasing out of interest rate ceilings, as the opportunity costs of holding M1 would be adjusted with each new "phase." Second, new money market instruments became available to households after deregulation, and the commercial banks simultaneously developed new product offerings in response to the less regulated environment. With new product offerings came adjustments in households' demands for M1 assets. Finally, in 1981 and 1982 the economy underwent its longest and deepest recession since the Great Depression. It coincided with a decline of more than 10 percent in inflation, and therefore in nominal interest rates, and induced an unusually large degree of income uncertainty. Both of those factors tended to raise money demand and, as suggested by the log-linear model of velocity developed in section 3.7, contributed to the decline in velocity during 1981–1982. Obviously, the demand for M1 became very unpredictable during period 3 and M1 was no longer a reliable definition of money for the Federal Reserve to use in its conduct of monetary policy. Whether or not it will ever regain sufficient stability to again become the primary definition of money used for monetary policy remains an open question.[19] However, the velocity of M1 is likely to continue to remain more volatile than it was in periods 1 and 2.[20]

3.9 THE VELOCITY OF M2

The velocity of M2 is plotted in Figure 3.5. In contrast to the trend in M1 velocity, the long-run trend in M2 velocity appears to be zero. Moreover, no secular changes can be clearly identified in the entire period from 1959 to 1991.

---

[19]A recent regulatory decision permitting banks to automatically "sweep" OCDs (other checkable deposit accounts) into MMDAs whenever the balance exceeds a given threshold (selected at the bank's discretion) could substantially reduce M1 in the future if such accounts prove popular.

[20]Mehra (1992) has argued that the legalization of NOW accounts will increase the interest elasticity of the demand for M1, and therefore induce more volatility into the velocity of M1.

Apparently improvements in the technology of the economy's payment system did not affect the overall economywide demand for M2. This empirical fact is potentially of great importance for the conduct of monetary policy. It implies that the Federal Reserve may be able to rely on the long-run relationship between real M2 balances and real GDP, or equivalently nominal M2 and nominal GDP, to avoid the problem of systematically over- or undersupplying money to the economy when secular changes in the demand for money occur unexpectedly, as happened in 1973 and 1980 for the demand for M1. Why did the factors that caused the secular changes in the demand for M1 not also cause secular changes in the demand for M2? In the period from 1973 to 1980, households, but primarily firms, were reducing the share of financial assets held in the form of transaction assets; for most of period 3 from 1980 to 1991, households were increasing the share of financial assets held in the form of transaction assets (for the reasons discussed above). Where were these funds going in the 1973 to 1980 period and where were they coming from in the 1980 to 1991 period? In both cases, the answer is (primarily) non-M1 components of M2. Households and firms were adjusting their financial asset portfolios by transferring funds from one set of components of M2 into other components of M2. For example, in the latter period after the nationwide legalization of NOW accounts (interest-bearing checking accounts), households began drawing funds from various short-term savings assets such as small CDs, MMMFs, and passbook savings and placing those funds in their checkable deposit accounts, which had some savings properties. The effect was to increase the demand for M1, but to leave the overall demand for M2 unchanged.[21]

Given the history of the velocity of M2 as presented in Figure 3.5, what can be said about the choice of M2 as the primary measure of money for the purpose of conducting monetary policy? The empirical fact that no secular changes occurred in the long-run zero trend in M2 velocity from 1960 to 1991 indicates that over the long term, the nominal supply of M2 and nominal GDP have the same average rates of growth. Hence, the Federal Reserve has a reference point for examining the long-run implications of policy decisions. If the Federal Reserve is concerned about the long-run average growth rate of nominal GDP, it can obtain information on that growth rate by approximating what the long-run growth rate of M2 would be under various policy choices.[22] However, as Figure 3.5 indicates, M2 velocity has significant short-run volatility,[23] which suggests that the relationship between M2 and nominal GDP may not be very predictable in the short run. Therefore, if the Federal Reserve is pursuing short-run policy objectives, such as keeping the economy continually at or near "full

---

[21]See Tatom (1983) for evidence of these portfolio adjustments.

[22]McCallum (1988) suggested that nominal GDP could actually be used as an intermediate target for monetary policy. Also note that a difference in the ability of the Federal Reserve to control the supply of M2 versus M1 must be considered.

[23]Note that Figures 3.4 and 3.5 are not directly comparable because of the difference in scale on the vertical axis.

employment" (the policy objective generally associated with "stabilization or countercyclical policy"), it is unlikely to be successful if it relies exclusively on the relationship between M2 and nominal GDP.

The more general implications of the unpredictability of the relationship between the Federal Reserve's principal definition of money (whether it is M1 or M2) and GDP are discussed at length in Chapter 14. Here we can simply note that since the mid-1980s, M2 has replaced M1 as the Federal Reserve's principal definition of money. The reason for the change was the erratic behavior of M1 velocity in response to the phasing out of interest rate ceilings on deposit accounts and the implementation of the other provisions of the DI-DMCA of 1980.

Recently, the predictability of M2 behavior has also become suspect, as evidenced in Figure 3.5 by the continual increase in M2 velocity since 1991. This recent behavior of M2 velocity has been attributed at least in part to the growing popularity of stock and bond mutual funds among households, which has attracted funds from M2 assets. The adjustments households are making to their overall financial asset portfolios may become a permanent feature in the aggregate demand for money. If so, there may be a once-and-for-all upward shift in M2 velocity. Alternatively, if the portfolio adjustments prove to be

Figure 3.5   Income Velocity of M2

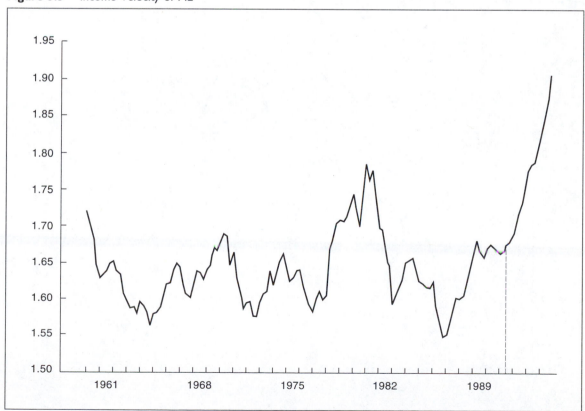

transitory, M2 velocity will eventually return to its historical long-run mean. In the meantime, the Federal Reserve is left without a reliable monetary aggregate to guide its policy deliberations.

 **3.10   OTHER VELOCITY MEASURES**

By varying the definition of money, we can construct alternative velocity measures. For example, dividing nominal GDP by the nominal supply of currency in the hands of the public gives the income velocity of currency. Figure 3.6 is a graph of this measure. The income velocities of M3, L, and currency plus demand deposits are plotted in Figures 3.7, 3.8, and 3.9, respectively. Because Federal Reserve policy influences the supply of each of these alternative definitions of money, they are all candidates for being the principal definition of money used by Federal Reserve in conducting monetary policy. In Figures 3.6, 3.7, and 3.8, we see from the general behavior of the velocities of currency, M3, and L that they would not be particularly good measures for the Federal Reserve use. The demand for currency appears to have followed the path shown in Figure 3.4 for the velocity of M1, and therefore has the same erratic behav-

Figure 3.6   Income Velocity of Currency

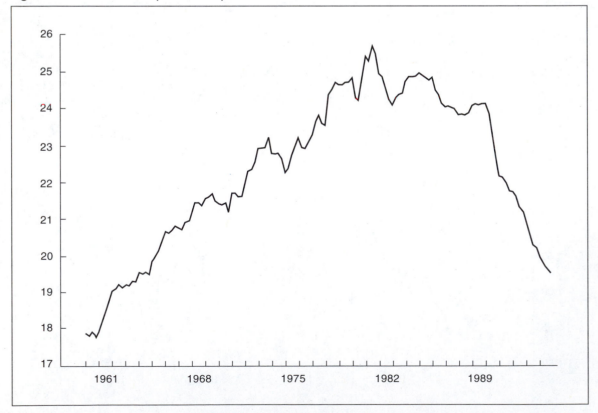

Figure 3.7 Income Velocity of M3

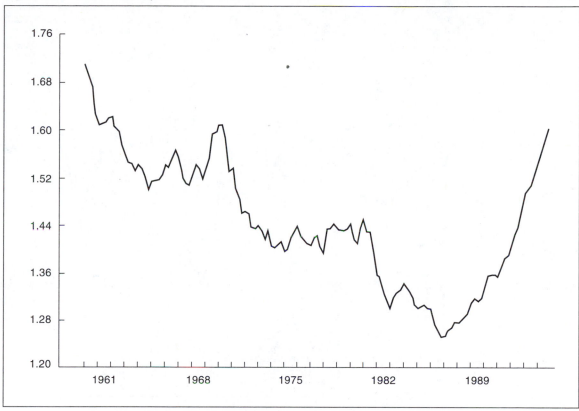

ior.[24] Similar abrupt secular changes in demands are apparent for M3 and L in the 1980s.[25]

In Figure 3.9, the velocity of an alternative "narrow" measure of money, currency plus demand deposits, is plotted (V1 old). Historically, the Federal Reserve redefined the monetary aggregates in 1980 (as discussed in Chapter 2) in recognition of the new money market instruments, such as MMMFs, that had emerged outside the banking system in the late 1970s and the new deposit

---

[24]The increase in the demand for currency in the 1980s is not fully understood. Part of the increase was undoubtedly due to the sharp decline in interest rates in 1981–1983, but much of the increase is unexplained. Some observers have speculated that it was due to the rise in the "underground economy," where currency transactions are more prevalent than in the economy generally. Others have noted a pickup in the demand for U.S dollars worldwide (where, as noted in Chapter 2, more than 50 percent of U.S. currency resides) as a hedge against political uncertainty, particularly in Eastern Europe and the countries created from the former Soviet Union.

[25]The sharp decline in L (in particular) accompanied the rise in consumer indebtedness during the 1980s. It began to reverse toward the end of the decade.

Figure 3.8   Income Velocity of L

account offerings that would develop within the banking system as a consequence of the DIDMCA of 1980. Prior to the redefinition, M1 was defined to be currency plus demand deposits. This aggregation is therefore often called "old M1."

As indicated in Figure 3.9, the velocity of old M1 essentially followed the velocity of M1 (V1) prior to 1980 because the two monetary aggregates were nearly the same during that period. The only difference was that M1 included NOW accounts in banks in a few New England states (before NOWs were made legal on a nationwide basis) and traveler's checks.

We see in Figure 3.9 that the velocities of M1 and old M1 began to diverge significantly after 1980. Interestingly, although the demand for old M1 was much more volatile in the post-1980 period than in the pre-1980 period, there do not appear to have been any secular changes in its long-run trend. The growth in old M1 velocity that is evident in the pre-1980 period appears to be largely unaffected in the post-1980 period. Hence, as in the case of M2, monetary policy decisions based on old M1 as the principal definition of money would not have caused the Federal Reserve to systematically over- or undersupply money during the 1980s although the greater volatility would have significantly lessened its usefulness for short-run policy purposes.

Figure 3.9 Income Velocity of Old MI and MI

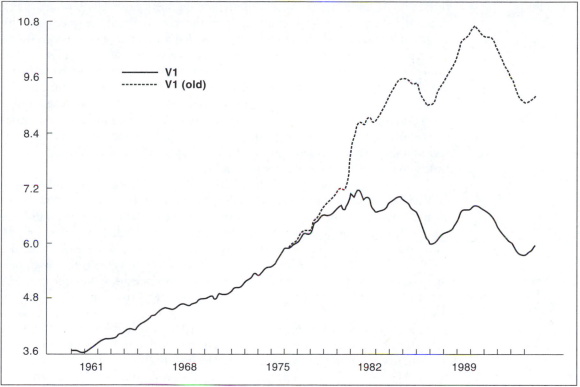

3.11 SUMMARY

When the Federal Reserve evaluates measures of money for their potential usefulness in policy deliberations, it tries to identify the monetary aggregate with the closest empirical (or statistical) relationship to the macroeconomic variables that are the object of its policies, such as output (real GDP) and the price level (CPI). Economic theory can be used to describe that relationship qualitatively. One such theory described in this chapter stresses the role of money as a medium of exchange in the economy. The theory of transactions demand for money predicts that the demand for nominal money balances increases with real income and the price level, and decreases with improvements in the efficiency of the payment system and higher interest rates. When net cash flows are uncertain because of income volatility or unpredictable expenditure patterns, the demand for money will rise for precautionary reasons as the level of uncertainty rises. This general theory applies equally well to households and to firms.

Transforming the theory into a quantitatively useful statistical model requires estimation of the relationship between nominal money balances and their determinants. The relationship can be estimated at various levels of aggregation. The level of aggregation that is of principal interest to the Federal Reserve is the macroeconomic or economywide level. Statistical models are used to estimate the relationship between a monetary aggregate, real GDP, prices (CPI), and interest rates. Empirical evidence from the models about the price elasticity of nominal money balances implies that the demand for money is based on its real purchasing power. In cases where the income (or real GDP) elasticity of money demand is unity, the demand for money can be represented by velocity, which is then a positive function of interest rates and a negative function of income uncertainty and improvements in the payment system. Because interest rates and income uncertainty have no long-run trends, their influence on velocity is short term and generally related to business-cycle fluctuations. In contrast, technological improvements in the payment system occur continuously over time and can induce a secular trend in velocity.

When we examine the velocity of M1 prior to 1980, the demand for M1 appears very stable and therefore predictable in both the short and long term, with the single exception of the break in the trend in 1973. Apart from the one break, this evidence suggests that the Federal Reserve could have relied on M1 as its principal measure of money in evaluating policy alternatives. After the DIDMCA of 1980, the behavior of M1 velocity became very erratic, with neither stable short-run nor well-defined long-run properties. Consequently, M1 lost much of its usefulness in macroeconomic analysis of monetary policy decisions.

The M2 velocity was more volatile than M1 velocity prior to 1980, but its behavior changed very little after 1980. The zero trend in M2 velocity prior to the DIDMCA continued throughout the 1980s. The long-run relationship between M2 and the real economy was relatively stable and could have provided helpful information for the monetary authorities. However, since 1991, the relationship seems to have gone awry. Whether this change is a transitory phenomenon, a one-time shift in asset portfolios of households, or the beginning of a period of unpredictable behavior of the M2 aggregate remains an open question. Meanwhile, the Federal Reserve has no single monetary aggregate with which it can reliably gauge the impact of its policy decisions on the economy. Consequently, the aggregates are given less emphasis in policy deliberations today than they were in the recent past, but they continue to be monitored closely.

REVIEW QUESTIONS

1. The theory of transaction demand for money is based on a model of an optimal cash management strategy adopted by households or firms. For the following scenarios, explain what adjustments an individual household makes to its short-run management of cash holdings and how that action affects the demand for money.
   (a) The household receives a raise in personal income.
   (b) The household's bank expands the number of ATMs.
   (c) The Federal Reserve tightens monetary policy, causing short-term interest rates to rise.
   (d) The household retires, its income declines, and it responds by reducing its savings rate.

2. Recently, some commercial banks have introduced a new feature of checking accounts whereby deposit balances above some threshold level, say $15,000, are automatically swept into MMDA accounts, which pay a higher interest rate but do not have checking privileges. Discuss how households may respond to the new "sweep accounts" and the effect on their demand for M1 balances, given that not all households are the same.

3. The recent behavior of M2 has led the Federal Reserve to attach less weight to the "signal" it receives from the growth rate of that aggregate.
   (a) Explain this concern in terms of velocity.
   (b) Three scenarios for the future behavior of M2 velocity are suggested in the text. Describe each one with reference to a likely path for M2 velocity.

*4. It has been suggested that old M1 may be a better definition of money than M2 for policy purposes.
   (a) Given the likely causes of the unusual behavior of M1 and M2, what must occur in the future for old M1 to become a more useful measure of money than M2?
   (b) Describe how the changes suggested in (a) would be reflected in the velocity measures of old M1 and M2. Remember that the Federal Reserve has both long-run and short-run policy goals.

*5. It has been suggested that a new aggregate called M2 +, which adds stock and bond mutual funds to the M2 aggregate, would be a better definition of money for policy purposes.
   (a) What characteristics must the velocity of M2 + satisfy for this to be true?
   (b) What does your answer in (a) imply about the demand for stock and bond funds?
   (c) Discuss the pros and cons of relying on M2 + exclusively.

3.1 APPENDIX

Optimal Solution to the Household's Cash Management Problem

Assume that the household's average propensity to consume, *apc,* is a constant. Then, for a given payment period, the value of its real consumption expenditures, *c,* is a constant fraction, *apc,* of its real income during the period, y_h. Nominal consumption expenditures, which are equal to the price per unit of consumption, *P*, times the number of units of consumption, *c*, is then equal to a constant fraction of nominal income, which is equal to the unit price of goods, *P*, times real income, y_h.

$$Pc = (apc)\, Py_h$$

The household's cash management problem, as described in the text, is to minimize the total cost of cash management, *TC*, by choosing the optimal level of average nominal money balances to hold during the payment period, $\overline{M}$. This decision determines the optimal number of portfolio conversions of the less liquid asset into money, n_b, at a nominal unit cost of Pb, where b is a real fixed cost per conversion and is independent of the size of the conversion. The total cost of cash management is then given by the sum of the opportunity cost of money holdings and the cost of converting liquid assets into money during the payments period.

$$TC = r_b \overline{M} + n_b Pb \tag{1}$$

where $r_b = (r_s - r_m)$, which equals the opportunity cost of holding one dollar in the form of "money," which pays a return of r_m, as opposed to "storing" the dollar in the less liquid asset, which pays a return of r_s. The household's optimization problem consists of choosing $\overline{M}$ to minimize TC while consuming Pc during the period.

To carry out the optimization, we must first express n_b in terms of $\overline{M}$ and Pc. We assume that consumption expenditures are carried out at a uniform rate over the payments period. Then, as is evident from Figure 3.1, the dollar volume of (nominal) consumption expenditures during the period must equal the size of each transfer, $M = 2\overline{M}$, times the number of transfers plus one (for the initial allocation of income to money balances, $n_b + 1$).

$$Pc = (n_b + 1) \, 2\overline{M} \tag{2}$$

Solving equation (2) for n_b and substituting into (1) gives an expression for TC as a function of $\overline{M}$.

$$TC = r\overline{M} + [(Pc/2\overline{M}) - 1]Pb \tag{3}$$

To find the optimal average per-period money balances, take the derivative TC with respect to $\overline{M}$, set it equal to zero, and solve for $\overline{M}$. This procedure yields (after a little algebra):

$$(\overline{M}/P) = [(apc)by_b/2r]^{1/2} . \tag{4}$$

Taking the log of both sides of equation (4) gives the following expression.

$$\log(\overline{M}/P) = (1/2) \log[(apc)b/2] - (1/2) \log(r) + (1/2) \log(y_b) \tag{5}$$

It is similar to the log-linear model of real money balances in the text, where

$$\log(\overline{M}/P) = \alpha - \alpha_1 \log r + \alpha_2 \log y_b \tag{6}$$

when the αs are defined as $\alpha = (1/2) \log[(apc)b/2]$ and $\alpha_1 = \alpha_2 = (1/2)$. As stated in the text, the theory gives us a good idea of what factors determine the demand for money, and what the signs of the elasticities ought to be, but because of the assumptions required for a theoretical model, the actual values of the elasticities are an empirical question. That is, α, α_1, and α_2 must be estimated statistically.

◼ REFERENCES

Baumol, William. 1952. "The Transactions Demand for Cash: An Inventory Theoretic Approach." *Quarterly Journal of Economics* 66 (November): 545–56.

Friedman, Milton. 1953. *Essays in Positive Economics.* Chicago: University of Chicago Press.

Hester, Donald. 1980. "Innovations and Monetary Control." *Brookings Papers on Economic Activity* 1981: 1, 141–90.

Ireland, Peter N. 1994a. "Endogenous Financial Innovation and the Demand for Money." *Journal of Economic Dynamics and Control* 18 (May/July): 815–48.

————. 1994b. "Money and Growth: An Alternative Approach." *American Economic Review* 84 (March): 47–65.

Marquis, Milton H., and Steven R. Cunningham. 1990. "Financial Innovations, Price Smoothing, and Monetary Policy." *Economic Inquiry* 28 (October): 831–50.

————and Williard E. Witte. 1989. "Cash Management and the Demand for Money by Firms." *Journal of Macroeconomics* 11 (Summer): 333–50.

McCallum, Bennett T. 1988. "Robustness Properties of a Rule for Monetary Policy." *Carnegie-Rochester Conference Series on Public Policy* 29 (Autumn): 173–203.

Mehra, Yash P. 1992. *Review.* Federal Reserve Bank of Richmond.

Miller, Merton H., and Daniel Orr. 1966. "A Model of the Demand for Money by Firms." *Quarterly Journal of Economics* 80 (August): 413–25.

Tatom, John A. 1983. "Money Market Deposit Accounts, Super-NOWs, and Monetary Policy." *Review.* Federal Reserve Bank of St. Louis (March).

Tobin, James. 1956. "The Interest Rate Elasticity of Transactions Demand for Cash." *Review of Economics and Statistics* 38 (August: 241–7.

Tsiang, S. C. 1969. "The Precautionary Demand for Money: An Inventory Theoretic Analysis." *Journal of Political Economy* 77 (January/February): 99–117.

Whalen, Edward L. (1966). "A Rationalization for the Precautionary Demand for Cash." *Quarterly Journal of Economics* 80 (May): 314–24.

CHAPTER 4

STOCK AND BOND VALUATION AND THE TERM STRUCTURE OF INTEREST RATES

The preceding chapter described the cash management problem that households (and firms) face when deciding how to manage their portfolios of short-term financial assets optimally between payment (or disbursement) periods. Their objectives are to ensure that they have enough money to meet transaction requirements while minimizing both the costs of frequent portfolio adjustments and the opportunity costs (forgone interest income) of holding idle cash balances. The theory developed in Chapter 3 abstracts from the household's decisions on how much of its wealth portfolio to invest in short-term financial assets versus long-term financial assets such as stocks and bonds. This chapter examines the selection of asset maturity as part of the household's optimal wealth portfolio allocation decision and the implications of that selection for the relationship between short-term and long-term interest rates.

Because liquidity has a lesser role in the demand for long-term assets than in the demand for short-term assets, the demand for the former is associated principally with the tradeoff between risk and return. There is a minimum rate of return that a household requires on any given asset if it is to have a positive demand for that asset. As described in this chapter, the minimum rate of return is based on the household's preferences in terms of willingness to postpone consumption through savings and its tolerance for risk. Because inflation affects the *ex post* returns on any asset, the household's expectations of inflation are also reflected in the minimum rate of return that it requires on its investments. In equilibrium, the nominal rate of return on an asset consists of the expected inflation rate and the real rate of return as consistent with the preferences of the individual household that represents the marginal investor in the asset.

To examine the basic determinants of the marginal investor's required nominal rate of return on any long-term asset, we can focus specifically on stocks and bonds. In particular, stock and bond valuation formulas that describe the determinants of the market value or market price of an individual stock and of an individual bond are derived in this chapter. Stock and bond prices are shown to vary inversely with their nominal rates of return.

The relationship between long-term interest rates and short-term interest rates affects households' willingness to place long-term financial assets in their wealth portfolios. For example, suppose stocks and bonds suddenly began yielding very high returns in relation to short-term assets such as money market mutual funds. Investors would be likely to sell their money funds and buy stocks and bonds. As a result, market interest rates would adjust to restore equilibrium in those markets. The increase in the demand for stocks and bonds would cause their prices to rise, making them less attractive to new investors as their rates of return decline. Simultaneously, the decrease in demand for money market mutual funds would cause borrowers in the money markets, who supply the underlying assets in which the mutual funds invest, to increase the rates of return they offer to continue to attract investors. Hence, long-term interest rates would decline and short-term interest rates would rise until some new equilibrium relationship between them is reached, whereby long-term interest rates may exceed short-term rates or vice versa. This equilibrium relationship is called the term structure of interest rates.

One theory of the term structure of interest rates, known as the expectations hypothesis, is described in this chapter. It is predicated on the belief that investors will adjust the composition of their financial asset portfolios to achieve a desired balance between short-term and long-term assets, taking into account the relative rates of return they would expect to receive on each of the alternative investments over a fixed time horizon. As the fundamental determinants of the investments change over time, the term structure of interest rates is also expected to change in accordance with the theory. The implication is that changes in the relationship between long-term and short-term interest rates indicate how investors' perceptions of such things as future inflation, risk, or the performance of individual firms have changed. Collectively, such perceptions are related to the overall performance of the economy and hence could give policy makers meaningful signals of future macroeconomic conditions.

4.1   HOUSEHOLD PREFERENCES AND THE REQUIRED RETURN TO SAVINGS

Consider a household that receives income today and must decide how much of it to consume and how much of it to save. The amount consumed today is valued by the household in terms of the utility produced in the current period. The level of utility is determined by a current-period utility function that partly characterizes household preferences. Referring to Figure 4.1, we see that the utility function for household a, denoted $U_a(c_t)$, has two important properties. The first is that a higher level of consumption at any date t, denoted c_t, yields more utility at that date. That is, utility is a positive function of consumption, or $U_a(c_t^+)$. Therefore, when consumption rises from c^* to c', or by Δc units of

Figure 4.1
Household
Preferences

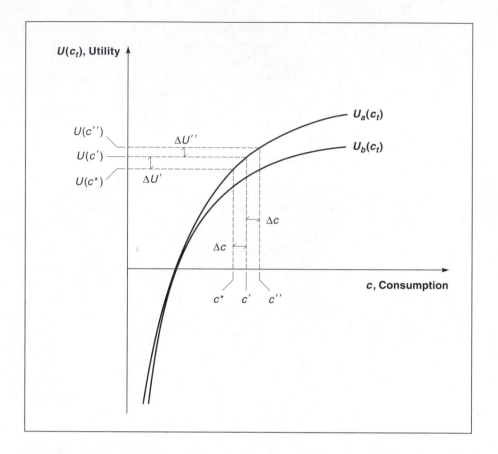

consumption, the utility received by household a at date t increases from $U_a(c^*)$ to $U_a(c')$, or by $\Delta U'$ units of utility. The second property is known as diminishing marginal utility in consumption, whereby a unit increase in consumption produces a lesser increase in utility at higher consumption levels than at lower consumption levels. This property is illustrated in Figure 4.1, where a rise in consumption from c' to c'', or by Δc units as before, raises household a's utility from $U_a(c')$ to $U_a(c'')$, or by $\Delta U''$ units of utility. Note that $\Delta U'' < \Delta U'$, indicating that less utility is received from the second increase in consumption by Δc units than is received from the first increase in consumption by Δc units.

Some households may experience diminishing marginal utility more rapidly than others. This situation is depicted graphically in Figure 4.1, where household b's utility function, denoted $U_b(c_t)$, is seen to have greater curvature than that of household a. This property of household preferences is related to the household's tolerance for risk and is known as the household's degree of risk aversion. Household b is more risk averse than household a and its lower tolerance for risk is reflected in a higher minimum expected return on investments.

An additional feature of household preferences is that households place a higher value today on utility received today than on utility to be received tomorrow. In this sense, they are said to discount the future. As a concrete example, suppose that at date $t = 0$ a household expects to consume c^* units of consumption both in the current period, or $c_0 = c^*$, and in the next period, or $c_1 = c^*$. The utility it receives from consumption at date $t = 0$ is $U(c_0) = U(c^*)$, which equals the utility it receives at date $t = 1$, or $U(c_1) = U(c^*)$. However, because the household must wait one period before consuming c_1, the value it places today on the utility to be received tomorrow is less than the value it places today on the utility received from the consumption of c_0 today. This valuation can be represented mathematically by stating that today's value of today's utility is simply $U(c_0) = U(c^*)$, but today's value of tomorrow's utility is only $\beta U(c_1) = \beta U(c^*)$, where $\beta \in (0,1)$. β is known as the household's discount factor. Households with a low discount factor, or a β much less than one, place a relatively low value on future utility and vice versa.

The discounting of future utility is illustrated graphically in Figure 4.2. Household a's utility function at date t is given by $U_a(c_t)$. The function is identical for date $t + 1$. However, for any level of utility received at date $t + 1$, the value to the household today is reduced by the discount factor β. Today's valuation of this future utility for any level of consumption at date $t + 1$ is represented graphically by the curve labeled $\beta U_a(c_{t + 1})$, where the utility function $U_a(c_t)$ is shifted downward by an amount determined by β. The more household a discounts the future, the lower is β and greater is the downward shift of the

Figure 4.2
Future Discounting
and Risk Aversion

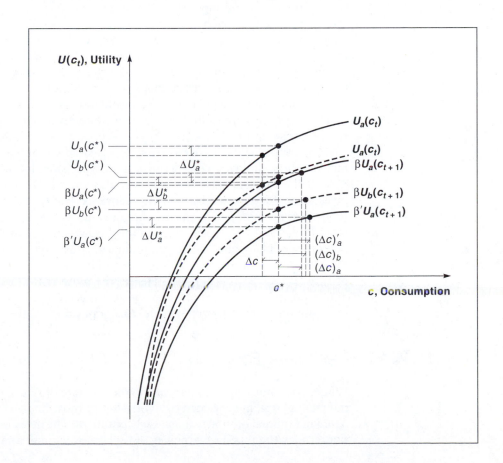

utility function measuring the value of tomorrow's consumption today. This effect is illustrated for the case when household a has a lower discount factor of $\beta' < \beta$. Also note that Figure 4.2 depicts the one-period discounting of future utility for household b, which is more risk averse than household a.

Figure 4.2 can be used to illustrate the effects of discounting and risk aversion on the household's consumption/savings decision. The decision to save more today is essentially a decision to postpone consumption. For the household to postpone consumption, it must be compensated by an amount that is determined by its preferences. Suppose household a has been following a consumption plan whereby it consumes c^* units each period, or $c_t = c_{t+1} = c^*$. However, at date t it considers whether it should reduce its date t consumption by Δc units to increase its savings. If the returns to the additional savings are used fully to increase consumption at date $t+1$, how much additional consumption must the household receive at that time to be willing to postpone current consumption by the designated amount, Δc?

From Figure 4.2, we see that household a loses utility in the current period in the amount of ΔU_a^*. If the household's discount factor is β, then reading the curve labeled $\beta U_a(c_{t+1})$ that represents today's valuation of next period's utility, we see that an equivalent offsetting gain in utility would require an increase in next period's consumption by $(\Delta c)_a$ units where $(\Delta c)_a > \Delta c$. The household therefore must receive a minimum real return on its investment of Δc, denoted r_a, in the amount given by $r_a = [(\Delta c)_a - \Delta c]/\Delta c$. If the return on the prospective investment is less than r_a, the household would not increase its savings rate because that return is insufficient to offset the amount by which the household discounts the future. If household a's preferences are characterized by a lower discount factor, β', a similar exercise would indicate that a still larger minimum real rate of return is required to entice the household to increase its savings and reduce consumption.

Now suppose the more risk-averse household b that has the same discount factor as household a is considering a similar decision. Its current consumption plans call for consuming c^* units in periods t and $t+1$, and it is evaluating an investment option whereby it would reduce its date t consumption by Δc units to increase its savings. How many additional units of consumption at date $t+1$ would household b require to make this investment? From Figure 4.2, we see that household b would require $(\Delta c)_b$ units of consumption at date $t+1$, where $(\Delta c)_b > (\Delta c_a)$, which corresponds to a minimum rate of return on the investment of $r_b = [(\Delta c_b) - \Delta c]/(\Delta c) > r_a$. Hence, the more risk-averse household b requires greater compensation than the less risk-averse household a (with the same discount factor β) to postpone consumption willingly.

4.2   THE FISHER EQUATION

Whereas the household is interested in the real rate of return on its investments, the income stream generated by ownership of most financial assets is denominated in nominal or money units, such as dollars. The investor knows that inflation erodes the purchasing power of dollars over time, and will demand full compensation for the anticipated effect of inflation on an asset's future income stream. This compensation is reflected in the market value of the asset and is captured by its nominal rate of return, or the nominal interest rate, denoted R. The nominal interest rate incorporates an inflation premium that is added to the real rate of return, denoted r, demanded by the investor. The inflation premium is (approximately) equal to the average rate of inflation that is expected to prevail over the life of the asset, denoted π^e. This important relationship is termed the Fisher equation.[1]

$$R = r + \pi^e$$

Therefore, an investor who revises expectations of future inflation upward by, say, one percentage point will demand that the nominal rate of return on investment also increase by one percentage point to keep the real rate of return intact. How these changes in investors' inflation expectations, as well as the changes in the factors that determine the expected real rate of return on financial assets, affect trade in the asset markets is discussed at length below. Because of the relative importance of bonds and stocks to financial markets, special attention is given to their valuation.

4.3 BOND VALUATION

When an individual purchases a 30-year U.S. Treasury bond on the day it is initially issued, what is he or she actually buying? Ownership of the bond represents claims against the issuer, which in this case is the U.S. government, but what form do the claims take? Upon issue, the Treasury pledges to make periodic payments to the bondholder for the life of the bond, and then to pay a lump sum equal to the face value of the bond at the time of maturity (after 30 years). The periodic payments are made semiannually and are called coupon payments because coupons literally must be removed from the bonds and sent to the Treasury for redemption. The coupons are for a fixed dollar amount that is specified at the time of issuance. Therefore, an investor who buys a 30-year Treasury bond at the time of issuance is acquiring claims in the form of 60 semiannual coupon payments and a payment equal to the initial face value of the bond to be received at maturity when the bond is redeemed. The nominal or dollar value of each of these claims to future payments is known by the investor at the time the investment is made. Therefore, the question is: How much

---

[1]The equation is named after the famous early twentieth century economist Irving Fisher. Note that of the three variables in this equation, only R is directly observable. However, if independent estimates of r and π^e can be obtained, this equation is not merely a definition, but a theory that is testable. That is, do the estimates of the real rate of return for a particular asset and the expected rate of inflation sum to the observed nominal rate of return on that asset? Many studies have addressed that question, and tend to support the Fisher equation as a good first approximation to the actual relationship between those variables. See Hamburger and Platt (1975) and the general discussion by Mishkin (1983).

will the investor pay for these claims? The answer is determined by the rate of return the investor wants to receive. The higher the return the individual investor demands, the lower the price the investor is willing to pay for the bond. Therefore, when the bond is sold in the market, an equilibrium bond price is determined. That price establishes the equilibrium rate of return on this asset, which corresponds to the long-term interest rate, or yield, on government bonds.

The relationship between the bond price and the bond yield is most easily illustrated in a simple example. Consider a hypothetical two-year bond that has a face value of $1000 and *annual* (to simplify the calculations) coupon payments of $40. In this case, the investor will receive two $40 coupon payments, one at the end of each year, and the redemption value of the bond, or $1000, at the end of the second year. Assume the investor wants to receive at least an 8 percent annual rate of return on the investment. How much is he or she willing to pay for the bond? To answer this question, first price each claim individually. That is, determine how much money would have to be invested today at 8 percent to return the value of the claim. The three investments can then be summed to determine the total value of the bond to the investor, which is the maximum price the investor is willing to pay for the bond.

Begin by placing a value today on the first $40 coupon payment. This value is termed the present value of the coupon payment. Let x_1 represent the dollar investment today that at an 8 percent rate of return will grow into $40 at the end of one year. This amount is found by solving the following equation.

$$x_1(1.08) = \$40$$

Therefore, the present value of the first $40 coupon payment today is $x_1 = \$40/(1.08) = \$37.04$. To determine the present value of the second coupon payment, the investor must discover the dollar investment today, say x_2 dollars, that at an 8 percent per year rate will return $40 in two years. Note that after one year this investment will have grown into $x_2(1.08)$ dollars. At the end of the second year, the return will be $[x_2(1.08)](1.08)$ or $x_2(1.08)^2$, dollars. Therefore, the investor must solve the following equation to determine the present value of the second coupon payment.

$$x_2(1.08)^2 = \$40$$

The second coupon payment is worth $x_2 = \$40/(1.08)^2 = \$34.29$ today to the investor. The final claim is the return of the face value of the bond, or the $1000 to be received at the end of two years. Because this claim is received at the same time as the second coupon payment, its present value in dollars, denoted by x_3, is found by solving a similar equation.

$$x_3(1.08)^2 = \$1000$$

This claim is valued today at $x_3 = \$1000/(1.08)^2 = \$860.28$.

The maximum price the investor is willing to pay for the bond, denoted b, can now be found by summing the present values of the claims that are being purchased.

$$b = x_1 + x_2 + x_3 = \$931.61$$

From this example, we obtain the general formula for computing the value of a two-period bond.

$$b = C/(1 + R) + C/(1 + R)^2 + M/(1 + R)^2$$

$$= \sum_{t=1}^{2} C/(1 + R)^t + M/(1 + R)^2$$

where C is the coupon payment ($40 in the example), R is the required rate of return on the investment (8 percent in the example), and M is the face value of the bond received by the investor at the time of maturity ($1000 in the example). Note that if the investor were willing to take a smaller return on the investment, say 4 percent, applying the bond valuation formula would yield a value of the bond for this investor of $1000, or the face value of the bond. In this case, the investor is said to be willing to pay the "par value" for the bond, which is said to be "priced to yield" 4 percent. This observation suggests an inverse relationship between bond prices and bond yields. The relationship can be shown to generalize to the equilibrium market pricing of all bonds that are actively traded, whether newly issued or not.

The formula can be extended to determine the relationship between the market value or equilibrium price of any bond, denoted B, and the bond rate per period or equilibrium bond yield, denoted R, when there are n periods remaining until maturity and each period represents the length of time between coupon payments.

$$B = \sum_{t=1}^{n} C/(1 + R)^t + M/(1 + R)^n$$

This expression is the general bond valuation formula.

Now consider what happens when a long-term government bond is initially sold at par, in which case it is said to have been "priced to yield R percent," and then continues to trade at par for some time thereafter. The equilibrium long-term bond rate, R, would remain virtually unchanged. However, if the bond then began to trade below par (if the price of the bond fell), the equilibrium long bond rate would rise. Moreover, for any bonds subsequently newly issued to sell at par, they must offer higher coupons to satisfy investor demands for a higher nominal rate of return. The converse is also true, implying that rising bond prices translate into lower long-term nominal interest rates and cheaper funds for the issuers. Hence, there is literally an inverse mathematical relationship between long-term bond yields and bond prices. If we know one, we also know the other.

4.4   STOCK VALUATION

The formula for pricing stocks is only slightly more complicated than the formula for pricing bonds. One share of stock represents part ownership of the assets of the firm that issued the stock. If one million shares of the firm are outstanding, ownership of one share of the firm's stock implies ownership of one millionth of the firm's assets. This ownership entitles the shareholder to one millionth of the profits the firm generates. The firm's profits can be deployed in various ways, but for simplicity they can be thought of as either paid out to the shareholders directly as dividends (usually quarterly) or reinvested by the firm. Whenever a firm retains its profits for reinvestment, it does so for the purpose of raising its future profits, which would enable it to pay out higher dividends in the future. Therefore, a firm's share price reflects today's value of the future stream of dividends that the firm is expected to pay.

A stock valuation formula can be constructed by first determining the present value of each claim to which the shareholder is entitled. These claims are to future dividends. The sum of the present values of future dividends equals the maximum price an investor would be willing to pay for a share of the stock. Two principal differences between stocks and bonds affect their pricing. One is that stocks do not have fixed maturity.[2] The firms are viewed as existing in perpetuity. Therefore, ownership of a share of stock in a firm represents claims to an infinite stream of future dividends, which can be denoted $D_0, D_1, \ldots$, where the subscript represents dates $t = 0, t = 1$, and so on at which the dividends are received. The second difference is that the investor does not know the nominal values of the dividends that the firm will pay in the future, and therefore must form expectations of what they are likely to be.

For example, suppose at date $t = 0$ a potential investor in a firm knows that as a shareholder he or she will receive a dividend of D_0, and expects the dividend to grow in the future at the rate of g per period. The expected dividend stream is $D_0, D_0(1 + g), D_0(1 + g)^2$, and so on. The investor must price these claims and sum them to determine the maximum amount to pay for the share of stock. The present value of the initial dividend, denoted x_0, is simply D_0 because it is received "today." However, if the potential investor demands a minimum rate of return on the investment of R each period, the present value of the next dividend, $D_1 = D_0(1 + g)$, expected at the end of the first period (at date $t = 1$), denoted x_1, is given by $x_1 = D_1/(1 + R) = D_0(1 + g)/(1 + R)$. The present value of the following dividend is $x_2 = D_2/(1 + R)^2 = D_0 [(1 + g)/(1 + R)]^2$, and so on. Therefore, the maximum price, s_0, that the potential investor is willing to pay for the share of stock at date $t = 0$ can be determined.

$$s_0 = x_0 + x_1 + x_3 + \ldots$$

$$= D_0 + D_0 (1 + g)/(1 + R) + D_0 [(1 + g)/(1 + R)]^2 + \ldots$$

$$= D_0 \sum_{t = 0}^{\infty} [(1 + g)/(1 + R)]^t$$

---

[2]Certain bonds issued by the British government to help finance the costs of World War II also have no maturity date. They are known as British "consols."

If this individual turns out to be the marginal investor for this share of stock, the formula also will determine the date $t = 0$ equilibrium share price, S_0.[3]

Given that dividends cannot be expected to grow (on average) more rapidly than the rate of return demanded by the marginal investor, denoted R—that is, $R > g$—the infinite sum in the valuation formula can be simplified.[4]

$$\sum_{t=0}^{\infty} [(1 + g)/(1 + R)]^t = (1 + g)/(R - g)$$

Therefore, the equilibrium share price for this stock is given by a simple valuation formula.

$$S_0 = D_0(1 + g)/(R - g)$$

When the market raises its expectations of dividend growth for an individual firm, or when g increases, the equilibrium share price rises. Conversely, if the market demands a higher return from the investment, or when R increases, perhaps because of a greater risk of not receiving the expected dividends, the share price falls. Such evaluations can be very complex. Financial analysts do them each day on a full-time basis. Many individual investors play hunches. If an individual either believes the growth outlook for a company is not fully reflected in the price of the stock or is willing to incur a risk greater than that attached to the firm's ability to meet a given expected dividend schedule, that person is a potential buyer of the stock. The maximum amount he or she is willing to pay for a share, say s_0, exceeds the equilibrium price, or $s_0 > S_0$. The individual from whom the stock is purchased would have been the previous marginal investor, who did not place as high a value on the stock. Therefore, in an improving economic environment, many potential investors will be revising their expectations of future earnings upward for many firms and the stock market will be rising. However, increasing uncertainty about the future can cause the stock market to fall.

4.5   BOND AND STOCK PRICE FLUCTUATIONS

As with any financial asset, the rate of return on stocks and bonds reflects the liquidity of the market for the asset, or how quickly the asset can be converted into cash without penalty, and the level of perceived risk of the asset, or the

---

[3] If the current share price is S_0 and reflects a given expected dividend stream, some shareholders would be willing to continue to hold the stock even at a higher rice of say $S_0^H > S_0$. However, potential new investors would require a lower price, say $S_0^L < S_0$, to purchase the stock. The marginal investor is the individual who is willing to pay up to S_0 for the stock, but no more.

[4] This expression can be found by defining $m = (R - g)/(1 + g)$ and noting that the infinite sum can be rewritten as $\sum_{t=0}^{\infty} [1/(1 + m)]^t$, which equals $1/m$, if $m \in (0,1)$.

likelihood that the future stream of income generated by the asset will not meet expectations. The liquidity of most assets is determined by the properties of the markets in which they are traded and is not likely to change rapidly. However, the perceived risk of not receiving the anticipated stream of returns attached to ownership of a particular asset may change abruptly with news about the firm (in the case of a private security), the economy, or government policy. For long-term investors in bonds who plan to hold them until maturity, the risk is that the issuer may go into bankruptcy and the coupon and redemption payments may not be made.[5] In most cases, this assessment of risk will not change quickly. However, bondholders with shorter investment horizons face the risk of capital losses when selling bonds prior to maturity. A bond's price may have fallen because of higher inflation expectations or a more rapid growth in the supply of bonds than in the demand for bonds, as typically occurs over the course of the business cycle. In both cases, the nominal interest rate rises and bond prices fall.

The dividends an investor purchases when buying a share of stock are not known at the time the stock is issued. Moreover, a stockholder cannot legally declare the firm bankrupt if the firm lowers or even eliminates its quarterly dividend. If a firm does go into bankruptcy and its assets are subsequently liquidated, the stockholders are (usually) last in line to get their share. Risk is therefore significantly higher for long-term stock investors than for long-term bond investors.[6] When projections of future economic growth are revised upward, expectations of corporate profits are also raised. The implied possibility of future dividend increases by most firms would be reflected in stock prices. Conversely, stockholders could have capital losses in their investments if an unexpected weakening of the economy were to reduce corporate profits and they sold their stock in fear of further declines. Funds fleeing the stock market or the bond market are likely to be placed in short-term investments, such as money market mutual funds.

4.6   THE TERM STRUCTURE OF INTEREST RATES: THE PURE EXPECTATIONS HYPOTHESIS[7]

An investor can freely choose the portion of his or her wealth to place in short-term versus long-term investments. If market conditions change after the deci-

---

[5]The most standard form of corporate bond is called a debenture. Owners of debentures can declare a firm that is delinquent in making coupon payments legally bankrupt. Upon liquidation of the firm's assets, they are first in line to receive claims against these assets.

[6]However, one could argue that if inflation were to accelerate substantially after the investment is made, the loss in purchasing power of the bond coupons could be substantially greater than the negative affect on dividends, which the firm may have to increase in nominal terms to keep up with inflation, thereby protecting the long-term investor.

[7]Among the voluminous writings on the expectations hypothesis of the term structure, see Shiller (1979), Singleton (1980), and Pesando (1983) for some early critical evaluations.

sion is made, for example, with long-term investments becoming more attractive, the investor will make a portfolio adjustment by selling short-term assets and buying long-term assets. If many investors attempt to realign their portfolios in that way, the greater demand for long-term assets will drive up their prices and reduce their yields. Similarly, the weaker demand for short-term assets will cause their prices to fall and their rates of return to rise. That process continues until an equilibrium is reached. At equilibrium, there is no further tendency for asset prices or interest rates to adjust unless and until the financial markets receive new information. The equilibrium relationship between a short-term interest rate and a long-term interest rate may reflect several factors, including essential differences in the liquidity and the risk characteristics of the underlying assets as described above for bonds and stocks. However, the difference in maturity of the assets also plays a key role, which can be illustrated best with a hypothetical example.

Assume Carol has $1000 that she wants to invest for a fixed period of two years. She contemplates two separate investment strategies. One strategy, call it investment L, is simply to purchase a two-year U.S. Treasury note and hold it to maturity. The annual rate of interest paid on this investment is denoted RL and is currently 8 percent. If Carol chooses this investment, she will receive $1000 (1 + RL)^2 = \$1166.40$ at the end of two years.

Alternatively, Carol could purchase a one-year U.S. Treasury bill and roll the investment over when it matures at the end of the first year, that is, reinvest the principal and interest income in another one-year T-bill. Call this investment S. If the current market rate on this asset, denoted RS_1, is 6 percent, what would Carol expect to receive at the end of two years from investment S? The answer depends on what she believes the interest rate on one year T-bills will be one year from today. Denote the expected value of this interest rate one year hence by $E(RS_2)$. Carol would expect to receive $\$1000(1 + RS_1)[1 + E(RS_2)]$ $= \$1000(1.06)[1 + E(RS_2)]$ at the end of two years from her initial $1000 investment.

Obviously, both investment strategies are available in the market. Because the underlying assets are issued by the U.S. government, they are free of any default risk and the strategies cannot be differentiated on that basis. If we assume that the investor does not value liquidity, then the marginal investor, who determines the equilibrium relationship between the current short-term interest rate, RS_1, and the current long-term interest rate, RL, should be indifferent between the two investment strategies. Otherwise, trading in these assets would occur as described above until an equilibrium is reestablished between RL and RS_1. The implication is that the following equilibrium relationship must be true.

$$\text{Return from Investment } L = \text{Expected Return from Investment } S$$
$$\$1000 (1 + RL)^2 = \$1000 (1 + RS_1)[1 + E (RS_2)]$$

Note from this equation that the relationship between the current short-term interest rate, RS_1, and the current long-term interest rate, RL, depends on the market's expectations of the future short-term interest rate, $E(RS_2)$, but is independent of the amount of money invested.

In the preceding example, $RL = 8$ percent and $RS_1 = 6$ percent. The market's expectations of next period's short-term interest rate is $E (RS_2) = (1 +$

$RL)^2/(1 + RS_1) - 1 = 10$ percent. Therefore, if the current short-term interest rate is below the current long-term interest rate, or $RS_1 < RL$, the market must be anticipating a rise in short-term interest rates in the future. If that were not the case, the asset markets would not be in equilibrium. Investment L would always be preferable and investors such as Carol would have an incentive to initiate the portfolio realignment process described above by selling short-term assets and buying long-term assets, thereby causing RS_1 to increase and RL to fall. Conversely, if $RS_1 > RL$, for the financial assets markets to be in equilibrium the marginal investor must be expecting short-term interest rates to fall in the future.

These results generalize to rates of return linking assets of any maturities. Let RL denote the current yield on an n-period asset and RS_i denote the interest rate on a one-period asset during the period i. The length of a period is therefore defined by the maturity of the latter asset. The rates are related by the following expression.

$$(1 + RL)^n = (1 + RS_1)[1 + E(RS_2)][1 + E(RS_3)] \ldots [1 + E(RS_n)]$$

When short-term rates are expected to be rising, or $E(RS_n) > E(RS_{n-1}) > \ldots > E(RS_2) > RS_1$, the current long-term interest rate is observed to be above the current short-term interest rate, or $RL > RS_1$. Because this relationship is true for any n, we might expect under these particular market conditions that the longer the maturity of the asset, the greater will be the rate of return on the asset. The converse is also true. When the markets are expecting short-term interest rates to fall, or $E(RS_n) < E(RS_{n-1}) < \ldots < E(RS_2) < RS_1$, the current long-term interest rate is below the current short-term interest rate, or $RL < RS_1$, and in general we would expect that the longer the maturity of the asset, the lower will be the interest rate paid on the asset. This relationship between rates of return on assets within the same risk class is called the *term structure of interest rates* and the theory that explains the relationship is the *pure expectations hypothesis*.

4.7 THE YIELD CURVE

What use can be made of this theory? Many morning newspapers, such as *The Wall Street Journal,* provide a list of interest rates, or yields to maturity, for securities issued by the U.S. Treasury that range in maturity from three months to 30 years. That information can be used to plot a graph of interest rates (or yields) versus maturity as in Figure 4.3. Such a graph is known as the *yield curve* or, more particularly, the *government securities* or *Treasury yield curve*. Note that all of the underlying assets are free of default risk. Similar yield curves could be drawn for debt issued by either municipalities or firms that have similar quality ratings. That is, the assets whose returns are being plotted as a yield curve must be within the same risk class. Maturity and liquidity are thus isolated as the only features that differentiate the assets.

Refer to Figure 4.3. Abstracting from the differences in liquidity of the assets, the expectations hypothesis indicates that when the Treasury yield curve is upward-sloping like yield curve A, the markets are expecting short-term interest

Figure 4.3
Alternative Shapes of
the Yield Curve
without the Liquidity
Premium ($\sigma^2 = 0$)

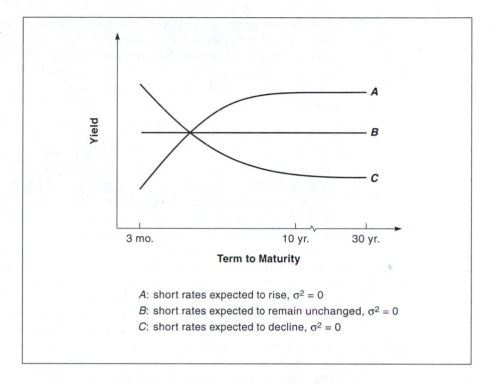

A: short rates expected to rise, $\sigma^2 = 0$
B: short rates expected to remain unchanged, $\sigma^2 = 0$
C: short rates expected to decline, $\sigma^2 = 0$

rates to rise. When the yield curve is flat like yield curve B, short-term interest rates are expected to remain unchanged in the future. When the yield curve is downward-sloping like curve C, short-term interest rates are expected to decline. All three shapes are possible and all three have occurred. What, then, is the *normal* shape of the yield curve, where "normal" means the slope on average over time? The answer depends on the typical pattern of movements in the short-term interest rate. Because observations over a sufficiently long period of time suggest that on average short-term interest rates neither rise nor fall, the yield curve would normally be flat like curve B when differences in liquidity are ignored. The next question therefore is: What effect do differences in liquidity have on the prediction of the normal shape of the yield curve that derives from the pure expectations hypothesis?

4.8 THE LIQUIDITY PREMIUM

Consider the example in which Carol contemplated the two investments L and S. Suppose she observes in the market that the long-term interest rate, RL, is identical to the short-term interest rate, RS_1. If she believes that short-term interest rates are not going to change in the future, which of those investments would she choose? If she values liquidity, she will choose investment S. In fact, she would have to be paid a premium to choose investment L and thereby tie up her money for a longer period of time. In other words, to invest willingly in the long-term asset, Carol would require RL to exceed RS_1. The implication is that, other things being equal, lenders want to lend short. What about the borrowers? Suppose the borrower is a firm considering whether it should finance a long-term project by issuing short-term debt or long-term debt. Returns from the project received over an extended period of time are to be used to retire the debt. If the firm issues short-term debt, it would have to roll the debt over when it comes due. Even though short-term interest rates are not expected to change, they may rise in the interim, thereby raising the financing costs to the firm. Short rates may also fall in the interim, but firms are typically risk averse and would therefore choose to issue long-term debt. The implication is that, other things being equal, borrowers want to borrow long. In sum, lenders demand a premium for lending long and many borrowers are willing to pay a premium to borrow long. Consequently, long-term interest rates have a built-in upward "bias" over and above short-term interest rates on assets of comparable risk. The bias is termed the liquidity premium.

The pure expectations hypothesis of the term structure of interest rates can be modified to reflect the liquidity premium. The general expression for the relationship between two assets drawn from the same risk class becomes $(1 + RL)^n = (1 + RS_1)[1 + E(RS_2)][1 + E(RS_3)] \ldots [1 + E(RS_n)] + \sigma^2, \sigma^2 > 0$, where RL is the one-period yield on an n-period asset; RS_i is the one-period return in period i on a one-period asset; and σ^2 is the liquidity premium. Note that when short-term interest rates are not expected to change in the future, or $RS_1 = E(RS_2) = E(RS_3) = \ldots = E(RS_n)$, the current long-term interest rate exceeds the current short-term interest rate, or $RL > RS_1$.

What effect does the liquidity premium have on the yield curve? Refer to Figure 4.4. Let RS_1 represent the current short-term interest rate paid on three-month Treasury bills and RL represent the yield on the 30-year Treasury bond. For the scenario in which the markets are expecting short-term interest rates to remain unchanged in the future, $RL > RS_1$. With $\sigma^2 > 0$, the slope of the yield curve would have an upward "bias" as indicated by comparing the "normally sloped" yield curve B' in Figure 4.4 with yield curve B in Figure 4.3 where the liquidity premium is absent, or $\sigma^2 = 0$. Therefore, if the markets are expecting short-term interest rates to rise, the slope of the yield curve must be not only positive, but steeper than "normal" as shown, for example, by yield curve A'. As noted in Figure 4.4, the flat yield curve D' indicates that markets are actually expecting short-term interest rates to fall and, in this case, to fall by just the amount necessary to offset the liquidity premium. When short-term interest rates are expected to decline by an even greater amount, the slope of the yield curve can become negative, as shown by curve C' in Figure 4.4. The result is what is known as an *inverted yield curve*, which is a source of anxiety for the financial markets as discussed below.

Finally, note that the yield curve is usually, fairly flat over the maturity range of 10 to 30 years.[8] The reason is twofold. Forecasts of short-term interest

---

[8]A premium often is paid on some Treasury securities in the two-year maturity range, which are said to be "on special." The cause of this premium is that forward markets may have committed heavily to the delivery of those particular assets, inducing a temporary shortage.

Figure 4.4
Alternative Shapes of
the Yield Curve with
the Liquidity Premium
$(\sigma^2 > 0)$

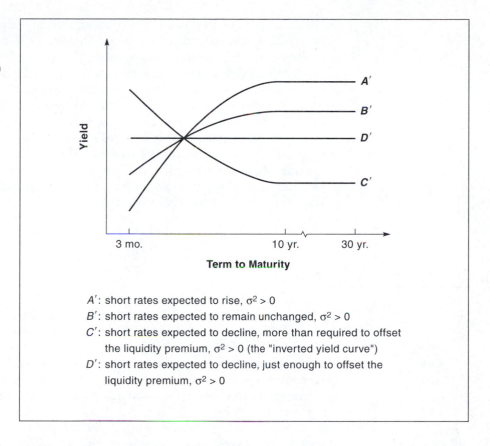

A': short rates expected to rise, $\sigma^2 > 0$
B': short rates expected to remain unchanged, $\sigma^2 > 0$
C': short rates expected to decline, more than required to offset
    the liquidity premium, $\sigma^2 > 0$ (the "inverted yield curve")
D': short rates expected to decline, just enough to offset the
    liquidity premium, $\sigma^2 > 0$

rates at time horizons beyond 10 years are so imprecise as to be indistinguishable. Moreover, the differences in the liquidity premium between assets whose maturities are so distant are essentially zero.

4.9 INTERPRETING THE SLOPE OF THE YIELD CURVE

Suppose the slope of the yield curve steepens abruptly. What would such a change portend for the economy and what effect would it have on the market value of stocks and bonds? From the expectations hypothesis of the term structure of interest rates, the steepening could be due either to an upward revision in the markets' expectations of future short-term interest rates in relation to the current short-term interest rate or to an increase in the liquidity premium. The Fisher equation suggests that an upward revision of expected future short rates would be due to either relatively higher anticipated real interest rates, r, or an increase in inflation expectations, π^e. Both may occur if the economy strengthens, which would be good news for stocks but not for bonds. A steepening of the yield curve could also reflect greater uncertainty about future economic activity, which would coincide with a larger liquidity premium and would have an adverse effect on both stock and bond prices.

An inverted yield curve implies that markets are expecting fairly sharp declines in short-term nominal interest rates. Such steep declines in short rates are often accompanied by a recession. During a recession, corporate earnings are obviously lower and dividend growth is likely to diminish. From the stock valuation equation, the reduction in expected future dividends is reflected in lower share prices. The effect of an inversion of the yield curve on bond prices depends on whether long rates have risen or fallen. More often than not, long-term interest rates decline in a recession. Therefore, an inversion of the yield curve usually, but not always, leads to a rise in bond prices.

4.10   SUMMARY

One of the important economic decisions for households is the allocation of wealth/income to consumption and savings. Households save to raise future consumption possibilities. Saving therefore represents postponed consumption. The willingness of a household to postpone consumption is determined largely by its preferences, which include the rate at which it discounts future utility and its tolerance for risk. The more it discounts future utility and the lower its tolerance for risk, the less willing it is to give up current consumption in anticipation of higher future consumption. To entice the household to postpone consumption through saving, borrowers must offer adequate compensation in the form of a minimum real rate of return on investments that constitute the household's savings. The minimum rate of return is determined by the preferences of each household. The equilibrium rate of return on a given asset is just equal to the minimum required rate of return for the marginal investor, whose preferences would preclude making the investment if the real return were any lower.

Financial assets generally yield a stream of income denominated in units of money such as dollars. Because inflation erodes the purchasing power of money over time, the required real rate of return of the marginal investor in a financial asset must be adjusted to compensate fully for inflation that is expected over the life of the asset. The equilibrium nominal rate of return on an asset is therefore equal to the minimum real rate of return demanded by the marginal investor plus the expected rate of inflation. As inflation expectations are revised upward, the nominal return on the asset must rise and the price of the asset falls.

Because financial markets are forward-looking, the prices of stocks and bonds reflect the anticipated stream of returns. For bonds, the returns are semiannual coupon payments and the face value of the bond received at maturity. Each of the returns is fixed in nominal terms and is known throughout the life of the bond. The bond price therefore reflects the present value of the stream of returns, where the future is discounted by the nominal rate of return on the bond or the bond yield. Hence, as long-term nominal interest rates rise, bond prices fall.

Stock prices are determined by the present value of the future expected dividend stream. Future dividend levels are unknown by investors, who therefore must forecast dividend growth. Many factors influence the forecasts, including news about the specific firm that issued the stock, news about the industry group of which the firm is a part, revisions in projections of future macroeconomic growth, and changes in government policies and regulations. Moreover, uncertainty about the factors that influence dividend forecasts tends to adversely affect stock prices because investors tend to be risk-averse and must be compensated for incurring increased risk.

Interest rates or yields on long-term assets are related to short-term interest rates through the portfolio choices made by investors and the alternative financing options of borrowers. This term structure of interest rates incorporates the average future expected path for short-term interest rates into the current long-term interest rate. When short-term interest rates are significantly below long-term interest rates, the financial markets are expecting short rates to rise in the future; otherwise, investors would flee short-term assets and buy long-term assets. The converse is also true. When current short rates exceed current long rates, short-term interest rates are expected to fall in the future.

The yield curve is a plot of interest rates, or yields, versus maturity for assets within the same risk class. Typically, this curve is upward-sloping, reflecting the belief that lenders prefer to lend short and must be compensated for the loss of liquidity when lending long, whereas risk-averse borrowers with long-run financing needs prefer to borrow long and are willing to pay a premium to lock-in financing costs in the future. Therefore, interest rates tend to increase as the maturity of the debt instrument lengthens. Under certain macroeconomic conditions, however, the yield curve can become inverted, with short-term interest rates exceeding long-term interest rates. The yield curve usually has such a shape prior to a recession in the macroeconomy.

REVIEW QUESTIONS

1. The minimum real rate of return necessary to induce a household to invest in a particular asset depends on both the rate at which the household discounts the future and the household's tolerance for risk.

   (a) Illustrate graphically a situation in which a more risk-averse household requires a lower rate of return on a given investment than a less risk-averse household. Determine the minimum rates of return.

   (b) The degree of risk aversion reflects the likelihood of not attaining a certain future level of utility. Relate it to the riskiness usually associated with investments in the stock market.

2. The stock market is often cited as a "leading indicator" of the U.S. economy.

   (a) How would you expect graphs of a stock market index and of the real GDP to compare?

(b) Explain how a firm that has good short-term growth prospects but poor long-term growth prospects could have a high share price.

(c) Explain how a firm that has good long-term growth prospects but poor short-term growth prospects could have a high share price.

3. Assume that the markets are expecting short-term interest rates to fall.
   (a) What are the possible shapes of the yield curve? Explain.
   (b) The Federal Reserve tightens policy and in response short-term interest rates rise while long-term interest rates fall. From the Fisher equation, what is a possible explanation of this response?

*4. Consider two alternative investments. Asset A represents claims to a stream of returns with $100 at the end of the first year and returns that grow by 5 percent received at the end of each of the next three years. Asset B yields $200 at the end of the first year and $50 in each of the following six years.
   (a) If you demanded a 6 percent annual rate of return on your investment, how much would you be willing to pay for each of these assets?
   (b) Suppose there is only a 50 percent chance that you would receive the $50 returns in years 2 through 6 on asset B and a 50 percent chance that you would receive no return in years 2 through 6. Would you prefer to own this asset rather than asset A? What are the odds that you would receive the $50 returns in years 2 through 6 that would leave you indifferent between assets A and asset B?

*5. Turn to the section of *The Wall Street Journal* that displays the yield curve.
   (a) Describe the shape of the yield curve, and what the markets' expectations of short-term interest rates are likely to be.
   (b) Has the slope of the yield curve changed significantly over the past four weeks? Speculate on why it may have done so.
   (c) Turn to the section on futures markets and explain whether your answer in part (a) is confirmed by interest rates futures.

REFERENCES

Hamburger, Michael J. and E. N. Platt. 1975. "The Expectations Hypothesis and the Efficiency of the Treasury Bill Market." *Review of Economics and Statistics* 57 (May): 190–99.

Mishkin, Frederic S. 1983. *A Rational Expectations Approach to Macroeconomics.* Chicago: National Bureau of Economic Research.

Pesando, James E. 1983. "On Expectations, Term Premiums and the Volatility of Long-Term Interest Rates." *Journal of Monetary Economics* 12 (March): 467–74.

Shiller, Robert J. 1979. "The Volatility of Long-Term Interest Rates and Expectations Models of the Term Structure." *Journal of Political Economy* 87 (December): 1190–1219.

Singleton, Kenneth J. 1980. "Expectations Models of the Term Structure and Implied Variance Bounds." *Journal of Political Economy* 88 (December): 1159–76.

PART II

Fundamentals of Monetary and Financial Institutions

CHAPTER 5

FINANCIAL INTERMEDIATION

When a household purchases a house or an automobile or when a firm purchases raw materials for production, it can borrow the needed funds from firms such as commercial banks that specialize in lending. The lending institution is not the ultimate source of the funds, however. The ultimate source is the net savers in the economy who have surpluses of funds that they want to invest. The institution therefore acts not only as a lender to parties that want to borrow, but also as a borrower from parties that want to invest. Collectively, the institutions then channel funds from areas in the economy where they are in surplus to areas of the economy where they are in deficit, anonymously matching borrowers with lenders. In other words, the institutions *intermediate* loans and therefore are called financial intermediaries.

Financial intermediation is costly. Moreover, imprudent lending practices by the financial intermediaries can lead to severe strains on the economy if many of the loans they make go into default.[1] Yet virtually all market-oriented economies have firms specializing in the function of financial intermediation, even though this third-party activity is not essential. Parties that want to borrow could instead go directly to parties that have funds to lend. The terms of each loan could be agreed upon by both parties and the transfer of funds could take place without the aid of an intermediary. Evidently financial intermediaries provide significant benefits to the economy, because otherwise the market for their services would simply not exist.[2]

---

[1]Such strains became very apparent in the U.S. economy during the 1980s, particularly within the savings and loan industry.

[2]Diamond (1991) examines the choice of the direct placement of debt, for example, when a firm considers issuing a bond instead of securing a loan intermediated through a bank. He argues that the greater the need for monitoring the use of the loan, which reflects the degree of uncertainty about the payback of the loan, the more likely it is that the loan will be intermediated. The financial intermediary will perform the monitoring tasks as a condition for the loan.

In this chapter, the benefits an economy derives from the services of financial intermediaries are described in the context of the island economy of Chapter 1. The set of trading frictions peculiar to intertemporal trades, which involve loans, are first described. These trading frictions restrict intertemporal trade by causing credit (or loan) markets to be missing or incomplete. Through specialization in the matching of borrowers with lenders, financial intermediaries reduce the costs of the trading frictions by completing many of the missing credit markets. This activity is welfare-improving because it results in a more efficient allocation of the economy's resources to their most highly valued use. Therefore, the average per capita utility level for the economy as a whole is increased.

The next chapter examines the generic classes of financial intermediaries that have arisen in modern monetary economies. Of special interest are the regulated financial institutions, such as commercial banks, that play crucial roles in the functioning of the money markets. Knowledge of their activities is central to an understanding of monetary theory and policy in practice.

5.1 FINANCIAL INTERMEDIATION IN AN ISLAND ECONOMY

In Chapter 1, the lack of a double coincidence of wants between potential trading partners is seen to be the basic trading friction that precludes certain bilateral trades. A description is given of how money can be introduced into the economy (at some cost) to resolve this problem by providing a common medium of exchange that completely decentralizes markets. Decentralization of trade enhances economic welfare. Specifically, the reallocation of perishable goods around the island by trade is accomplished more efficiently because markets are no longer missing. Greater incentives for home production and increased consumption of market-traded goods (perishable goods produced at distant homesites and acquired through trade) raise levels of utility.

In the economy described in Chapter 1, durable investment goods are not traded. In this chapter, such trades are permitted and a set of trading frictions associated with their intertemporal nature is described. The trading frictions introduce costs that deter households from engaging in intertemporal trades. The result is missing markets. The trading frictions and their attendant costs provide a role in the economy for financial intermediaries. Through specialization, financial intermediaries reduce the trading costs and thus enable more intertemporal trades to occur. The number of missing markets is reduced, and the economy's resources are allocated more efficiently toward their most productive (and highly desired) use. As a consequence, output, consumption, and welfare increase.

5.2 FINANCIAL INTERMEDIATION AND THE MATCHING OF INTERTEMPORAL PREFERENCES

In opening the island economy to trade in durable investment goods, we must ask the fundamental two-part question associated with any exchange: Is there any incentive for such trades to take place and are any such trades feasible? In answering that question, we assume that the island economy is in the state at which we left it at the end of Chapter 1. Fiat money is circulating in the economy and resolves the lack of double coincidence of wants by perfectly decentralizing exchange markets. With that trading friction eliminated, we can examine the special intertemporal nature of trade in durable investment goods by first finding the set of incentives on both sides of the exchange that would make a trade desirable, and then identifying the trading frictions that must be resolved for the desired trades to be feasible.

Suppose a miller on the island, designated household i, has a positive demand for a set of durable investment goods that includes new gears for his grist mill, machine tools for installing and maintaining the new equipment, and special lubricants that are needed to operate the new gears. All of these investment goods are produced at distant homesites on the island. In the notation of Chapter 1, these durable investment goods are represented by the set x_i^t depicted in Figure 5.1. Obviously, the miller's demand for these goods is not based on the direct utility he receives from them, which is zero.[3] Instead, they represent part of an investment project that the miller undertakes to make more efficient use of his (home-produced) capital and (quality-adjusted) labor in the production process. This project will enable him to produce more flour in the future that he can sell in the market.

To acquire the investment goods x_i^t today through a monetary transaction, the miller would have had to increase his output and reduce his consumption in the previous period by an amount sufficient to generate enough savings (say, in the form of money acquired from the sale of home-produced perishable goods) to make the purchase. If units of x_i^t are sufficiently costly, the miller may have to save for many periods before making the purchases. However, if he could acquire x_i^t today, the greater productivity resulting from the investment project could be expected to generate higher income in the form of greater output in the future. Therefore, as an alternative to multiperiod saving to finance the investment project, the miller could avoid lowering his consumption during those periods by pledging, or borrowing against, a portion of the higher expected future income resulting from the acquisition of additional units of investments goods x_i^t. Of course, he must find a lender who is agreeable to those terms.

Suppose a household, say j, on the island produces all three of the investment goods—gears, machine tools, and lubricants—that the miller needs for the project. This condition is depicted in Figure 5.1, where x_i^t is a subset of household j's home-produced durable investment goods x_j^h. One necessary, but not sufficient, condition for household j to enter into the lending arrangement with the miller (household i) is its willingness to forgo consumption and leisure today in exchange for consumption and/or leisure in the future. That is, it must produce today the additional units of the investment goods that the miller wants to ac-

---

[3]We retain the assumption made in Chapter 1 that no durable consumption goods are produced on the island. Their presence in the artificial economy would complicate the story without providing additional insights.

Figure 5.1

Trade in Durable Investment Goods

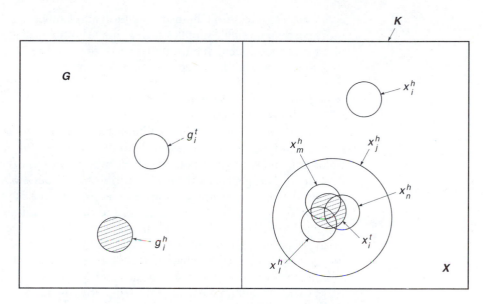

G = set of perishable goods produced in the economy

X = set of durable investment goods produced in the economy

g_i^h = set of home perishable goods produced by household i

g_i^t = set of perishable goods not produced by household i,

    but in demand by household i

x_i^h = set of home durable goods produced by household i

x_i^t = set of durable goods in demand by household i,

    but produced elsewhere in the economy

quire, x_i^t, without receiving any payment from the miller until some time in the future. This trading friction must be resolved. It is akin to the intraperiod double coincidence of wants problem that was resolved with money in Chapter 1.

Once the miller finds a supplier such as household j that produces the investment goods he wants, there must be an appropriate matching of preferences whereby the miller does not want to postpone consumption and his supplier wants to plan for higher future consumption at the expense of current consumption. That is, the miller (household i) is a net borrower and his supplier (household j) is a net saver. As described in Chapter 4, the preferences of the saver, household j, will determine a minimum required rate of return that it must receive for extending credit to the miller. Conversely, the project the miller is contemplating must be expected to enhance his productivity sufficiently that he can afford to pay the minimum rate of return demanded by household j. Therefore, both of those factors determine whether such a project is feasible.

For the miller and his supplier, household j, to find one another involves a costly search. It is completely analogous to the search process of households in Chapter 1 when trade in perishable goods is restricted to bilateral exchanges without intermediate transactions. Engaging in search diverts time (an economic resource) from home production and from leisure. The search is even more costly if no single supplier such as household j produces all of the durable, investment goods in x_i^t that the miller needs to complete his project. In that case, the miller must search for separate suppliers for each of the investment goods.

Referring to Figure 5.1, suppose household k produces the new gears, which are therefore designated as x_k^b, household l produces the machine tools, x_l^b, and household m produces the lubricants, x_m^b.

As in the case of the miller and household j, there must be an appropriate matching of preferences between the miller and each of his suppliers (households k, l, and m). In addition, the miller must coordinate the trades. He cannot acquire the new gears and the machine tools from households k and l until he is certain that he can secure the lubricants needed to operate the new equipment from household m. Similarly, the gears and the lubricant are of no use without the machine tools needed to install and maintain the new equipment. Obviously, as the number of potential lenders increases, the search and coordination costs could rise dramatically.[4] If the costs are too great, the search process would simply not be initiated and the corresponding trades in durable investment goods would not be made. Consequently, the miller would not undertake the investment project and his production process would not become more efficient. His inability to increase the future production of flour through a more productive use of his share of the economy's resources would result in a lower level of welfare than the economy could otherwise have attained.

Note that this situation is more of a problem for the miller, who is the borrower, than for household j or households k, l, and m, the savers. The reason is that the savers can still save. That is, they can produce more perishable goods today to trade for money, and the money can be carried over to future periods to facilitate consumption at that time. However, this is not the preferred method of saving for two reasons. First, the increase in supply of the savers' home-produced perishable goods would depress the market values of those goods in the current period. (Remember that households derive diminishing marginal utility from consuming these goods.) Second, the return to money holdings is the negative of the inflation rate, and is likely to be less than the return the households could receive from the miller for making the loans.[5]

Search costs introduce incompleteness in loan or credit markets that households on both sides of the market would like to see eliminated or at least minimized. Reducing search costs is one role of the financial intermediary. If no uncertainty were associated with the ability and willingness of borrowers to repay loans, the financial intermediary could specialize in anonymous matchings of borrowers and lenders. In the example, the intermediation process could

---

[4]This point is emphasized here because most financial intermediaries typically bundle a large number of small savings into larger loans. The exceptions are small finance companies and some venture capitalists.

[5]If the inflation rate were just equal to the negative of the real interest rate, the household would be indifferent between holding money and making the loan. This is the optimal money rule of Friedman (1969) and is discussed in more detail in Chapter 15.

proceed as follows. Suppose the miller wants to acquire investment goods x_i^t from households k, l, and m. However, the miller is not be able to work out a satisfactory repayment schedule with all of the suppliers. That is, a fundamental mismatch of intertemporal preferences cannot be resolved in the related collection of bilateral agreements. The miller can go to an intermediary and request a loan in the form of a line of credit, or claims against the intermediary that the intermediary stands ready to honor. The two parties can agree on a single repayment schedule with an appropriate interest payment to compensate for the time value of the loan. The miller can relinquish claims against the financial intermediary to households k, l, and m in exchange for the new gears, x_k^b, the machine tools, x_l^b, and the lubricants, x_m^b, respectively. Those three households then have claims against the intermediary. However, they are net savers and they must receive a minimum required return on their savings as determined by their preferences. Because the intermediary cannot honor the claims immediately, a loan agreement could be struck between the three households and the intermediary whereby, in exchange for the households' claims against the intermediary, alternative liabilities in the form of interest-bearing deposit accounts are issued. The difference between the interest received from the miller and the interest the intermediary pays on the deposit accounts represents income to the intermediary. This income must be sufficient to cover the costs of intermediation.

At any point in time, the intermediary is intermediating loans between many borrowers and many lenders. As long as the interest income received from the borrowers exceeds the interest payments to the lenders plus any net withdrawals from the deposit accounts, the intermediary remains solvent and credit markets that may otherwise have been missing are complete. The net effect on the economy is that more durable investment goods are produced and traded, which expand and enhance production processes. The resultant increases in output and consumption raise overall welfare levels in the economy.

5.3   RISK ASSESSMENT, AGENCY COSTS, AND UNCERTAIN INVESTMENT PROJECTS[6]

Just as money perfectly decentralizes exchange markets for intraperiod trade, financial intermediation perfectly decentralizes credit markets for interperiod trade. It performs an anonymous matching of borrowers with lenders in the same way as money performs an anonymous matching of trades in perishable goods.

---

[6]The following example is constructed to match the island economy of Chapter 1 with literature on costly communication and delegated monitoring of investment projects by financial intermediaries, and the associated literature on credit rationing. See, for examples, Townsend (1983), Diamond (1984, 1989), Lacker and Weinburg (1989), Williamson (1986, 1987), and Bernanke and Gertler (1989).

However, a trading friction is associated with the interperiod nature of trades involving durable investment goods: uncertainty of payback. The very nature of a loan (or an extension of credit) is that one household or firm is giving up claims on wealth today in exchange for a promise from another household or firm to return the wealth (in some form) in the future plus interest payments, the latter reflecting the time value of the wealth. Such agreements always carry the risk that, either through fraud or miscalculation, the borrower will be unable to repay the loan in the future at the terms agreed to by both parties. The terms are generally set forth in a formal contract. The purpose of the contract is to prevent deception by the borrower and to provide the greatest assurance to the lender that the loan will be repaid. Therefore, contracts often include provisions such as collateralization of all or part of the loan, which explicitly state that a transfer of ownership of wealth from the borrower to the lender will take place in the event of default. Even so, the lender almost always (with the exception of certain bizarre cases) wants the terms of the contract to be fulfilled by a successful repayment of the loan. But what about the borrower?

Consider the example in which the miller undertakes an investment project to upgrade his grist mill. The project requires new gears, machine tools, and lubricants contained in the set of durable investment goods x_i^t, all of which are produced by household j. (That is, x_i^t is a subset of x_j^b as in Figure 5.1.) Suppose the miller wants to acquire these investment goods by borrowing against the future income that the investment project is expected to generate. The simplest agreement that would enable the miller to make this type of acquisition would be an extension of "trade credit" by his supplier, household j, whereby household j agrees to transfer ownership of the goods x_i^t to the miller today in exchange for claims against the miller's future production of flour, which in the notation of Chapter 1 is given as g_i^b in Figure 5.1. Note that it is not necessary for household j to demand any flour for its own consumption (in which case the intersection of g_j^t and g_i^b is the null set, as shown in Figure 5.1). Because fiat money is circulating in the economy and has decentralized the markets for perishable consumption goods, either household j could take its portion of the flour produced by the miller to the market and exchange it for money or the miller could sell the flour in the market and repay the loan with the money received from the sale. What could prevent such an agreement from taking place?

The agreement cannot occur unless the miller has an incentive to repay the loan. If he is to complete the transfer of claims on his future home production of flour to household j as promised, some form of communication must be established between the miller and household j in the future. Without a guarantee of a future communication link, the miller could receive the goods x_i^t from household j and then become anonymous. Would there be any incentive for the miller to repay the loan? If he does not plan to borrow again, the answer is clearly no. The miller would simply acquire the investment goods x_i^t from household j and vanish. The miller would become wealthier at the expense of household j.

Of course, the decision by the miller not to repay the loan would have consequences. It would certainly preclude him from ever again being able to obtain credit from household j. Moreover, household j communicates with other households on the island and would inform them that the miller is a bad credit risk, further reducing his ability to obtain credit in the future. Hence, the miller would choose not to repay only if the value of the investment goods x_i^t received today exceeds the value he places on having his access to trade credit reduced in the future as a consequence of that decision. The larger the network of households that add the miller to their list of bad credit risks, the greater will be the cost to the miller.[7] (We are ignoring the deterrant effect of the threat of legal action in the case of default.)

The miller's failure to repay the loan might be due to outright fraud. That is, the miller could secure credit from household j under the false pretense of utilizing the investment goods x_i^t in an investment project, when in fact he acquires the goods to sell to a third party for money with no intention of repaying. However, his failure to repay the loan could also be due to his miscalculation of the potential benefits associated with the prospective investment project. The latter possibility introduces a second dimension into the assessment by the potential lender, household j, of the miller's loan request. Uncertainty is associated with any investment project; events could simply render the borrower incapable of meeting the agreed-upon repayment schedule. Household j must both assess that risk and determine how to allocate the risk between itself and the borrower.

Various loan arrangements can be used to allocate risk, depending on the relative levels of risk tolerance of the respective borrower and lender. They range from full collateralization and no profit-sharing, whereby the borrower assumes nearly all of the risk, to no collateralization and full profit-sharing, whereby the lender assumes nearly all of the risk. However, what is important to stress here is that risk assessment itself is a costly activity. It involves not only some expertise about the proposed investment project, but also a monitoring of the past and present behavior of the potential borrower. Much of the lender's information about the potential success of a project is provided by the borrower. In the example, the miller has the greatest amount of relevant information about the project. He understands the operation of the grist mill and the quality of the machinery, and is in the best position to assess the likely productivity improvements due to installation of the new gears. Unless the miller reveals his knowledge to others, it remains his private information. If the information would be detrimental to the granting of the loan request, the miller would have incentive *not* to reveal the information to the lender, household j. The withholding of private information that is relevant to the risk assessment of the loan creates agency costs, which make risk assessment even more difficult for the lender, such as household j, and thus increase the need for monitoring. As monitoring activity increases, monitoring costs rise and increase the overall cost of providing loans. The result is that fewer loans are granted.

---

[7]Bernhardt (1989) examines this tradeoff in a general equilibrium model where agents are spatially separated and have such itineraries that they do not all meet with one another. Some communication structure reflecting the credit histories of potential borrowers is therefore needed for loans to be extended.

5.4   FINANCIAL INTERMEDIATION AND RISK REDUCTION THROUGH DIVERSIFICATION

In the absence of private information about risky investment projects, the borrower (such as the miller) and lender (such as household j) would structure their agreement (or contract) to match the allocation of risk between them with their relative tolerances for risk. In general, individual households are risk averse and require a high expected return on investments that have inherently high risk. That requirement raises the cost and reduces the potential profitability of borrowers' investment projects. Therefore, fewer loans are made in the economy. How could a financial intermediary lower such costs by reducing the overall level of risk for lenders?

Consider again the miller's investment project requiring trade credit from multiple suppliers, such as households k, l, and m (see Figure 5.1). Suppose the amount of trade credit granted by each of the three lenders represents a major share of their individual savings. If a future event, such as a fire that destroys the mill, results in a default on the loans by the miller, households k, l, and m will lose a large proportion of their savings (ignore any provisions for collateralization of the loans or possible fire insurance). Suppose that instead of entering into bilateral trade credit contracts with the miller, the lending households k, l, and m deposit their savings with a financial intermediary which in turn bundles the funds into loans. Further suppose that the financial intermediary makes loans for investment projects to many households in addition to the miller, and the lending households receive shares of the total investment income (in proportion to the size of their deposits) that the borrowing households pay to the financial intermediary.

For simplicity assume that all investment projects undertaken by households that borrow from the intermediary have the same level of risk, but each project has its own idiosyncratic risk. In the case of the miller's project, a fire at the grist mill that leads to a loan default by the miller may have no effect on the ability of the other borrowing households to fulfill the terms of their loan contracts with the financial intermediary. Other events, however, could alter the ability of all households to repay, such as a hurricane that sweeps across the island and damages all ongoing construction projects financed by the intermediary. In the case of the grist mill fire, when only the miller defaults on the loan, there would be a relatively small effect on the return to the savings of households l, k, and m, which are now depositors at the financial intermediary. That would not be the case had the lending households entered into separate bilateral trade credit contracts with the miller. Only if all of the borrowers were adversely affected by an economywide event such as a hurricane would the households not benefit from using the intermediary to channel their savings to the net borrowers. This example illustrates an important contribution of financial intermediaries. They can nearly eliminate idiosyncratic risks through diversification of the investments of small savers. The lowering of risk to the lenders reduces the cost to the borrowers of acquiring a loan and, for the economy as a whole, the quantity of loans or the amount of credit extended is increased. In effect, intermediation more efficiently allocates resources in the economy over time and results in overall welfare gains.

5.5   FINANCIAL INTERMEDIATION AND DELEGATED MONITORING

Borrowers' private information about their investment projects introduces agency costs into the risk assessment of loans. Such costs are manifested as the need for monitoring of the past and present behavior of borrowers. The higher the monitoring cost introduced by the trading friction associated with private information, the smaller the number of loans that will be made and the less efficient the intertemporal allocation of resources. The result is lower welfare levels in the economy. How can financial intermediaries reduce these costs to the economy and thereby engage in welfare-improving activities?

First, in the absence of financial intermediaries, note that the monitoring costs incurred by the economy as a whole rise as the number of borrowers per lending household increases. Even if the savings of individual households were large enough for them to engage in diversified investments without the aid of a financial intermediary, they would separately incur the monitoring costs associated with *all* of the households to which they extended trade credit. As in the example of the miller who receives trade credit from three suppliers, each of the lenders would perform the same monitoring activity. That monitoring activity would be costly in terms of using resources such as time that could otherwise be devoted to production or consumed as leisure. It is clearly in the interests of the miller's three lenders to delegate monitoring responsibility to one party, say household k. The resources that households l and m had been devoting to monitoring could then be reallocated to alternative uses. The result would be higher overall welfare levels in the economy.

We can easily see that significant economies of scale are possible in monitoring activity. The need for such scale economies has created a market for firms that specialize in monitoring services. Such services are another function performed by financial intermediaries. They act as delegated monitors of the past and present activities of the borrowers in the economy to give the lenders the greatest possible assurance that their loans will be repaid.[8]

One method of reducing monitoring costs associated with the borrower's private information is to structure the loan agreement or contract to provide incentives for the borrower to reveal as much private information about the project as possible.[9] The greater the borrower's stake in the success of the

---

[8]Scale economies are also associated with specializing in particular types of loans. For example, a commercial bank specializing in real estate lending in Orange County, California, would process a loan request from a builder in that area more efficiently than a commercial bank unfamiliar with the market.

[9]See Lacker and Weinberg (1989) for a discussion of contracts that are rendered optimal by clauses that satisfy compatibility constraints.

project, the less incentive the borrower has to withhold private information from the lender. Therefore, collateralization of loans can reduce the monitoring costs to the lender by shifting the risk of default to the borrower. This practice would facilitate approval of loan requests, but would require the borrower to have a sufficient amount of (unpledged) collateral to back the loan, which is not generally the case.

When loans are not fully collateralized, the lender must look for alternative assurances that the borrower will repay. It does so by monitoring the past and present activities of the borrower to identify signals that would aid in assessing the overall riskiness of the loan. One important signal that the lender obtains is the reputation the potential borrower has established in prior loan commitments. The information can be negative if the borrower has defaulted or been delinquent in payments on previous loans, it can be positive if the borrower has successfully fulfilled the terms of loan contracts in the past, or it can be uninformative if the borrower has no prior credit history.

Monitoring of the potential borrower's past activities gives the potential lender very valuable information that determines not only whether the loan is made, but also the terms of the loan. Households or firms with positive credit histories may receive low interest rates on loans simply because they represent a low credit risk. Reputation therefore is literally an asset and reputation building is a costly investment. If the household or firm has a sufficiently strong reputation as a good credit risk, the lender may rely very heavily on that signal, perhaps even to the exclusion of all others. In such cases, monitoring costs are substantially reduced. If those costs were sufficiently low, the services of the financial intermediary as a delegated monitor would no longer be required, although it may continue to intermediate the loan for reasons other than agency costs.[10]

When the prospective loan is not to be fully collateralized and the reputation of the potential borrower is not sufficient to merit granting the loan, the lender can look for other signals that could provide additional information to use in assessing the riskiness of the loan. One important signal is the net worth of the borrower. For example, suppose the miller has been extended credit by a financial intermediary that has been delegated by depositors, such as households *k, l,* and *m,* to monitor the miller's activities as the ultimate borrower of their savings. The project was a new design for the blades in the water wheel that runs the grist mill. The new blades were supposed to increase the efficiency of the mill, but the new design was a failure. Rather than realizing an improvement, the mill's efficiency worsened. The investment project for which the miller used the credit actually reduced his production of flour to such an extent that

---

[10]A good example is the commercial paper market as described in Chapter 2. In that market, large blue chip firms such as IBM or GM can issue short-term notes and place them directly in the portfolios of investors rather than borrowing from commercial banks as smaller and less well-known firms must do. The large denomination of commercial paper issues precludes direct investment by small savers. This indivisibility of the issues requires intermediation by firms such as MMMFs.

he was unable to meet his interest payments from revenues generated by the mill. If the miller had a large net worth, he could sell assets to absorb the losses. However, if the assets were not pledged as collateral against the loan (ignore possible legal action that could be taken against the miller in the case of default), is there any reason for the miller to continue to honor the terms of the loan agreement? The answer is yes if he values access to credit markets in the future. If the miller were unwilling to give up tangible real assets to honor the contract, he would suffer a loss of reputation which, in the extreme, could preclude any future borrowing. The threat of being effectively cut off from the credit markets (or of being forced to pay very high interest rates on future loans) makes net worth an important signal to lenders of the likelihood that a loan will be repaid.

Clearly, credit histories can be very important to the intermediation process. The more thorough the credit histories are on individuals in the economy, the more valuable they are as signaling devices. Moreover, the more efficient and accurate the system that assembles the credit histories, the greater lenders' reliance on them. Borrowers therefore have a great incentive to maintain a good reputation in terms of their perceived creditworthiness, which in turn enhances the value of other signals processed by the lender such as the borrower's overall net worth.

In general, financial intermediaries deal with many borrowers at any point in time, and in addition may process many loan applications from individual borrowers over time. Intermediaries therefore have an incentive to maintain accurate and complete information on the credit histories of all past borrowers, as they may become potential borrowers again at some future date. The need for scale economies in the compilation of credit histories has created a market for specialization in that activity and an additional role for financial intermediaries. By reducing the monitoring costs associated with the trading friction due to withholding of private information by borrowers, credit histories contribute to a more efficient intertemporal allocation of the economy's resources and thereby enhance welfare levels for the economy as a whole.

5.6 SUMMARY

Introducing money into a pure exchange economy resolves the basic trading friction that arises in intraperiod trade because of a mismatching of preferences that results in a lack of double coincidence of wants between trading partners. By completely decentralizing trade, money effectively performs an anonymous matching of preferences. A similar trading friction arises in interperiod trade, where borrowers with preferences for current consumption must be matched with lenders who want to postpone their consumption until some future date. Moreover, lenders must have the resources or commodities that the borrowers want to obtain, such as durable investment goods that a borrower needs for a particular investment project. In the absence of an intermediary, the matching of preferences would involve a costly search by both the borrowers and the lenders, and the search costs would rise if the investment projects involved many lenders for each borrower. Financial intermediation can resolve the mismatching of preferences and in the case of multiple lenders per borrower can realize economies of scale in performing that function. Hence, there is a market for firms that specialize in resolving the trading friction associated with matching the intertemporal preferences of borrowers and lenders. The activities of such firms can be welfare improving.

Another trading friction associated with intertemporal trades is the risk that a loan will not be repaid at a future date. Default can be due to either fraud or miscalculation on the part of the borrower, either of which affects the borrower's willingness and/or ability to repay the loan in the future. In the absence of private information, when borrowers and lenders have exactly the same knowledge of the prospects for repayment, the risk assessment of a loan is strictly an evaluation of the likelihood that future events will make it impossible for the borrower to repay. Every investment project has a certain amount of idiosyncratic risk of this type that must be incurred by the borrowers and lenders, and various contractual arrangements can be written whereby risk-sharing between them is based on their individual risk tolerances. However, in the absence of an intermediary, small savers (the lenders) may not be able to insulate themselves from idiosyncratic risks through a diversified investment strategy. Financial intermediaries can perform that function well and can realize scale economies in the process. The overall reduction in risk to the lenders in the economy enhances the ability of borrowers to receive credit, which in turn increases the volume of intertemporal trade. The result is further welfare improvements for the economy through a more efficient intertemporal allocation of the economy's resources.

In actual economies, borrowers and lenders do not have the same information about the likelihood of future repayment. Borrowers have private information relevant to the risk assessment of loans that lenders are unable to take into account. Lenders know that, in general, borrowers have an incentive to withhold private information if it is detrimental to their chances of being granted the loan or to the terms of the loan. One way to handle the resultant agency costs is through collateralization of the loans. However, borrowers may not have enough unpledged assets to collateralize the loans fully. Lenders therefore have incentive to monitor the past and present activities of borrowers to achieve the maximum assurance of being repaid.

Past credit histories establish borrowers' reputations, which lenders rely on as important signals of the likelihood of future repayment. A good reputation can be viewed as an asset because it enables a household not only to have greater access to the credit markets, but also to receive more favorable terms on loans. Consequently, other signals such as the borrower's overall net worth become even more valuable to the lender in assessing the riskiness of a loan. Financial intermediaries can achieve economies of scale in their monitoring activity and in the assemblage of complete and accurate credit histories of potential borrowers. They fill a market niche by acting as delegated monitors of the borrowers' activities on behalf of the lenders. The result is a more efficient intertemporal allocation of resources in the economy and enhancement of welfare.

■ REVIEW QUESTIONS

1. In the island economy, assume the miller and household *j* meet for the first time in a neutral location that is equally distant from their respective home-sites. In their meeting household *j* discovers that the miller has an investment project in mind that would significantly increase the productivity of his flour mill. What role could household *j* play in the financing of the miller's investment project under the following scenarios? In each case, state the sufficient conditions for the financing arrangement to be feasible.
   (a) Household *j* produces the investment goods that the miller needs and is a net saver.
   (b) Household *j* produces the investment goods that the miller needs, but is not a net saver.
   (c) Household *j* does not produce the investment goods that the miller needs, but is a net saver.
   (d) Household *j* does not produce the investment goods that the miller needs and is not a net saver.

2. Assume the miller in the island economy needs investment goods from three separate suppliers, households *k, l,* and *m,* all of which are net savers. The miller proposes his project to each supplier, states his expected rate of return on the project, and offers his assessment of the project's risk. Suppose household *k* is the least risk averse, followed by household *l,* and then household *m,* which is the most risk averse.
   (a) If the risk and expected return features satisfy household *m,* what type of financing arrangements could the miller obtain?
   (b) If the risk and expected return features satisfy only household *k,* what type of financing arrangements might the miller obtain?
   (c) Suppose the risk and expected return features as described by the miller are satisfactory to all three households, but they feel that the miller knows more about the project than he is revealing. In what ways could the financing arrangements be affected?

3. Discuss the effects that a system of extensive credit histories (versus no credit histories) would have on the following loan applications.
   (a) The miller applies for funds to rebuild his grist mill after a fire destroys a renovation project that he was undertaking with funds he had secured in his only prior loan agreement.
   (b) The miller applies for funds to reinstall his old water wheel design after the new design proves woefully inefficient and forces him to use some of his personal wealth to retire the loan that he had secured to install the new design. Assume that he has a long record of successfully repaying investment loans.
   (c) In the same situation as in (b), assume the miller has no personal wealth to use for repayments and therefore needs the new loan not only to reinstall the old water wheel design, but also to retire the previous loan that he used to install the unsuccessful new design.

(d) The miller applies for a loan to fund the installation of a new set of gears to run the grist mill. He has never borrowed in the past.

*4. The information revolution has afforded relatively easy access to individual credit histories.

(a) In what ways is this development a good thing? Can you cite evidence in the credit markets that is consistent with what theory would predict?

(b) Discuss the negative side of this development. To what extent should the misuse of credit histories be self-correcting through market forces?

(c) Given your answers in (a) and (b), discuss the pros and cons of government regulation of the use and dissemination of credit histories.

*5. The term "agency costs" is often applied to upper management decisions in publicly held firms.

(a) Discuss how private information about the firm that is known by upper managers could cause their decisions to be at variance with the best interests of the shareholders who own the firm.

(b) What incentives could be given to upper managers to make their decisions compatible with both the shareholders' interests and their own self-interests? Do you observe the mechanism(s) of such incentives operating in the U.S. economy?

▨ REFERENCES

Bernanke, Ben and Mark Gertler. 1989. "Agency Costs, Net Worth and Business Fluctuations." *American Economic Review* 79 (September): 14–31.

Bernhardt, Dan. 1989. "Money and Loans." *Review of Economic Studies* 56 (January): 89–100.

Diamond, Douglas W. 1984. "Financial Intermediation and Delegated Monitoring." *Review of Economic Studies* 51 (July): 393–404.

———————— . 1989. "Reputation Acquisition in Debt Markets." *Journal of Political Economy* 97 (August): 828–62.

———————— . 1991. "Monitoring and Reputation: The Choice Between Bank Loans and Directly Placed Debt." *Journal of Political Economy* 99 (4): 689–721.

Friedman, Milton. 1969. *The Optimal Quantity of Money and Other Essays*. Chicago: Aldine Publishing Company.

Lacker, Jeffrey M. and John A. Weinberg. 1989. "Optimal Contracts under Costly State Falsification." *Journal of Political Economy* 97 (December): 1345–63.

Townsend, Robert. 1983. "Financial Structure and Economic Activity." *American Economic Review* 73 (December): 895–921.

Williamson, Stephen D. 1986. "Costly Monitoring, Financial Intermediation and Equilibrium Credit Rationing." *Journal of Monetary Economics* 18 (September): 159–79.

———————— . 1987. "Financial Intermediation, Bank Failures and Real Business Cycles." *Journal of Political Economy* 95 (December): 1196–1216.

CHAPTER 6

FINANCIAL INSTITUTIONS

Chapter 5 describes how trading frictions associated with intertemporal trades create a market for firms that perform the functions of financial intermediation. Such firms match the intertemporal preferences of borrowers and lenders in terms of their consumption timing and relative risk tolerance. In addition, they enable small savers to diversify their investments to an extent that could not be achieved otherwise when borrowers are generally seeking funding for large and indivisible investment projects. Finally, such firms act as delegated monitors of borrowers' past and present activities, thus minimizing the agency costs associated with borrowers' incentives to selectively withhold private information that is relevant to the risk assessment of potential loans.

In modern economies, financial institutions have emerged to perform all of the functions of intermediation described above to some degree. However, specialization of activities has produced a variety of financial institutions that have successfully differentiated their products or the services they offer. They focus narrowly on specific groupings of preference-matching, investment portfolio diversification, and monitoring activities, often by specializing in certain types of loans, such as housing, or in certain maturity classes of assets, such as money market instruments (described in Chapter 2). In addition, government regulation has played a role in segregating classes of financial institutions. Of particular interest are the depository institutions, the largest category of which is commercial banks.

In this chapter, generic classes of financial institutions are described in terms of the specialized markets they serve. Then commercial banks and the regulations that govern their day-to-day operations are discussed in more detail.[1]

---

[1]A study of the distortionary effects of the excessive regulation of the depository institutions in the United States after the banking crisis of the 1930s would be very instructive. However, for the purposes of this textbook, the long view is taken that mutual savings banks and mutual thrift institutions will have a smaller share of the market in the future, and stock-based thrifts and commercial banks will become increasingly similar in terms of the regulations that govern them. The focus is therefore on the commercial banking industry. Credit unions are becoming the financial institution of choice for an increasing number of depositors, but at the time of this writing their overall market share was still small.

6.1 FINANCIAL INTERMEDIATION IN STOCKS AND BONDS

The money and capital markets can be conveniently differentiated in terms of the maturity of the financial instruments created and traded in those markets. Short-maturity assets are generally considered to be money market instruments. They are described in Chapter 2. Capital market instruments generally have longer maturities. The maturity cutoff that separates money and capital market assets is somewhat arbitrary, but is usually taken to be approximately one year. Assets of longer maturity are considered to be capital market instruments. Notable exceptions are two- to five-year CDs, which are considered to be monetary assets.

A full discussion of the capital markets is beyond the scope of this book. However, the financial intermediation of stocks and bonds is relevant to subsequent discussions. The valuations of stocks and bonds are described in Chapter 4. For the purposes of this chapter, the intermediation process associated with these assets is described briefly.

Stocks and bonds are issued by firms that want to acquire funds to finance long-term investment projects. Bonds can range in maturity from 10 to 30 years, whereas stocks have infinite duration. Many stocks and bonds are placed directly into the asset portfolios of the lenders with only the aid of an agent who facilitates the exchange. For example, suppose a publicly held corporation wants to issue a number of new shares of stock and a household wants to purchase a fixed number of those shares. The household can simply call a broker and place the order, and on the date of issuance the order will be filled. Note that the broker in this example performs none of the functions of an intermediary, but simply acts as an agent for the lender to facilitate the investment.

Alternatively, the broker could intermediate the transaction by selecting new issues for a lender whose preferences are known. In this case, the broker would be matching the preferences of the lender and the borrower. In addition, a broker who is managing an investment portfolio for a lender could assist the lender in achieving diversification of the investments. This portfolio management activity of the broker would include a delegated monitoring role. For example, if adverse information about a large investment project of an individual firm were to be revealed, the broker should inform the lender or make adjustments in the lender's investment portfolio (if authorized to do so). The increased riskiness of the investment may cause the riskiness of the overall investment portfolio to exceed the risk tolerance of the lender.

The cost of managing individual household portfolios can be relatively high. To reduce the cost, mutual funds have been created wherein a single portfolio of, say, stocks of a certain risk class, such as technology stocks, is managed by a firm. The matching of preferences is accomplished by the household's selection of the particular fund in which to invest. In recent years, the number and variety of mutual funds have increased dramatically. The household can avoid some of the costs of intermediation by picking the fund, or a broker can assist in the selection for a fee. Similar options are available for the acquisition of new issues in the bond market.

Once new issues of stocks and bonds have been placed, or acquired by lenders, events could unfold whereby those financial assets no longer match the owners' preferences in terms of maturity and/or risk tolerance. The lenders would want to exchange those assets for others that match their preferences. Such exchanges of stocks and bonds take place in the so-called secondary markets. All of the forms and degrees of financial intermediation, whether through a broker or a mutual fund, are available to facilitate the trades.

Pension funds are similar to mutual funds in performing the functions of financial intermediation, but with further specialization. That is, they collect individual household savings and purchase (and manage) portfolios of stocks and bonds (and money market assets) to match preferences, achieve diversification, and monitor borrowers. The additional specialization is in preference matching, as the investments made with the savings are explicitly intended to provide future retirement income for the lenders. Consequently, certain contractual arrangements have emerged that limit the lenders' control over these savings in terms of the quantity paid into the funds, the lenders' access to the funds, and how the funds are invested.

Historically, many pension plans were established as part of a firm's employee benefit package and were managed by the firm as an in-house trust fund exclusively for its own employees. The plans were rigidly structured and contributions were made by the employer in amounts that were non-negotiable.[2] The plans also had vesting provisions that required an individual to be employed by a firm for, say 10 years before becoming eligible for the pension. Finally, the investments made by the employer-managed pension trust funds were generally of low risk and long maturity, and hence were an appropriate match with the preferences of many lenders (the employees) who were saving for retirement.

However, as the ultimate lenders in pension plans, households differed in their levels of risk tolerance. If they wanted to assume a higher risk than that of the investment portfolios in their employer's pension trust fund—that is, if they wanted a higher expected return on their investments—they had to supplement their retirement savings with additional high-risk investments. That meant raising their overall level of retirement savings, which many did not want to do. Because of the failure of employer-managed trust funds to satisfactorily solve the basic intertemporal trading friction associated with preference matching, a market niche was created for firms that could specialize in intermediating such loans.

Beginning in the 1970s, that niche was filled by private pension funds. The structure of pension plans in the United States changed dramatically. Rather than continuing to manage separate trust funds for their employees, many firms chose to pay their employee pension contributions to the private pension funds. One immediate benefit was the relaxation, and in many cases outright elimination, of vesting requirements. Although the employees could not receive payments from the pension plan until they satisfied some age or retirement provision, they could become eligible for the retirement program immediately

---

[2]The terms could be periodically renegotiated as part of a union contract, for example.

upon employment. The retirement income was tied to the employer's contributions to the pension plan on the employee's behalf.

The specialization of pension funds enabled them to offer a great variety of investment plans to the contributing firm's employees. The employees could have some say about how the funds were invested by choosing between investment portfolios that differed in maturity and risk. Because the private pension funds collected employer contributions from many firms, they were able to exploit economies of scale by maintaining a large offering of investment portfolios. By the end of the 1980s, the pension funds had become very large. On a given day, their trading activities in stocks and bonds may account for most of the trading that takes place on organized exchanges such as the NYSE, AMEX, or NASDAQ. Note that it was the basic intertemporal trading friction associated with the need to coordinate preference matching between borrowers and lenders that produced the important market that the pension funds are able to fill.[3]

6.2 THE FINANCIAL INTERMEDIATION OF DEPOSITORY INSTITUTIONS

Depository institutions are a class of financial institutions that accept deposits of small savers and aggregate them into large loans that are made to borrowers. They resolve intertemporal trading frictions identical to those in the Chapter 5 example, where anonymous preference matching by the intermediary involved many lenders per borrower. As described in that chapter, a firm that intermediates many such loans can realize economies of scale in both its preference matching and its monitoring activities, and can achieve risk reduction through portfolio diversification.

However, the specialized intermediation that depository institutions perform has an additional dimension. The depositors (the lenders) prefer very short maturities and their risk tolerance for the deposited funds is very low. Essentially, they want to have easy access to the funds and they want to be assured that the funds are readily convertible into consumption purchases. In terms of the general characteristics of assets as described in Chapter 2, depositors are seeking assets with high liquidity and low risk, which they understand have a low expected return.

To match the maturity preferences of this group of lenders to their asset offerings, depository institutions have created a class of highly liquid assets called demand deposits (a variant of which is the NOW account). As implied by the name, the intermediary must honor requests by lenders (depositors) to access the funds on demand. Recall the household cash management problem

---

[3]In other contexts, this basic trading friction gives rise to markets for other specialized financial intermediation such as that performed by life insurance companies, finance companies, and venture capitalists.

described in Chapter 3: consumption expenditures are continuous over time, but income is received periodically in lump sums. Demand deposits are one major means by which households can store the portion of their income that is dedicated to consumption between successive payment periods.

From the intermediary's perspective, the demand deposits are liabilities that it must stand ready to honor on demand, and demand by individual lenders could fluctuate drastically. That is, each household periodically makes deposits and withdrawals, the timing and magnitude of which can vary over time. To the extent that the fluctuations are idiosyncratic, or specific to the household, the financial intermediary can insulate itself from them by offering demand deposits to many households. This is a form of diversification, because a positive net withdrawal by one household will often occur at the same time as a negative net withdrawal by another household. The overall net effect on the total volume of demand deposits at the depository institution is zero. However, events that cause depositors to demand more positive net withdrawals than negative net withdrawals and vice versa could induce fluctuations in the institution's overall deposit levels. The deposit levels represent the volume of funds that the institution has available for intermediating loans. Therefore, the anticipated volatility in deposit levels affects the selection of the institution's asset portfolio as well as the total volume of loans that it chooses to intermediate. That is, the institution must also satisfy the lenders' (depositors') relatively low tolerance for risk.

The risk that concerns depositors is the likelihood that the depository institution will be unable to meet their demands for withdrawals. Such a situation could occur if the institution's asset portfolio is too illiquid or if a sufficient number of the loans it made go into default. Depository institutions minimize illiquidity risk in two ways. First, a portion of the funds placed on deposit with the institution are not loaned out. They are held in reserve to absorb any unexpected net withdrawal demands. In general, as the anticipated volatility in deposit levels increases, the depository institution has a greater incentive to increase its reserves as a percentage of its asset portfolio. However, the idle reserves generate no interest income for the institution. For the economy as a whole, they represent an inefficiency in the intertemporal allocation of resources associated with matching borrowers with lenders. Therefore, to reduce reliance on reserves as a means of ensuring the liquidity of their asset portfolios, depository institutions minimize risk in a second way. They specialize in intermediating loans that are either of short maturity or for which there is an active secondary market. Maintaining a low average maturity in the asset portfolio increases its liquidity, because at any point in time a large number of the loan agreements will be expiring, freeing funds to meet withdrawal demands if the need arises. If there is an active secondary market for individual assets that the depository institution acquires, the maturity of the assets is less important in determining the overall liquidity of the asset portfolio. The intermediary will be able to sell the assets on short notice without penalty (that is, at their true market value) and acquire additional reserves in exchange.

Depository institutions must always maintain sufficient liquidity in their asset portfolios to meet withdrawal demands, because even infrequent failures to do so would deter small savers from making deposits.[4] Then fewer loans would be intermediated by the institutions, and intertemporal allocation of the economy's resources would be less efficient. However, a potentially greater deterrent to depositors is the risk that loans made by the intermediary will go into default. Depository institutions minimize this risk in several ways. The most obvious is by selecting assets (making loans) that have inherently low risk. Assets with short maturities and, to a lesser extent, those with an active secondary market, are in this category.[5]

A second obvious way to reduce default risk is through diversification. Future events could produce a high default rate in one category of assets, such as real estate loans, without affecting repayment from other assets in the institution's portfolio. If that category of assets represents only a small portion of the institution's asset portfolio, the impact on the institution's ability to meet withdrawal demands would be minimal. However risk reduction achieved through diversification involves a tradeoff. Depository institutions perform delegated monitoring of the ultimate borrowers of their depositors' savings. As described in Chapter 5, specialization in selected markets leads to economies of scale that reduce monitoring costs and improve the efficiency of the intermediation in those markets. The tradeoff between diversification and specialization is accomplished in part by increasing the share of assets that have no default risk (such as U.S. government securities) as the degree of specialization increases.[6]

Despite these measures, the risk of default is not eliminated. Over time, loan defaults will occur. The depository institution effectively loses an asset when a loan goes into default. To the extent that the loan was collateralized, the lost asset is replaced by another asset, the collateral. Even when loans are collateralized, however, a loan default generally results in a net reduction in the total assets held by the depository institution.[7] As a consequence, it no longer has enough assets to honor all of the potential withdrawal demands of the depositors. The liabilities of the depository institution exceed the value of its assets, a condition that places the institution in technical default. Essentially, the institution would be unable to meet all of its contractual agreements with depositors, even if it could costlessly and instantaneously liquidate all of its assets, but only if all of its depositors (or at least a very large fraction, depending on how

---

[4]Even the expectation that a depository institution may temporarily suspend its obligation to meet withdrawal demands could precipitate a "run" on the institution that could drive it into insolvency. Diamond and Dybvig (1983) describe the ingredients for such an event.

[5]Corporate stocks, in which banks cannot invest, obviously have very active secondary markets, but are nonetheless relatively risky assets.

[6]This tradeoff is clearly demonstrated by Rhoades and Rutz (1982) in their test of Hicks' "quiet life" hypothesis. They show that small commercial banks with loans concentrated in local markets tend to have a much higher share of secondary reserves than large banks with more diversified loan portfolios.

[7]For collateralized loans, the cost of the ultimate disposition of the collateral, such as a repossessed automobile, reduces its value to the depository institution.

seriously deficient the assets are) simultaneously pressed their legitimate withdrawal demands.

To avoid that eventuality, depository institutions must provide tangible assurance to the depositors that their deposits are safe, even though loan defaults will surely occur. The owners of the institutions (or the managers acting on the owners' behalf) therefore retain some of the accumulated interest income that they receive on their loans (net of operating costs) within the institution rather than dedicating it to other purposes, such as consumption. When loans go into default, these funds can be used to cover the asset losses. Thus, the depositors are effectively insulated from much of the risk to their deposits from loan defaults. The larger the stock or quantity of such funds in the institution, the lower is the risk borne by depositors.

6.3 MUTUAL VERSUS STOCK-BASED OWNERSHIP OF DEPOSITORY INSTITUTIONS

The stock of accumulated net interest income retained by depository institutions to insulate deposit funds from the risk of loan defaults represents an amount of wealth that the owners of the institution have reinvested in the activities of the firm. If the depository institution is owned by the depositors, these so-called retained earnings are the institution's total capital and represent the amount of owners' equity in the firm. Over time, as (net) interest income flows into the institution, a portion of it is added to total capital in the form of retained earnings and the remainder is paid out as dividends to the depositors/owners in proportion to their relative shares of total deposits in the institution. Institutions with this form of ownership organization are called mutuals. In the United States, credit unions, mutual savings banks, and some savings and loans have this form of organization.

Alternatively, a depository institution can issue shares of stock that represent fractional ownership in the firm. The shares need not be bought by the depositors. The income received from the sale of stock is added to retained earnings to constitute the total capital of the institution, and hence the amount of owners' equity in the institution. The net interest income received by the firm is allocated between retained earnings and dividends, with the latter distributed in proportion to the fraction of shares held by the owners. If the stock is traded on a secondary market, such as the NYSE, the firm is said to be publicly held. Otherwise, the firm is said to be privately owned.[8] In the United States, commercial banks and most savings and loans are stock-based firms.

---

[8]An advantage of a publicly held firm is its ready access to the capital markets if, for example, it needs to raise equity for an expansion of its activities. However, in the United States, private firms are exempt from the regulatory oversight of the Securities and Exchange Commission and can therefore avoid the costs of regulatory compliance, including both the reporting requirements and possible restrictions on their activities. As a general rule, although there are exceptions, privately owned depository institutions in the United States are relatively small firms as measured by total assets.

6.4   DEPOSITORY INSTITUTIONS IN THE UNITED STATES

Depository institutions play key roles in the smooth functioning of the economy's payment system and in the transmission of monetary policy changes to the overall economy. An understanding of those aspects of the economy therefore requires some detailed knowledge of the specific markets in which these institutions participate, the regulations under which they operate, and the central decisions their individual managers must make to fulfill their functions in the economy as financial intermediaries.

In the United States, four types of financial intermediaries are regulated as depository institutions: commercial banks, savings and loans, credit unions, and mutual savings banks. Of the four, the commercial banks have the largest market share, followed by the savings and loans. As seen in Table 6.1, commercial banks and savings and loans together dominate the market. Moreover, federal regulation enacted in the early 1980s was designed to phase out the regulatory distinctions between commercial banks and savings and loans,[9] a process that is still ongoing. For those reasons, the requisite background knowledge of depository institutions can be obtained by examining the commercial banking industry as being representative of such financial intermediaries.

6.5   A CLOSER LOOK AT COMMERCIAL BANKING

Table 6.2 is the consolidated balance sheet of domestically chartered commercial banks in the United States. The assets and liabilities are subdivided into categories that are convenient for highlighting the actual decisions made by bank managers as they carry out their tasks of financial intermediation, and for

Table 6.1   Relative Size of Depository Institutions in the United States*

DEPOSITORY INSTITUTION	TOTAL ASSETS (billions of dollars)	MARKET SHARE (percent)
Commercial banks	2807	61.1
Savings and loans	1347	29.3
Mutual savings banks	258	5.6
Credit unions	179	3.9

*Source: Federal Reserve.

[9]The two important pieces of legislation were the Depository Institutions Deregulation and Monetary Control Act (DIDMCA) of 1980 and the Garn–St. Germaine Amendment of 1982.

Table 6.2   Assets and Liabilities of Domestically Chartered Commercial Banks in the United States (in billions of dollars)*

ASSETS	
Primary Reserves	227.0
Vault cash	27.9
Deposits at the Federal Reserve	26.7
Cash items in process of collection	106.6
Other cash assets	65.9
Secondary Reserves	516.1
U.S. government securities	345.9
Other	170.2
Federal Funds Sold	131.5
Total Loans	1,779.2
Commercial and industrial	515.5
Real estate	683.2
Individual	363.5
Other	217.0
Other Assets	133.6
TOTAL ASSETS	2,806.6

LIABILITIES	
Total Deposits	2,103.0
Transaction deposits	618.7
Savings deposits	507.1
Time deposits	977.2
Borrowings	383.0
Federal funds bought	131.5
Borrowings from the Federal Reserve	251.5
Other Liabilities	120.9
TOTAL LIABILITIES	2,606.9
CAPITAL ACCOUNT	199.7

*Source: *Federal Reserve Bulletin*, October 1989. Data for the last Wednesday of May 1989.

illustrating how those decisions are affected by specific sets of regulations. The regulations of primary concern are reserve requirements, which are intended to give the Federal Reserve some control over the supplies of the various forms of money defined in Chapter 2, and capital requirements, which are intended to insulate bank deposits from the risks associated with loan defaults.

In Table 6.2, total deposits are broken down into three groupings of money market instruments (described in greater detail in Chapter 2). Transaction deposits are demand deposits and other checkable deposit accounts. Savings deposits consist of passbook savings and MMDAs, and time deposits are essentially CDs. All are highly liquid assets, and the bank can expect short-run volatility in these account balances due to unexpected net withdrawals, both positive and negative. To stand ready to honor the withdrawal demands, the bank maintains a stock of highly liquid assets in the form of primary reserves. They consist of currency in its vaults, deposits that it holds with the Federal Reserve, and demand deposits at other commercial banks (which account for most of "other cash assets"). At any point in time it will also have a large number of uncleared checks, which are represented by the accounting entry "cash items in process of collection." As a matter of policy, the Federal Reserve is prohibited from paying interest on the deposits of its member banks, and commercial banks are not permitted to pay interest on the demand deposit accounts maintained by other banks (largely for the purpose of check clearing), although the latter are deducted from the volume of deposits against which the banks must hold reserves. Because primary reserves are non-interest-bearing, commercial banks have an incentive to minimize the share of their total assets held in the form of primary reserves. Reserve requirements therefore give the Federal Reserve some control over the supplies of money in the economy.

Federal law authorizes the Federal Reserve to establish minimum reserve requirements (within prescribed limits) for selected groupings of bank deposits that must be met regularly by commercial banks. For the purpose of meeting those requirements, bank reserves are defined as vault cash plus the bank's deposits with the Federal Reserve. Commercial banks must maintain a minimum quantity of bank reserves, although they can choose how to allocate them between vault cash and deposits at the Federal Reserve. This minimum quantity of bank reserves is termed required reserves. Excess reserves are defined as the quantity of willingly held bank reserves that exceeds the required minimum.

The deposit accounts on which the Federal Reserve has the discretion to impose reserve requirements are: all transaction assets (less the demand deposits held at other banks), one category of CDs (termed nonpersonal time deposits of short maturity), and Eurodollar deposits. The current reserve requirements are 10 percent against transaction deposits and zero percent against both nonpersonal time deposits and Eurodollar deposits.[10] The requirements establish a fixed relationship between the total quantity of the deposit accounts and the quantity of required reserves and are referred to as reserve requirement ratios. Growth in the quantities of the deposits is reflected as growth in the various measures of money, that is, in the monetary aggregates. The Federal Reserve

---

[10]The reserve requirements against nonpersonal time deposits and Eurodollar deposits were reduced from three to zero percent in January 1990. The reason given was that financial innovation had provided a sufficient variety of substitutes for these assets that the requirements had become anachronistic and were ineffectual.

can exercise control over the total quantity of bank reserves in the economy. The mechanics of the process by which the Federal Reserve maintains control are discussed at length in Chapters 7, 16, and 17. Of special interest here is how control of total bank reserves relates to limited control of the money supply and how that in turn leads the Federal Reserve to select reserve requirements.

To the extent that the numerical relationship between total bank reserves and the monetary aggregates remains relatively constant and predictable over time, the Federal Reserve has the ability to regulate the total supply of money by adjusting the stock of bank reserves in the economy. Two sources of weakness in the linkages between bank reserves and the monetary aggregates can cause the numerical relationships to change unexpectedly. One source of weakness is changes in households' preferences for how they want to hold their wealth. Such changes could be due to changing economic conditions, which could be temporary or permanent, or to the introduction of new financial instruments (as discussed at length in Chapter 2).[11] The other source of weakness is unpredictable fluctuations in the quantity of excess reserves held by the banks.[12] It has a bearing on the criteria that should be used in selecting the optimal reserve requirement ratios.

If there were no reserve requirements, banks would still hold some reserves to meet unexpected net withdrawal demands even though such assets do not generate any interest income. Moreover, the numerical relationship between the reserves and, say, transaction deposits could be allowed to fluctuate as economic conditions alter the incentives for banks to hold reserves. Now suppose the Federal Reserve imposes reserve requirements on transaction deposits but at very low levels, say, .1 percent. How would the banks respond? In all likelihood they would already be meeting the requirement, so there would be no change in bank management practices and the relationship between bank reserves and transaction deposits would be as variable as before. That is, the reserve requirement is simply not binding.

What this example illustrates is that if the Federal Reserve wants to strengthen its control of the money supply, it must choose reserve requirement ratios that are high enough to be binding. High reserve requirement ratios effectively force banks to hold more reserves than they want to hold. The non-interest-bearing asset characteristic of reserves provides an incentive for bank managers to keep their excess reserves as low as possible at all times. Under these circumstances, bank reserves, over which the Federal Reserve may exercise very good control, are nearly equal to required reserves, which are numerically linked to the total volume of certain deposits, such as transaction

---

[11]The significance of these issues for monetary control is discussed in more detail in subsequent chapters.

[12]Banks also hold reserves for clearing interbank transactions (such as those associated with check clearing) through the Federal Reserve, where one bank's account is debited and the other bank's account is credited.

deposits. The higher the reserve requirement ratios, the more carefully the bank monitors its excess reserves by attempting to keep them as close to zero as possible.

However, as discussed previously in this chapter, reserve holdings represent inefficiencies in intertemporal trading in the loan markets. The higher the reserve requirement ratios, the greater will be the welfare losses. Therefore, the Federal Reserve faces a tradeoff. It must maintain reserve requirement ratios that are high enough to ensure good monetary control, but not so high as to cause unnecessary welfare losses due to the greater inefficiencies in the loan markets.[13]

Reserve requirement regulations are strictly enforced. Most large commercial banks must file reports with the Federal Reserve each week to provide evidence that they were in compliance with the requirements over a biweekly period called the reserve maintenance period.[14] The banks' problem in meeting reserve requirements on a biweekly basis is that the quantity of their individual bank reserves fluctuates with unexpected net deposit withdrawals. One way to cope with this problem is to hold excess reserves that can be used to meet any unexpected withdrawal demand, thus preventing the bank from becoming reserves deficient. The cost of this option is the forgone interest income.

Alternatively, if a bank is reserves deficient at the end of the reserve maintenance period, it can acquire additional reserves by either selling assets or incurring additional liabilities.[15] Assets that are useful for this purpose must be highly liquid, that is, they must be easy for the bank to sell on short notice at their true market value. Such assets are listed in Table 6.2 as secondary reserves. They consist of U.S. government and government agency securities and municipal bonds. Because assets with high liquidity and low default risk yield relatively low rates of return, one cost of maintaining a large stock of secondary reserves for this purpose is forgone interest income. A second potential cost is the risk of incurring capital losses on the sales. If long-term interest rates have risen between the time the bank acquired the securities and the time it decides to sell them, their market value will have declined and the bank will be selling them at a loss.

Commercial banks have other asset management options that can be used to maintain compliance with reserve requirements. Large secondary markets have arisen in the United States over the past few decades for the resale of real estate loans, in particular home mortgages, and for the resale of automobile loans, which comprise the largest share of individual loans (see Table 6.2). In

---

[13]Friedman (1960) and Sargent (1988) discuss the consequences of the Federal Reserve's policy of not paying interest on reserves.

[14]Smaller banks have different reporting requirements. Some file quarterly reports, some file annual reports, and some are exempt from reporting requirements.

[15]The Federal Reserve does allow some carryover of reserve surpluses or deficiencies from one maintenance period to the next.

addition, many short-term business loans that constitute the category of commercial and industrial loans (Table 6.2) have call provisions whereby the commercial bank can demand full and immediate repayment of the loan. However, none of those forms of loan liquidations are used frequently for the purpose of meeting reserve requirements.

Since the 1960s, commercial banks have increased their reliance on liability management techniques to meet reserve requirements.[16] With the lifting of interest rate ceilings on most deposit accounts in the 1980s as described in Chapter 2, banks are free to compete with each other for deposits by making explicit adjustments in deposit interest rates.[17] However, that is not a very efficient or reliable way to raise reserves on short notice. Reserves-deficient banks have therefore simply turned to borrowing money directly for the express purpose of replenishing reserves.

Because unexpected net withdrawal demands are idiosyncratic, or bank specific, on any given week some banks will have unexpected positive net withdrawals that deplete their reserves and could cause them to become reserves deficient whereas other banks will have unexpected negative net withdrawals that build up their level of excess reserves. Consequently, a market has emerged that enables banks that are reserves deficient to borrow from banks that have excess reserves to lend. It is called the federal funds market and the interest rate charged on the loans is termed the federal funds rate. This market has grown dramatically since 1960 and is very efficient at allocating bank reserves among banks, keeping excess reserves for the banking system as a whole to a minimum.[18] As an alternative, domestic commercial banks that are reserves deficient can rely on nondeposit sources of funds, including bank repurchase agreements and Eurodollar deposits (described in Chapter 2). These sources of funds grew dramatically during the 1980s.

When unexpected net withdrawals for the banking system as a whole are positive, not all reserves-deficient banks may be able to meet their reserve requirements through the federal funds market. If the quantity of excess reserves

---

[16]Evidence can be seen in the sharp decline in securities holdings in the banking system as a percentage of total assets. For the banking system as a whole, the share fell from approximately 50 percent in 1959 to 30 percent in 1994. There has been a rebound in secondary reserve holdings of banks in recent years in the aftermath of the drop in the real estate market that weakened the loan portfolios of many commercial banks and more particularly the S&Ls.

[17]When this form of competition was prohibited, the competition for deposits simply took an alternative implicit form, such as offering kitchen utensils or cutlery as bonuses for opening a new deposit account or for increasing balances in existing accounts. As inflation and therefore market interest rates rose in the late 1970s, these bonuses began to take the form of gold necklaces and earrings. See Klein (1971) for a discussion of these implicit costs.

[18]Since 1960, total excess reserves in the banking system as a percentage of total assets has fallen from over 3 percent to less than 1 percent.

in the banking system as a whole is insufficient, and given that nondeposit sources of funds are limited, an additional infusion of reserves into the system is necessary to meet the demands. Some of these reserves may come from asset sales, particularly from the sale of secondary reserves. An additional primary source of borrowed funds for the express purpose of meeting reserve requirements is the discount window at the Federal Reserve. By law, the Federal Reserve is the so-called lender of last resort and is required to make short-term loans to banks that are short of reserves at the end of the reserve maintenance period. The interest rate it charges on such loans is called the discount rate. Unlike the federal funds rate, it is an administered rate and its value is determined by the Federal Reserve as a matter of policy.

As a practical matter, reserves-deficient banks have the option of borrowing in the federal funds market or at the discount window, although the Federal Reserve actively discourages excessive reliance on the discount window as a means of complying with weekly reserve requirements. Because the federal funds rate and the discount rate represent the banks' costs of raising funds, the two interest rates, and the relationship between them, play principal roles in the transmission of monetary policy decisions to the rest of the economy. That process is discussed in detail in subsequent chapters.

6.6   LOAN DEFAULT RISK, DEPOSIT INSURANCE, AND CAPITAL REQUIREMENTS

The banking system just described is a "fractional reserve system." Banks take in deposits and create deposit accounts. The deposit accounts represent liabilities to the banks, many of which must be honored on demand. Banks withhold a fraction of the deposits as reserves and loan or invest the rest. As described previously, to insulate deposits from the possibility of an inordinately large number of loan defaults, banks retain some of their earnings. The retained earnings are added to the capital paid into the firm by its stockholders. Together the retained earnings and capital paid in constitute the bank's capital account as in Table 6.2.[19] If enough loan defaults were to occur to put the bank into technical default, that is, if the value of its remaining assets were less than the value of its liabilities, the depletion of the capital account would leave the bank vulnerable to excessive withdrawal demands by its depositors. It simply could not cover them all. If the depositors learned of the bank's precarious position, they would have an incentive to withdraw their funds as quickly as possible and a "run" on

---

[19]For the purpose of regulation, banks are able to issue subordinated debentures, which are also considered to be bank capital. In effect they are corporate bonds whose owners, in the event of bankruptcy, have claims to shares of the bank's assets only after depositors' claims have been fully met.

the bank could ensue. Once all of the bank's assets were exhausted, the remaining depositors would lose their funds.

To preclude the possibility of bank runs, the United States Congress established a system of federal deposit insurance whereby the federal government fully insures deposits of the system's member banks (which collectively hold more than 99 percent of the deposits in the banking system) up to a legal maximum (currently $100,000 per account). The insurance system is financed by premiums paid into a fund by member banks. The fund is managed by an agency of the federal government.[20]

In the absence of federal deposit insurance, depositors would have to perform a monitoring function on their commercial bank's loan and investments policies. They would incur agency costs associated with the financial intermediary's private information on the relative risk of the bank's asset portfolio, which it has no incentive to reveal to depositors. However, the federal government's deposit guarantees shift loan default risk away from depositors and toward the owners of the financial institution and the federal government. Consequently, depositors no longer have any incentive to monitor the bank's lending practices (unless they happen to be the owners of the institution). Such monitoring activities have been assumed by the federal agency managing the deposit insurance fund.

To reduce monitoring costs, the federal government has established a set of capital requirements that commercial banks must meet. Essentially, commercial banks must maintain a minimum quantity of capital as a percentage of total assets.[21] This requirement reduces monitoring costs in two ways. First, the larger the quantity of bank capital, the greater is the volume of loan defaults that the bank can absorb before it exhausts its capital and goes into technical default. Second, because bank capital represents the owners' equity in the financial institution that is placed at risk, owners incur a greater share of the monitoring costs as the stock of capital increases. Note, however, that the greater the stock of capital as a percentage of total assets, the lower is the expected rate of return to that capital. Therefore, banks must raise the interest rate they charge on loans to attract capital investment in the financial institution. Higher loan rates would reduce the quantity of loans intermediated. Hence, reducing the federal government's monitoring costs by imposing capital requirements causes inefficiencies in the loan markets. The inefficiencies lead to welfare losses due to the reduction in the overall volume of intertemporal trades being intermediated.

---

[20]Several government agencies are actually involved in the U.S. deposit insurance system, a detailed discussion of which is beyond the scope of this book. Moreover, at the time of writing, the deposit insurance system was undergoing major reform and what the final structure of the system would be was not clear.

[21]Since 1992, capital requirements have been adjusted for the level of risk inherent in the bank's assets. This risk assessment is made by a federal regulatory agency.

6.7 SUMMARY

The economic function of financial intermediaries is to channel funds from areas in the economy where they are in surplus to areas where they are in deficit. Intermediaries obtain funds from net savers and place the funds with an appropriate set of net borrowers. That activity involves matching the preferences of savers with the preferences of borrowers in terms of willingness to postpone consumption and relative tolerance for risk. The terms of the loan embody the tradeoffs of risk, expected return, and liquidity. The preference matching done by the financial intermediary may or may not involve anonymity between parties on one or both sides of the loan agreement. Anonymity of the borrower to the lender requires the intermediary to be the lender's delegated monitor of the borrowers' uses of the funds. Intermediation activities are costly, but the costs can be reduced if financial institutions specialize in intermediating certain types of loan agreements.

Households can invest directly in the liabilities of a publicly held firm by buying the firm's stocks and bonds with the aid of a broker, who performs none of the preference-matching or monitoring roles of a financial intermediary but merely places the order for the household. Alternatively, the broker could help the household select a portfolio of stocks and bonds that match its preferences for liquidity, risk, and expected return, and could keep the household abreast of developments in the financial markets, the economy, or the specific firms in which the household has invested. In that case, the broker is performing the preference-matching and monitoring roles of an intermediary, for which he or she receives a fee.

Depository institutions specialize in intermediating loans from funds representing the portion of savings for which households prefer high liquidity and minimal risk. Assets are created by the depository institution in the form of its deposit liabilities, many of which the household can access on demand without penalty. The household pays for high liquidity and low risk by receiving a relatively low rate of return on its funds. To match their depositors' preferences with those of potential borrowers, the depository institution must maintain liquidity and safety in its investment and loan portfolios. Depository institutions therefore invest a relatively large part of their deposit funds in short-term assets, and reduce risk further through portfolio diversification. As a buffer against the possibility of default on a significant number of their loans, depository institutions retain some of their earnings, which are added to owners' equity. In mutuals, depositors own the depository institution and share this risk. In stock-based depository institutions, bank capital insulates depositors from this risk, which is borne by the shareholders.

The most liquid of a commercial bank's assets are its primary reserves, which consist of vault cash and deposits at the Federal Reserve. They are used to meet the normal fluctuations in net withdrawal demands by depositors. Because such assets are non-interest-bearing, the bank does not want to maintain excessive holdings of reserves. However, to control the money supply, the Federal Reserve imposes reserve requirements whereby banks must maintain mini-

mum levels of reserves in proportion to selected deposit liabilities. For large banks, the required reserves generally exceed the amounts they would willingly hold to meet normal withdrawal demands. The banks' forgone interest income due to excess reserves, often called the reserve tax, causes inefficiency in the intertemporal allocation of resources associated with loan-making by raising the cost of financial intermediation. Because of the reserve tax, the Federal Reserve faces a tradeoff when setting reserve requirement ratios. As the ratios become higher, it is likely to have more control over the money supply, but the economic inefficiency of the intermediation process increases.

When a bank is short of the reserves it is required to maintain, it most frequently turns to the federal funds market where it borrows from other banks that have excess reserves to lend. Overnight loans are negotiated at the so-called federal funds rate. That interest rate is extremely sensitive to economywide credit conditions, because it reflects the availability of reserves in the banking system as a whole. When those reserves are inadequate to meet the reserve needs of the entire banking system, banks may choose to borrow directly from the Federal Reserve at its discount window facility. The interest rate banks pay to borrow from the Federal Reserve is an administered rate determined as a matter of policy. The relationship between the discount rate and the federal funds rate is a central concern in the formulation and implementation of monetary policy in the United States. Because of their importance, issues relating to the discount rate and the federal funds market in general are discussed at length in subsequent chapters.

REVIEW QUESTIONS

1. Describe the specialized financial intermediation provided by each of the following institutions.
   (a) Depository institutions.
   (b) Stockbrokers.
   (c) Money market mutual funds.
   (d) Pension funds.

2. When the Federal Reserve increases the reserve requirement ratios, the so-called reserve tax increases.
   (a) How are a large commercial bank's depositors likely to be affected?
   (b) How are individuals who receive loans from the bank likely to be affected?
   (c) How are the shareholders of the bank likely to be affected?

3. The Federal Reserve may increase capital requirements on a bank when it sees an increased risk that the bank will become illiquid.
   (a) What effect would such action have on bank depositors?
   (b) What effect would such action have on households in need of a bank loan?
   (c) What effect would such action have on the shareholders of the bank?

*4. The Federal Depository Insurance Corporation (FDIC) manages the federal deposit insurance system for commercial banks and savings and loans in the United States. Depository institutions pay periodic insurance premiums that are assessed as a percentage of the institution's insurable deposits.

(a) How would higher premiums be likely to affect depositors?

(b) How does the existence of federal deposit insurance affect bank management decisions about the asset portfolio?

(c) Should all banks be assessed the same fee? Why or why not?

(d) Given your answers to (a), (b), and (c), discuss reforms to the federal deposit insurance system that may address the problems you have identified.

*5. Since 1992, the Federal Reserve has required banks to maintain a certain level of capital in relation to the risk of the assets in their asset portfolios.

(a) What is the problem with setting capital requirements to be a maximum allowable value for a bank's leverage ratio, which is the ratio of total assets to total capital?

(b) If banks had no capital requirements to maintain, what would restrain any individual bank's leverage ratio?

(c) Discuss why high capital requirements should reduce the need for monitoring of a bank's activities *by the regulatory agency*. Who are the other interested parties?

REFERENCES

Diamond, Douglas, and Phillip Dybvig. 1983. "Bank Runs, Deposit Insurance, and Liquidity." *Journal of Political Economy* 91 (June): 401–19.

Friedman, Milton. 1960. *A Program for Monetary Stability*. Bronx, NY: Fordham University Press.

Klein, Michael. 1971. "A Theory of the Banking Firm." *Journal of Money Credit and Banking* 3 (May): 205–18.

Rhoades, Stephen A. and Roger D. Rutz. 1982. "Market Power and Firm Risk: A Test of the Quiet Life Hypothesis." *Journal of Monetary Economics* 9 (January): 73–85.

Sargent, Thomas R. 1984. "Interest on Reserves." *Journal of Monetary Economics* 15 (3): 1–17.

CHAPTER 7

THE MONEY SUPPLY PROCESS

The reserve requirements described in Chapter 6 that commercial banks (and other depository institutions) must meet are a regulatory instrument that enhances the central bank's control over the supplies of the monetary aggregates. The central bank can alter the money supply either by changing reserve requirements directly or by adjusting the total volume of reserves in the banking system through so-called open market operations. To the extent that there is a known mathematical relationship between the volume of bank reserves and the stock of a monetary aggregate such as M1, the Federal Reserve can effectively determine the economywide supply of that aggregate. However, such relationships are not completely predictable and perfect control over the money supply by the central bank is not attainable.

In this chapter we examine the ability of the Federal Reserve to control the outstanding stock of selected monetary aggregates in the United States. The basic principles carry over to other Western economies that have a fractional reserve banking system.[1] Three factors limit the Federal Reserve's ability to control the aggregate money supply. One is the decision by commercial banks to hold reserves in excess of those required by the Federal Reserve. Another is the household portfolio decision about how to allocate wealth across various short-term financial assets, of which some are reservable bank deposits and some are not. The third factor is the extent to which banks are able to raise funds through so-called managed liabilities that include large time deposits and nondeposit sources of funds such as bank RPs. Those sources enable banks to fund loans without relying on reservable deposits.

---

[1] For theoretical arguments against the need for reserve requirements for sufficient monetary control, see Black (1975) and Fama (1980). In 1992, reserve requirements on commercial banks were eliminated in Canada. However, Canadian banks still demand reserves for the purpose of clearing transactions, thus enabling the Bank of Canada (the Canadian central bank), to affect the money supply by altering the supply of reserves in the banking system.

This chapter begins with a description of the various measures of reserve aggregates and how they are related to the reserve requirement regulations of the Federal Reserve. To facilitate the latter discussion, the items on the consolidated balance sheet of the District Federal Reserve Banks are examined.[2] An open market operation is then described to illustrate how the Federal Reserve exercises a high degree of control over the total volume of reserves in the banking system. When the Federal Reserve changes the volume of bank reserves, commercial banks and households respond with changes in their asset portfolios that induce changes in the aggregate quantity of money in supply in the economy. In an economy with a fractional reserve banking system, that process is known as multiple deposit creation, whereby a one-dollar increase in total bank reserves leads to a larger than one-dollar increase in the volume of bank deposits, and therefore to a larger than one-dollar increase in the monetary aggregates. Multipliers for transaction deposits and for two of the most commonly used measures of reserves, nonborrowed reserves and the monetary base, are derived that give the mathematical relationships between increases in the stocks of those deposits and reserve aggregates and the size of an open market purchase. Money multipliers for M1 and M2 are also derived that relate the stocks of those monetary aggregates to nonborrowed reserves and to the monetary base. The relationships can be used to quantify the impact on M1 and M2 of a specific open market operation. How the relationships are affected by decisions made by commercial banks and households is discussed.

7.1 RESERVE AGGREGATES

Total reserves in the banking system (TR) in the United States are defined as the sum across all banks of the first two items on the asset side of the banks' balance sheets: vault cash (VC) and deposits at the Federal Reserve (FD).

$$TR = VC + FD \tag{1}$$

Each bank chooses the mix of vault cash and deposits at the Federal Reserve that makes up its reserve holdings. Let f represent the fraction of total reserves that the bank wants to hold as deposits at the Federal Reserve. Then $FD = f(TR)$, and from equation (1) the following relationship can be obtained.

$$VC = (1 - f)(TR) \tag{2}$$

Because VC and FD are the only two items on a bank's balance sheet (apart from real assets such as structures) that are non-interest-bearing, banks prefer to minimize their reserve holdings.[3] To examine a bank's decision on its

---

[2]The United States is partitioned geographically into 12 Federal Reserve Districts, each of which has a Federal Reserve Bank that services the commercial banks in its district.

[3]For discussions of how reserve requirements act as a unit tax on commercial banking activities, see Diamond (1984), Ramakrishnan and Thakor (1984), and Boyd and Prescott (1986).

Figure 7.1
Definitions of
Measures of Reserves

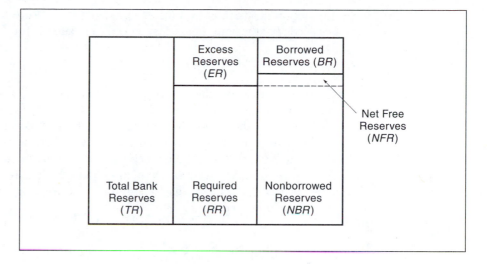

reserve position, it is useful to divide TR into required reserves (RR) and excess reserves (ER).

$$TR = RR + ER \qquad (3)$$

(See Figure 7.1. Also, refer to Table 7.1 for the relative magnitudes of the reserve aggregates.) Required reserves are the volume of reserves that banks must hold in proportion to certain deposit liabilities (which are assets to the depositors): transaction deposits (demand deposits and other checkable deposit accounts, such as NOWs), DD; nonpersonal time deposits (of short maturity), TD; and Eurodollar deposits, ED. (See Chapter 3 for a discussion of those money market assets.) As a matter of policy, the Federal Reserve sets the fraction of the deposits that banks must retain in the form of bank reserves. The fractions are known as the reserve requirement ratios, and are denoted r_D for

Table 7.1   Aggregate Reserves of Depository Institutions and the Monetary Base

BASE	BILLIONS OF DOLLARS
Required Reserves (*RR*)	41.55
Excess Reserves (*ER*)	1.25
Non-borrowed Reserves (*NBR*)	41.70
Borrower Reserves (*BR*)	.53
Net Free Reserves (*NFR*)	.15
Total Reserves (*TR*)	42.80
Currency in the Hands of the Public (C)	167.46
Monetary Base (*MB*)	210.26

Source: Federal Reserve Bulletin.

transaction deposits, r_T for time deposits, and r_E for Eurodollar deposits. With knowledge of the bank's deposits, we can calculate the total volume of required reserves.

$$RR = r_D DD + r_T TD + r_E ED \tag{4}$$

The bank decides the quantity of reserves that it wants to hold in excess of the minimum quantity required. It may choose to hold excess reserves to avoid having to incur the costs of borrowing funds or liquidating other assets on short notice to meet reserve requirements whenever there is an unanticipated net withdrawal of deposits. Alternatively, reserve requirements may simply not be binding. A bank may want to retain more than the legally required reserves to meet the needs of its day-to-day operations.[4] Let e represent the fraction of total reserves held in excess.

$$ER = e(TR) \tag{5}$$

Substitute from equation (5) into equation (2) to obtain

$$RR = (1 - e)(TR) \ . \tag{6}$$

Reserve requirements are rigorously enforced. Most commercial banks must be in compliance with reserve requirements at the end of every two-week period, termed the reserve maintenance period. The banks must file weekly reports with the Federal Reserve to validate their compliance with the regulations.[5] However, central banks in general act as the "lender of last resort" for commercial banks. When a bank is short of reserves at the end of the biweekly reserve maintenance period, it must find a way to obtain the additional reserves.[6] One option is to borrow directly from the Federal Reserve (actually one of its District Federal Reserve Banks) at the so-called "discount window." The Federal Reserve must grant such loans, but does not want to become a regular source of funds for any individual bank. It therefore discourages discount-window borrowings by two methods. It charges an interest rate on the loans, called the discount rate, that is an administered rate set by the Federal Reserve as a matter of policy. It also applies administrative pressure to banks that are deemed to be abusing the borrowing privilege. The latter method can be effective, given the extensive regulatory authority that would enable the Federal Reserve to micromanage the bank if it chose to do so (it seldom does).

---

[4]The majority of banks in the United States willingly hold vault cash in quantities that exceed their legal minimum reserve requirements. However, they tend to be the smaller banks. Nearly all large commercial banks with assets exceeding $1 billion would prefer to reduce their reserves below the legal minimum. Such banks are called bound banks. For a lucid discussion of the many issues relating to reserve requirements in the United States, see Feinman (1992).

[5]Actual reporting requirements vary across banks, with the larger banks generally being required to sumbit more detailed and more frequent reports.

[6]To some extent, banks are permitted to carry over reserve surpluses and deficiencies from one maintenance period to the next.

For any given reserve maintenance period, a number of commercial banks will have borrowed from the Federal Reserve for the explicit purpose of meeting reserve requirements. The fact that incentives for banks to borrow at the window change over time suggests another useful way of dividing total bank reserves. They can be divided into the portion borrowed from the Federal Reserve, termed borrowed reserves (BR), and the remainder, termed nonborrowed reserves (NBR) (see Figure 7.1).

$$TR = NBR + BR \qquad (7)$$

A comparison of nonborrowed reserves with required reserves is considered by some observers to be a useful measure of how "tight" or "loose" credit conditions are for the economy as a whole. They watch a measure called net free reserves (NFR), which is the difference between the two.

$$NFR = NBR - RR \qquad (8)$$

The argument is that a large positive number for NFR suggests that banks are holding excess reserves without having simultaneously incurred temporary obligations to the Federal Reserve through discount window borrowings, and therefore are more likely to turn those non-interest-bearing assets into loans.[7]

7.2   THE FEDERAL RESERVE'S BALANCE SHEET

The Federal Reserve is the central bank for the United States. In that role, it differs in an important way from commercial banks in its ability to supply liquidity to the economy. Commercial banks are limited in supplying liquidity by the total quantity of funds available to them. The total is determined primarily by their deposit bases, but includes managed liabilities. Also, reserve requirements limit the banks' ability to leverage certain of their deposits into loans. A central bank with authority to operate the printing press for fiat currency is under no such limitations. It can expand the nominal quantity of money and credit in the economy without limit. The fact that supplying money in excess of the economy's liquidity needs will cause inflation places an upper limit on how rapidly the *real* money supply can grow.

The Federal Reserve attempts to regulate the stock of money in the economy by supplying reserves to the banking system in managed quantities and by supplying currency on demand. To understand the process, we need to have some knowledge of the Federal Reserve's balance sheet. Refer to Table 7.2. The largest liability of the Federal Reserve is Federal Reserve notes (paper money).[8]

---

[7] A more thorough discussion of discount rate policy and the administration of the discount window is postponed until Chapter 16.

[8] The Federal Reserve keeps track of the quantity of assets it possesses that are "held" as collateral against the notes: gold, SDRs, and that portion of its U.S. government and U.S. government agency securities needed to equal the amount of notes outstanding. The notes are therefore 100 percent collateralized.

Table 7.2   Consolidated Balance Sheet of the Federal Reserve District Banks[a]

ASSETS	
Gold[b]	11,090
Special drawing rights	4,618
Coin	486
Loans to depository institutions	1,567
Federal agency obligations	8,257
U.S. government treasury securities	167,095
Treasury bills	76,286
Treasury notes	67,066
Treasury bonds	23,743
Total loans and securities	176,919
Cash items in process of collection	7,394
Foreign currencies	4,493
Other assets	10,082
Total assets	215,082

LIABILITIES	
Federal Reserve notes	171,286
Deposits	
Depository institutions (FD)	26,253
U.S. treasury department	2,656
Foreign official accounts	274
Other	323
Total deposits	29,506
Other liabilities	10,177
Total liabilities	210,969
Capital accounts	4,113

Source: Federal Reserve Bulletin.
[a]Figures are in millions of dollars.
[b]Gold is officially valued at $43.33 per fine ounce.

They comprise the nation's fiat money and constitute the vast majority of its currency (the rest being coin minted by the U.S. Treasury Department). The second largest item on the liability side of the Federal Reserve's balance sheet is deposits of depository institutions, which are the assets of commercial banks (*FD*) that along with vault cash constitute total bank reserves. Other deposit accounts are those of the U.S. Treasury Department (essentially a checking account for the U.S. government) and of foreign governments and international organizations.

On the asset side of the balance sheet, the principal asset is U.S. government Treasury securities. By some measures, U.S. government debt represents the single largest securities market in the world, and the Federal Reserve, which owns approximately 8 to 10 percent of the debt obligations, is a very important participant in that market. As described in detail below (and in Chapters 16 and 17), the activities of the Federal Reserve in that market are central to an understanding of the mechanics of monetary policy. A second important asset of the Federal Reserve that is related to the conduct of its monetary policy is loans to depository institutions. Such loans include the short-term borrowings at the discount window, which represent the reserve aggregate described as borrowed reserves (BR).[9] Other assets are coin, minted by the U.S. Treasury Department and provided by the Federal Reserve to member banks as a service; cash items in process of collection, or uncleared checks, reflecting the central role of the Federal Reserve in the nation's check-clearing system;[10] gold, special drawings rights (SDRs) at the International Monetary Fund, and foreign exchange, all of which are available for use in the international settlement of accounts resulting from international trade or for use when the U.S. government intervenes in the foreign exchange markets to influence the exchange value of the dollar; and finally the debt obligations issued by federal agencies other than the Treasury Department.

7.3 OPEN MARKET OPERATIONS

When the Federal Reserve wants to change the supply of money or, more specifically, the stock of one of the monetary aggregates in the economy, it can do so by buying or selling U.S. government securities in the open market. When it wants to increase the money supply, it buys government securities. That action leads to an increase in the quantity of bank reserves in the economy, and eventually to an increase in the monetary aggregates. A sale of U.S. government securities has the opposite effect. This process of money creation can be explained by answering three basic questions. First, when the Federal Reserve engages in open market activities, with whom is it dealing? Remember that the transactions are potentially very large, in the billions of dollars per week. Therefore, what guidelines have been established to determine precisely who gets this (quasi-) governmental business? Second, what is the sequence of events that eventually causes a bond purchase by the Federal Reserve to raise the money supply, regardless of how we choose to measure money? Finally, how much does the money supply increase for each dollar of U.S. government securities that the Federal Reserve purchases and how predictable is that figure?

---

[9]Some longer term loans are made to commercial banks for special purposes, other than meeting short-term liquidity needs. Therefore, borrowed reserves in Table 7.1 total less than the quantity of loans indicated in Table 7.2.

[10]The Federal Reserve competes with private clearinghouses for this business. The latter have grown significantly over the past 15 years, but the Federal Reserve continues to receive the largest share of the market.

Open market operations are conducted in a single room in the Federal Reserve Bank of New York. A desk manager is in charge of the operations and has some discretion in structuring the purchases in terms of the quantity, maturity, and timing of the securities to be bought and in the selection of the seller(s). However, those decisions must be consistent with broad guidelines passed down in the form of a policy directive from the Federal Open Market Committee, which is one of the policy-making arms of the Federal Reserve System. A description of the details of that part of the process (how policy is formulated and the steps of implementation down to the desk manager's decisions on the quantity, composition, and timing of purchases) is postponed until Chapters 16 and 17. The part of the process taken up here begins with the desk manager's decision about who the Federal Reserve's counterparties in the transactions should be.

Nearly all of the Federal Reserve's open market operations are conducted with authorized primary government securities dealers. A government securities dealer is essentially a private firm that manages a portfolio of government securities and is a "market maker" in the particular issues of government securities (differentiated by date of issue and maturity) that it holds in its portfolio. As a market maker, the government securities dealer stands ready at all times to add to its portfolio a given security at a preannounced price, termed the "bid price," and to sell from its portfolio the same security at another (higher) preannounced price, termed the "ask price." Hence, the firm is making a market for anyone who wants to buy or sell that particular security. The difference between the ask and bid prices, termed the "bid-ask spread," is the gross profit margin demanded by the dealer for turning over a dollar's worth of the security in its portfolio. For securities that are low in risk and high in liquidity, as U.S. government securities are, the bid-ask spreads are very small. The markets for the so-called "over-the-counter stocks" listed on the National Association of Securities Dealers Automated Quotation system (or NASDAQ) also consist of a collection of market makers, but bid-ask spreads on the stocks, such as Apple Computer, are significantly larger than those for U.S. government securities.

There are both primary and secondary government securities dealers. The distinction is that primary government securities dealers are authorized to be counterparties to the Federal Reserve in open market operations. To become an authorized primary government securities dealer, of which there are currently only 39, a firm must meet criteria in three areas: capitalization, expertise, and capacity. The purpose is to ensure that the Federal Reserve can engage in large transactions with the firms without fear that they will be unable to complete them competently. The firms are required to maintain a minimum level of capital, provide current information on market activities, and both participate in open market operations and underwrite Treasury securities when new issues of government debt are "brought to market" through public auctions. Obviously, the Federal Reserve is buying from and selling to only a handful of very large financial firms, including large commercial banks and brokerage firms.

To choose between the authorized primary government securities dealers (hereafter GSDs) when making an open market purchase of government securities, the Federal Reserve requires knowledge of the ask prices of all GSDs. In fact, the Federal Reserve employs agents who continuously monitor the dealers' bid and ask prices for selected issues. The monitoring takes place even when no open market operation is planned. It is intended in part to supplement other "market intelligence" supplied by the dealers that is made available to the policy makers to keep them abreast of ongoing market conditions. Should extraordinary events begin to unfold in the markets, the key policy makers at the Federal Reserve can take quick action if necessary. More routinely, however, if the Federal Reserve is buying securities, it seeks the GSDs with the lowest ask prices. Conversely, if the Federal Reserve is selling securities, it wants to receive the highest return from the sale and seeks the dealers with the highest bid prices. Other criteria also may be used in the selection of a seller or buyer. Moreover, because the dollar volume of the Federal Reserve's open market operations can be fairly large, more than one GSD is normally used to complete the transaction.[11]

7.4   THE RELATIONSHIP BETWEEN OPEN MARKET OPERATIONS AND TOTAL BANK RESERVES

When the Federal Reserve purchases U.S. government securities in the open market, many of the ensuing transactions are done electronically. However, it is instructive to examine them individually. Assume the Federal Reserve is buying a fixed quantity of, say, $10 billion in government bonds from a single GSD and that it pays the GSD with a check that it writes against itself. Eventually, the check will be presented back at the Federal Reserve to clear. (One of the advantages of controlling the printing press for the nation's fiat money supply is always being able to honor such a check!) This process involves a sequence of financial transactions between the Federal Reserve, the GSD, and a commercial bank. We can trace the transactions with the aid of "T-accounts," which show the changes to the assets and/or liabilities on the balance sheets of the parties in an individual transaction.

Refer to Table 7.3. Initially, the Federal Reserve purchases $10 billion in government bonds, thereby acquiring an asset as shown in Table 7.3A. The GSD loses this asset on its balance sheet. However, because balance sheets are a form of double-entry bookkeeping, offsetting entries are associated with the transaction. The Federal Reserve has incurred an additional liability in the form of the outstanding check of $10 billion. This check becomes a new asset for the GSD. Obviously, the GSD wants to turn the paper claim against the Federal Reserve into a usable asset. It does so by taking the check to its bank (GSD's Bank) and placing it on deposit. This transaction shows up in Table 7.3B as a loss of an asset by the GSD in the form of the check. The check becomes an asset

---

[11]Most of the daily open market operations conducted by the Federal Reserve involve temporary repurchase agreements versus outright purchases; the latter occur only four to six times a year. However, the effect on reserves is the same for either transaction. The details of these transactions are described at length in Chapter 17.

Table 7.3   T-Accounts for the Transactions of an Open Market Purchase by the Federal Reserve of $10 Billion

A. Federal Reserve purchases $10 billion in U.S. government securities (GS) from an authorized primary government securities dealer with a check that it writes against itself

FEDERAL RESERVE		GOVERNMENT SECURITIES DEALER (GSD)	
Assets	Liabilities	Assets	Liabilities
+ $10B (GS)	+ $10B (check)	− $10B (GS)	
		+ $10B (check)	

B. Government securities dealer deposits check in GSD's Bank

GOVERNMENT SECURITIES DEALER (GSD)		GSD'S BANK	
Assets	Liabilities	Assets	Liabilities
− $10B (check)		+ 10B (cash items in process of collection, the check)	+ $10B (GSD's demand deposit account)
+ $10B (demand deposit account)			

C. GSD's Bank sends check to Federal Reserve to clear

FEDERAL RESERVE		GSD'S BANK	
Assets	Liabilities	Assets	Liabilities
	− $10B (check)	− $10B (cash items in process of collection, the check)	
	+ $10B (deposits of GSD's Bank)	+ 10B (deposits at the Federal Reserve)	

of the GSD's Bank and is entered on the balance sheet under "cash items in process of collection." The offsetting entries associated with the transaction are the addition of the $10 billion deposit as an asset to the GSD and as a liability to the GSD's Bank.

Note that the GSD's Bank has increased its required reserves (RR) by $10 billion times the required reserve ratio for transactions assets (r_D). Assume that r_D is 10 percent. If the GSD's Bank had no excess reserves (ER) prior to the deposit, it would be short of reserves by $1 billion just after the deposit. Like the GSD, the bank wants to transform the check into so-called usable funds. Therefore, it sends the check to the Federal Reserve to clear. It thus initiates the final transaction of the money supply process that necessarily involves the Federal Reserve. Refer to Table 7.3C. When the Federal Reserve is presented the check by the GSD's Bank, it can destroy the check and thereby write off the liability. The bank, in turn, relinquishes the check as an asset and its cash items in process of collection are reduced by $10 billion. The Federal Reserve compensates the GSD's Bank for the loss of this asset by honoring its check with a credit to the deposit account of the bank at the Federal Reserve. The Federal Reserve replaces one liability (the check) with another (deposits of GSD's Bank); the bank replaces one asset (the check) with another (deposits at the Federal Reserve). However, there is a significant difference between the two bank assets. The latter (FD) is eligible to count as bank reserves (TR) and the former is not. Therefore, the initial result of the open market purchase of $10 billion is to raise total bank reserves by an equal amount.

7.5 MULTIPLE DEPOSIT CREATION: A SIMPLE EXAMPLE

In the example, the GSD's Bank's deposits and total reserves increased by $10 billion. However, its required reserves rose by only $1 billion, leaving the bank with $9 billion in excess reserves that were not earning interest income. Assume that the bank wants to maintain excess reserves in an amount of 1 percent of total reserves, that is, $e = .01$. How much will the GSD's Bank increase its initial lending as a consequence of the open market purchase? The answer to this question depends on whether the bank chooses to use the funds to expand its loan (and/or securities) portfolio or to reduce its liabilities, or both.

First consider the case in which the bank chooses to expand its loan portfolio. We now can answer the question with the help of some algebra. Begin with the fact that transaction deposits have initially risen by $10 billion ($\Delta DD_0$). (The notation Δ indicates "change in" and the subscript 0 indicates that the change is due to the initial deposit of the GSD resulting from the open market operation.) The bank will eventually loan out that amount less what it retains to meet reserve requirements (ΔRR_0), and additional desired excess reserves (ΔER_0).

$$\text{New Loans}_0 = \Delta DD_0 - (\Delta RR_0 + \Delta ER_0) \tag{9}$$

Using equations (3), (4), and (5), we can rewrite equation (9) in the following form. (This is left as an exercise for the reader.)

$$\text{New Loans}_0 = [(1 - e - r_D)/(1 - e)]\ \Delta DD_0 \tag{10}$$

Therefore, the open market purchase of $10 billion generates an initial $8.99 billion in new loans from the GSD's Bank.

However, this is not the end of the financial transactions that result from the open market purchase. In what form are the new loans given to the recipients? That is, what new assets do they acquire? One possibility is that the

GSD's Bank will give them a cashier's check. Another is that the recipients' demand deposit (or NOW account) balances will be raised. Still a third possibility, although remote for large purchases, is that the recipients will simply receive cash in the full amount of the loans. In any case, the recipients are likely to use their newly acquired assets to purchase a new car or boat or for whatever purchase the loans were initially acquired. Regardless of the form of the assets received from the bank, the ultimate effect of the initial open market operation on the aggregate deposit levels in the economy is the same.

For simplicity, assume that individuals always take their new loans in the form of cash, which is used to make a purchase from another individual in the economy. Further assume that reserve requirement ratios on nonpersonal time deposits and Eurodollar deposits are zero (as they are at the time of this writing).[12] The individual who receives the cash transforms a portion of it into other financial assets. Divide those financial assets into two classes: transaction deposit accounts (DD), which are subject to reserve requirements, and other liquid assets (LA), such as time deposits, MMMFs, and so on. This division reflects household asset portfolio decisions, which can be represented by the following ratios. For every dollar of transaction deposits, the household chooses to hold c dollars in currency (C) and a dollars in other liquid assets (LA).

$$C = c(DD) \text{ and } LA = a(DD) \qquad (11)$$

The number c is called the currency-deposit ratio.

Now return to the example. After a good, say a new boat, has been purchased with the funds acquired in the bank loan, the seller of the boat will make a portfolio allocation of the new assets in accordance with the preceding ratios. Assume all sellers make the same portfolio decision. (The subscript 1 indicates the change due to the portfolio decision of the sellers of the goods to the recipients of the first round of bank loans generated by the open market purchase.)

$$\text{Funds Distributed as New Loans}_0 = \Delta DD_1 + \Delta C_1 + \Delta LA_1 \qquad (12)$$

Substituting from equations (10) and (11) into equation (12), we can express the volume of bank deposits held by the sellers, or households 1, in terms of the size of the original open market operation.

$$\Delta DD_1 = \{(1 - e - r_D)/[(1 - e)(1 + c + a)]\} \Delta DD_0 \qquad (13)$$

If each household chooses to hold one dollar in currency and two dollars in other liquid assets for every dollar that it maintains in a transaction deposit account, which corresponds to values of $c = 1$ and $a = 2$, the increase in transaction deposits of households 1 can be calculated to be \$2.25 billion.

Again, the sequence of financial transactions resulting from the original open market purchase does not end here. The banks that received the deposits

---

[12]One reason given by the Federal Reserve for the elimination of the reserve requirements on those two types of deposit accounts is that financial innovations both within the United States and in the international financial markets have rendered such regulations obsolete, which suggests that the reserve requirement ratios on those assets should be permanently set to zero. However, the Federal Reserve retains the statutory authority to reimpose reserve requirements on those two classes of bank liabilities.

of households 1 in the amount $\Delta DD_1 = \$2.25$ billion are now holding reserves that exceed desired reserves. Their total reserves have risen by $\Delta DD_1 = \$2.25$ billion and required reserves have risen by $r_D (\Delta DD_1) = \$225$ million. If these banks want to maintain excess reserves in an amount equal to 1 percent of total reserves, $e = .01$, they face the same decisions as the GSD's Bank made previously. How much of the additional reserves should be used to fund new loans? If they all chose to expand their loan portfolio, the same formula, equation (10), applies. (The subscript 1 is used here to identify the first bank deposits and set of loans generated subsequent to the initial deposits by GSD and set of decisions by the GSD's Bank.)

$$\text{New Loans}_1 = [(1 - e - r_D)/(1 - e)] \, \Delta DD_1 \qquad (14)$$

Equation (14) reveals that the quantity of new loans created by these banks equals $2.02 billion. A portion of the funds distributed by the new loans again appears as transaction deposits in commercial banks 2. Assuming that these banks also choose to expand their loan portfolio, the quantity of new deposits is related to the additional deposits in the previous banks 1, denoted ΔDD_1, by an expression similar to equation (13).

$$\Delta DD_2 = \{(1 - e - r_D)/[(1 - e)(1 + c + a)]\} \, \Delta DD_1 \qquad (15)$$

This calculation yields a value of $50.5 billion in new deposits at commercial banks 2.

Note the pattern that has emerged in the volume of new transaction deposits at each successive group of banks. The volume is reduced by the fraction given by $\{(1 - e - r_D)/[(1 - e)(1 + c + a)]\}$. We now can determine the total increase in transaction deposits associated with the initial deposit of the GSD (ΔDD_0) resulting from the open market operation of the same amount under the assumption that all banks choose to expand their loan portfolio, and not to reduce their liability. We simply add up the succession of new deposits.[13]

$$\text{Total Deposit Creation} = \Delta DD_0 + \Delta DD_1 + \Delta DD_2 + \ldots$$

$$= \Delta DD_0 + \{(1 - e - r_d)/[(1 - e)(1 + c + a)]\}\Delta DD_0$$

$$+ \{(1 - e - r_d)/[(1 - e)(1 + c + a)]\}^2 \Delta DD_0$$

$$+ \{(1 - e - r_d)/[(1 - e)(1 + c + a)]\}^3 \, \Delta DD_0 \ldots$$

$$= \Delta DD_0 \sum_{j=0}^{\infty} \{(1 - e - r_D)/[(1 - e)(1 + c + a)]\}^j$$

$$= \{(1 - e) (1 + c + a)/[(1 - e)(q + c + a) - (1 - e - r_D)]\} \, \Delta DD_0 \qquad (16)$$

---

[13]In the derivation, the following identity for infinite sequences is used:

$$\sum_{j=0}^{\infty} r^j = 1/(1 - r), \text{ for } |r| < 1$$

Hence, the total quantity of transaction deposits created by the initial open market purchase of $10 billion is found from equation (16) to equal $12.9 billion. For every $1 in bonds purchased by the Federal Reserve in the open market, therefore, an additional $1.29 in transaction deposits is created in commercial banks.

The process just described is generally known as the multiple deposit creation mechanism and is associated with a fractional reserve banking system. The ratio of new transaction deposits created per dollar of open market purchases is called the deposit multiplier, m_D. In the case where all banks choose to expand their loan portfolio with the additional deposits, an expression for the deposit multiplier can be found from equation (16).

$$m_D = (1 - e)(1 + c + a)/[(1 - e)(1 + c + a) - (1 - e - r_D)] \quad (17)$$

In the example, the deposit multiplier is 1.29.

7.6 RESERVE AGGREGATE MULTIPLIERS

In conducting monetary policy, the Federal Reserve is often interested in exercising close control over one of the monetary aggregates, such as M1 or M2. However, its control over the money supply is limited. Rather than attempting to control the money supply directly, it may choose to regulate the outstanding stock of one of the reserve aggregates. The usual choice is either nonborrowed reserves (NBR) or the monetary base (MB). To decide how rapidly the reserve aggregate should grow to achieve a certain monetary growth rate, it estimates the relationship between the reserve aggregate and the selected monetary aggregate. We therefore need to determine the relationship between an open market operation and the stocks of nonborrowed reserves and the monetary base.

For simplicity, assume that reserve requirements on nonpersonal time deposits and Eurodollar deposits are zero. Then, when the level of BR remains unchanged, equations (3), (4), (5), and (7) for the reserve aggregates can be manipulated to yield an expression between the change in nonborrowed reserves and the change in the quantity of transaction deposits.

$$\Delta NBR = [r_D/(1 - e)] \Delta DD \quad (18)$$

From the preceding discussion, we know that a one-dollar open market purchase by the Federal Reserve increases DD by m_D dollars when banks choose to expand their loan portfolio. In this case, NBR should rise by $[r_D/(1 - e)]$ times m_D per dollar of the open market purchase, thus defining an NBR multiplier for open market purchases, m_{NBR}.

$$m_{NBR} = r_D(1 + c + a)/[(1 - e)(1 + c + a) - (1 - e - r_D)] \quad (19)$$

In the example, $m_{NBR} = .130$. The $10 billion open market purchase raises the total volume of nonborrowed reserves by $1.30 billion.

An alternative reserve aggregate that is closely watched by many economists and potentially used by the Federal Reserve as an alternative to nonborrowed reserves is the monetary base (MB). The monetary base is defined as the total volume of reserves in the banking system (TR) plus the total volume of currency outstanding (C).

$$MB = TR + C \tag{20}$$

One reason for the interest in this aggregate is that the Federal Reserve can control its magnitude exactly if it chooses, because it represents the bulk of liabilities on the Federal Reserve's balance sheet. The monetary base is often called "high powered" money.

From equations (11), (18), and (20), we can derive a relationship between a change in the monetary base and a change in the total volume of transaction deposits.

$$\Delta MB = \{[r_D + c\,(1 - e)]/(1 - e)\}\,\Delta DD \tag{21}$$

Obtaining the monetary base multiplier for an open market purchase, m_{MB}, is analogous to obtaining the multiplier for NBR when banks choose to expand their loan portfolio.

$$m_{MB} = [r_D + c\,(1 - e)]\,(1 + c + a)/$$

$$[(1 - e)\,(1 + c + a) - (1 - e - r_D)] \tag{22}$$

In the example, $m_{MB} = 1.42$, and the \$10 billion open market purchase raises the monetary base by \$14.2 billion.

7.7 MONEY MULTIPLIERS

As emphasized in Chapters 2 and 3, historically the two most important measures of the money supply for Federal Reserve policy have been the monetary aggregates M1 and M2. When the Federal Reserve seeks to control the supply of money in the economy, it is explicitly seeking to control the stock of one of those two aggregates. Therefore, it needs to estimate the amount by which the money supply will change in response to an open market purchase. As previously stated, the Federal Reserve usually separates this relationship into two sequential links between open market operations and the money supply. (A detailed discussion of why this approach is often useful is postponed until Chapter 16.)

First, how much does a particular reserve aggregate change in response to the open market purchase? Second, how much does the selected monetary aggregate change in relation to the change in the particular reserve aggregate? We have already derived the first set of relationships. Here we derive the second set, which consists of the M1 and M2 multipliers for both nonborrowed reserves (NBR) and the monetary base (MB).

The monetary assets that make up M1 consist of all transactions assets in the economy as described in detail in Chapter 2. In the notation of this chapter, they include currency (C) and transaction deposits (DD).[14] From this definition

---

[14]Traveler's checks are ignored.

of M1, we can derive a relationship between M1 and DD by using the currency-deposit ratio (c).

$$M1 = DD + C = (1 + c)\ DD \tag{23}$$

The desired relationship between M1 and NBR can be found by substitution from equation (18) that links changes in DD to changes in NBR.

$$\Delta M1 = [(1 + c)\ (1 - e)/r_D]\ \Delta NBR \tag{24}$$

The M1 multiplier with respect to nonborrowed reserves, $m_{M1/NBR}$, is then given by the following expression.

$$m_{M1/NBR} = [(1 + c)\ (1 - e)/r_D] \tag{25}$$

In the example, a one-dollar increase in nonborrowed reserves leads to an increase in M1 of $19.80.

The detailed description of the assets that make up M2 is given in Chapter 2. In the notation of this chapter, let LA represent the composite of all non-M1 components of M2, which are highly liquid nontransactions assets such as MMMFs, small CDs, and so on.[15] Using the currency-deposit ratio (c) and the ratio of liquid assets to transaction deposit (a), we can determine the relationship between M2 and DD.

$$M2 = DD + C + LA = (1 + c + a)\ DD \tag{26}$$

The relationship between changes in M2 and nonborrowed reserves can then be found from equations (18) and (28).

$$\Delta M2 = [(1 + c + a)\ (1 - e)/r_D]\ \Delta NBR \tag{27}$$

The M2 multiplier for nonborrowed reserves, $m_{M2/NBR}$, is given by the following expression.

$$m_{M2/NBR} = [(1 + c + a)\ (1 - e)/r_D] \tag{28}$$

For the example, a one-dollar increase in nonborrowed reserves raises the stock of M2 by $39.60.

Similar derivations can be made of the M1 and M2 multipliers for the monetary base. Denote these multipliers as $m_{M1/MB}$ and $m_{M2/MB}$, respectively.

$$m_{M1/MB} = (1 + c)\ (1 - e)/[r_D + c(1 - e)]$$

$$m_{M2/MB} = (1 + c + a)\ (1 - e)/[r_D + c(1 - e)]$$

In the example, $m_{M1/MB}$ is 1.82 and $m_{M2/MB}$ is 3.63.

Finally, to determine how much the stocks of M1 and M2 rise in response to a one-dollar open market purchase, we can use the sequential linkages from

---

[15]Overnight bank RPs comprise a small portion of M2. Their volume is determined primarily by the bank's decision on the structure of its liabilities, and not by the household's portfolio allocation decision. The role of such managed liabilities is discussed later in the chapter.

open market purchases to reserves and from reserves to the money supply. When banks choose to expand their loan portfolios, the M1 and M2 multipliers associated with an open market purchase are then given by the following expressions.

$$m_{M1} = m_{M1/NBR}\, m_{NBR} = m_{M1/MB}\, m_{MB}$$

$$= [(1 + c + a)\,(1 + c)\,(1 - e)]/[(1 - e)\,(1 + c + a) - (1 - e - r_D)]$$

$$m_{M2/NBR}\, m_{NBR} = m_{M2/MB}\, m_{MB}$$

$$= [(1 + c + a)^2\,(1 - e)]/[(1 - e)\,(1 + c + a) - (1 - e - r_D)]$$

In the example, the $10 billion open market purchase by the Federal Reserve raises the M1 money supply by $26.67 billion and the M2 money supply by $53.33 billion.

7.8   THE SOURCES OF IMPERFECT MONETARY CONTROL

If the values of all of the multipliers just derived were known with certainty to the Federal Reserve, it could exercise perfect control over the nominal money supply in the economy, with money defined as either M1 or M2, provided the banks did not actively manage their liabilities described in Section 7.9. In this case, the Federal Reserve would need to know the currency-deposit, liquid asset to transaction deposit, excess reserves to total reserves, and required reserve ratios (c, a, e, and r_D). In reality, only the last of these ratios is known, because it is set by the Federal Reserve as a matter of policy. Households choose c and a when they make their money market portfolio decisions and commercial banks choose e when selecting their reserves position. All three ratios (c, a, and e) vary over time and not always in predictable ways. Therefore, in its efforts to exercise control over the money supply, the Federal Reserve can only estimate the ratios and use the estimates to guide its open market operations.

In practice, the excess reserves to total reserves ratio, e, is the most stable and therefore the most predictable of the ratios. Banks typically hold less than 1 percent of total *assets* in the form of excess reserves, which corresponds to values of e in the range of 2 to 3 percent. For the data reported in Tables 7.1 and 7.2, $e = .029$, whereas excess reserves are only .58 percent of total assets for the banking system as a whole. The numbers tend to vary from week to week, but do not drift far on average over the course of one or two months. The implication is that fluctuations in excess reserves can contribute to lack of control over the money supply in the very short run, but are not a major problem for monetary control over longer periods.

The currency-deposit ratio, c, and the liquid asset to transaction deposit ratio, a, are greater problems for monetary control. From monetary data compiled at the same time as the bank data reported in Tables 7.1 and 7.2, $C = 166.8 billion, $DD = 425.7 billion, and $LA = $1,897$ billion. The ratios for that month were $c = .392$ and $a = 4.456$, which are typical numbers.

However, they tend to vary slightly more than *e* over week-to-week periods, the interval over which they are most frequently compiled. Perhaps more important is the fact that the averages of these numbers over longer periods of up to four to six months can also exhibit a significant drift, either up or down. The changes are not so drastic as to prevent the Federal Reserve from exercising sufficient control over either M1 or M2 to conduct a successful monetary policy. However, they represent important *behavioral* changes on the part of commercial banks, households, and firms of which the Federal Reserve must be mindful if it is to avoid unnecessary monetary control errors that adversely affect the economy.[16]

7.9   ENDOGENOUS MONEY SUPPLY

Suppose an exogenous event occurs in the economy that causes output to rise. The greater output stimulates overall economic activity and commercial banks experience an increase in loan demand. How could they respond? One possibility is that the Federal Reserve could increase bank reserves through open market operations. Alternatively, the banks could draw down their excess reserves (*e* falls). In either case, deposits increase and the money supply rises.

Another option for the commercial banks is to increase their reliance on managed liabilities. They could raise funds by issuing overnight or term RPs, or more aggressively marketing their large time deposits by raising the interest rates on them. Note that managed liabilities are included in M3, but not all are included in M2. Such an endogenous response of the banking system to the increase in loan demand would tend to increase the overall deposit base. Although the Federal Reserve could offset the endogenous money supply growth with appropriate open market operations, provided that the behavioral parameters *c, a,* and *e* remain fixed, this example shows how banks may be able to accommodate fluctuations in loan demand to a limited extent by shifting their reliance toward managed liabilities. It suggests a mechanism whereby the economy is able to generate liquidity without the assistance of a Federal Reserve policy response designed to alter the availability of bank reserves.[17]

7.10   SUMMARY

The Federal Reserve exercises control over the money supply by closely managing the total quantity of reserves in the banking system. However, the rela-

---

[16]Even perfect control over one or more of the monetary aggregates would not ensure a successful monetary policy, because success also requires a predictable link between changes in the monetary aggregate of choice and the real economy. This issue constitutes a much more difficult problem for policy makers. It was described briefly in Chapter 3 and is discussed more thoroughly in Parts III, IV, and V of the book.

[17]An endogenous response by the banks to shocks that originate in the real sector of the economy weakens the effectiveness of monetary policy. This topic has been an active area of research in recent years. Early work includes that of King and Plosser (1984) and Plosser (1990).

tionships between bank reserves and various measures of the money supply, such as M1, M2, and M3, fluctuate over time, limiting the Federal Reserve's monetary control. To enhance monetary control, the Federal Reserve imposes reserve requirements on selected liabilities of commercial banks.

Banks can meet the requirements by holding reserves in the form of vault cash and deposits at their respective Federal Reserve District Banks. Because neither of those bank assets are interest bearing, banks tend to minimize their reserve holdings. However, banks normally maintain reserves in excess of their legal minimum, either as a cushion against unexpected net deposit withdrawals that could cause them to become reserves deficient or because their day-to-day operating need for currency exceeds the required reserve levels. The extent to which banks alter their demand for reserves introduces a degree of flexibility in the relationships between the quantities of reserves in the banking system and reservable deposits, thus weakening the central bank's control of the money supply. However, the total amount of excess reserves is relatively small and its volatility is not a major problem for monetary control over long periods of time such as a month or more.

More troubling for the Federal Reserve are households' adjustments in the composition of their liquid asset portfolios. The adjustments could entail a shifting of funds between reservable deposits and nonreservable deposits or even monetary assets outside M2. Such portfolio adjustments have occurred in the past and often extend over periods of several months. To the extent that the adjustments are unpredictable, monetary control is impaired.

Commercial banks are able to "create" money without an open market purchase of Treasury securities by the Federal Reserve. To meet an increase in loan demand, the banks could raise additional funds through managed liabilities that appear in the monetary aggregates principally as non-M2 components of M3. Such action would produce a multiplier effect that would eventually increase the deposit base unless the Federal Reserve conducted offsetting open market operations. An endogenous money supply response by the banking system is likely to affect the monetary aggregates M1, M2, and M3 differently, and hence may compound the monetary control problem of the Federal Reserve.

■ REVIEW QUESTIONS

1. Let the reserve requirement ratios be 10 percent for transaction deposits and zero for time and Eurodollar deposits. Assume the banks choose an excess reserves ratio of 1 percent and that households select liquid asset portfolios consistent with a currency-deposit ratio of 1.1 and a liquid asset to transaction deposit ratio of 1.8. Further assume that banks choose to use additional reserves supplied by the Federal Reserve to expand its loan portfolio.
   (a) How much would a $10 billion open market operation by the Federal Reserve increase nonborrowed reserves and the monetary base, if borrowed reserves remained unaffected?
   (b) How much would a $10 billion open market purchase increase M1 and M2?

   (c) How would your answers to (a) and (b) differ if banks simultaneously increased their borrowings at the discount window by $1 billion?

   (d) Suppose the Federal Reserve wants to increase M2 by the amount determined in (b) but, unknown to the Federal Reserve, household preferences changed and the liquid asset to transaction deposit ratio rose to 2. By how much would the Federal Reserve miss its M2 target?

2. Use T-accounts to trace the initial impact of a $10 billion sale of Treasury securities by the Federal Reserve to a government securities dealer that pays for the securities with a check drawn on its bank. What is the likely effect on the availability of bank loans?

3. In the mid-1980s, the Federal Reserve had set reserve requirements at 12 percent for transaction deposits and 3 percent for both nonpersonal time deposits (of short maturity) and Eurodollar deposits. These reserve requirement ratios were subsequently reduced to 10 percent for transaction deposits and zero for both nonpersonal time deposits and Eurodollar deposits.

   (a) Discuss the consequences of these reserve requirement changes for the monetary aggregates if the Federal Reserve made no adjustments in its open market operations.

   (b) What adjustments in open market operations would be needed to accommodate these reserve requirement changes?

   (c) Describe the change in the magnitude of the M2 response to an open market purchase of Treasury securities of $10 billion by the Federal Reserve when the reserve requirement ratio on transaction deposits is reduced from 12 percent to 10 percent under the following assumptions: reserve requirement ratios on nonpersonal time deposits (of short maturity) and Eurodollar deposits are both zero, the excess reserves ratio is 1 percent, the currency-deposit ratio is 1, and the liquid asset to transaction deposit ratio is 2.

   (d) Given your answer in (c), should anything be added to your response to (b)?

*4. The banking system has some ability to supply money endogenously by relying more heavily on managed liabilities to meet an increase or decrease in loan demand that would accompany a pickup or slowdown in economic activity, as described in this chapter. However, banks are limited in this response by the willingness of investors to acquire and hold their liabilities.

   (a) Describe how a central bank could assist in this type of response by altering the money supply elasticity over the course of a business cycle.

   (b) Is the central bank policy that you described in (a) consistent with the current practices of the Federal Reserve? Explain.

*5. Unlike the Federal Reserve, the central bank of Germany, the Bundesbank, owns private-sector debt obligations.

   (a) Could the Federal Reserve conduct open market operations by buying and selling corporate bonds rather than government bonds?

(b) Use T-accounts to describe how such a bond purchase by the Federal Reserve might take place. Is a financial intermediary necessary?

(c) Discuss any potential problems that may arise with open market operations of the type you described.

REFERENCES

Black, Fischer. 1975. "Bank Funds Management in an Efficient Market." *Journal of Financial Economics* 2 (December): 323–340.

Boyd, John H., and Edward C. Prescott. 1986. "Financial Intermediary Coalitions." *Journal of Economic Theory* 38 (April): 211–233.

Diamond, Douglas W. 1984. "Financial Intermediation and Delegated Monitoring." *Review of Economic Studies* 51 (July): 393–414.

Fama, Eugene. 1980. "Banking in the Theory of Finance." *Journal of Monetary Economics* 6 (January): 39–57.

Feinman, Joshua. 1993. "Reserve Requirements: History, Current Practice, and Potential Reform." *Federal Reserve Bulletin* 79 (June): 569–589.

King, Robert G., and Charles I. Plosser. 1984. "Money, Credit, and Prices in a Real Business Cycle." *American Economic Review* 74 (June): 363–380.

Plosser, Charles I. 1990. "Money and Business Cycles." *NBER Working Paper Series*. Working Paper No. 3221.

Ramakrishnan, R. T., and A. V. Thakor. 1984. "The Valuation of Assets Under Moral Hazard." *Journal of Finance* 39 (March): 229–238.

CHAPTER 8

INSTITUTIONS OF MONETARY CONTROL: HISTORICAL ROLE OF THE FEDERAL RESERVE IN THE UNITED STATES

The Federal Reserve was created by an act of Congress in 1913. Since that time, the institution has assumed increasingly larger roles as a principal regulator of the depository institutions described in Chapter 6 and a principal architect of the nation's macroeconomic policy. The two roles are not completely independent. The ability of the Federal Reserve to affect the real economy through monetary policy decisions is derived in part from its regulatory authority, in particular from binding reserve requirements. Conversely, its role as regulator is to ensure the safety and soundness of the depository institutions, which in turn can be affected by changing macroeconomic conditions. This interdependence is best understood within the context of the Federal Reserve's role in the money supply process.

The purpose of this chapter is to describe how the process of money creation has evolved in the United States and the role of the Federal Reserve in that process. The role played by the Federal Reserve today was not envisioned in the Federal Reserve Act of 1913. Moreover, the decision-making structure within the Federal Reserve System has been fundamentally altered over the years as its mandate in determining monetary policy has expanded. This chapter traces the principal events that led to the evolutionary changes in both the structure and the mandate of the Federal Reserve as they relate to the institution's role in the money supply process in the United States.

8.1 THE PROBLEM OF AN INELASTIC MONEY SUPPLY[1]

Before we examine the role of the Federal Reserve in the money supply process that was envisioned by the Federal Reserve Act of 1913, we need to note important historical changes in the money and financial markets. In 1913, one primary medium of exchange for households was gold and silver coins minted and issued by the Treasury Department. They were commodity money as described in Chapter 1. The Treasury Department also issued representative commodity money in the form of circulating gold and silver certificates, which were backed 100 percent by the gold and silver holdings of the Treasury Department. In addition, national bank notes circulated as paper currency. They were issued by nationally chartered banks and backed by holdings of U.S. government securities that those banks kept on deposit at the Treasury Department. The bank notes could be redeemed for gold from the Treasury Department. (See Appendix 7.1 for a discussion of how and why national bank notes came into existence.) Together with the gold and silver coins and certificates, the national bank notes represented what was termed "lawful money." Today's paper money, Federal Reserve notes, did not exist.

Firms, unlike households, relied heavily on (interest-bearing) checking accounts for their business transactions.[2] Commercial banks were required to hold reserves against a fraction of those deposits in the form of gold and "lawful money."[3] If "money" is defined here as the collection of assets most closely associated with media of exchange, that is, the quantity of "lawful money" in circulation plus the volume of demand deposits held in accounts at commercial banks, then for a given stock of bank reserves this type of fractional reserve banking system (as discussed in Chapter 7) fixes an upper limit on the supply of money.[4] To raise the upper limit, the volume of bank reserves must be

---

[1]The general historical information in the chapter is drawn freely from Goldenweiser (1925), Willis (1936), James (1940), Friedman and Schwartz (1963), and Wicker (1966).

[2]Money privately issued by commercial banks had largely vanished because of the imposition of a stiff tax in 1863 that effectively rendered them uncompetitive with national bank notes issued by the Treasury Department.

[3]Reserve requirements varied among states for state chartered banks, and across categories of nationally chartered banks, in terms of both the reserve ratios and the classes of deposits requiring reserves. See James (1940) for an account of these differences. In addition, some state statutes were ambiguous on whether or not national bank notes could be considered legal reserves. See Friedman and Schwartz (1963).

[4]This would hold absolutely if there were no changes in either the currency-deposit ratio or the ratios of deposit accounts with different (positive) reserve requirements. See Chapter 7.

increased. When reserves consist exclusively of gold and "lawful money," as in 1913, the upper limit is determined by the stock of gold acquired directly by the commercial banks or the stock of gold and silver acquired by the federal government and either introduced into the economy directly as commodity money (gold and silver coins) or held as backing for representative commodity money (gold and silver certificates) which is then injected into the economy.[5] The growth in domestic gold supplies, either from new gold discoveries or from the inflow of gold from abroad to settle international payments accounts, would in turn limit how rapidly "lawful money," and therefore reserves, could be expanded. In practice, most banks held excess reserves to be able to meet the liquidity needs of their business customers, which were subject to business-cycle and seasonal fluctuations.

The system of money creation had two fundamental problems. First, there was no formal mechanism in place to control the price level. The supply of bank reserves was effectively determined by the domestic supply of gold, and the relative price of gold to, say, a basket of other commodities would fluctuate with the stock of domestic gold supplies. Because the dollar value of gold was fixed, the fluctuations in gold supplies would automatically induce changes in the dollar value of commodities, and hence in the price level.[6] The basic connection between bank reserves, the money supply, and the price level was not well understood at the time, when central banking in the United States was still in its infancy. Therefore, the problem of price level control was not addressed by the Federal Reserve Act of 1913, but was the source of major debates over U.S. monetary policy after World War I. Those debates fundamentally changed the nature of central banking in the United States.

The second problem with the money supply system was the relatively inelastic response of the supply of reserves to business-cycle and seasonal fluctuations in money demand. The inelasticity tended to exaggerate periods of credit expansion and contraction and induce larger swings in real economic activity associated with the accompanying fluctuations in money demand. Most banks held excess reserves in normal times to accommodate the varying liquidityneeds of businesses, although their willingness to do so was limited by the fact that reserves were non-interest-bearing. However, when the economy undergoes a normal cyclical downturn, reserves must be drawn down as the demand for money, in the form of bank deposits, falls. Once the legal reserves minimum is

---

[5]This was not strictly true, because deposits that banks held in certain New York banks could also be counted by the holders of those accounts as reserves. However, this option was severely limited. See James (1940).

[6]Obviously, fluctuations in the demand for gold would have similar effects. They are more important today than in nineteenth century America, when new gold discoveries were common, and during World War I and World War II, when European financing of military hardware from the United States led to massive gold inflows. In each of those cases, the economy was susceptible to rapid inflation.

reached, banks must call in loans to restore reserve balances, which contracts the money supply even farther and sharpens the downturn. A symmetrical response can occur during periods of expansion, although it would be cushioned somewhat by a buildup of excess reserves. Virtually no deposit insurance schemes were in effect during the late nineteenth and early twentieth centuries, so periods of severe contraction were accompanied by numerous "bank runs." Two such periods of so-called "bank panics" that occurred in 1893 and 1907 were blamed largely on the inelasticity of the money supply process. They led to the creation of the Federal Reserve, which was to have as a principal objective the provision of an elastic money supply that would systematically rise and fall with business-cycle and seasonal fluctuations in money demand.[7]

8.2   ENDOGENOUS MONEY SUPPLY

The Federal Reserve Act of 1913 established a system of 12 largely autonomous regional District Federal Reserve Banks whose activities were to be very loosely coordinated by a central Federal Reserve Board. The regional banks offered membership to commercial banks in their district.[8] The commercial banks were required to put up capital (in the form of gold and gold certificates) in rough proportion to their size to establish the initial operating capital of the Federal Reserve. Effectively, they were the owners of the Federal Reserve and received dividends corresponding to a fixed (and low) rate of return from the profits generated by Federal Reserve operations.[9]

The elastic money supply process was designed to operate as follows. By virtue of Federal Reserve membership, the member banks were able to present first class commercial paper, purchased from the issuing firms at a discount, to the Federal Reserve to be rediscounted in exchange for Federal Reserve notes (paper currency) and member bank deposits at the Federal Reserve. As described in Chapter 2, commercial paper is a short-term IOU issued by a firm. The proceeds received by the firm are used to cover short-term "working capital" requirements, such as payroll expenses and inventory financing. These short-term liquidity needs fluctuate with the level of business activity. Member

---

[7]James (1940) argues that proper management of gold reserves would have provided the necessary elasticity of the money supply. Moreover, Willis (1936) provides some evidence that Federal Reserve notes did not provide currency elasticity as intended.

[8]Federally chartered banks were required to be members of the Federal Reserve, but they were free to seek a change in their charter through application to their respective states. Many availed themselves of that opportunity.

[9]Eventually, provisions were made to remit excess profits to the Treasury. As discussed later in the chapter, those profits enabled the federal government to engage in inflationary finance of its gross expenditures.

banks were required to meet reserve requirements as they are today.[10] However, reserve assets at member banks consisted of "lawful money" (less national bank notes), that is, Treasury Department issues of gold and silver coins and certificates, plus the deposits carried by the banks at their respective District Federal Reserve Banks.

When commercial paper was presented to a Federal Reserve Bank by a member bank for rediscounting, the member bank would receive in exchange either Federal Reserve notes that would be available to go into circulation or a credit to its deposit balance. The latter would add to the bank's reserves; to the extent that the reserves were in excess of required reserves, the bank could extend additional credit (leading to the multiple deposit creation process described in Chapter 7).[11] Therefore, both the money supply and bank credit would automatically increase in response to the initial increase in the demand for money by the firm that had originally issued the commercial paper.

An important aspect of this process was that the expansion of bank reserves, and therefore of money and credit, was self-liquidating. As the short-term commercial paper matured, the commercial bank would have to use up reserves to reclaim the commercial paper, just as the firms redeemed them after repaying the bank by drawing down deposit account balances. Therefore, for the economy as a whole, the volume of currency and deposits would rise and fall in accordance with the fluctuating liquidity needs of businesses. The system would produce an elastic, endogenous money supply that accommodated fluctuations in money demand.[12]

Monetary policy therefore did not consist of an exogenous determination of the optimal volume of money and/or credit in the economy, but rather how the endogenous response of the money supply ought to be implemented. It es-

---

[10]Nonmember state-chartered banks, which were more numerous than state and federally chartered member banks, also had to meet reserve requirements according to state laws. In fact, the different requirements continued until the Depository Institutions and Deregulation Act of 1980 was passed, when reserve requirements at all depository institutions, including savings and loans and state-chartered commercial banks, were made uniform. However, many states simply deferred to the federal regulations in establishing reserve requirments. See James (1940) for an account up to the mid-1930s. See Cargill and Garcia (1982) for an analysis of why uniform reserve requirements were desirable in terms of providing the Federal Reserve greater monetary control.

[11]Beginning in 1959, the Federal Reserve was authorized to allow member banks to meet reserve requirements with any combination of member bank deposits at the Federal Reserve and Federal Reserve notes (vault cash).

[12]The elasticity envisioned for this system was primarily in the supply of Federal Reserve notes that would serve as representative commodity money with gold backing. Eventually, those notes were intended to replace national bank notes as the nation's principal paper currency. Moreover, the Federal Reserve was to engage actively in the process of removing national bank notes from circulation.

sentially involved two sets of objectives. One was to ensure the high quality of commercial paper that was being rediscounted. The other was to regulate the degree of elasticity of the money supply by adjusting the rediscount rate. The higher the rediscount rate charged to commercial banks, the less likely commercial banks would be to grant credit (or the higher would be their initial discount rate charged to firms), and the less elastic the money supply would become.

8.3 UNINTENDED CONSEQUENCES OF OPEN MARKET OPERATIONS, 1917–1921

The framers of the Federal Reserve Act envisioned a Federal Reserve System that would function in the national interest. However, they also believed that private-sector control over the Federal Reserve's operations was essential. They initially conceived of the 12 Federal Reserve Banks as institutions owned by and operated for the benefit of the banks in the local districts. Although the Federal Reserve Banks were not intended to be profit-maximizing institutions and therefore would not be attractive investments, membership was not required of commercial banks. The goal was to entice banks to join the Federal Reserve System of their own accord by offering them a modest return on their capital investment in the Federal Reserve and by providing valued services such as check-clearing and, more importantly, access to reserves to meet short-run demand fluctuations.

To achieve that goal, the Federal Reserve Banks were given a high level of regional autonomy. They were authorized to engage in asset management, as seemed prudent to maintain adequate reserves against the principal liabilities, which were Federal Reserve notes and member bank deposits, while also managing the investment funds of their owners, the member banks.[13] They were given the latitude to purchase and sell private-sector securities in the open market. Although they were not prohibited from the purchase and sale of government securities in the open market, that activity was not initially seen to be a significant part of their open market operations. In relation to monetary policy, open market purchases and sales were primarily of private-sector securities, because the purpose of the purchases and sales was to "make effective" the rate at which commercial paper was being rediscounted by the Federal Reserve and thus establish the desired degree of elasticity of the money supply process. For example, if a Federal Reserve Bank lowered the rediscount rate to increase the elasticity, but failed to elicit enough willingness by the commercial banks in its

---

[13]To ensure "prudence," each Federal Reserve Bank was required to maintain a minimum gold reserve of 40 percent against Federal Reserve notes in circulation and 35 percent against member bank deposits. In practice, that requirement was never binding. When it threatened to become so in 1945, Congress reduced the minimum requirement to a uniform 25 percent against both Federal Reserve notes and member bank deposits.

district to accept commercial paper and extend credit to businesses, the Bank could simply increase the demand for commercial paper itself by purchasing it directly in the open market from firms. Such purchases were expected to be very infrequent in the normal course of operations of the Federal Reserve.

Before the Federal Reserve System was even fully operational, World War I broke out in Europe. Almost immediately the Federal Reserve undertook an active role in the U.S. government's assistance to the Allies in financing their war effort. That role was greatly expanded with the entry of the United States into the war in 1917.[14] The Federal Reserve's experience during this period eventually led to a greater understanding of how central bank policies affect the real economy. Its war financing activities had two important consequences that altered many views about what the proper role of the Federal Reserve in the economy ought to be.

One consequence was the massive inflow of gold to the United States from Europe in payment for war material the United States sold to its allies. So much of the gold found its way into the vaults of the Federal Reserve Banks that gold reserves far exceeded their legal minimum required under the Federal Reserve Act.[15] However, because the increase in domestic gold supplies depressed the dollar value of gold, the Federal Reserve Banks were obliged to increase the supply of Federal Reserve notes in circulation to restore the former gold price. The result was a rapid increase in the dollar price of all other commodities. That is, in 1919–1920, the U.S. economy underwent a sharp inflation.

The second consequence of the war financing was a very large increase in the stock of U.S. government securities issued by the Treasury Department. As often noted, the financing of the war continued after the Armistice was signed and the fighting had stopped in 1918. Over the next several months, large costs were incurred in the restoration of a peacetime economy both in the United States and abroad, much of which was financed by U.S. government debt obligations. A large volume of the U.S. government securities went into commercial bank portfolios, as well as into the asset holdings of the Federal Reserve Banks.[16] By 1919, a theory had emerged that the inflation in the economy was due not to the gold inflows and the gold standard, but to the presence of U.S. government debt in the portfolios of commercial banks and the Federal Reserve. The theory was based on the prevalent view of the elastic money supply process that the Federal Reserve was intended to provide. That is, as business activity

---

[14]Wicker (1966) provides an engaging discussion of the numerous methods of finance that were contemplated and the friction that arose between the Treasury Department and the Federal Reserve over which of the methods should be implemented and what their implications were for Federal Reserve operations.

[15]For much of this period, the Federal Reserve's gold reserves were more than 70 percent of Federal Reserve notes and member bank deposits.

[16]The Federal Reserve had been offering low interest loans to member banks to assist them both in meeting established quotas in their holdings of U.S. government securities and in extending credit to households to enable them to purchase U.S. government securities.

created demand for money, the commercial banks, through the elastic response of central bank reserves, would just accommodate the increase in demand through the discounting of commercial paper. Government debt was believed to have interfered with this natural process. Therefore, the solution to the inflation problem was seen to lie in purging government debt from the portfolios of commercial banks and the Federal Reserve and shifting it into the savings portfolios of the public. Such action was expected to lead to a resumption of the normal prewar pricing relationships.

The Federal Reserve Banks began selling government securities to the public from their portfolio holdings. To purchase the securities, households and firms drew down their money balances and commercial bank reserves contracted. Commercial banks then called in loans to meet reserve requirements, which reduced the volume of credit in the economy and led to further declines in the supply of money. As the Federal Reserve continued its sale of government securities into 1920, the credit contraction dramatically slowed overall economic activity and led to the severe recession of 1920–1921. Of course, inflation did come down!

The link between the Federal Reserve's open market operations and the overall volume of credit in the economy is well understood today, but that was not the case in 1919. Ironically, although it was primarily a subsequent reversal of the Federal Reserve's open market operations that brought an end to the recession, the principal reason for the reversal was not concern about the overall health of the real economy, but concern about the Federal Reserve Banks' own profits![17] In the process of selling off government securities, the Federal Reserve Banks were losing large volumes of their earnings assets. They were giving up not only interest-bearing government securities from their portfolios, but also much of the income-generating commercial paper that they had been rediscounting for the commercial banks, and were being left with increasing percentages of assets in the form of gold. Their ability to pay dividends to their member banks was thereby impaired. To restore earnings assets to their portfolios, they reversed their open market operations policy and began buying back outstanding government securities by issuing Federal Reserve notes. That action led to an expansion of money and credit, and by the end of 1921 began to lift the economy out of the recession.

8.4   THE CENTRALIZATION of MONETARY POLICY DECISION MAKING, 1921–1935

When it became clear that the Federal Reserve Banks would have to play a large role in the U.S. government's financing of World War I, the heads of the District Banks, at the time given the title of governor, recognized the need to coordinate

---

[17]For evidence that the profit motive loomed large in the rationale for reversing their stance on Federal Reserve portfolio holdings of government securities, see Wicker (1966).

their activities. Rather than allowing their decisions to be coordinated by the Federal Reserve Board, as would have been consistent with the Federal Reserve Act, they established a separate committee for that purpose. It was known as the Council of Governors. The council in turn established another committee, the Open Market Investment Committee, to specifically coordinate open market operations. It consisted of five of the governors and was headed by the very influential Benjamin Strong, governor of the New York Federal Reserve Bank. This committee, and not the Federal Reserve Board, directed the open market operations for the Federal Reserve System as a whole.

The experience of the post-World War I business cycle fundamentally altered the Federal Reserve's views toward open market operations. Its views did not change instantaneously, but certainly many people in the Federal Reserve, particularly the members of the Open Market Investment Committee, had become aware of a strong link between open market operations and credit availability in the economy and the relationship of open market operations to the price level. Those relationships were officially acknowledged in the *Tenth Annual Report* of the Federal Reserve in 1923, in which the Federal Reserve interpreted its mandate more broadly to include, for the first time, determining the volume or *quantity* of Federal Reserve credit outstanding and not merely ensuring the *quality* of the paper that it was discounting and determining the *elasticity* of the money supply process. The new mandate ultimately opened the possibility of the Federal Reserve engaging in an active countercyclical policy designed to "smooth out" business cycles, in contrast to its original mandate of passively accommodating fluctuations in money demand with an endogenous elastic supply of Federal Reserve credit.

Some evidence suggests that the Open Market Investment Committee pursued countercyclical policy during the mild recessions of 1923 and 1927. However, with the death of Governor Strong in 1928, the Council of Governors lost its leadership and the Federal Reserve Board was neither willing nor fully capable of assuming that role. A period of indecisive policy moves followed. By 1930, the composition of the Open Market Investment Committee had been expanded to include all 12 of the Federal Reserve Bank governors and was renamed the Open Market Policy Conference. The new members largely opposed the policies of Governor Strong, and internal disagreements led to a substantial weakening of the group as the Federal Reserve's principal policy-making entity.

Over the next several tumultuous years encompassing the Great Depression, the Federal Reserve Board continued to exert a greater influence over the decisions of the Open Market Policy Conference through its legal powers of "review." The diffusion of responsibility for setting policy, along with an inadequate understanding of the influence of open market operations on the real economy, has been blamed for the succession of policy blunders that turned what was otherwise likely to have been a manageable recession into the longest sustained period of negative economic growth in the U.S. economy's history. Moreover, the sharp contraction in the U.S. economy spread overseas and helped to precipitate a worldwide depression.

What policies did the Federal Reserve adopt during that period? Between 1929 and 1933, the Federal Reserve engaged in open market operations that contracted the money supply in the United States by more than one third! The process continued unabated over the period, even as the economy was sharply contracting. Why? Two basic reasons were given officially.[18] The first was the desire to stem speculation in the securities markets. Speculation was believed to have artificially elevated stock prices and led to the collapse of the stock market in 1929. After that event, banks became much more cautious in lending, and significantly increased their own bank reserves as well as the share of their asset portfolios in government securities. The effect was a sharp reduction in the quantity of credit outstanding in the economy. Fear of continued speculation led the Federal Reserve to a further tightening of credit through securities sales in the open market. That action exacerbated the developing "liquidity" crisis as many banks exhausted their large reserve holdings, and eventually resulted in a significant number of bank closures.[19]

The second official reason for the further tightening of credit by the Federal Reserve was the departure of Britain from the gold standard in 1931 subsequent to a series of "runs" in Europe on the British pound for conversion into gold. Speculation quickly shifted to the United States and led to a belief that the U.S. dollar would rapidly follow suit. Because of extensive outflows of gold from the United States, the Federal Reserve felt obliged to take dollars out of circulation to maintain the dollar value of gold. That process was accompanied by large open market sales of government securities that further restricted the availability of credit in the United States.[20] Consequently, the economy grew weaker and the number of bank failures increased alarmingly as households rushed to withdraw their funds from commercial banks before they closed. Finally, in 1933, the wave of bank runs reached such proportions that "bank holidays" were declared for both state and federal banks and emergency legislation was passed to reassure depositors that their funds were not threatened.

The flood of subsequent banking legislation included the enabling legislation establishing the Federal Deposit Insurance Corporation, the Federal Home

---

[18]Eichengreen (1992) has blamed the poor policy decisions of the Federal Reserve during the period on a stubborn adherence to the gold standard. Although not at variance with that view, Bernanke and James (1991) have argued that the world financial system was in a very fragile state and that the Federal Reserve's contractionary policies merely preceipitated a worldwide contraction that was likely to have occurred in any case.

[19]Wicker (1966) examined transcripts of official Federal Reserve documents and unofficial communications between persons involved in policy decision making at the time, and concluded that the failure to appreciate the commercial banks' precautionary reasons for maintaining large bank reserves was one of the principal causes of the Federal Reserve's subsequent policy mistakes. Friedman and Schwartz (1963) and Brunner and Meltzer (1968) also emphasize the Federal Reserve's incorrect view that large excess reserves represented slack loan demand.

[20]Friedman and Schwartz (1963) have argued that there was no need for the Federal Reserve to have engaged in open market sales of government securities. The gold reserves at the Federal Reserve were very large at the time, far in excess of legal minimums, and could easily have accommodated the speculative purchases.

Loan Banks, and the separation of commercial and investment banking. The decision-making apparatus of the Federal Reserve System was drastically overhauled. The general thrust of the reorganization under the Banking Act of 1935 was to centralize decision making and to place the decision makers under closer governmental control. Those changes were accomplished by downgrading the policy role of the heads of the 12 Federal Reserve Banks, whose title was changed from governor to president, and shifting more of the authority to the Federal Reserve Board, which received the more expansive title of the Board of Governors of the Federal Reserve System. The Open Market Policy Conference was dissolved and replaced by the two policy-making groups in the Federal Reserve that still exist today.

One group, located in Washington, DC, is the Board of Governors. It consists of seven individuals who are appointed by the President and confirmed by the Senate to single staggered 14-year terms. It must maintain adequate regional representation[21] in composition. The chairman and vice chairman of the Board of Governors are appointed by the president and confirmed by the Senate to four-year terms, but can serve more than one term in those capacities. The governors were given broad powers to set the discount rate and to set, within limits, the reserve requirements of member banks.[22] They were also given veto power over the selection of Federal Reserve Bank presidents and the authority to veto the Federal Reserve Banks' implementation of policy decisions.[23]

The second policy-making group in the Federal Reserve is the Federal Open Market Committee (FOMC) that replaced the Open Market Policy Conference. It consists of 12 members: the chairman, who is selected from among the members of the FOMC, but has always been the chairman of the Board of Governors, the remaining six governors from the Board of Governors, the president of the Federal Reserve Bank of New York, and four rotating members drawn from among the presidents of the remaining 11 Federal Reserve Banks. The 12 individuals have the mandate to determine the open market operations of the Federal Reserve System. The special status accorded the Federal Reserve Bank of New York reflects its role as the institution where all open market operations of the Federal Reserve, as well as all foreign exchange market transactions of

---

[21]The single long terms are intended to provide some insulation from excessive political influence in policy deliberations; the staggered terms are intended to prevent one administration from appointing an overwhelming majority of the governors. In practice, this framework has not worked as well as originally planned, as the average tenure of governors is less than seven years. The requirement for regional representation stipulates that no two governors can be residents of the same Federal Reserve District.

[22]They were authorized to as much as double existing reserve requirements. Although the requirements were not uniform across all member banks, this legislation effectively imposed an upper limit on reserve requirements of approximately 25 percent.

[23]In practice, when the position of president of one of the Federal Reserve Banks becomes vacant, the Board of Governors nominates a candidate to fill the vacancy. The nomination is voted on by the directors of the bank. However, there is usually only one name on the ballot.

the Federal Reserve, are conducted. The autonomy of the 12 Federal Reserve Banks that was originally envisioned in the Federal Reserve Act of 1913 disappeared. Moreover, "ownership" of the Federal Reserve Banks by the member commercial banks in their respective districts became merely symbolic. In addition to reflecting a greater concern with macroeconomic policy matters, the centralization of policy making shifted the focus of policy away from regional banking concerns and toward ensuring the "safety and soundness" of the nation's banking system as a whole.

8.5   THE GOLD PURCHASE PROGRAM AND TREASURY DEPARTMENT DOMINANCE, 1933–1937

Ironically, the centralization of decision-making authority at the Federal Reserve coincided with a weakening of the institution's role in formulating monetary policy. With one very important exception described subsequently, the Federal Reserve acted largely as a passive agent in accommodating decisions taken by the Treasury Department. Those decisions effectively determined the nation's monetary policy in the first few years of the post-1933 New Deal era.

Three reasons generally have been given for the subordination of the Federal Reserve to the Treasury Department during this period.[24] One was the obvious failure of the Federal Reserve System to mitigate the business-cycle contraction of 1930, which ultimately culminated in the Great Depression. We understand today that the Federal Reserve's actions during this period exacerbated the contraction of the economy, but at the time the Federal Reserve was believed to be largely impotent to slow the contraction. That view was reinforced by a second argument that is often cited for the abdication of policy-making responsibilities by the Federal Reserve. During this period, there was a growing acceptance of the ideas that were later to become formalized in early Keynesian theories. They held that fiscal policy measures have dominant influences and monetary policy measures have weak influences on the real economy. Finally, the continued disagreements among policy makers within the Federal Reserve, coupled with the lack of leadership after the death of Benjamin Strong, created an atmosphere of indecision and drift that affected the official policy positions taken by the system.

The emergence of the Treasury Department as the principal monetary authority was a direct consequence of a policy decision taken in 1933 to stimulate the U.S. economy's recovery from the Great Depression. Acting under the powers granted him by the Emergency Banking Act, President Roosevelt announced

---

[24]See Friedman and Schwartz (1963) and Wicker (1966) for more detailed discussions with supporting evidence.

that the U.S. government would embark on a deliberate policy of domestic price inflation that would be initiated by a devaluation of the dollar against foreign currencies. Such action was expected to stimulate domestic production by raising export demand and reducing import demand.[25] It was to be achieved by increasing the dollar price of gold.[26] The president's plan had four aspects. One was reduction of the gold content of the dollar, which he was authorized to cut by as much as 50 percent. The second was the nationalization of gold.[27] Private holdings, including those of commercial banks, of gold bullion, coins, and certificates were to be relinquished to the Federal Reserve Banks and the Treasury Department by January 17, 1934, at an exchange value of $20.67 per ounce. On that date, the market price for gold had risen to $33 per ounce. The third was a gold embargo to preempt the flight of gold out of the country. The fourth was a massive gold purchase program that was to be undertaken by the Treasury Department. The relative success or failure of this program has been the subject of debate,[28] but what is of particular interest is the effect it had on determining the money supply process in the United States. In fact, the Federal Reserve's passive compliance in the implementation of the gold purchase program is what effectively placed monetary control in the hands of the Treasury Department.

Under the provisions of the Gold Reserve Act of 1934, the official dollar price of gold was fixed at $35 per ounce. To support that price, the Treasury Department agreed to purchase any amount of gold offered to it, although gold sales were restricted to the settlement of international accounts. This devaluation produced large "paper profits" for the Treasury, which previously had valued its substantial gold holdings at $20.67 per ounce. The profits were used to create a "stabilization fund" to support the gold purchase program. The Treasury Department would pay for gold purchases by drawing against its deposit balance at the Federal Reserve. A portion of the funds would circulate back into reserves through deposits at commercial banks and a portion would show up as an increase in currency in the form of Federal Reserve notes outstanding.

---

[25] A particular concern was the promotion of exports of U.S. agricultural products and raw materials, which had undergone severe deflation over the preceding three years of economic contraction and for which there were large foreign markets.

[26] Additional legislation was necessary for some of the initiatives. Congress quickly complied.

[27] Private holdings of gold were limited to small amounts needed for industrial and artistic purposes and to collections of rare coins deemed to have significant numismatic value. Individuals were permitted up to $100 per person in gold coins and certificates. However, that provision was subsequently revoked by the Gold Reserve Act of 1934.

[28] Friedman and Schwartz (1963) provide some evidence that the increase in the domestic money supply that accompanied the gold purchase program tended to produce the desired positive effect on the trade balance because of the dollar devaluation. However, the pre-World War II saber-rattling led to a capital flight from Europe to the United States, which increased the demand for U.S. dollars and lessened the effect of the trade balance.

That is, there would be an increase in the supply of money.[29] The Treasury Department would then replenish its Federal Reserve account balance by issuing gold certificates to the Federal Reserve, which would credit the Treasury's account. On balance, the amount by which U.S. official gold holdings increased represented the quantity that had been removed from the gold markets. There was also an increase in the volume of Federal Reserve notes outstanding. The reduction in the supply of gold and increase in the supply of Federal Reserve notes led to the devaluation of the U.S. dollar in relation to foreign currencies.[30]

The Federal Reserve could have nullified the effect of the Treasury Department's gold purchases on the money supply by engaging in offsetting open market operations. That is, when forced to raise the Treasury's deposit account by buying gold certificates, it could simultaneously have sold U.S. government securities of an equal amount. Such action would have just cancelled the impact of the gold purchase program on the total volume of commercial bank reserves, and therefore on the money supply. It would have precluded the commodity price inflation and the corresponding U.S. dollar devaluation that the gold purchase program was intended to achieve. In fact, such *sterilization* was performed, but not by the Federal Reserve. In 1937, the Treasury Department determined that some of its gold sales were expanding bank reserves too rapidly and therefore financed the purchases by issuing government securities, which negated the effect on the volume of total bank reserves. Thus, the Treasury Department was acting as the nation's monetary authority.

8.6 UNINTENDED CONSEQUENCES OF RESERVE REQUIREMENT CHANGES, 1937–1938

In the years after the onset of the gold purchase program, the Federal Reserve virtually relinquished the use of its principal policy tools for monetary control—the discount rate and open market operations—to the Treasury Department. However, it received a new tool under the Banking Act of 1935. For the first

---

[29] The effects on the money supply due to currency holdings versus bank deposits differ as a result of the multiplier effect associated with deposits in a fractional reserve banking system. During this period, the deposit/currency ratio was rising, which tended to raise the money supply for a given stock of bank reserves. However, banks were also increasing their holdings of excess reserves, which tended to reduce the money supply.

[30] The currencies that had remained on the gold standard during this time, most notably the French franc, would necessarily appreciate in relation to nongold commodities. That is, countries that retained the gold standard would be undergoing deflation unless they also devalued their currency in relation to gold, as most of them did. In fact, many countries abandoned the gold standard altogether.

time, the Federal Reserve was authorized to set reserve requirements for member banks.[31] It was quick to make use of the new tool.

The large gold inflows throughout the mid-1930s were accompanied by a large runup in bank reserves. During that period, commercial banks began to hold unusually large excess reserves for precautionary reasons.[32] The Federal Reserve incorrectly viewed the excess reserves as slack loan demand and feared that banks would begin promoting loans for speculative purposes. The recent history of the 1929 stock market crash and the widespread speculation that had preceded it were very much on the minds of the policy makers at the Federal Reserve. Against the backdrop of recent history, the large reserve holdings in commercial banks were seen to be potentially dangerous and to warrant an active policy designed to absorb the excess liquidity they were perceived to represent.

To achieve that goal, the Federal Reserve engaged in three successive changes in the required reserve ratios that effectively doubled reserve requirements.[33] The policy changes were so severe that they induced an outright contraction in the volume of money and credit in the economy and precipitated the recession in 1937–1938. Like the Federal Reserve's first active use of open market operations in 1919 to "purge government debt" from the portfolios of commercial banks and the Federal Reserve, its first active use of reserve requirements in 1936–1937 to "absorb excess liquidity" had a much greater influence on the real economy than it had anticipated.[34]

8.7 WORLD WAR II AND THE U.S. GOVERNMENT BOND PRICE SUPPORT PROGRAM, 1939–1945

The rebound in the economy began to take hold in 1938 and was attributable to the events leading up to the early stages of World War II. Those events were accompanied by large gold inflows to the United States, as had occurred just

---

[31]The act also authorized the Board of Governors of the Federal Reserve System to regulate interest rate ceilings on selected deposit accounts at commercial banks. In addition, under provisions of the Securities and Exchange Act of 1934, the Board of Governors was empowered to set margin requirements on loans for the purchase of stocks and bonds through members of national securities exchanges and for the purchase of stocks from commercial banks.

[32]Friedman and Schwartz (1963) point out that the discount rate was significantly above market rates during that period, so commercial banks reduced their reliance on the discount window borrowings to meet short-term liquidity needs. Also, see footnote 19.

[33]This was the maximum increase allowed by the Banking Act of 1935.

[34]The restrictive monetary policy coincided with the onset of the sterilization of the Treasury's gold purchase program, which minimized the effect of gold inflows to the United States on the domestic money supply.

prior to World War I, both to pay for war material supplied by the United States and to escape the uncertain investment climate in Europe. The Treasury Department did not sterilize these purchases, which caused a large increase in the domestic money supply and subsequently in the price level.

After the United States entered the war in 1941, the Treasury Department significantly stepped up its issuance of new government debt to finance the war effort. To ensure that the large increase in the supply of U.S. government securities would not depress their price and thereby raise the interest cost to the Treasury, the Federal Reserve agreed to engage in a price support program for U.S. government securities. It was accomplished through massive open market purchases by the Federal Reserve that raised the demand for Treasury bills (of various maturities) sufficiently to keep the interest rates down to predetermined levels. The interest rate pegs (actually, ceilings) were periodically adjusted upward as inflation rose. The adjustments were advocated by the Federal Reserve and reluctantly agreed to by the Treasury Department with the knowledge that most of the interest payments made by the Treasury on the debt to the Federal Reserve would be returned to the Treasury as excess profits of the Federal Reserve System.[35] During this period, the gold inflows to the United States diminished. However, the rapid expansion of bank reserves that accompanied the open market purchases by the Federal Reserve led to a correspondingly rapid monetary expansion and eventually to a continuation of the high inflation that previously had been attributed to gold.[36] This monetization of the debt was the mechanism of inflationary finance of the war. Again, the fiscal decisions of the Treasury Department, not the monetary considerations of the Federal Reserve, determined the nation's monetary policy.

8.8   THE TREASURY—FEDERAL RESERVE ACCORD: TRUCE AND SETTLEMENT, 1945–1952

The U.S. government bond price support policy continued after World War II. It remained a source of contention between the Federal Reserve and the Treasury Department that took the form of debates over the appropriate support price, or interest rate ceiling, at which the Federal Reserve was obliged to intervene in the open market with government bond purchases. The dispute came to a head with the outbreak of the Korean War in 1950. That event caused a mild speculative economic boom that was accompanied by gold outflows associated with the pur-

---

[35]See Friedman and Schwartz (1963) for evidence of this *quid pro quo* for the Treasury's acquiescence in the rate increases.

[36]Much of the inflation associated with monetizing the government debt issues used to finance the war did not actually set in until after the war had ended. Part of the reason for the post-war price surge was increased spending by consumers that was reflected by a sharp increase in the deposit-currency ratio, which had a multiplier effect on the money stock.

chase of war material from abroad. Market interest rates rose significantly, thereby reducing the demand for low-yielding government bonds. At the same time, the Treasury's financing requirements for the war effort led to an increase in new issues of government debt, which placed an extremely large burden on the Federal Reserve to buy government bonds in the open market. If left unchecked, the open market purchases would lead to excessive monetary growth that would exacerbate the sharp inflation that accompanied the speculative boom. Those conditions eventually resulted in the well-publicized Treasury–Federal Reserve Accord of 1951, whereby the Federal Reserve was relieved of its responsibility for maintaining a support price for U.S. government debt.

The disconnection of the Federal Reserve's open market operations from the Treasury financing requirements ended the Treasury Department's virtual dominance of monetary policy that had begun in 1935, although the Treasury Department did continue to influence policy decisions. The accord forced the Federal Reserve to reinterpret its legislative mandate and to redefine its basic policy objectives. That redefinition was contained in its *Annual Report* in 1952, where for the first time it officially recognized the significant of monetary policy in terms of exercising control over the *quantity of money* in addition to its more traditional official concern with credit policy. That is, ever since the *Tenth Annual Report* of 1923, its policy had been expressed in terms of exercising control over the *quantity of credit* in the economy. The 1952 document sketched the broad outlines of Federal Reserve policy. Monetary growth was to be regulated in a manner consistent with zero inflation on average, and the expansion and contraction of credit was to be regulated to smooth out business cycles. The specifics of how those fundamental policy goals could be achieved were left to the discretion of the policy makers at the Federal Reserve and hence were susceptible to the Treasury's influence. Nonetheless, the Federal Reserve clearly had reestablished itself as the principal institution responsible for the nation's monetary policy.

8.9 THE COLLAPSE OF THE BRETTON WOODS AGREEMENTS, 1952–1973

By the end of World War II, the economies of Europe had been totally devastated. Rebuilding would require massive capital investment. The United States economy had been converted to a wartime footing, but otherwise had survived the war relatively unscathed. As a result, it would become the source of much of the capital needed to rebuild Europe (and many affected economies in other parts of the world). To ensure monetary stability in those economies during the rebuilding period, however, it was deemed necessary to guarantee a stable purchasing power for their currencies. Virtually all of the countries had abandoned gold and silver standards either before or during the war. It was decided that to implement such a guarantee, a return to a managed gold standard would be optimal, whereby gold could serve as an anchor for the international monetary system. The system was embodied in an international set of commitments made in 1945 known as the Bretton Woods Agreements. The agreements established a system of fixed exchange rates for all major Western currencies in relation to the U.S. dollar, which in turn was pegged to gold at the exchange value of $35 per ounce. Effectively, all currencies had a known value in relation to gold.

The Bretton Woods Agreements withstood various strains over the years, and were never seriously threatened until late in the 1960s. In the early 1960s, the United States became involved in the civil war in Vietnam. As in previous wars, the Treasury Department issued large amounts of U.S. government debt to finance the military expenditures, which increased dramatically in 1965. At the same time, President Johnson's antipoverty programs (the Great Society programs) were initiated. They too required a very large increase in federal expenditures. The unwillingness of the president and Congress to raise taxes to finance both the war effort and the new domestic programs left only two financing options. Either the federal government would go into debt with new bond issues without Federal Reserve accommodation or the Federal Reserve would buy up the new Treasury securities, thereby monetizing the debt.

The latter option would involve large open market operations that would be inflationary, just as they had been in the financing of the Korean War. The problem of inflationary finance was what had led to the Treasury-Federal Reserve Accord in 1951. Nonetheless, President Johnson applied pressure on the Federal Reserve to again monetize the debt. Beginning in 1965, the Federal Reserve accommodated the president's wishes and relinquished much of its control over the money supply to the Treasury Department.[37] Predictably, the ensuing inflation precipitated market pressure on the dollar for a devaluation against all other major Western currencies. To enforce the fixed exchanged rates agreed to under Bretton Woods, however, European central banks were forced to intervene in the exchange markets to support the dollar. They did so by purchasing dollars with their own currencies. The intervention removed dollars from circulation outside central bank vaults, thereby making them somewhat more scarce and hence more valuable while having the opposite effect on European currencies. The transactions by the Federal Reserve and other central banks increased inflation, not only in the United States, but also in the countries that intervened in the foreign exchange markets to enforce the Bretton Woods exchange rates. The United States was said to be *exporting inflation*.[38]

That process continued for several years, until the resulting inflation in European countries began to strain their domestic policy goals. France and West

---

[37]There was a difference between the Federal Reserve's accommodation of the Treasury's financing requirements in the late 1960s and that in pre-1951 Accord years. In the earlier period, there was a clear support price for Treasury debt obligations that the Federal Reserve attempted to achieve. In the late 1960s, government securities had no such clear interest rate ceiling and the authority for setting monetary policy was blurred substantially.

[38]Once the Federal Reserve had oversupplied dollars, other central banks would buy them with their own currencies only up to the point where the original exchange rate was reestablished. The result was an excess in the supplies of both dollars and the other foreign currencies.

Germany, in particular, became increasingly reluctant to further inflate their economies by purchasing U.S. dollars. Their central banks, along with those of other European countries, collectively threatened to ask for gold redemption of their very large holdings of U.S. dollars in accordance with the Bretton Woods Agreements. The Treasury Department feared that the resultant sizable loss from its gold stock could lead to an international run on the dollar that could threaten to deplete its gold reserves. In response to that threat, the United States unilaterally broke its international commitments and took the dollar off the gold standard. In 1971, the "gold window" was closed and the dollar could no longer be exchanged for gold at $35 per ounce. By 1973, the system of fixed exchange rates that was the final remnant of the Bretton Woods Agreements was abolished. All of the affected currencies were allowed to "float" against each other so that the market forces of supply and demand would determine their relative exchange values. Moreover, all of the central banks were issuing purely fiat money. That is, none of the currencies were backed by gold and there was no longer any anchor for the international monetary system.

8.10   POST–BRETTON WOODS AND THE HUMPHREY-HAWKINS FULL-EMPLOYMENT ACT

After the collapse of the Bretton Woods Agreements, the Federal Reserve was again faced with having to reinterpret its mandate. The new environment under which it operated left open the question of price control. The discipline enforced by the gold standard was gone. The Vietnam War had ended, and with it the need for the Federal Reserve to acquiesce in the Treasury's policy of inflationary finance of military expenditures. The Federal Reserve was back in control of the nation's monetary policy, but just how and to what end was monetary policy to be conducted?

By 1973, the Federal Reserve had become fully engaged in countercyclical monetary policy. In that year, the Organization of Petroleum Exporting Countries (OPEC) cartelized world oil prices by restricting supply. Fearing a recession, which in fact did occur, the Federal Reserve continued the monetary policy of rapid monetary growth that it had begun in 1965. The result was continued inflation, as gold prices rose to more than $200 per ounce. In an atmosphere of recession and rising inflation (the new term "stagflation" was coined), Congress became increasingly concerned with monetary policy, and initially passed a Joint House-Senate Resolution in 1974 requiring the Federal Reserve to report routinely to Congress the anticipated growth rates for the money and credit aggregates.[39] That provision was eventually incorporated into a major piece of legislation termed the Humphrey-Hawkins Full-Employment Act of 1978. The

---

[39]The Federal Reserve had been providing such information to the President's Council of Economic Advisors on a regular basis. The Resolution therefore simply required that Congress, which has direct oversight responsibility for the Federal Reserve, also receive the information.

purpose of the legislation was to state explicitly what the Federal Reserve's mandate over monetary policy was to be (in the aftermath of the Bretton Woods Agreements), and to establish a system of congressional oversight. Within broad parameters, the Federal Reserve was charged with pursuing a "full-employment" countercyclical policy while maintaining low inflation. The act effectively reaffirmed the relative independence of the Federal Reserve in establishing and implementing monetary policy. Its policy decisions were not intended to be subordinate to the Treasury Department, but were instead to be subject to review by Congress.

Under the provisions of the legislation, the chairman of the Board of Governors of the Federal Reserve System was required to submit semi-annual reports to Congress before the appropriate House and Senate committees. The reports were to include the System's macroeconomic forecasts, a description of current Federal Reserve policy, and a list of target ranges for the growth in the monetary and credit aggregates.[40] A principal reason for requiring the Federal Reserve to report target ranges for the monetary aggregates was to establish accountability for Federal Reserve policy in controlling the price level, because the dollar was no longer required by law to be pegged to gold. However, the Congressional initiatives failed miserably during the first five year period, 1975–1980. The Federal Reserve dutifully reported target ranges every six months but completely ignored them in practice, and for five consecutive years the money supply exceeded the Federal Reserve's own targets.[41] By 1979, the consequence of the first decade of the Federal Reserve's policy without the discipline of the gold standard was double-digit inflation.

High inflation was seen to be such a severe problem that the Federal Reserve reversed course very abruptly in October 1979 and adopted a very tight monetary policy. The money supply actually declined for an extended period. The result, from mid-1981 through 1982 was the most severe contraction in the economy since the Great Depression. The inflation rate fell dramatically, from a 12-month annual rate of 14 percent in 1980 to 4 percent in 1984. Since then the inflation rate has generally remained in a band of approximately 3 to 7 percent. In 1985, with the disinflation experience behind it, the Federal Reserve explicitly stated that price stability, initially defined as zero average inflation, was its long-run policy objective. In the absence of the discipline imposed by the gold standard, however, the Federal Reserve has been unable to achieve that goal.

---

[40]Currently, the Federal Reserve reports target ranges for M2 and M3 and a monitoring range for total consumer credit. See Chapters 2 and 16.

[41]That situation led to a problem known as "base drift" whereby, whenever the Federal Reserve reestablished its target ranges for future monetary growth, it would completely ignore how far it had missed the targets in the past and simply set new target growth ranges based on the current stock of money. Any monetary control errors accumulated, and the money supply and the price level randomly drifted upward. This issue is discussed in more detail in Chapter 16. Also, see Poole (1976), Walsh (1986), and Goodfriend (1987).

Nonetheless, the Federal Reserve has firmly established its independence in setting policy goals and in determining the methods it employs in implementing policy. Its decisions are actually made behind closed doors. Until recently, they were revealed to the public only after a long delay, by which time new policy decisions had often already been made.[42] The Federal Reserve receives criticism from many quarters, but its independence does not appear to be seriously threatened.

8.11 SUMMARY

The Federal Reserve was created by an act of Congress in 1913. Its principal purpose was to provide an elastic money supply for the U.S. economy that would accommodate seasonal and business fluctuations in money demand. Establishing a credit facility for commercial banks that would enable them to expand or contract their loan portfolios systematically in response to business conditions was expected to reduce the amplitude of business cycle swings, which had encompassed two severe recessions around the turn of the century. The credit facility would enable banks to sell short-term debt obligations that they had acquired from firms to the central bank in exchange for bank reserves. Under a fractional reserve banking system, the reserves could be leveraged into an expansion of the bank's loan portfolio. As economic activity slowed, the demand for working capital loans to businesses would fall and central bank credit to commercial banks would be reduced automatically. This self-liquidating property of central bank credit provided the vehicle for increasing the elasticity of the money supply. Monetary policy was essentially limited to verifying the quality of the business loans the Federal Reserve was acquiring and "making effective" the degree of elasticity of the money supply that it deemed appropriate. The Federal Reserve achieved the latter objective principally by setting the rediscount rate at which it purchased business loans from commercial banks, although it also retained authority to buy short-term debt obligations directly from firms in the open market if it felt the banks were not responding adequately to the economy's liquidity needs.

Because of regional variation in business conditions, 12 separate Federal Reserve Banks were established and given a significant level of regional autonomy in tailoring policy to fit the needs of their districts. Over time, as experience with central banking in the United States grew, policy making became increasingly centralized and the policy mandate of the Federal Reserve expanded. Its first extensive sales of Treasury securities that it had acquired during World War I precipitated a major recession in 1920–1921. The connection between open market operations and the real economy was not well understood at that time, but the recession led to the creation of the Council of Governors and even-

---

[42]In 1994, the Federal Reserve broke with its tradition of silence by releasing information on policy decisions immediately after the FOMC meetings.

tually to the Open Market Investment Committee that coordinated open market operations for the Federal Reserve System as a whole. The policy mandate of the Federal Reserve shifted to encompass a determination of the volume of Federal Reserve credit outstanding.

In the early 1930s, the Federal Reserve engaged in extensive sales of Treasury securities that contracted the money supply in the United States by more than one third. That action has been widely cited as precipitating the Great Depression. Two significant events led to misguided policy. One was the stock market crash in 1929, after which the Federal Reserve wanted to reduce the reserves and Treasury securities holdings of commercial banks that it feared could be used to fuel another round of speculation in the stock market. The other was the run on the British pound that eventually led to its removal from the gold standard, after which the Federal Reserve wanted to strengthen the value of the dollar. The response to the Federal Reserve's bond sales after each of those events led to banking panics. The second of the panics was so severe that President Roosevelt declared a "bank holiday" and initiated a series of reforms that were intended to restore depositor confidence in the banking system, while simultaneously combating the continual decline in economic output. As part of those reforms, the Federal Reserve System was given expanded powers and policy-making authority was further centralized. Ironically, with one notable exception, the increase in statutory authority coincided with the relinquishment of monetary policy decisions to the Treasury Department, first under the gold purchase program that began in 1934 and then under the Treasury bond price support program that lasted from 1938 until 1951. The exception was in 1936–1937, when the Federal Reserve used its newly acquired authority to effectively double the reserve requirements of member banks in yet another effort to head off speculation in the stock market. The recession of 1937–1938 followed.

Not until the Treasury–Federal Reserve Accord of 1951 did the Federal Reserve regain control of monetary policy. However, it was still susceptible to fiscal policy imperatives. In 1965, government spending requirements associated with the Vietnam War and the antipoverty programs of the Johnson administration brought pressure on the Federal Reserve for inflationary finance through monetarization of government debt. The ensuing domestic U.S. inflation spread to other countries, which attempted to support the Bretton Woods international monetary agreements. Eventually, the strain on the international monetary system caused it to collapse. In 1973, the U.S. dollar was removed from the gold standard. Once again a reinterpretation of the Federal Reserve's policy mandate was needed. The interpretation was ultimately given legislative expression in the Humphrey-Hawkins Full-Employment Act of 1978, which remains in effect today. Under its provisions, the Federal Reserve is charged with conducting monetary policy in a manner most consistent with full employment and low inflation. However, the wide scope allowed in the interpretation of the mandate has enabled the Federal Reserve to exercise extensive discretion and to maintain a high degree of independence in its conduct of the nation's monetary policy.

■ REVIEW QUESTIONS

1. The Federal Reserve was established in 1913 for the express purpose of increasing the elasticity of the nation's money supply in the context of real economic activity.
   (a) Explain the problem created by an inelastic money supply.
   (b) Describe in detail how the operations of the Federal Reserve as they were originally envisioned would increase the elasticity of the money supply. Why is a central bank necessary?
   (c) Contrast the original policy mandate of the Federal Reserve with its policy mandate today.

2. During several episodes in U.S. monetary history, the Federal Reserve appears in retrospect to have made poor policy decisions. Discuss the policy mistakes it made in each of the following periods and alternative policies that it could have pursued.
   (a) The period just prior to the 1920–1921 recession.
   (b) The years between the 1929 stock market crash and the bank holiday in 1933.
   (c) The year 1937.

3. The Federal Reserve has existed for more than 80 years. However, for a significant party of that time, monetary policy was effectively determined by the Treasury Department. Describe in detail how that was done in each of the following cases.
   (a) The gold purchase program in the 1930s.
   (b) The government bond price support program.
   (c) The inflationary finance of government expenditures in the late 1960s.

*4. Some economists argue that monetary and fiscal policies should be coordinated to achieve common macroeconomic objectives, but others disagree.
   (a) What evidence from U.S. monetary history can you cite to support the view that monetary policy should be independent of decisions taken by the fiscal authorities?
   (b) Can you give examples of similar problems in other countries?

*5. After the breakup of the Soviet Union, the great uncertainty about the future of Russia was reflected in the value of the ruble.
   (a) Many Western economists advised the Russian government to place the ruble on the gold standard. What are the advantages and disadvantages of such action?
   (b) The new republics created from the former Society Union had to decide whether to create their own currencies or continue to use the ruble. What are the advantages and disadvantages of a new currency? How should the decision be influenced by a Russian decision to place the ruble on the gold standard?

8.1 APPENDIX

Circulating Currencies in the United States from the Civil War to the Creation of the Federal Reserve, 1860–1913.

In 1860, more than 1600 private bank notes or currencies were in circulation, in the United States. The federal government's contributions were restricted to the Treasury issues of gold and silver coin and certificates. Three problems were associated with a monetary system involving multiple issuers of currency. One was inefficiency. A set of market exchange rates, which took the form of different rates of discount at which the private bank notes would trade, was necessary to value the currencies against each other correctly. The currencies were all denominated in dollars (that is, there was a common unit of account), but there was no assurance that the issuing bank could redeem its notes. State bank reserve requirements helped, but the number of bank failures each year indicated that the risk was substantial. The risk of default on bank notes was the second major problem with the system of private note issues. Some arrangements among banks in the private sector, such as the Bank Safety Fund in New York, attempted to reduce the risk through the maintenance of a collective deposit insurance fund. However, only a small number of banks actually participated. The third problem was the difficulty of redemption. In general, bank notes could be redeemed only at the issuing bank. Consequently, the more distant the monetary transaction was from the issuing bank, the greater was the discount at which the bank notes traded. Private banks tried several arrangements to establish centralized redemption centers for currencies circulating in their region, such as the Suffolk Bank system in New York. However, redemption difficulty was an endemic problem because of the relatively primitive state of technology of information systems and transportation. Finally, demand deposit accounts did not play a large role in the nation's monetary system. They were used almost exclusively by businesses for large intrabusiness transactions.

The events of the Civil War led to the collapse of many private banks, and their note issues disappeared from circulation. In addition, the National Bank Act of 1863–1864 carried provisions for consolidating private bank note issues into a single currency in the form of national bank notes. The system for issuing national bank notes relied on the established bank structure. Private commercial banks (with national charters) were authorized to issue national bank notes once they had purchased government securities in the amount of the issue and placed them on deposit with the Treasury Department.[43] To encourage the replacement of private currencies with national bank notes in circulation, the National Bank Act imposed a tax of 200 percent on new issues of private bank

---

[43]For analysis of the potential for large profit opportunities that the issuance of these national bank notes afforded comercial banks, see Friedman and Schwartz (1963), Goodhart (1965), James (1976), Cagan and Schwartz (1991), Kuehlwein (1992), and Champ, Wallace, and Weber (1992).

notes.[44] By 1875, nearly all circulating paper currency consisted of national bank notes and gold certificates. Private bank notes had effectively been taxed out of existence.

REFERENCES

Bernanke, Ben S., and H. James. 1991. "The Gold Standard, Deflation, and Financial Crisis in the Great Depression: An International Comparison." In *Financial Markets and Financial Crises*. R. Glenn Hubbard, ed. Chicago: University of Chicago Press for NBER.

Brunner, Karl, and Allan H. Meltzer. 1968. "What Did We Learn from the Monetary Experience of the United States in the Great Depression?" *Canadian Journal of Economics* 1 (May): 334–348.

Cagan, Phillip, and Anna J. Schwartz. 1991. "The National Bank Note Puzzle Reinterpreted." *Journal of Money, Credit and Banking* 23 (August): 293–308.

Cargill, Thomas F., and Gillian G. Garcia. 1982. *Financial Deregulation and Monetary Control: A Historical Perspective and Impact of the 1980 Act*. Stanford, CA: Hoover Institution Press, Stanford University.

Champ, Bruce, Neil Wallace, and Warren Weber. 1992. "Resolving the National Bank Note Paradox." *Federal Reserve Bank of Minneapolis Quarterly Review* 16 (Spring): 13–21.

Eichengreen, Barry. 1992. *Golden Fetters: The Gold Standard and the Great Depression, 1919–1939*. Oxford, England: Oxford University Press.

Friedman, Milton, and Anna Jacobsen Schwartz. 1963. *A Monetary History of the United States, 1867–1960*. Princeton, NJ: Princeton University Press.

Goldenweiser, Emanuel Alexandrovich. 1925. *Federal Reserve System in Operation*. New York: McGraw Hill Publishing Company.

Goodfriend, Marvin. 1987. "Interest Rate Smoothing and Price Level Trend-Stationarity." *Journal of Monetary Economics* 19 (May): 335–348.

Goodhart, C.A.E. 1965. "Profit in National Bank Notes: 1900–1913." *Journal of Political Economy* 73 (October): 516–522.

James, F. Cyril. 1940. *The Economics of Money, Credit and Banking*, 3rd ed., New York, Ronald Press Company.

James, John A. 1976. "The Conundrum of the Low Issue of National Bank Notes." *Journal of Political Economy* 84 (April): 359–367.

Kuehlwein, Michael. 1992. "The National Bank Note Controversy Reexamined." *Journal of Money, Credit and Banking* 24 (February): 111–127.

Poole, William. 1976. "Interpreting the Fed's Monetary Targets." *Brookings Papers on Economic Activity* (1): 247–59.

Walsh, Carl E. 1986. "In Defense of Base Drift." *American Economic Review* 76 (September): 692–700.

Wicker, Elmus R. 1966. *Federal Reserve Monetary Policy: 1917–1933*. New York: Random House.

Willis, Henry Parker. 1936. *The Theory and Practice of Central Banking with Special Reference to the American Experience, 1913–1935*. New York: Harper & Brothers.

---

[44]See James (1940) for a discussion of pre-Federal Reserve Act banking in the United States.

EQUILIBRIUM ANALYSIS

CHAPTER 9

"FULL EMPLOYMENT" AND MONETARY POLICY NEUTRALITY

Monetary policy decisions can be directed at a potentially large set of economic objectives. However, the most enduring principal policy goals pursued by central banks in market-oriented economies around the world, albeit with varying degrees of success, are stable growth and stable prices. For that reason alone, those policy objectives warrant study. The purpose of this chapter is to provide a theoretical framework for systematically examining the pursuit of those objectives. The remainder of the text covers issues ranging from the desirability of the objectives, to the feasibility of attaining them, to the mechanics of implementing the policy decisions on a day-to-day basis.

This chapter begins with development of a short-run equilibrium model of the macroeconomy. The model is used to provide an economic definition of "full employment," which is completely determined by household preferences, technology, and the factor endowments of capital and time, and is unaffected by monetary policy. To illustrate this property of the model, a process is described whereby a change in the money supply filters through the economy and ultimately determines a new equilibrium price level. The process is called the *transmission mechanism*. However, in this particular application of the model, the only effect of a change in the nominal money supply is to induce equiproportional changes in nominal variables while leaving the real economy unaffected. This ineffectiveness of monetary policy, or the inability of a change in the level of the nominal money supply to affect the real economy, is termed *monetary policy neutrality*.[1] It is a basic theoretical result that recurs in a variety

---

[1]Examples of research on neutrality include the work of Lucas (1972, 1973, 1975), Kydland and Prescott (1977), and Barro (1976, 1980). Note, however, that this neutrality result may apply only to the central bank's open market operations. For example, in the United States, the Federal Reserve also sets reserve requirements, which effectively act as a tax on deposit accounts, and a change in reserve requirements can therefore have real effects. For an argument that the latter is the *only* means by which the Federal Reserve affects the real economy, see Plosser (1990).

of models and is used in this text as a point of departure for the subsequent analysis of monetary policy issues.

9.1 MODELING THE ECONOMY AS A COLLECTION OF AGGREGATE MARKETS

The economies of even small, remote island communities are extremely complex. Economists use a theoretical construct, the aggregate market, to systematically think through the nexus of economic decisions and interactions that continually take place in an economy. An aggregate market is merely an approximation to reality that can be constructed by identifying items in the economy that share certain intrinsic characteristics, even though they may differ in others. For example, a money market could be constructed by defining money as M1 or alternatively by defining money as M2. For the U.S. economy, a unit of M1 is a representative portfolio of currency, demand deposits, other checkable deposits, and traveler's checks that is valued at one dollar, where the weights given to the four assets in the portfolio reflect their respective shares of M1 in the economy. A unit of M2 is constructed similarly, but the portfolio includes additional assets such as savings and MMDAs (see Chapter 2 for the details). A similar approach could be taken for the goods market. A unit of goods would be a representative marketbasket of all goods produced in the economy, and the price of a unit of goods would be the money price of the representative marketbasket such as the consumer price index (CPI) or the gross domestic product (GDP) implicit price deflator. In this context, an aggregate market can be thought of as a grouping of similar items for which meaningful supply and demand schedules can be obtained, such that an equilibrium price and quantity can be determined.

With this theoretical construct, the economy can be partitioned into a collection of aggregate markets and a systematic analysis can be made of how those markets interact. The interaction summarizes in a convenient form the complex set of activities that take place in a market economy. Although the summary is only an approximation of what is really going on the economy, it can be a useful tool for understanding the macroeconomic effects of policy- or non-policy-related shocks.

Obviously, there is no unique way to partition the economy into aggregate markets. The finer the partitions, the greater will be the number of aggregate markets in the model, and the more intractable the model will become. The principle of parsimony is usually good to apply in theoretical modeling: when constructing a theoretical model, one should keep the model as simple as possible by omitting any detail that is extraneous to the analysis of the issues the model is being built to examine. In this chapter, the principle of parsimony is employed in the construction of a short-run equilibrium model of a macroeconomy that is helpful in analyzing the effects of a change in monetary policy on employment, output, and prices. Those macroeconomic variables are used to define the policy objectives. In subsequent chapters, the model is used to examine the economy's response to productivity and preference shocks. Without such shocks, there would be no business cycle and no role for monetary policy.

One partition of the economy that has proven useful to economists in the past consists of five aggregate markets: (1) money, (2) goods, (3) labor, (4) bonds, and (5) physical capital. This partition is a great simplification of actual economies, but still produces a model that is generally very complex and in need of greater parsimony. Let the short run be defined as approximately one year. In that case, it is useful to restrict attention to the class of bonds known as "one-period" bonds that pay interest only upon maturity. Let one period equal one year, which corresponds to both the length of maturity of a newly issued bond and to the definition of the short run.

A second useful assumption that is internally consistent with the stated objectives of the model is that the stock of physical capital is held fixed. Note that this is *not* a claim that the capital stock is not changing significantly over time; it is a claim that once a firm makes a decision to build new plant and equipment, the length of time needed to get it up and running exceeds one year. If the government injects money into the economy today that alters firms' decisions to invest in new plant and equipment, those decisions will not affect the stock of productive capital in the economy in the short run.[2] Therefore, the model needs to pertain only to the markets for money, goods, labor, and bonds, in which equilibrium quantities may change over the time horizon of the analysis.

Another simplifying assumption is that the response of international trade to changes in monetary policy has negligible effects on the short-run equilibrium of the economy. Therefore, the model represents a closed versus an open economy. There is neither foreign trade (exports and imports are zero) nor any foreign exchange markets. The central bank's concern is the value of the domestic currency (for example, the dollar) in terms of its purchasing power for domestically produced goods, which is measured by an aggregate price level such as the CPI.[3]

9.2 THE PRINCIPAL ECONOMIC AGENTS AND THEIR ROLES IN DETERMINING EQUILIBRIUM

The three groups of decision-makers in the economy are households, firms, and the government. They have different objectives and each participates in a different subset of the four markets of the economy. It is the pursuit of their objectives that leads to "optimal" decisions that determine the shapes of the supply and demand schedules in the markets where the groups interact.

---

[2]Although policy makers should be concerned about the long-run consequences of their actions, an abundance of historical evidence shows that short-run economic considerations have frequently dominated monetary policy decisions. The long-run consequences of myopic policy making are discussed in subsequent chapters.

[3]This is not an unreasonable assumption for the U.S. economy, where exports represent only about 11 to 12 percent of GDP. However, it is a less useful assumption for the German economy, where exports are closer to 50 percent of GDP.

Households.   The objective of households is to maximize utility, which is derived from consumption and leisure. Households do so by making three important decisions. The first is the consumption/savings decision. They decide how much of their real income to allocate to consumption today and how much to save to increase consumption opportunities tomorrow. This decision determines the demand for consumption goods in the economy, thereby affecting aggregate demand. It simultaneously determines the total quantity of domestic savings in the economy, often called the supply of real loanable funds. The second decision of households is how to allocate their savings between the two available financial assets, money and one-period bonds. Households demand money to make consumption purchases in accordance with the money demand schedule derived in Chapter 3. The quantity of savings not allocated to money holdings determines the household's (and the aggregate) demand for bonds. Finally, households make the labor/leisure decision. They choose how much of their available time (which is a real resource) to enjoy as leisure and how much to make available for production. This decision determines the aggregate labor supply schedule.

Firms.   The objective of firms is to maximize profits. They make two important decisions. The first is how much investment to make in new plant and equipment to raise future production possibilities. To finance such investments, firms must borrow from households in the bond market. This borrowing determines the aggregate supply schedule for one-period bonds. Firms use the revenues raised from newly issued bonds to purchase investment goods, thus affecting aggregate demand in the goods market. Second, firms make short-run production decisions, which require selecting the optimal quantities of labor input (the capital stock is fixed in the short run). These decisions simultaneously determine aggregate supply in the goods market and the labor demand schedule for the economy as a whole.

Government.   As the purpose of the model is to examine the short-run effects of monetary policy on the economy, it is useful to abstract from fiscal policy by assuming there is no fiscal government. Hence, government expenditures on goods are zero and there are no taxes and no government bonds. The only role of government is to supply money. Applying the principle of parsimony, we can model the money supply process by restricting the central bank's operations to simply printing money and injecting it into the economy through direct transfers to households.[4] By altering the rate at which the monetary injections are

---

[4]This characterization greatly simplifies the actual open market operations process without affecting the qualitative results derived here. It essentially allows the model to abstract from the roles of financial intermediaries, the policy groups within the Federal Reserve, and the government securities market. Those features of the process are important for the issues relating to monetary control and the interaction of the financial markets with monetary policy decisions and decision makers, and are taken up in subsequent chapters.

made, the government seeks to achieve its short-run macroeconomic policy objectives of stable growth and stable prices. The stable growth objective can be defined as the attempt to keep the economy as close as possible to "full employment" in the short run. Therefore, we need to have a clear definition of "full employment," which the model developed in this chapter provides.

Under the stated assumptions, we can construct a parsimonious model of the economy that enables us to examine the effects of certain monetary policy decisions on the economy. The type of analysis conducted here is termed *comparative statics*. It begins with the economy in a general equilibrium in which all markets are simultaneously in equilibrium. The economy is then subjected to shocks that may affect one or more markets. For example, shocks could result from a change in the production technology in the goods sector, a shift in household preferences, or a change in monetary policy. The shocks produce a disequilibrium in one or more of the markets and a process of adjustment to a new equilibrium takes place that may spill over to other markets in the economy. Eventually, all markets once again clear and the economy attains a new general equilibrium. The comparative statics analysis consists of comparing the price and quantity variables in all of the markets in the economy before and after the shocks to determine the effect on the economy.

9.3   HOUSEHOLD PREFERENCES

Households are utility maximizers. They derive utility from consumption and from leisure. At any point in time, they prefer more consumption to less consumption and more leisure to less leisure. However, for a given amount of leisure, successive increases in consumption yield smaller increases in utility. Similarly, for a given level of consumption, successive increases in the amount of leisure produce smaller increases in utility. Thus, household preferences are characterized by *diminishing marginal utility in consumption* and *diminishing marginal utility in leisure*.

Economists typically believe that household preferences have the property of diminishing marginal utility and that the preferences tend to be stable. Stable preferences imply that over any sufficiently long period of time, changes in the amount of utility that a household receives are determined exclusively by the household's levels of consumption and leisure. However, at any point in time, the preferences of an individual household may change in such a way that the enjoyment received from given amounts of consumption and/or leisure exceeds the average, or vice versa.

For an individual household, say, the jth household in the economy, the relationship between today's utility, denoted by u^j, consumption, c^j and leisure, l^j, can be characterized by a utility function.

$$u^j \; (\overset{+}{c^j}, \; \overset{+}{l^j}, \; \overset{+}{\gamma^j}, \; \overset{+}{\lambda^j}) \tag{9.1}$$

where γ^j and λ^j capture the relative intensity of household preferences for consumption and leisure, respectively.[5] In a period when the household enjoys consumption more than usual, γ^j increases and the household receives greater utility per unit of consumption. Similarly, if household preferences shift toward a greater enjoyment of leisure, λ^j increases and the household's utility per unit of leisure time rises.

If an aggregation of preferences across households is performed to approximate an average of household preferences across the economy, the utility function of a single representative household can be constructed (as in preceding chapters).[6]

$$U(\overset{+}{c}, \overset{+}{l}, \overset{+}{\gamma}, \overset{+}{\lambda}) \tag{9.2}$$

where c and l can be taken to represent aggregate consumption and leisure time, or

$$c = \sum_{\text{all households}} c^j \text{ and } l = \sum_{\text{all households}} l^j \,,$$

and γ and λ are average intensities of preferences γ^j and λ^j across households. With stable household preferences, there will generally be more variation in γ^j and λ^j for individuals households than in the averages γ and λ, because some households may increase the intensity of their preferences for consumption or leisure while others are simultaneously doing the opposite, thereby canceling the effects of the preference shifts in the aggregate.

We can examine the representative household's preferences by referring to Figure 9.1. When the intensity of preference for leisure and the amount of leisure time taken are held fixed, the relationship between the level of consumption and utility can be portrayed as in the upper panel of the figure. Each curve in the figure shows the amount of utility received by the household from various levels of consumption at a given intensity of preference for consumption. For example, with preference set by γ_0, the level of consumption c_0 yields utility in the amount U_0. The slope of the curve is the marginal utility of consumption, labeled $MU(c_0, \gamma_0)$. Note that as consumption increases, to say c_1, utility rises to U_1 but the marginal utility of consumption declines to $MU(c_1, \gamma_0)$, as indicated by the flatter slope of the utility function at c_1. An increase in the intensity of preference for consumption, from say γ_0 to γ_1, shifts the utility function up, so that the utility produced by the level of consumption c_0 increases to U_2. Also note that the marginal utility of consumption at c_0 increases to $MU(c_0, \gamma_1)$, as

---

[5]A common utility function that fits this characterization is logarithmic utility, where $u(c,l,\gamma,\lambda) = \gamma \ln c + \lambda \ln l$. Note that shifts of γ and λ in opposite directions can produce intratemporal preference shocks, whereas shifts of γ and λ in the same direction can produce intertemporal preference shocks identical to shocks to the rate at which households discount the future. These are the generic forms of preference shocks examined in the text.

[6]For conditions under which this aggregation may be reasonable, see Mas-Colell, Whinston, and Green (1995).

Figure 9.1
Household
Preferences: The
Utility Function

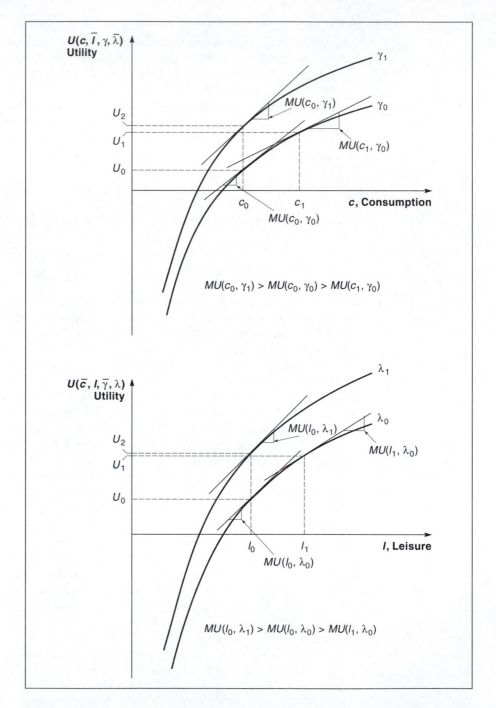

indicated by a steeper slope of the utility function associated with the greater intensity of preference for consumption.

The lower panel in Figure 9.1 shows similar properties of the utility function for leisure, l, and the intensity of preference for leisure, λ, when the level of consumption and the intensity of preference for consumption are fixed. When the intensity of preference for leisure is set at λ_0, an increase in leisure from l_0 to l_1 raises utility from U_0 to U_1 and reduces the marginal utility of leisure from $MU(l_0,\lambda_0)$ to $MU(l_1,\lambda_0)$, as indicated by the flatter slope to the utility function at l_1 than at l_0. An increase in the intensity of preference for leisure from λ_0 to λ_1 increases utility derived from l_0 from U_0 to U_2 while raising the marginal utility of leisure to $MU(l_0,\lambda_1)$, as indicated by the steeper slope to the utility function associated with λ_1.

▌9.4 THE CONSUMPTION/SAVINGS DECISION

Periodically, the household receives real wage income from the labor services it provides and real interest income on the bonds it purchases with its savings. The household dedicates a portion of this income to consumption and saves the remainder to enhance future consumption possibilities. The consumption/savings decision depends on the relative intensity of the household's preference for consumption in the current "period," given by γ. Denote the household's consumption share of the income by $\phi(\gamma)$, or

$$\overset{+}{\phi}(\gamma) = c/y, \ \phi(\gamma) \in (0,1) \ , \tag{9.3}$$

where y represents the household's total real income for the period. The share of income allocated to savings, or the savings rate, is therefore given by $1 - \phi(\gamma)$, or

$$1 - \phi(\gamma) = (S/P)/y \tag{9.4}$$

where (S/P) is the household's volume of real savings denominated in units of goods. It is found by deflating the nominal or money value of savings, S, by the money price of goods or the price level, P.

Equation (9.3) implies that the household allocates the same share of income to consumption each period unless the intensity of its preference for current consumption changes. If the household's intensity of preference for consumption rises, it allocates more of its income to consumption in the current period and its savings rate declines. If the appeal of consumption in the current period is reduced, the household is more willing to postpone consumption and, as indicated by equation (9.4), its savings rate rises. These relationships between consumption, savings, income, and preferences can be illustrated graphically. Solve equations (9.3) and (9.4) for income, y.

$$y = [1/\phi(\gamma)] \ c \quad \text{and} \quad y = \{1/[1 - \phi(\gamma)]\} \ (S/P) \tag{9.5}$$

The expressions in (9.5) are depicted graphically in Figure 9.2, where income is plotted against consumption in the left panel and against savings in the right panel. Note that because neither consumption nor savings can exceed income, the plots are bounded below by 45° rays from the origins. When the household receives income in the amount y_0, its consumption is c_0 and its savings is $(S/P)_0$ if its intensity of preference for consumption is γ_0. When its desire for current consumption γ rises to say γ_1, its consumption increases to c_1 and its savings falls to $(S/P)_1$.

Figure 9.2
Household's
Consumption/Savings
Decision

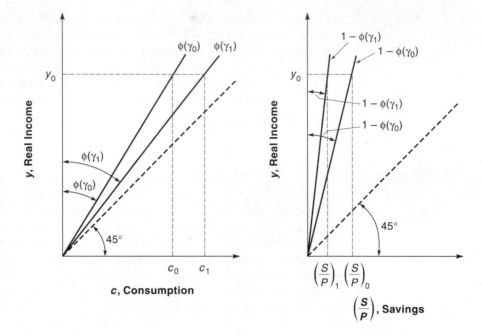

9.5 THE PORTFOLIO ALLOCATION DECISION

Once the volume of savings is determined, the household must decide how its savings should be allocated between its two financial assets, money and bonds. The household must maintain a certain quantity of money to meet its planned consumption expenditures while minimizing the cost of cash management, as described in Chapter 3. The household therefore demands real money balances in the amount denoted by $(M/P)^d$, which rises with planned consumption expenditures, c and declines with the opportunity costs of holding money as determined by the bond rate, r.

$$(M/P)^d = M^d(\overset{-}{r}, \overset{+}{c}) \tag{9.6}$$

Equation (9.6) is depicted graphically in Figure 9.3, where the relationship between the bond rate and real money demand is plotted for given levels of consumption. Note that when planned consumption increases from say c_0 to c_1, the money demand schedule shifts to the right. This shift implies that for any given interest rate, such as r_0, the household wants to increase its real money balance, which rises in this case from $(M/P)_0$ to $(M/P)_1$. The increase in planned consumption could be due either to an increase in real income, y, or to an increase in the intensity of preference for current-period consumption, γ.

The portion of savings that the household does not retain as money is used to purchase one-period bonds that are issued by firms and sold at a discount.

Figure 9.3

Household's Portfolio Allocation Decision: The Demand for Money

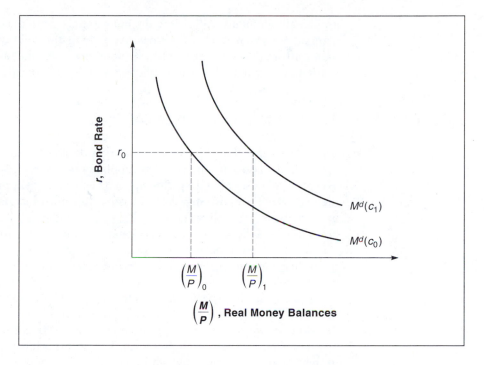

The firm agrees to pay the household the face value of the discount bonds at the end of the period. Let the face value of these bonds when priced in units of goods be represented by $(B/P)^d$, where the superscript d indicates that this is the quantity of real bonds in demand by the household. In exchange for these funds, the household must receive a rate of return, r, on the investment. Therefore, the household is willing to lend the firm the discounted (or present) value of the claims on $(B/P)^d$ units of goods at the end of the period, which equates to $(B/P)^d/(1 + r)$ units of goods today (see Chapter 4). The loan is then equal to the household's savings, (S/P), minus the change in its real money balance, denoted $\Delta(M/P)^d$.

$$(B/P)^d/(1 + r) = (S/P) - \Delta(M/P)^d \qquad (9.7)$$

Equation (9.7) indicates that an increase in household savings, (S/P), raises the household's demand for bonds. In addition, a higher bond rate increases the opportunity cost of holding money, which causes a portfolio adjustment by inducing households to shift wealth from money to bonds. Therefore, the household's bond demand function can be expressed in the following form.

$$(B/P)^d = B^d \overset{+\quad+}{[r, (S/P)]} \qquad (9.8)$$

Note that an increase in savings, (S/P), could be due either to an increase in real income, y, or to a decrease in the intensity of preference for current consumption, γ, where the latter increases the household's savings rate, $1 - \phi(\gamma)$.

The relationship given in equation (9.8) between the household's real bond demand, $(B/P)^d$, the bond rate, r, and the level of savings, (S/P), is depicted graphically in Figure 9.4, where the bond rate is plotted against the real bond demand for given levels of savings. At a bond rate of say r_0, an increase in savings from $(S/P)_0$ to $(S/P)_1$ shifts the bond demand schedule to the right as the household's demand for real bonds rises from $(B/P)_0$ to $(B/P)_1$.

9.6 THE LABOR/LEISURE DECISION

The role of households in the labor market derives from their decision on the optimal allocation of time between supplying labor services and taking leisure. To entice a household into giving up some leisure and supplying more labor to the market, the opportunity cost of leisure time must be raised. It can be raised by increasing the real wage rate, because a higher real wage enhances the household's ability to increase its consumption (and therefore utility) in the future for each additional hour worked. Therefore, a higher real wage rate causes the utility-maximizing household to reduce its leisure time and increase its supply of labor.

Suppose an improvement in technology in the goods sector permanently increases the productivity of labor. How would the household's labor/leisure decision be affected? From the household's perspective, the improved technology represents an increase in its wealth. That is, firms have a permanent increase in their demand for labor, which implies that the household's resource of time

Figure 9.4
Household's Portfolio
Allocation Decision:
The Demand for
Bonds

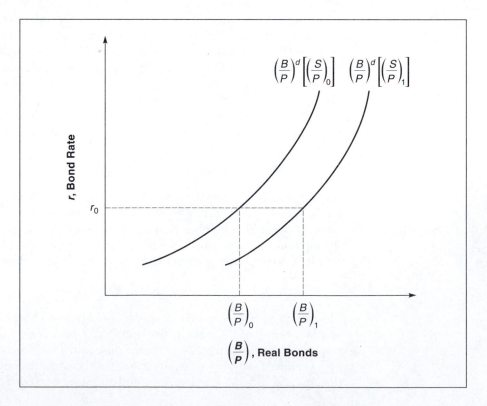

has a higher market value. In response to the permanent increase in labor demand, the household reduces its supply of labor at any real wage rate, thereby increasing its amount of leisure time. Improved technology therefore reduces the household's supply of labor.

A final factor that can affect the labor/leisure decision is a shift in preferences. The household could increase the intensity of its preference for current-period leisure, which corresponds to a higher λ. In that case, the household would have to be offered a higher real wage to continue supplying labor in the same quantity. The shift in preference toward current-period leisure reduces the household's supply of labor.

If we assume that an aggregation of preferences across households is possible, the effects of these factors on the aggregate labor supply schedule can be represented by the following expression:

$$N^s = N^s[(W/P)), \overset{+}{\theta}, \overset{-}{\lambda}] \tag{9.9}$$

where the quantity of labor supplied, denoted N^s, rises with the real wage rate, (W/P), where W denotes the nominal or money wage (given an aggregation to a single economywide wage rate as described in section 9.8); declines with technological improvements, where the level of technology is measured by θ (whose aggregation is also discussed in section 9.7); and falls with an increase in the intensity of household preference for current-period leisure, λ. These relationships are depicted graphically in Figure 9.5, where the real wage rate is plotted against the quantity of labor supplied to the market for given levels of technology and intensity of preference for current-period leisure. Note that its slope reflects the diminishing marginal utility of consumption associated with higher real wages.

Figure 9.5
Household's Labor/
Leisure Decision: The
Supply of Labor

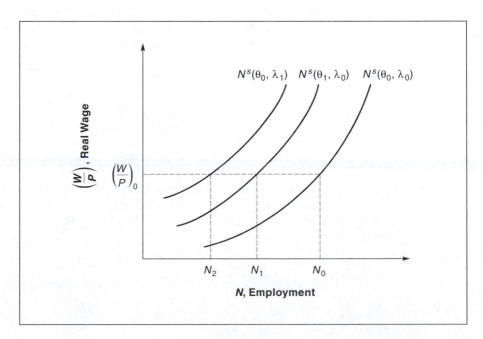

For the given real wage rate, $(W/P)_0$, and given preference for current period leisure, λ_0, the labor supply schedule shifts to the left with an improvement in technology characterized by an increase in θ from θ_0 to θ_1, and the supply of labor falls from N_0 to N_1. Similarly, a decline in labor supply from N_0 to N_2 accompanies an increase in the intensity of preference for current-period leisure, as measured by an increase in λ from λ_0 to λ_1, when real wages and technology are held fixed at $(W/P)_0$ and θ_0, respectively.

9.7 TECHNOLOGY OF THE GOODS-PRODUCING FIRMS

The next step in constructing the model is to characterize the economy's technology for transforming the factor inputs of capital and labor into output in the goods market. Output for an individual firm, say the ith firm in the economy, can be represented by a production function.

$$\text{output } (i) = \overset{+\ +}{\theta^i f^i} (k^i, n^i), \quad \theta^i > 0 \ , \tag{9.10}$$

where k^i is the stock of physical capital, or plant and equipment, used by the ith firm and n^i is the quantity of labor services employed, measured as manhours or number of workers employed, by the ith firm. Increases in either capital or labor raise output. However, as technology improves over time, the same quantities of capital and labor produce more output. The level of technology for the ith firm at a given point in time is represented by θ^i. As technology improves, θ^i increases and capital and labor become more productive for the firm.

In a macro model, our interest is in relating the total stock of capital in the economy and the total level of employment in the economy to the economy's total output, or real GDP, which is denoted by y^s. Begin by equating y^s to the sum of output across all firms.

$$y^s = \sum_{\text{all } i \text{ firms}} \text{output } (i) \tag{9.11}$$

To proceed, we must confront the aggregation problem again because all firms in the economy have different production processes or production functions. Therefore, we must make an assumption to approximate the relationship between y^s and the total stock of capital and total level of employment in the economy. A useful assumption is that the production function of the ith firm is representative of the average technology available to firms in the economy. The aggregate production function can then be obtained.

$$y^s = \overset{+\ +}{\theta F(K,N)} \tag{9.12}$$

where the total stock of capital in the economy is given by

$$K = \sum_{\text{all } i \text{ firms}} k^i \ ,$$

the total level of employment in the economy is denoted by

$$N = \sum_{\text{all } i \text{ firms}} n^i \; ,$$

and the level of technology that transforms K and N into aggregate output is determined at a point in time by $\theta = \theta^i$. Therefore, output for the economy as a whole rises with an increase in total plant and equipment, an increase in employment, or improved technology.

Because the purpose of constructing this model is to analyze the effects of monetary policy changes on employment, output, and prices in the short run, the assumption of a fixed aggregate capital stock that was discussed previously can now be imposed. Let $K = \overline{K}$, which is a constant. Then for a given level of technology, that is, for a given value of θ, the aggregate production function is a function of a single variable, N.

$$y^s = \theta F(\overset{+}{\overline{K},N}) \tag{9.13}$$

The implication is that given the level of technology, firms can raise output in the short run only by increasing the level of employment. Moreover, equation (9.13) states that, for a given level of technology, once the equilibrium level of employment is known, output for the economy as a whole is known. The relationship between output and employment is plotted in Figure 9.6 for two levels of technology, θ_0 and θ_1. Note that this function has an inflection point, which for $\theta = \theta_0$ is at $\hat{N}$, such that the slope of the curve is increasing with increasing

Figure 9.6
Firm's Production
Technology: Aggregate
Production Function

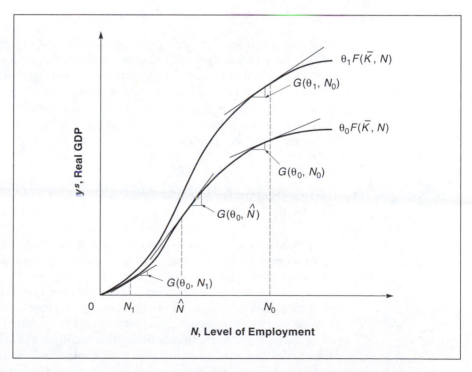

N for $N < \hat{N}$ and decreasing with increasing N for $N > \hat{N}$. The economic interpretation of this slope is that it represents the addition to output (in real terms) contributed by the last unit of labor employed. This is the familiar *marginal product of labor,* denoted *MPL.* Whenever $N < \hat{N}$, there are increasing returns to labor, and a competitive, profit-maximizing firm will continue to hire additional units of labor, because each new unit of labor employed is more productive than the last. However, once N exceeds $\hat{N}$, *diminishing marginal returns to labor* set in, and each additional unit of labor employed is less productive than the last. Therefore, firms will always hire somewhere in the region of diminishing marginal returns, where $N > \hat{N}$.

Note that the slope of the production function at $N = N_0$ increases as θ increases from θ_0 to θ_1, implying that the marginal product of labor increases with improved technology. Therefore, the marginal product of labor is a negative function of employment and a positive function of the level of technology.

$$MPL = G(\overset{-}{N}, \overset{+}{\theta}) \; . \tag{9.14}$$

In the long run, firms plan for expansion by increasing their investment in plant and equipment. An important factor that determines the level of investment is technology. Just as improved technology raises the productivity of labor, it raises the productivity of capital. This relationship can be expressed by a function similar to equation (9.14), where the *marginal product of capital, MPK,* is a positive function of the level of technology, θ, and a negative function of the quantity of capital employed, K, for a given level of labor employed.

$$MPK = H(\overset{-}{K}, \overset{+}{\theta}) \tag{9.15}$$

This function reflects *diminishing marginal returns to capital.* For a given level of technology and labor employment, successive increases in the capital stock used in production increase output but at a decreasing rate. Although this relationship governs firms' long-run decisions about future expansion, it is of interest in the short-run equilibrium to the extent that shocks to the economy today may affect the productivity of capital in the future and thus alter investment decisions in the short run.

9.8   THE PRODUCTION AND LABOR DEMAND DECISION

Recall from the micro theory of the firm that firms employ factors of production up to the point where the marginal factor costs equal marginal revenues. In this short-run model, once the level of technology is given, the production decision is completely determined by employment because the other factor of production, capital, is held fixed. The optimal hiring criterion of the ith firm can therefore be written in nominal terms by setting the marginal revenue product of labor, mrp^i, equal to the nominal marginal factor cost of labor, mfc^i. The firm's mrp^i is the amount of revenue raised by the last unit of labor employed. It is equal to the firm's product price, p^i, which is the price of each unit sold, times the marginal product of labor, denoted by the lowercase letters $mpl^i = g^i(\overset{-}{n^i},\overset{+}{\theta^i})$, which is the number of units produced by the last worker hired. The nominal marginal factor cost of labor is simply the nominal wage, or the cost per unit of labor paid by the ith firm, w^i. The hiring criterion for the ith firm can then be stated as follows.

$$p^i g^i(\overset{-}{n^i},\overset{+}{\theta^i}) = w^i$$

(9.16)

$$mrp^i = mfc^i$$

In perfectly competitive product and factor (in this case, labor) markets, the firm is too small for its production and labor demand decisions to affect the equilibrium product price, p^i, or the equilibrium nominal wage rate, w^i. Therefore, the firm takes p^i and w^i, as well as the level of technology, θ^i, as given when it sets its labor demand schedule.

Given the representative firm assumption, we can rewrite the ith firm's optimal hiring criterion to reflect economywide variables. The marginal product of labor is given by the slope of the aggregate production function as $G(\overset{-}{N},\overset{+}{\theta})$. The product price is taken as the average price of a marketbasket of goods produced in the economy, or the CPI, denoted P. Again, given the representative firm assumption, a competitive economywide labor market yields a single average nominal wage, denoted W. This aggregation assumption allows the hiring criterion to be characterized by the following useful relationship.

$$P\,G(\overset{-}{N},\overset{+}{\theta}) = W$$

(9.17)

Solving equation (9.17) implicitly for N yields the aggregate labor demand schedule.

$$N^d = N^d[(\overset{-}{W/P}),\overset{+}{\theta}]$$

(9.18)

Therefore, as real wages in the economy fall or as the level of technology rises, the demand for labor will rise according to the profit-maximizing relationship given above. The relationship is displayed graphically in Figure 9.7, where real wages are plotted against the aggregate quantity of labor in demand in the economy for given levels of technology. Note that the slope represents the fact that hiring will always take place in the region of diminishing marginal returns, and that improvements in technology are represented by rightward shifts of the aggregate labor demand schedule, N^d. The latter is illustrated for a real wage (W_o/p_u). An improvement in technology from t_0 to t_1 increases the demand for labor from N_0 to N_1.

9.9 THE INVESTMENT AND BOND SUPPLY DECISION

Over time, the firm's stock of productive capital depreciates. The loss of plant and equipment erodes the capacity of the firm to produce goods. To avoid loss

Figure 9.7
Firm's Labor Demand
Decision: The
Demand for Labor

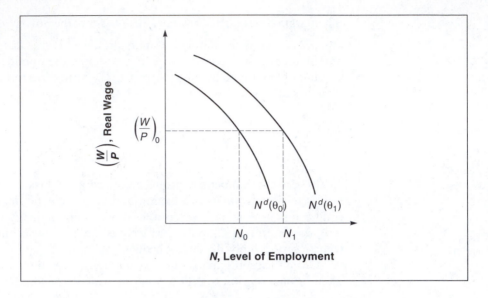

of capacity, the firm must invest in new plant and equipment. In addition, if the firm wants to expand its capacity, its level of investment must exceed the rate at which its current capital stock is depreciating. It determines the optimal level of investment by equating its real marginal factor cost of the investment to its marginal product of capital. From equation (9.15), its marginal product of capital is seen to be a negative function of the stock of capital (because of diminishing marginal returns to capital) and a positive function of the level of technology, which establish the productivity of capital. As described below, the firm's marginal factor cost is the interest rate paid on funds raised for investment purposes, termed the *cost of capital*. Therefore, in the short run, the ith firm in the economy can determine the benefits of an investment of amount i^i by observing the level of technology, θ^i, and accounting for the diminishing returns to capital, given its stock of capital, k^i, and its cost of capital, r^i.

$$i^i = i^i(\overset{-}{k^i}, \overset{+}{\theta^i}, r^i) \tag{9.19}$$

Assuming that the ith firm is representative of all firms in the economy, we can express the aggregate level of investment across all firms, $i = \sum_{\text{all firms}} i^i$, as a function of the aggregate capital stock, K, and the average level of technology in the economy, θ, and the market-average cost of capital, r.

$$i = i(\overset{-}{K}, \overset{+}{\theta}, \overset{-}{r}) \tag{9.20}$$

For simplicity, the representative firm is assumed to finance these investments exclusively with the proceeds from the sale of one-period bonds that are sold at a discount. When the bonds mature, the firm agrees to pay the household that purchased the bonds an amount equal to the face value of the bonds, $(B/P)^s$, when priced in units of goods, where the superscript indicates supply. As previously described, in exchange for these future claims to be received at the end of the period, the household is willing to lend $(B/P)^s/(1 + r)$ units of goods to the firm today. Upon maturity, the household receives $r (B/P)^s/(1 + r)$ as its total return on its bond investment, and the firm can purchase investment goods totaling $(B/P)^s/(1 + r)$ units.

$$i(\overset{-}{K}, \overset{+}{\theta}, \overset{}{\bar{r}}) = (B/P)^s/(1 + r) \qquad (9.21)$$

For a given capital stock, K, equation (9.21) determines the aggregate bond supply schedule.

$$(B/P)^s = B^s(\overset{-}{r}, \overset{+}{\theta}) \qquad (9.22)$$

The relationship between the aggregate supply of bonds, the bond rate, and the level of technology given by equation (9.22) is depicted graphically in Figure (9.8), where the bond rate, r, is plotted against the real bond supply, $(B/P)^s$, for given levels of technology. Note that for a bond rate of r_0, an improvement in technology measured by an increase in θ from θ_0 to θ_1 causes the supply of bonds to increase from $(B/P)_0$ to $(B/P)_1$ as the bond supply schedule shifts to the right. The rationale for this increase in the supply of bonds by firms is that the improvement in technology is seen to be permanent, and hence is expected to increase the productivity of capital permanently. Firms respond by increasing their investment, which requires a larger bond issuance to fund the additional expenditures on investment goods.

Figure 9.8
Firm's Investment
Decision: The Supply
of Bonds

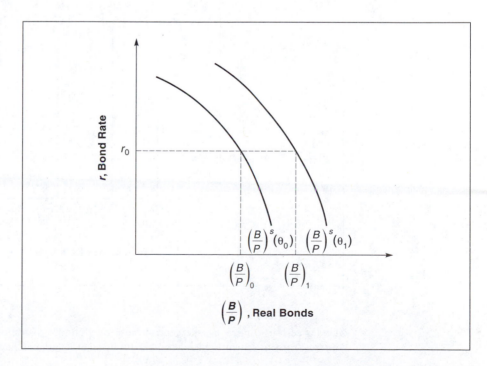

9.10   THE GOVERNMENT'S MONEY SUPPLY DECISION

Thus far, financial asset demand and supply in the economy have been expressed in real terms. That is, the quantities of money and bonds in demand by households and the quantity of bonds issued by firms have been measured in units of goods. The government determines the nominal values of money and bonds in the economy in its role as the economy's monetary authority. It does so by printing money, which it then injects into the economy through direct transfers to households. This action increases the household's nominal savings and can thereby affect its portfolio allocation decision. Over time, the accumulation of monetary injections into the economy establishes the economy's money supply, denoted M^s, and ultimately determines the price level, P.

The real stock of money in supply in the economy is found by deflating the nominal money supply by the price level, which equates to (M^s/P). Because the nominal money supply is determined exogenously as a matter of policy, the money supply schedule is assumed to be perfectly inelastic with respect to the bond rate.[7] When the bond rate is plotted against real money balances as in Figure 9.9, the money supply schedule, (M^s/P), is vertical. Note that an increase in the nominal money supply from, say, M_0 to M_1 in the absence of a change in

Figure 9.9
Government's Money
Supply Decision

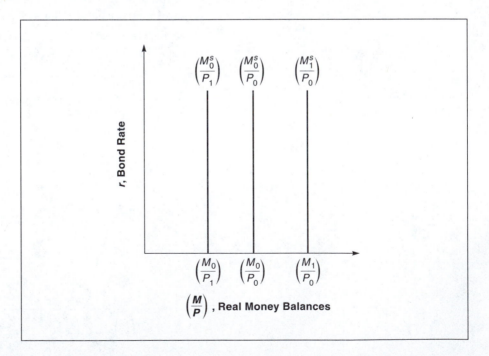

[7]Under certain conditions, the central bank may choose to respond systematically to interest rate movements. Such action is discussed at length in Chapter 16.

prices increases the real money supply from (M_0/P_0) to (M_1/P_0) and the money supply schedule shifts to the right. Conversely, an increase in the price level from, say, P_0 to P_1 with no change in the nominal money supply reduces the real money supply from (M_0/P_0) to (M_0/P_1) and the money supply schedule shifts to the left.

9.11   GENERAL EQUILIBRIUM

A general equilibrium occurs in the economy when households make consumption/savings, labor/leisure, and portfolio allocation decisions that are consistent with their utility-maximizing objective and firms make production and investment decisions that are consistent with their profit-maximizing objective, given the resources in the economy (of capital and time) and a monetary policy, such that all markets in the economy are simultaneously in equilibrium. Those conditions can be fully characterized by the set of equilibrium prices and quantities that clear the goods, labor, money, and bond markets.

We can display the general equilibrium graphically by assembling the components of the short-run macro model developed in this chapter. Refer to Figure 9.10. Beginning in the lower left panel, equilibrium in the labor market is illustrated for a given level of technology, θ, and a given intensity of preference for current-period leisure, λ. In this case, there is a unique level of employment, N_0, and a unique real wage, (W_0/P_0), that clear the market. At this equilibrium level of employment, the upper left panel indicates the quantity of output goods produced in the economy, y_0^s, for the given level of technology, θ. The market value of those goods represents the total revenues to firms. Firms use the revenues to pay their wage bill and retire their maturing debt. Households receive the firms' wage payments as labor income and the firms' interest payments as the return on their bond holdings. Therefore, the value of the economy's output, y^s, equates to the households' real income, y. In Figure 9.10, $y_0 = y_0^s$.

The households' consumption/savings decision is represented graphically in the upper middle and upper right panels of Figure 9.10. The households' real income, y_0, is decomposed into purchases of consumption goods, c_0, shown in the upper middle panel, and savings, (S_0/P_0), shown in the upper right panel. This decomposition corresponds to a given intensity of preference for current consumption, γ.

The lower middle and lower right panels show the supply and demand conditions in the financial markets. Those market conditions reflect the portfolio allocation decision of households, the investment decision of firms, and government's money supply decision. The money market is represented in the lower middle panel. The level of consumption, c_0, establishes the money demand schedule, denoted $(M/P)^d (c_0)$. The money supply schedule is determined by the nominal money supply, M_0^s, and price level, P_0, such that the real money supply is given by (M_0^s/P_0). When the money market is in equilibrium, the real money supply coincides with the unique bond rate, r_0. This bond rate must clear the bond market. The demand schedule for bonds is determined by the volume of household savings. When household savings equal (S_0/P_0), the bond demand

Figure 9.10   Short-Run Macro Model of the Economy in a General Equilibrium at "Full Employment"

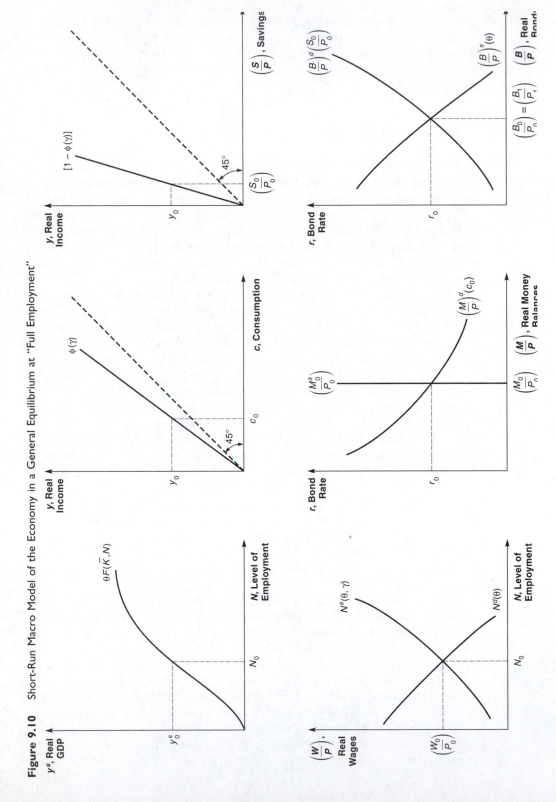

schedule is represented by $(B/P)^d$ (S_0/P_0). Firms determine the supply of bonds in accordance with their investment needs, which depend on the bond rate and the level of technology, θ. Therefore, the bond supply schedule is represented by $(B/P)^s$ (θ). For the level of savings, (S_0/P_0), a bond rate of r_0 corresponds to an equilibrium real supply of bonds of (B_0/P_0), as shown Figure 9.10.

For the economy to be in general equilibrium, all markets in the economy must simultaneously clear. Hence, for this model, the money, bond, labor, and goods markets must all be in equilibrium. In Figure 9.10, the prices and quantities that simultaneously clear the money, bond, and labor markets are shown explicitly. However, when those three markets are in equilibrium, the goods market must also be in equilibrium. This is an application of Walras' Law, which states that in an economy consisting of a number of markets equal to N, if $N - 1$ of the markets are in equilibrium, the Nth market must also be in equilibrium. Therefore, when the economy is in general equilibrium, a macroeconomic shock to one market disturbs the equilibrium in at least one other market. In response, the economy will adjust to a new general equilibrium that could induce movements in prices and/or quantities in many markets throughout the economy. The impact of the shock must be examined by comparing the prices and quantities between the initial and final equilibria in *all* markets.

The prices and quantities that correspond to the general equilibrium portrayed in Figure 9.10 can be partitioned into real and nominal variables. Equilibrium in the goods market consists of output, y_0^s, and the money price of goods, P_0. In the labor market, an equilibrium level of employment, N_0, corresponds to an equilibrium real wage rate, (W_0/P_0). However, for a given goods price, P_0, the equilibrium employment level also corresponds to an equilibrium nominal or money wage, W_0. This distinction is important in Chapters 11 and 12, where prices and nominal wages are not permitted to adjust rapidly to their new equilibrium values after the economy is subjected to a shock.

The bond rate, r_0, represents the "price variable" in the financial markets. As discussed in Chapter 4, the bond rate and the bond price are linked inversely to one another and carry precisely the same information. That is, the value of a bond can be expressed equally well in terms of the bond rate or the bond price. At the bond rate r_0, the equilibrium real stock of bonds is (B_0/P_0), which could be decomposed into the nominal or money price of the outstanding stock of bonds in the economy, B_0, and the goods price, P_0. However, such decomposition does not prove to be useful in the study of monetary policy. There is no intrinsic policy interest in the nominal stock of bonds outstanding in the economy, and the nominal value of the bonds plays no special role in the transmission of monetary policy from its initial impact on the money market to ultimate effects on the real economy.

The bond rate also serves as a "price variable" for real money balances by representing the opportunity costs of holding money. In the money market, at the bond rate r_0, the equilibrium quantity variable is the level of real money balances, (M_0/P_0). Unlike decomposition of the equilibrium real quantity of bonds, the decomposition of the real money balances, (M_0/P_0), between the nominal stock of money, M_0, and the price level, P_0, is essential to the analysis of monetary policy, because price stability is one of the central bank's objectives that is to be analyzed.

That is, the central bank determines the nominal money supply in circulation in the economy, but the demand for money is in real terms. Therefore, for a given monetary policy, equilibrium in the money market determines the price level.

The general equilibrium for the economy as displayed in Figure 9.10 can be summarized as follows. Given the capital stock, $\overline{K}$, preferences, γ and λ, and the level of technology, θ, the general equilibrium consists of the set of nominal variables for money, bonds, savings, wages, and prices: M_0^s, B_0, S_0, W_0, and P_0; the set of real variables for money, bonds, savings, wages, employment, and output: (M_0^s/P_0), (B_0/P_0), (S_0/P_0), (W_0/P_0), N_0, and y_0^s; and the bond rate: r_0, such that households are maximizing utility and firms are maximizing profits. The analysis in the next few chapters consists of introducing shocks into the economy in the form of changes in technology (changes in θ), changes in preferences (changes in γ and/or λ), and changes in monetary policy (changes in the M^s), and then determining how the variables that describe the general equilibrium change as the economy absorbs the shocks.

9.12   "FULL EMPLOYMENT"

The level of employment that clears the labor market in the model in Figure 9.10 has an important and specific economic interpretation. The labor demand schedule in the lower left panel is a graph of equation (9.18), which corresponds to the firms' optimal hiring criterion. That is, given the level of technology, as long as the real wage in the market and the level of employment in the economy are on that curve, firms are maximizing profits. They are constrained only by the level of technology and the current stock of capital used in their production process. Similarly, for the labor supply schedule, at a given level of technology, households are maximizing utility whenever the real wage in the market and the level of employment in the economy are on the supply curve. They are constrained only by their own preferences and by time. Therefore, the intersection of the two curves yields a unique equilibrium real wage and employment level where both firms and households are simultaneously optimizing, subject to the level of technology and the intensity of household preference for current-period leisure. In that sense, the unique level of employment, denoted N_0 in Figure 9.10, is the underlying economic definition of "full employment" for the level of technology θ and the intensity of household preference for current-period leisure, λ.

This definition does *not* imply that the level of unemployment associated with full employment is zero. Firms would gladly hire additional labor (either more workers or additional hours for current employees) if individuals were willing to work for less than the market-clearing wage of (W_0/P_0) in Figure 9.10. However, households are unwilling to supply additional labor at real wages below (W_0/P_0) because they value their leisure time. The lower real wages are simply not high enough to entice them out of leisure and into supplying more labor. The positive level of unemployment associated with "full employment" is often called the "natural rate of unemployment."

As the economy evolves over time with changing technology and preferences, both the level of employment associated with full employment conditions and the natural rate of unemployment will change. Therefore, when the government pursues a traditional short-run stabilization policy, which includes an attempt to keep the economy as close as possible to "full employment" in the short run, its policy goal is based on an economic definition of full employment that is unobservable. Even when policy makers use all of the economic data available to them, they are unable to identify clearly when the economy is at "full employment" or even what "full employment" is at any point in time and thus are hindered in designing a successful stabilization policy. This very practical problem is given considerably more attention in subsequent chapters.

9.13   MONETARY POLICY NEUTRALITY

The principal objectives of monetary policy pursued by many central banks around the world are stable growth and stable prices. In terms of the short-run macro model constructed in this chapter, those objectives translate into attempting to keep the economy as close to full employment as possible while minimizing fluctuations in the price level. In many cases, those objectives may be in conflict with one another. Efforts to achieve stable growth may produce instability in the price level and vice versa. The consequent policy tradeoff for the central bank is discussed in the next few chapters. However, under certain circumstances, the central bank may face the possibility that any policy it adopts will have no effect on the real economy, in which case it cannot successfully pursue stable growth objectives. That phenomenon recurs in many theoretical macroeconomic models, including the model developed in this chapter, and is referred to as *monetary policy neutrality*.

To illustrate the presence of monetary policy neutrality in the model, we can analyze a monetary policy change that consists of a one-time increase in the nominal money supply. Begin with the economy in a general equilibrium at full employment as shown in Figure 9.11, where the initial values of the macroeconomic variables are denoted with the subscript zero. Note that there is no need for the central bank to change its policy. The economy is already at full employment and there is no disturbance such as a technology shock or a preference shock that could induce changes in either the levels of output and employment or the price level. However, it is instructive to examine how this economy responds to a change in monetary policy.

Suppose the central bank alters its monetary policy by printing money in an amount ΔM^s, which it transfers directly to the households. The nominal money supply increases to $M_1 = M_0 + \Delta M^s$. Before prices have had a chance to adjust, the real money supply rises to (M_1/P_0). This increase in real money balances is represented in the lower middle panel by a rightward shift of the money supply schedule. At the same time, the household's nominal savings rise from S_0 to $S_1 = S_0 + \Delta M^s$. Before any price adjustment occurs, the monetary transfer raises the household's real savings to (S_1/P_0) and its real demand for bonds increases, as represented in the lower right panel of Figure 9.11 by a rightward shift in the bond demand schedule. A bond rate of r_0 is now too high to clear either of the financial markets. That is, households are left with an

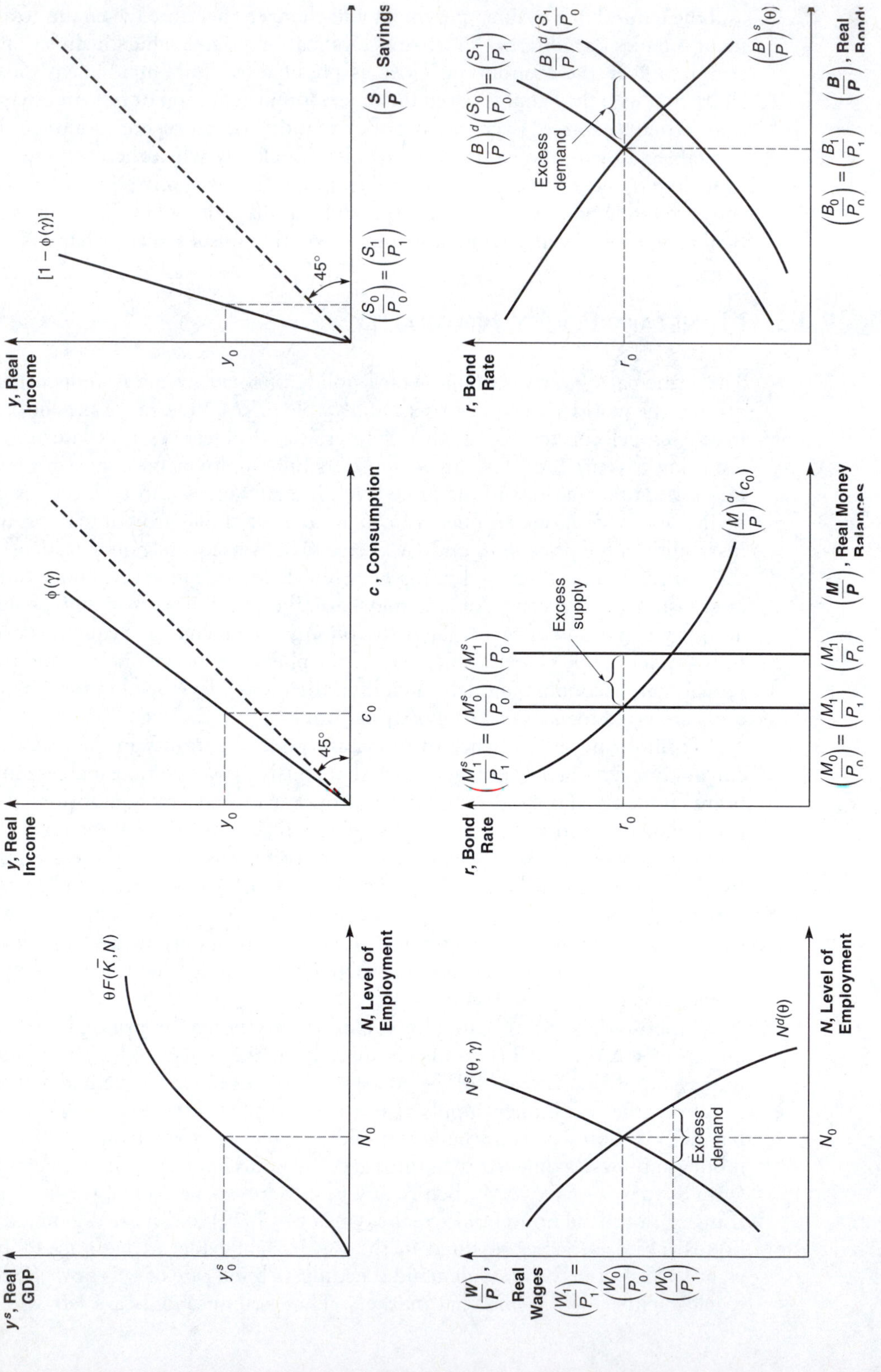

Figure 9.11   Analysis of a Monetary Policy Change: Neutrality

imbalance in their financial asset portfolios, which consist of too much money and too few bonds. The imbalance translates into excess supply in the money market and excess demand in the bond market as illustrated in Figure 9.11. Households respond by attempting to exchange money for bonds. The price of bonds is bid up and the bond rate begins to fall.

How could such adjustments in the financial markets affect the real side of the economy? Firms would observe the decline in the bond rate and realize that their cost of borrowing from the household sector for the purpose of investment is falling. Their demand for investment goods would rise, producing an excess demand in the goods market that causes prices to rise. However, as prices rise to a level such as P_1, the real wage rate falls to (W_0/P_1). At the lower real wage, firms increase their demand for labor while households simultaneously withdraw their labor services from the market because the opportunity cost of leisure has fallen. This process results in an excess demand for labor as shown in the lower left panel of Figure 9.11. To clear the labor market, firms bid for workers by increasing the nominal or money wage. Once the money wage has risen sufficiently, say to W_1, to restore the real wage rate to its initial level, or (W_1/P_1) = (W_0/P_0), the excess demand for labor is eliminated and once again the labor market clears. However, the new equilibrium level of employment is equal to the original equilibrium level of employment, N_0. Therefore, output is also unchanged at y_0^s, and consequently the demand for investment goods by firms must have been restored to its initial level. This can only be true if the bond rate has returned to its initial equilibrium value of r_0. For the bond rate to clear the financial markets, the price rise from P_0 to P_1 had to reduce the real money supply by exactly the amount that the original monetary injection had increased it. That is, (M_1^s/P_1) = (M_0^s/P_0). The real savings of the household are then also restored to their original level, or (S_1/P_1) = (S_0/P_0). Consequently, both the money supply schedule and bond demand schedule shift back to the left to the original positions observed before the monetary policy change took place.

What effect did the change in monetary policy have on the economy? Compare the final and initial equilibrium values. It is evident that all of the nominal variables, including the money supply, M, the nominal value of bonds outstanding, B, nominal savings, S, the nominal wage rate, W, and the price level P, rose. However, the real variables, including the real money supply, (M^s/P), the real stock of bonds outstanding, (B/P), real savings (S/P), the real wage rate, (W/P), output, y^s, and employment, N, are all unchanged. The bond rate, r, is also unaffected. In sum, the increase in the nominal money supply resulting from the monetary injection induced equiproportionate changes in all nominal variables and had no effect on the real economy.

The preceding exercise illustrates monetary policy neutrality. Prior to the policy change, the economy was in a general equilibrium characterized by full employment. After the economy absorbed the policy change, it returned to full employment. Obviously, there was no need for the monetary policy action that was taken. In fact, its effects were detrimental to the stable price objective because it caused prices to rise. However, in subsequent chapters, modifications are made to the macro model of this chapter that induce a non-neutral short-run response of the real economy to changes in monetary policy. Unlike the model in this chapter, those conditions may provide a rationale for the central bank to pursue its stable growth objective, in which case it must be able to influence the real economy.

9.14 SUMMARY

In this chapter, a basic short-run macro model is constructed to examine the effects that monetary policy actions may have on the economy. Three principal categories of agents in the economy make decisions that determine the allocation of the economy's resources. Households make consumption/savings, labor/leisure, and portfolio allocation decisions to maximize utility. Firms make production and investment decisions to maximize profits. The government determines the nominal quantity of money in circulation in the economy in accordance with its macroeconomic policy objectives. Exchange takes place between these agents in four separate markets. In the goods market, households demand consumption goods and firms demand investment goods. The goods are supplied by firms, which demand labor services as a factor input to production. Labor services are supplied by households. Firms also issue bonds and use the proceeds to purchase investment goods to offset depreciation and for future expansion of their production facilities. Households purchase the bonds and use the interest income they generate along with their labor income to purchase consumption goods in the current period and establish savings that can be used for future consumption. Households demand money to facilitate their consumption purchases. The money is supplied by the government, which prints the money and injects it into the economy with direct transfers to households. For a given level of technology, a given set of preferences by households, and a given monetary policy, the allocation of the economy's resources of capital and time establishes a general equilibrium in which all four markets simultaneously clear.

This general equilibrium is consistent with an economic definition of "full employment" in which households' optimizing decisions are constrained only by their own preferences and time and firms' optimizing decisions are constrained only by technology and the present capital stock. Monetary policy changes that consist of monetary injections into the economy produce equiproportional changes in all nominal macroeconomic variables, leaving the real economy, including output and employment, unaffected. This result is called monetary policy neutrality.

The most enduring policy objectives of central banks around the world are stable growth and stable prices. Inability to affect the real economy would render the first of those policy objectives infeasible. In the next chapter, the equilibrium model is used to examine the pursuit of the objective of stable prices when the economy undergoes technology and preference shocks. In subsequent chapters, the model is modified in ways that enable monetary policy to become nonneutral, and the role of monetary policy is reexamined.

■ REVIEW QUESTIONS

1. In constructing a model of an economy, one must identify the various agents in the economy that have control over the economy's resources, and what the economic objectives of those agents are when they decide how to allocate the resources.

   (a) For the model in this chapter, identify the agents, the resources they control, their objectives in the allocation of those resources, the decisions they make, and how those decisions are constrained.

   (b) Define the markets in the model economy of this chapter and which agents are on the demand and supply sides of each market.

   *(c) Suppose you want to modify the model to include a banking sector with a representative banking firm. What objectives would you give the bank and what resources would it control? What other modifications would you have to make to the model?

2. Assume the economy is in a general equilibrium that coincides with "full employment."

   (a) Using the model developed in this chapter, sketch the six graphs that show the general equilibrium.

   (b) Suppose the central bank mistakenly believes that the employment level in the economy is above the natural rate. What monetary policy would it be likely to adopt? Show the policy change on the appropriate graph from your answer to (a).

   (c) With the aid of the model, describe in detail how the economy absorbs the monetary policy change.

3. The measured unemployment rate that coincides with the economic definition of "full employment" may vary over time.

   (a) Describe how the "full-employment" level or natural rate of unemployment in the United States varied over the past 30 years and the cause(s) of the variation. What problems, if any, did this change in the natural rate of unemployment pose for the Federal Reserve?

   (b) Discuss the difficulty of measuring the natural rate of unemployment. What problems does it pose for the Federal Reserve?

   (c) Are there any actual unemployment problems in the U.S. economy that the model with a representative household and a representative firm cannot capture? Should any of those problems be addressed by monetary policy? Why or why not?

*4. In the discussion of the economy's response to a change in monetary policy, a potentially lengthy transmission mechanism was described that ultimately resulted in policy neutrality.

   (a) Would households and firms respond differently if they fully anticipated the policy change? What would be the effect on the length of time it would take the economy to absorb the policy change?

   (b) Given your answer to (a), is there a message for central bankers about how they conduct policy?

*5. In the model in this chapter, a modeling choice was made that allows firms to own the capital and to make the capital investment decisions.
   (a) Explain how the model accounts for the profits of the firm.
   (b) Describe how the model could have been designed to allow households to own the capital and to make the capital investment decisions. How would that alternative modeling choice change the accounting of the firm's profits?

REFERENCES

Barro, Robert J. 1976. "Rational Expectations and the Role of Monetary Policy." *Journal of Monetary Economics* 2 (January): 1–32.

───────────── . (1980). "A Capital Market in an Equilibrium Business Cycle Model." *Econometrica* 48 (September): 1393–1417.

Kydland, Finn E., and Edward C. Prescott. 1977. "Rules Rather than Discretion: The Inconsistency of Optimal Plans." *Journal of Political Economy* 85 (3): 473–493.

Lucas, Robert E. 1972. "Expectations and the Neutrality of Money." *Journal of Economic Theory* 4 (April): 103–24.

───────────── . 1973. "Some International Evidence on Output-Employment Tradeoffs." *American Economic Review* 63 (June): 326–364.

───────────── . 1975. "An Equilibrium Model of the Business Cycle." *Journal of Political Economy* 83 (December): 1113–1144.

Mas-Colell, Andreu, Michael D. Whinston, and Jerry Green. 1995. *Microeconomic Theory*. New York: Oxford University Press.

Plosser, Charles I. 1990. "Money and Business Cycles." *NBER Working Paper Series*, Working Paper No. 3221.

CHAPTER 10

ECONOMIC FLUCTUATIONS AND MONETARY ACCOMMODATION

Many modern macroeconomic theories attribute a large share of the short-run economic fluctuations that collectively constitute the business cycle to unexpected changes in productivity. Such changes are variously known as productivity shocks, technology shocks, or simply supply shocks.[1] Productivity shocks can have many causes. They may be macroeconomic, such as the negative oil supply shocks of 1973, 1979, and 1990 that preceded major recessions in the U.S. economy. Alternatively, the shocks could be concentrated in specific industry groups, such as a positive shock associated with the introduction of new technology that ripples throughout the economy and eventually raises the aggregate level of output.[2] However, what such shocks have in common is that they alter the quantity of output obtained from given quantities of factor inputs (capital and labor) in the production process. Capital and labor productivity are affected, which in turn may alter the consumption/savings, portfolio allocation, and labor/leisure decisions of households and the investment and labor demand decisions of firms. Moreover, as there is no particular pattern to the rate at which the shocks occur, their randomness may induce elements of

---

[1]The related literature is too vast to catalogue. However, the seminal articles include those of Kydland and Prescott (1982) and Long and Plosser (1983). For general discussions that provide overviews of the early research, see Hoover (1988) and Lucas (1987).

[2]See Horvath (1994) for an analysis of how relatively small supply shocks at the industry level alone can be amplified as they propagate throughout the economy, and eventually induce aggregate output fluctuations on the order of magnitude of those observed in the U.S. data.

randomness in the equilibrium prices and quantities that clear the aggregate markets, such as the labor market or the goods market. However, a random productivity shock can elicit systematic responses *among* macroeconomic variables. For example, a positive productivity shock is likely to cause not only an increase in output, but also a rise in real wages. The study of the normal relationship among these macroeconomic variables occupies much of the modern research on business cycles.

A second source of short-run macroeconomic fluctuations is random variation in household preferences. The value households place on current consumption and current leisure can change over time. Like productivity shocks, preference shocks induce changes in the consumption/savings, labor/leisure, and portfolio allocation decisions of households, and the equilibrium prices and quantities in the affected markets of the economy adjust. However, unlike productivity shocks, which are generally observed to have a high degree of persistence, preference shocks are short lived and their effects on the economy tend to average out to zero over time. In that sense, economists understand preferences to be "stable." [3]

The purpose of this chapter is to describe qualitatively the economy's equilibrium response to productivity and preference shocks in the context of the basic model described in Chapter 9. To preserve parsimony in the basic model, a positive productivity shock is represented by a sudden once-and-for-all increase in the technology parameter, θ, in the aggregate production function, $\theta F(K, N)$. This increase represents a permanent improvement in technology, which remains fixed unless a new shock occurs. The decisions of households and firms in their responses to the shock are then examined. Three empirical facts are used to determine the relative magnitudes of the responses (for example, how much the labor supply schedule shifts in relation to the shift in the labor demand schedule). One is that the average length of the workweek in the U.S. economy has not changed substantially since World War II. [4] Another is that over long time periods, the savings rate in the United States has not shown a tendency to rise or to fall. The third is that the real interest rate on capital assets in the United States has not shown a tendency to rise or to fall over a long time horizon. With these three facts, we can identify the new equilibrium and can conduct an equilibrium analysis of the economy's response to a productive shock. The implications of productivity shocks for a monetary policy pursuing the objectives of stable output growth around full employment and stable prices are discussed in the event that the economy adjusts relatively quickly to the shocks.

Preference shocks are random variations in households' objectives that affect their calculus of current and future utility. Two such shocks are described.

---

[3] For expositional purposes, all productivity shocks are viewed as permanent, whereas preference shocks are characterized as purely transitory.

[4] There has actually been a modest increase in the length of the workweek, but that is not expected to be an important trend and in any case is subject to a upper limit.

One is intratemporal, a change in the utility value the household places on current consumption in relation to current leisure. The second is intertemporal, a change in the rate at which the household discounts the future, or its willingness to forgo current utility in exchange for increasing its opportunities for future utility. Because these shocks are short lived and transitory, they do not generally call for a monetary policy response. However, preference shocks may frustrate policy makers, as they can easily be confused with productivity shocks to which a monetary policy response is appropriate.

10.1 TOTAL FACTOR PRODUCTIVITY SHOCKS

The economy's technology for transforming capital and labor into output goods is characterized by the short-run aggregate production function, where the stock of capital is held fixed at $\overline{K}$.

$$y_0^s = \theta_0 \; F(\overline{K}, \overset{+}{N_0})$$

The subscript zero is used to identify the initial equilibrium values for the level of output, y_0^s, the level of employment, N_0, and the level of technology, θ_0. The initial equilibrium is plotted in the graph of the aggregate production function labeled $\theta_0 F(\overline{K}, N)$ in the upper left panel of Figure 10.1.

Recall that the marginal product of labor, MPL, is defined as the additional output contributed by the last unit of labor employed. As described in the last chapter, the MPL is a negative function of the level of employment, N, because of diminishing marginal returns to labor, and a positive function of the level of technology, θ.

$$MPL = G(\overset{-}{N}, \overset{+}{\theta})$$

Thus, MPL is simply the slope of the aggregate production function, which is drawn on the graph for the initial equilibrium and labeled $MPL_0 = G(N_0, \theta_0)$.

When a positive productivity shock occurs, θ increases and the short-run aggregate production function shifts up. This shift is proportional to the level of output prior to the shock. That is, if θ increases to $\theta_1 > \theta_0$, output increases to y_1^s, or by the amount $y_1^s - y_0^s$, if the initial employment level is N_0. However, if the initial level of employment is less than N_0, the increase in output attributed to the productivity shock would be smaller than $y_1^s - y_0^s$. In fact, if the initial level of employment is zero, the level of output must be zero regardless of the level of technology in the economy. This somewhat subtle point is important in the graphic depiction of the effect of productivity shocks on the economy, because the productivity shock tends to increase the MPL. That is, the increase in θ to θ_1 from θ_0 causes the slope at the level of employment N_0 to rise to $MPL_1 = G(N_0, \theta_1) > G(N_0, \theta_0) = MPL_0$. Therefore, for the same level of employment, N_0, an increase in the level of technology raises labor productivity.

A similar phenomenon occurs for the marginal product of capital, denoted MPK. That is, capital is also more productive as a result of the improved

Figure 10.1 Analysis of a Positive Productivity Shock Without Monetary Accommodation

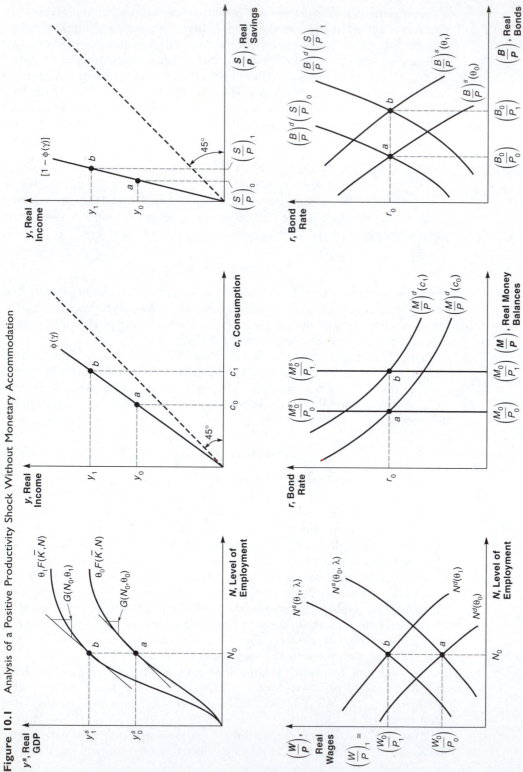

technology. An *MPK* function similar to the *MPL* function can be written as $MPK = H(\overset{-}{K}, \overset{+}{\theta})$. This expression states that there are diminishing marginal returns to capital, but improved technology raises capital productivity. In this short-run macro model, the capital stock is held fixed but its productivity is not. Therefore, an increase in θ raises the productivity of both capital and labor and, in fact, the productivity improvements of the two factors of production are equiproportionate. For that reason, increases or decreases in θ are called *total factor productivity shocks*.[5]

10.2   THE RESPONSE OF FIRMS TO A POSITIVE PRODUCTIVITY SHOCK

When a positive total factor productivity shocks occurs, firms want to increase their employment of both capital and labor. We saw in the preceding chapter that the aggregate demand for labor is a negative function of the real wage rate, (W/P), and a positive function of the level of technology, θ.

$$N^d = N^d[(\overset{-}{W/P}), \overset{+}{\theta}\ ]$$

This function can be represented graphically by a set of curves, each expressing the relationship between the real wage and the quantity of labor demanded for a given level of technology. As the level of technology changes, the curve shifts. In the lower left panel of Figure 10.1, the initial equilibrium position of the labor demand schedule is shown and indexed by the initial level of technology, θ_0. An improvement in technology associated with the productivity shock shifts the labor demand schedule to the right, as indicated by the curve labeled $N^d(\theta_1)$.

For this analysis to be useful, we must answer the question: How far does the N^d curve shift for a given increase in θ? Recall the firm's optimal hiring criterion that appeared in the aggregate as an equilibrium relationship ensuring that workers receive real wages that just reflect their contribution to the profits of the firms.

$$(W/P) = MPL = G(N, \theta)$$

That is, a worker's real wages reflect the marginal product of labor, or the productivity of the marginal worker. Hence, the initial equilibrium real wage, (W_0/P_0), is just equal to the slope of the initial aggregate production function when evaluated at the initial level of employment, or $G(N_0, \theta_0)$. By extension, after the productivity shock occurs, the upward shift of the aggregate production function from $\theta_0 F(\overline{K}, N)$ to $\theta_1 F(\overline{K}, N)$, as indicated in Figure 10.1, increases the *MPL* for the same level of employment to $G(N_0, \theta_1) > G(N_0, \theta_0)$. This implies, for example, that if the same equilibrium level of employment were to

---

[5]This is the most common representation of productivity shocks in the modern theoretical literature. However, to address certain issues, some economists have used factor-specific productivity shocks. For example, see King and Rebelo (1990).

occur after the productivity shock, there must be a corresponding increase in the real wage rate. At the level of employment equal to N_0, the new real wage, $(W/P)_1$, should equal $G(N_0,\theta_1)$. Therefore, one possible "point" on the new aggregate labor demand schedule is given by the triple $[(W/P)_1,N_0,\theta_1]$, where $(W/P)_1 = G(N_0, \theta_1)$. This determines the magnitude of the shift in the labor demand schedule as indicated in Figure 10.1

Firms also increase their demand for capital, which has become more productive. However, building new plant and equipment and making it operational takes time. That is, raising the stock of productive capital takes time. The first step in the process of increasing the capital stock is greater investment; firms increase their demand for investment goods. The additional investment goods are purchased with the funds raised by firms from bond sales. As the firms' desire to issue new bonds increases, the bond supply schedule shifts right from $(B/P)^s(\theta_0)$ to $(B/P)^s(\theta_1)$, as shown in Figure 10.1

10.3 THE RESPONSE OF HOUSEHOLDS TO A POSITIVE PRODUCTIVITY SHOCK

Households make three important decisions. One is how to allocate their time between labor and leisure, where utility is derived today from leisure, but may be increased in the present and in the future by an additional allocation of time to labor. Increasing the supply of labor services to the market today causes labor income to rise. The higher income increases the household's ability to raise consumption and thereby raise utility both today and in the future through additional savings. When a positive productivity shock occurs, the market value of the households' real resource time increases. The real wage that households could earn rises with the increase in their productivity and might entice them to work more, but households could work less and increase their leisure time without reducing their labor income, thus maintaining their current and future levels of planned consumption. The former is a "substitution effect," that is, from leisure to labor, and corresponds to a movement along the labor supply schedule. The latter is an "income or wealth effect" and corresponds to a leftward shift of the labor supply schedule. Again, how much does the curve shift?

The answer is based on the empirical fact that there has been very little change in the length of the workweek since World War II, even though labor productivity has continued to increase. The implication is that the income and substitution effects are largely offsetting. Therefore, once the new equilibrium is reached after the productivity shock has been fully absorbed, the level of employment should return to its previous equilibrium level, N_0. This outcome is shown in the lower left panel of Figure 10.1, where the initial position of the labor supply schedule is identified by $N^s(\theta_0,\lambda)$ and the final position of the labor supply schedule, farther to the left is identified by $N^s(\theta_1,\lambda)$. The final equilibrium in the labor market is now defined by the real wage and level of employment, $[(W/P)_1,N_0]$, that clear the labor market given the level of technology θ_1 and the intensity of preference for leisure λ. At this level of employment, we see in the upper left panel of Figure 10.1 that output under the new technology rises from y_0^s to y_1^s. The revenues firms receive from the sale of the output are paid to households as labor and interest income, which therefore rises from y_0 to y_1.

The upper middle and upper right panels of Figure 10.1 illustrate the impact of the productivity shock on the consumption/savings decision. When the intensity of preference for current consumption, γ, is unchanged, the savings rate does not change. This response of the savings rate to the productivity shock is consistent with the empirical fact that the average savings rate in the United States, $[1 - \phi(\gamma)]$, has shown no systematic tendency either to increase or decrease since World War II. If the productivity shock is permanent as assumed, the increase in real income engenders equal percentage increases in consumption and savings in the final equilibrium.[6] Consumption rises from c_0 to c_1 and savings increases from $(S/P)_0$ to $(S/P)_1$.

We can determine the portfolio allocation of the additional savings between money and bonds by first examining the bond market. At the higher level of savings, $(S/P)_1$, the demand for bonds rises and the bond demand schedule shifts to the right. Once again, we must ascertain the magnitude of the shift to determine the new equilibrium in the bond market. The empirical fact that, over a sufficiently long time horizon, real interest rates tend neither to rise nor to fall suggests that once the economy absorbs the productivity shock, the bond rate should return to r_0. For that outcome to occur, the increase in household savings must coincide with a rightward shift in the bond demand schedule from $(B/P)^d(S/P)_0$ to $(B/P)^d(S/P)_1$, given the rightward shift of the bond supply schedule as shown in the lower right panel of Figure 10.1.

The higher level of consumption expenditures increases the households' demand for money, as represented in the lower middle panel by a rightward shift of the money demand schedule from the curve labeled $(M/P)^d(c_0)$ to the curve labeled $(M/P)^d(c_1)$. For households' asset portfolios to return to equilibrium balance, the money market as well as the bond market must clear at the bond rate r_0. The increase in the demand for money would cause the bond rate to rise unless there is a corresponding increase in the supply of real money balances. The nominal money supply is unchanged, however, as there has been no response by the monetary authorities to the positive productivity shock. Therefore, the equilibrium balance in the households' asset portfolios can be restored only by a decline in the price level, P. The fall in the price level must be sufficient to increase the real money supply from (M_0/P_0) to (M_0/P_1) as shown by the rightward shift of the money supply schedule in the lower middle panel of Figure 10.1.

10.4   THE DETERMINATION OF NOMINAL WAGES

As part of the economy's response to a positive productivity shock, real wages increase. However, real wages may rise because of an increase in the nominal

---

[6]An additional important feature of modern macroeconomic theories, which keeps them generally in agreement with empirical observations, is the desire of households to "smooth" consumption patterns over time. Any transitory shocks to real income tend to be more heavily absorbed by adjustments in the savings rate.

wage and/or a decrease in prices. At this point, we have no way to apportion the change in real wages, which has been identified quantitatively (in a graphic sense), between changes in these two nominal variables. In modern theoretical macroeconomic models, the decomposition of real wages is possible once the general preferences of households that ultimately determine their labor/leisure, consumption/savings, and portfolio allocation decisions have been given an explicit mathematical formulation. We can make an assumption that is consistent with a broad class of preferences that are in common use in theoretical research:[7] once the productivity shock is fully absorbed, nominal wages appear unchanged. Therefore, the positive productivity shock that is unaccompanied by a change in the money supply ultimately leads to an increase in real wages that is due solely to a fall in the price level. This outcome is represented in the lower left panel of Figure 10.1 by an increase in the equilibrium real wage from (W_0/P_0) to (W_0/P_1).

10.5 EQUILIBRIUM ANALYSIS OF A POSITIVE PRODUCTIVITY SHOCK WITHOUT MONETARY ACCOMMODATION

All of the information needed to conduct the equilibrium analysis of the economy's response to a positive productivity shock is contained in Figure 10.1 where the initial equilibrium values are plotted as points a and the final equilibrium values as points b. The total factor productivity shock occurs, which improves technology as characterized by the upward shift of the aggregate production function in the upper left panel. In the labor market, shown in the lower left panel, firms respond by increasing their demand for labor, represented by the rightward shift of the labor demand schedule, and households respond by decreasing their labor supply schedule, represented by a leftward shift of the labor supply schedule. These shifts are exactly offsetting and the equilibrium level of employment remains unchanged at its initial level, N_0. Output rises, as indicated in the upper left panel, from its initial level of y_0^s to y_1^s. In addition, labor productivity increases to MPL_1 from its initial level of MPL_0. The higher level of labor productivity is reflected in an increase in real wages from the initial equilibrium value of (W_0/P_0) to the final equilibrium value of (W_0/P_1), which is brought about by the decline in prices from P_0 to P_1.

Households' labor income rises from its initial equilibrium level of y_0 to its final equilibrium level y_1. With no change in household preferences, the additional income is apportioned to consumption and to savings in accordance with the long-term savings rate, $[1 - \phi(\gamma)]$, as shown in the upper middle and upper right panels of Figure 10.1. The increase in household savings raises the demand for bonds. The increase in bond demand is just sufficient to meet the

---

[7]This class of preferences includes time-separable utility functions that are log-linear in consumption and leisure. See Long and Plosser (1983).

additional financing needs of firms that are expanding their capital investment. The new equilibrium bond supply, (B_0/P_1), requires no change in the equilibrium bond rate, which remains at r_0 as shown in the lower right panel. The increase in consumption from c_0 to c_1 raises the households' demand for money. The increase in transaction requirements of households is just met by the rise in the equilibrium stock of real money balances from (M_0/P_0) to (M_0/P_1) that results from the decline in the price level, such that the opportunity cost of holding money, measured by the bond rate, remains unchanged.

In summary, the results from the equilibrium analysis indicate that the productivity shock produces changes in some of both the real and nominal variables. That is, among the set of real variables, real income, output, real wages, and real money balances rise and the level of employment and the bond rate remain unchanged. Among the nominal variables, the price level falls and the nominal money supply and nominal wages do not change.

10.6   EQUILIBRIUM ANALYSIS OF A POSITIVE PRODUCTIVITY SHOCK WITH MONETARY ACCOMMODATION

In Chapter 9, the policy objectives of the central bank are described as stabilizing output growth around full employment while maintaining a stable price environment. In the preceding example, the economy is subjected to a positive productivity shock. It responds by fully absorbing the shock and moving to a higher level of output, but one that remains consistent with full employment. Therefore, no policy response by the central bank is necessary to meet its short-run policy objective for the real economy. However, prices have not remained stable. The permanent productivity shock induces a permanent shift in the price level. Such permanent shifts in the price level are perceived by the central bank to be inconsistent with the second of its policy goals, maintaining a stable price environment. The central bank simply failed to supply a sufficient quantity of money to the growing economy to prevent a decline in the price level.

To recognize the policy objectives of the central bank formally in the model, we must identify the central bank as a third decision maker in the economy. It chooses the nominal quantity of money to supply the economy to achieve the objectives of stable growth around full employment and stable prices. Hence, the nominal money supply depends on the level of technology in the economy, or the value of θ. With this modification to the model, we can reexamine the economy's response to a positive productivity shock, as in the preceding example.

In this case, the firms and households must take into account the central bank's decisions. Refer to Figure 10.2. The initial full-employment equilibrium values for the economy are identified by the subscript zero and plotted as points a. A positive productivity shock occurs and the aggregate production function in the upper left panel shifts up. In response to the increase in labor productivity, firms increase their labor demand and households decrease their labor

Figure 10.2   Analysis of a Positive Productivity Shock with Monetary Accommodation

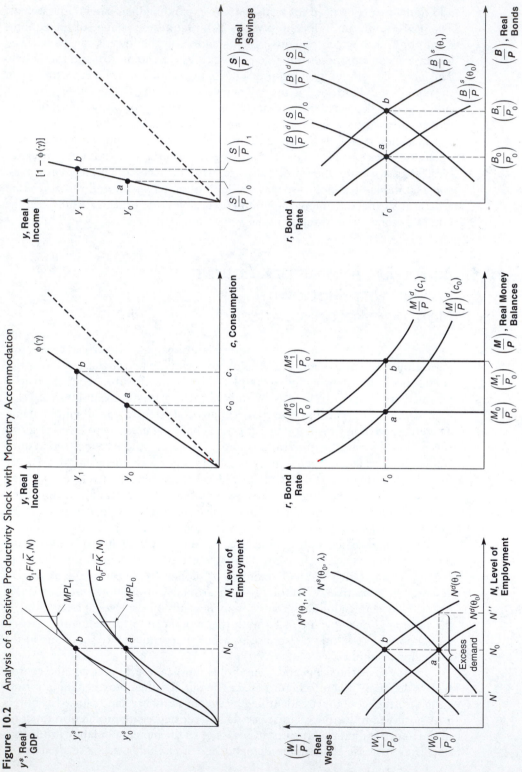

supply, corresponding to a rightward shift of the N^d schedule and leftward shift of the N^s schedule in the lower left panel. The equilibrium level of employment remains at its initial full-employment level, N_0. At that level of employment, output rises to y_1^s, reflecting the increase in productivity to MPL_1 from its initial value of MPL_0, as shown in the upper left panel. Real income therefore increases to y_1, which households apportion between consumption, which rises to c_1, and savings, which rises to $(S/P)_1$, as indicated in the upper middle and upper right panels. As shown in the lower right panel, the higher level of savings shifts the bond demand schedule to the right by the same amount that firms have increased their supply of bonds to finance the additional capital investment expenditures. The higher level of consumption increases the demand for money, as the transaction requirements of households increase. This is shown in the lower middle panel by the rightward shift of the money demand schedule to $(M/P)^d(c_1)$.

At this point, we have no way to differentiate the economy's adjustment in the new environment, in which the central bank wants to alter the money supply to achieve explicit policy objectives, from the economy's adjustment in the preceding example, when the central bank had no money supply response to the productivity shock. In the preceding example, the increase in the households' demand for money was met by a fall in the price level, which increased real money balances. The magnitude of the decline in the price level was such that real wages rose to reflect fully the higher level of labor productivity, and the increase in real money balances was just sufficient to restore the initial equilibrium bond rate at r_0. In the new environment, the central bank achieves the same increase in real money balances by increasing the nominal money supply. That is, the increase in the demand for money is fully accommodated by the central bank with a corresponding increase in the nominal money supply, which rises to its final value of M_1 from its initial value of M_0, and prices remain at their initial equilibrium levels. This outcome is represented graphically in the lower middle panel by a rightward shift in the money supply schedule, where the final equilibrium price level is given by P_0 and the final equilibrium level of real money balances is (M_1/P_0).

What are the implications of the policy response to the productivity shock for the equilibrium nominal wage? In the preceding example, the nominal wage did not change. Real wages rose solely as a result of a decline in prices. In this case, the price level does not change. If nominal wages also do not change, the real wage equals its initial equilibrium value of (W_0/P_0). However, at that real wage rate, households are willing to supply labor only in the amount equal to N', as indicated in Figure 10.2, whereas firms demand labor in the amount equal to N''. Therefore, an excess demand for labor must be absorbed for the equilibrium to be restored to the market. Equilibrium occurs when firms bid up the nominal wage to a level equal to W_1 such that real wages rise to reflect fully the higher level of labor productivity given by MPL_1.

Note that in both examples the real wage rises to clear the labor market as a result of the knowledge by households and firms that there has been an increase in labor productivity. In the latter example, the increase in the nominal wage reflects not only the knowledge that there has been an increase in labor productivity, but also the knowledge that the central bank will respond to the increase in productivity by increasing the nominal money supply in circulation in the economy by the amount required to prevent the price level from declining. None of the decision makers in the economy—the firms, the households, and the central bank—is assumed to have superior knowledge about the nature of the shock and all are assumed to know the objectives the other groups in the economy are trying to achieve. The new equilibrium for the economy as a whole therefore reflects full information on the part of all agents. It also reflects the lack of any impediments to the adjustment process as the economy absorbs the productivity shock and moves from its initial equilibrium to its final equilibrium.

10.7   PREFERENCE SHOCKS

Most economic theories are built on the belief that household preferences are stable. However, stability does not imply that in the aggregate, random fluctuations in preferences, or preference shocks, are not present, but only that such shocks are purely transitory. Unlike productivity shocks, which are permanent (that is, once they occur they are seen to be lasting), preference shocks dissipate quickly. Over a relatively short period of time, their effects average out to zero. The transitory nature of preference shocks implies that the central bank has little reason to alter its policy to counteract their effects.[8] The problem with preference shocks is that they are easily confounded with productivity shocks, to which the central bank does want to respond. Therefore, when the central bank monitors incoming economic data to identify the permanent productivity shocks that have taken place in the economy, the "signals" it receives from the data are made "noisy" by the presence of the transitory preference shocks. The "noise" complicates the central bank's economic analysis and may become the source of mistakes in monetary policy decisions.[9]

To illustrate how preference shocks may be manifested as fluctuations in observable economic data, two types of preference shocks are described with the aid of the model. An intratemporal shock is an increase in any period in a household's utility for consumption in relation to its utility for leisure. An intertemporal shock is an increase in the rate at which the household discounts future utility in general, whether derived from consumption or leisure. In this

---

[8]Some economists believe that preference shocks are of sufficient duration to warrant a short-term monetary policy response. Many of the same economists also stress the importance of possible short-run rigidities in the economy, such as long-term nominal wage contracts and the presence of physical capacity constraints on output, which can amplify the effects of preference shocks on the economy. These issues are discussed in Chapter 12.

[9]For a modern macroeconomic model in which preference shocks of the type described here play important roles in terms of their impact on monetary policy decisions, see Leeper and Sims (1994).

case, the household resists giving up either consumption or leisure time today in exchange for raising the opportunities to increase them in the future. With each of these preference shocks, households' principal economic decisions (consumption/savings, labor/leisure, and portfolio allocation) are affected. The altered decisions in turn introduce transitory equilibrium fluctuations into the economy.

10.8   INTRATEMPORAL PREFERENCE SHOCKS

When an intratemporal preference shock occurs, households may increase their intensity of preference for current consumption while simultaneously decreasing their intensity of preference for current leisure. In Figure 10.3, this type of preference shock is represented by an increase in γ from γ_0 to γ_1 and a decrease in λ from λ_0 to λ_1. The household increases its demand for consumption goods and reduces its demand for leisure. The reduction in the intensity of preference for current leisure coincides with an increase in the supply of labor, which is represented in the lower left panel of Figure 10.3 by a rightward shift of the labor supply schedule from $N^s(\theta,\lambda_0)$ to $N^s(\theta,\lambda_1)$. The excess supply of labor that results is absorbed by a rise in the level of employment to N_1 and a decline in the equilibrium real wage to $(W/P)_1$. As indicated in the upper left panel, the increase in employment raises output from y_0^s to y_1^s and reduces labor productivity from MPL_0 to MPL_1, where the latter is reflected in the lower real wage rate. In conjunction with the greater level of output, real income rises from y_0 to y_1. However, as indicated in the upper middle and upper right panels, the greater intensity of preference for current consumption, represented by an increase in γ, lowers the savings rate, $[1 - \phi(\gamma)]$.

The question central to identifying the new final equilibrium is: What has happened in the goods market? Output has increased, so the total quantity of goods produced is greater, but what is the compositional split of output between consumption and investment goods? Two effects are at work. The higher real income tends to raise both consumption and savings, where the latter ultimately determines the equilibrium level of investment. However, the preference shock favors consumption over savings. Therefore, although consumption unambiguously rises, the effect on savings and investment is ambiguous. Whether they increase, decrease, or remain unchanged depends on the magnitude of the output response resulting from the effect of the preference shock on the labor/leisure decision, that is, how much the N^s schedule shifts in relation to the magnitude of the effect of the preference shock on the consumption/savings decision, or how much the savings rate declined. Only when these two effects are exactly offsetting in decisions on the quantities of savings and investment will the effects of the preference shock be purely intratemporal. Otherwise, the changes to the current decisions caused by the preference shock will affect the household's opportunities for consumption and leisure in the future.

The case of a purely intratemporal preference shock favoring consumption over leisure is depicted in Figure 10.3. In the upper right panel, the positive effect on real savings of the increase in real income from y_0 to y_1 is exactly offset

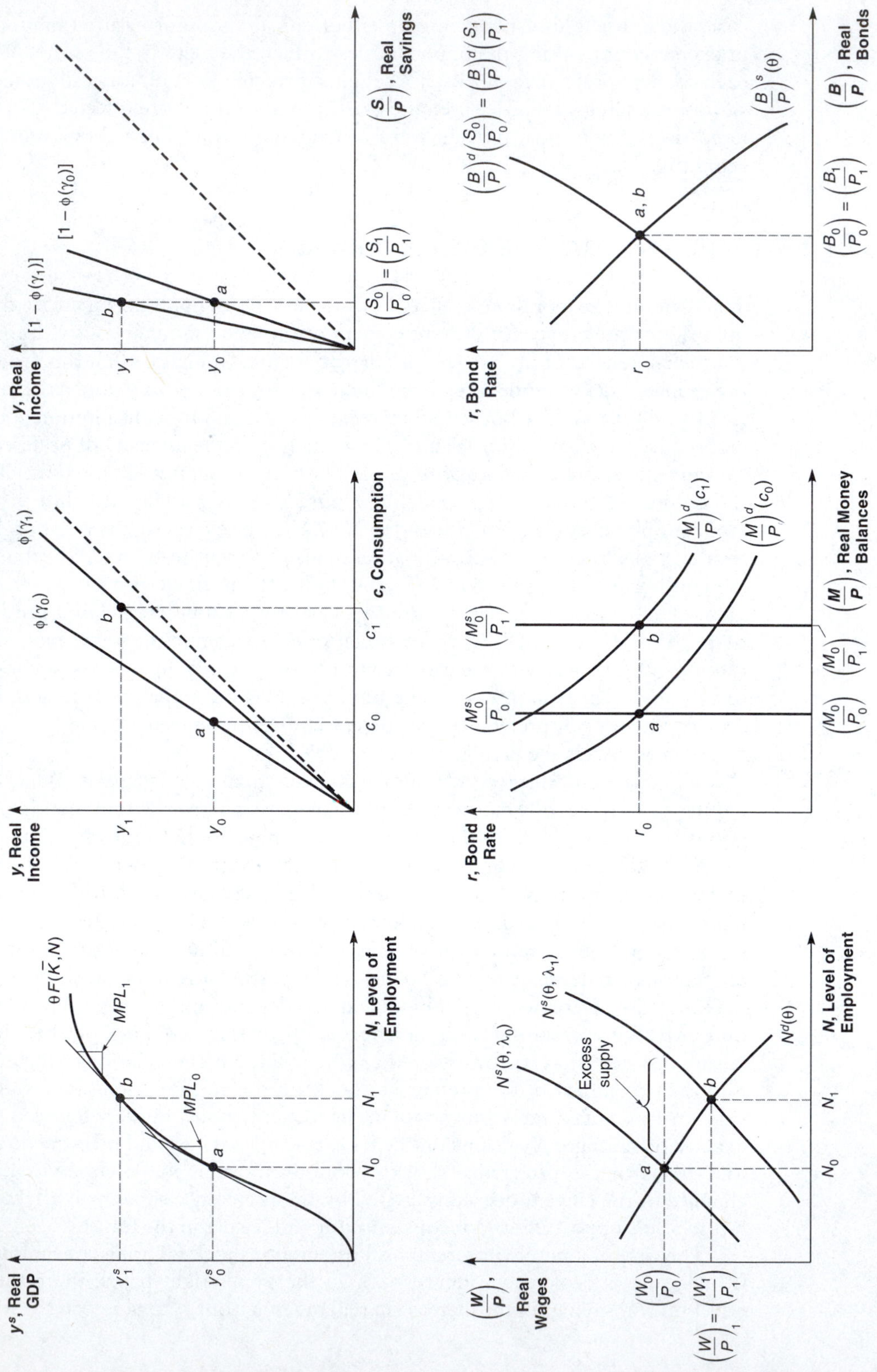

Figure 10.3   Analysis of an Intratemporal Preference Shock Favoring Consumption over Leisure

by the decline in the savings rate from $[1 - \phi(\gamma_0)]$ to $[1 - \phi(\gamma_1)]$. As a result, there is no change in the households' demand for bonds. Because there has been no change in technology, firms have not changed their demand for investment goods, which implies that their financing needs and hence the bond supply schedule remain unchanged. Therefore, neither the equilibrium supply of real bonds nor the bond rate is affected by the purely intratemporal preference shock.

In this case, households are working more and producing more and all of the additional output is consumed within the current period. The increase in consumption raises the households' demand for money, as indicated in the lower middle panel by a rightward shift in the money demand schedule from $(M/P)^d(c_0)$ to $(M/P)^d(c_1)$. With no change in monetary policy, the nominal money supply remains fixed. Therefore, to clear the money market at the equilibrium bond rate, r_0, prices must fall sufficiently to raise the households' real money balances from (M_0/P_0) to (M_0/P_1) to accommodate fully the increase in demand as shown in Figure 10.3. Note that the decline in the price level to P_1, where $P_1 < P_0$, must be accompanied by identical percentage declines in nominal savings to S_1, where $S_1 < S_0$, and in nominal bonds to B_1, where $B_1 < B_0$. However, the nominal wage rate must fall by a larger percentage than prices, because the final equilibrium real wage rate, (W_1/P_1), is less than the original equilibrium real wage rate, (W_0/P_0), as a result of the purely intratemporal preference shock that favors consumption over leisure.

The results of the equilibrium analysis of the purely intratemporal preference shock can now be described with reference to Figure 10.3. In the real sector of the economy, employment, output, income, and real money balances rise; real savings, real bonds, and the bond rate remain unchanged; and the real wage rate falls. On the nominal side of the economy, prices, nominal savings, nominal bonds, and the nominal wage rate fall and the nominal money supply remains unchanged.

10.9   INTERTEMPORAL PREFERENCE SHOCKS

When an intertemporal preference shock occurs, households become more impatient to receive utility. They place greater value on current consumption and current leisure, and the demand for both rises. There is an increase in the intensity of preference for current consumption, such that γ rises from γ_0 to γ_1, and an increase in the intensity of preference for current leisure, such that λ increases from λ_0 to λ_1. The greater intensity of preference for current consumption leads households to adjust their consumption/savings decisions by increasing the portion of current income used for consumption, and the savings rate falls. This situation is represented in the upper middle and upper right panels of Figure 10.4. In the labor market, households adjust their labor/leisure decisions by requiring greater compensation to give up leisure in the current period because they now value leisure more highly. This situation is represented in the lower left panel of Figure 10.4 by a leftward shift in the labor supply schedule from $N^s(\theta, \lambda_0)$ to $N^s(\theta, \lambda_1)$. The result is an excess demand for labor that is absorbed by an increase in the real wage from (W_0/P_0) to (W_1/P_1) and a decline in employment from N_0 to N_1. At the lower level of employment, output falls from y_0^s to y_1^s, as shown in the upper left panel of Figure 10.4, and labor productivity increases from MPL_0 to MPL_1, reflecting the higher wage rate. With the decline in output, real income falls from y_0 to y_1. Therefore, the decline in household savings as a result of the preference shock favoring current consumption over savings is exacerbated by the loss of real income due to the negative effect of the preference shock favoring current leisure that reduces the supply of labor and lowers output and real income.

The question that is again of interest is: What is happening in the goods market? Output is lower, but how is it divided between consumption and investment goods? The decline in output and income coupled with an increased desire for consumption unambiguously implies that the level of household savings and hence the level of investment by firms has fallen. However, the fall in income tends to reduce consumption, whereas the preference shock that favors consumption over savings tends to raise consumption. The net effect of the preference shock on the household's level of current consumption is therefore ambiguous. In the special case illustrated in Figure 10.4, these two effects on consumption are assumed to be exactly offsetting and the net effect of the intertemporal preference shock on current consumption is zero.

As the level of savings declines, the demand for bonds also declines as shown in the lower right panel by a leftward shift of the bond demand schedule from $(B/P)^d(S_0/P_0)$ to $(B/P)^d(S_1/P_1)$. Because technology has not changed, the bond supply schedule remains fixed and the bond rate is forced to rise from r_0 to r_1 to clear the bond market. The higher bond rate must also clear the money market if balance is to be maintained in the asset portfolios of households. With no change in consumption expenditures, the money demand schedule is unchanged, and with no change in monetary policy, the nominal money supply remains fixed. However, given the greater opportunity costs of holding money at the higher bond rate, real money balances must decline for the money market to clear, which causes prices to rise from P_0 to P_1. The result is a leftward shift in the money supply schedule and a decline in real balances from (M_0/P_0) to (M_0/P_1). Note in the lower left panel that real wages had to rise to clear the labor market, and prices were rising simultaneously. The implication is that the percentage increase in nominal wages from W_0 to W_1 exceeded the percentage increase in prices.

The equilibrium analysis of an intertemporal preference shock whereby households discount the future more heavily (or place a lower value on the utility that they expect to receive from future consumption and leisure) shows declines in employment, output, and investment, and increases in productivity (and real wages), the bond rate, and the price level. In general, the net effect on consumption is ambiguous and depends on whether the change in the labor/leisure decision that reduced output and income dominated the change in the consumption/savings decision that favors current consumption over savings. In the special case when these two effects are exactly offsetting, households' desire to raise current utility at the expense of the possibilities for future consumption and leisure is fully manifested as an increase in the amount of current leisure taken and a reduction in savings and investment. Households are therefore

Figure 10.4   Analysis of an Intertemporal Preference Shock Favoring Current Consumption and Current Leisure

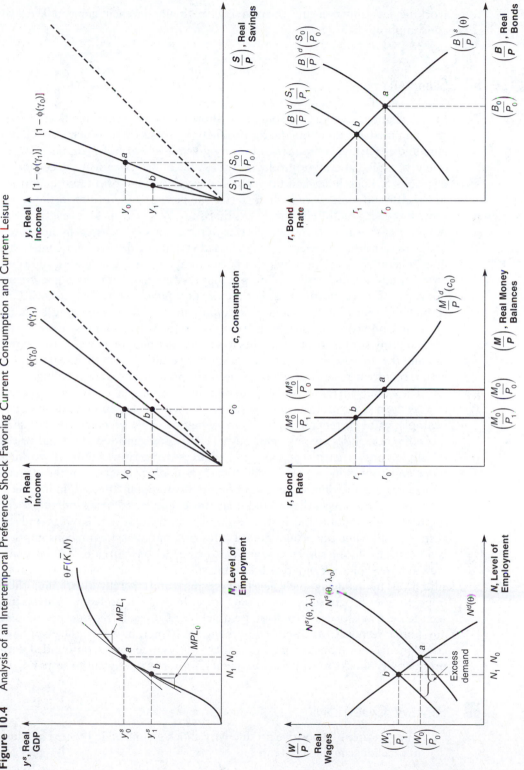

working less and reducing their savings to maintain their current levels of consumption.

10.10   SUMMARY

In this chapter, two generic sources of short-run macroeconomic fluctuations are examined. One is a total factor productivity shock. When such a shock occurs and is positive, output rises for any given levels of factor inputs. Consequently, capital and labor productivity rise. Such changes affect the economic decisions of households and firms and induce changes in prices and quantities of the affected markets that characterize the general equilibrium of the economy. By relying on the empirical facts that since World War II the length of the workweek, the savings rate, and the rate of return on capital assets in the United States have neither increased nor decreased systematically, we can identify the new general equilibrium to which the economy adjusts. The new equilibrium corresponds to a higher level of output that is consistent with full employment, but requires a decline in prices. For a monetary policy whose objectives are to stabilize output growth around full employment while maintaining a stable price environment, the appropriate response to the shock is a passive one when the economy's adjustment to the shock is rapid. It would merely seek to accommodate the increase in the demand for money resulting from the greater transaction requirements of a growing economy to prevent prices from falling.

The other generic source of short-run macroeconomic fluctuations is preference shocks. In purely intratemporal preference shocks, households may, for example, value current consumption more highly than current leisure. The shift in preference causes employment, output, and consumption to rise and prices to fall, but has no net effect on savings and investment. Households are working more and consuming all of the additional fruits of their labors in the current period, leaving their future consumption opportunities unaffected. In intertemporal preference shocks, households may, for example, become more impatient for both consumption and leisure. Employment, output, and savings and investment fall while prices and interest rates rise, but the effect on consumption is ambiguous. In the special case in which current consumption remains unaffected, households are working less while sustaining their level of current consumption by reducing their level of savings and thereby restricting their opportunities for consumption in the future. In general, preference shocks are seen to be transitory and to dissipate quickly. As a result, they do not require any policy response. As discussed in the next chapter, however, they can have consequences for monetary policy, as they can become easily confounded with productivity shocks to which the monetary authority does want to respond.

◼ REVIEW QUESTIONS

1. The example of a positive productivity shock examined in the text resulted in no change in the bond rate.

(a) Discuss the factors in a firm's investment decision that limit the amount of capital investment purchases it is willing to make at any point in time.

(b) Discuss the factors that limit the quantity of savings a household is willing to establish at any point in time.

(c) Show that the equilibrium bond rate is also unaffected by a negative productivity shock by conducting the graphic analysis similar to that in the text.

2. The example of an intratemporal preference shock examined in the text resulted in no change in the bond rate.

(a) Illustrate with the graphic analysis of a preference shock how the equilibrium bond rate is affected when an increase in the intensity of preference for current consumption dominates a decrease in the intensity of preference for leisure with respect to household savings.

(b) Is this shock purely intratemporal? Explain.

(c) What effect would this shock have on employment and the price level in comparison with the intratemporal shock examined in the text?

3. The example of an intertemporal preference shock examined in the text resulted in a higher bond rate.

(a) Give an intuitive explanation for this rise in the bond rate.

(b) Illustrate the effect of an intertemporal shock on the general equilibrium of the economy in the case where an increase in the intensity of preference for consumption is dominated by an increase in the intensity of preference for leisure with respect to the level of current consumption.

(c) What effect does the shock examined in (b) have on employment and prices in comparison with the intertemporal shock examined in the text?

*4. Suppose the economy underwent a purely *transitory* positive productivity shock.

(a) How would the shock be likely to affect households' decisions?

(b) How would it be likely to affect firms' decisions?

(c) Would it have any affect on the bond rate?

*5. Suppose the intratemporal preference shock described in the text is permanent rather than transitory.

(a) How would the shock be likely to affect the decisions of the monetary authority?

(b) What is likely to happen to the economy's long-run performance?

REFERENCES

Hoover, Kevin D. 1988. *The New Classical Macroeconomics: A Skeptical Inquiry.* Oxford and New York: Basil Blackwell.

Horvath, Michael T. K. 1994. "Circularity and Cyclicality: Aggregate Fluctuations from Independent Sectoral Shocks." Unpublished manuscript.

King, Robert G., and Sergio Rebelo. 1990. "Public Policy and Economic Growth: Developing Neoclassical Implications." *Journal of Political Economy* 98 (October): S126–S150.

Kydland, Finn E., and Edward C. Prescott. 1982. "Time to Build and Aggregate Fluctuations." *Econometrica* 50 (November): 1345–1370.

Leeper, Eric M., and Christopher A. Sims. 1994. "Toward a Modern Macroeconomic Model Usable for Policy Analysis." Unpublished manuscript.

Long, John B., and Charles I. Plosser. 1983. "Real Business Cycles." *Journal of Political Economy* 91 (February): 39–69.

Lucas, Robert E., Jr. 1987. *Models of Business Cycles*. Oxford and New York: Basil Blackwell.

CHAPTER 11

STABILIZATION POLICY WHEN FIRMS SET PRICES IN ADVANCE

In Chapter 10, the economy's response to total factor productivity shocks is described in the context of a model in which all economic agents (households, firms, and the government) have full information and adjustment costs are assumed to be zero. Under those assumptions, the economy is demonstrated to adjust rapidly to full employment, which implies that the first of the two objectives of monetary policy is always met. In addition, a monetary policy response to the shock exists that can simultaneously generate the second policy objective of a stable price level without compromising the full-employment objective. This model also carries predictions on the short-run behavior of the labor market. One prediction is that employment fully adjusts to productivity shocks within the time horizon of interest for the study of monetary policy. That time horizon is assumed to be approximately one year and corresponds to the duration of a single "period" in the model over which the comparative statics analysis is performed. However, in actual economies, output tends to fluctuate around its full-employment level over longer time periods, during which the level of employment is found to be positively correlated, or to rise and fall, with the short-run fluctuations in output.

One potential cause of short-run employment fluctuations could be the "stickiness" of good prices. For example, if firms set prices in advance of, say, a positive productivity shock, households will not experience the increase in real money balances that would otherwise accompany the price decline (as occurs, for example, in the model described in Chapter 10). Such inflexibility in real balances imposes a liquidity constraint on households that limits their ability to raise consumption to obtain higher levels of utility.[1] However, households may

---

[1] In modern macro models, this corresponds to a "cash-in-advance" constraint on consumption purchases. See Grandmont and Younes (1972) and Lucas (1980) for early descriptions of the rationale for this constraint and how it is used in modeling.

partially loosen the constraint by increasing the velocity of money. An increase in velocity implies that a greater volume of real transactions is conducted for a given level of real money balances. Such response places a greater demand on the households' resource time, which reduces their willingness to offer labor services to the market. Therefore, in equilibrium, employment falls to a level below full employment and output is correspondingly lower than it otherwise would be had prices been allowed to adjust fully.

If such a situation persists for a sufficiently long period of time, the monetary authority may have a role to play in relaxing the households' liquidity constraint. That is, with prices fixed in the short-run, an increase in the nominal supply of money will increase real money balances and households' consumption can rise. In fact, if the monetary authority is able to supply just the right amount of additional liquidity (or money) to the economy, the labor/leisure decision will not be affected in the short run. Households will make that decision in a way consistent with full employment. It turns out that this quantity of money also coincides with an unchanged price level. Therefore, in this particular case, monetary policy achieves both of its policy objectives of maintaining full employment and a stable price level. In a sense, the "stickiness" of goods prices is rendered optimal by the actions of the monetary authority. These results are illustrated by two examples, one in which the monetary authority does not respond to the productivity shock and one in which it does.

In the final sections of this chapter, the complication of preference shocks is added to the model. In that case, the monetary authority faces a "signal extraction" problem because the productivity shock is confounded with the preference shock. Consequently, its policy actions may induce levels of employment, output, and prices that do not fully achieve the policy objectives. If the mistakes in the policy are severe enough, the economy can actually be made worse in terms of the policy objectives than it would have been had no policy action been taken.

11.1   PRICE SETTING BY FIRMS[2]

In the preceding chapter, firms' decisions are based on full information, which includes knowledge of the current period's productivity level. Refer to Figure

---

[2]From the micro theory of the firm, price-setting behavior is associated with monopoly power, because firms that are competitive in the product markets are price-takers in those markets. One branch of the literature on "sticky prices" assumes that firms produce unique products and thus command some degree of monopoly power to set prices. That monopoly power is mitigated by the existence of close substitutes for the firms' products. See, for example, Yun (1994). A second branch of this literature maintains the assumption of competitive but long-lived firms that set prices at values that are expected to clear the respective product markets. For example, see King (1990), Cho and Cooley (1992), and Ireland (1994). A third branch of this literature has firms continually monitoring the demand for their products and setting prices sequentially as trading takes place. See Lucas and Woodford (1993) and Eden (1994).

11.1(A). With that information, firms make their labor demand and investment decisions. The equilibrium goods price and nominal wage rate are determined jointly by these decisions of firms and the decisions made by households and by the monetary authority. However, firms may incur some costs when changing prices that would preclude them from making quick price adjustments each period.[3] The slow adjustment process can be characterized in the model by having firms set their price of goods at the beginning of each period *prior* to the realization of any shocks for the period, such as the productivity shock and perhaps a preference shock. Refer to Figure 11.1(B). Because productivity shocks are permanent, firms predict that the level of productivity for the upcoming period is unchanged over whatever it was in the previous period. Preference shocks are assumed to be transitory and to dissipate before the end of the period, so that preferences are always treated as if they were invariant from period to period. With prices set, firms observe their own productivity shock and use that information to select their labor demand schedule and make their investment decision. Then adjustments follow in the nominal wage, the bond rate, and quantities in various markets that result in a new short-run equilibrium for the economy.

For the purpose of analysis, assume that at the beginning of the period, the firms in the model set their product prices to yield a price level of P_0. They then

Figure 11.1

The Timing of New Information and Decisions (A) Without Price Setting and (B) With Price Setting, in the Absence of Preference Shocks

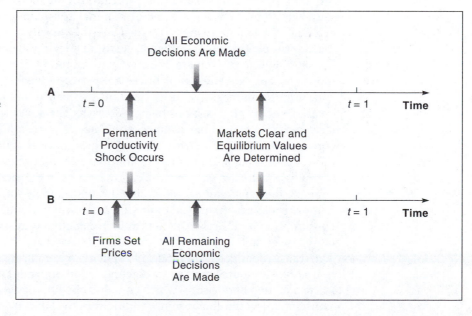

---

[3]The literature is somewhat divided on the causes of sluggish price adjustment. In some models, the costs are treated literally as adjustment or transactions costs and are called "menu costs." Other models treat the firms' preannounced product prices as implicit contracts between firms and households that deter firms from making rapid price adjustments. Either of these potential sources of price "stickiness" is consistent with the qualitative theoretical results of this chapter.

observe a positive total factor productivity shock, such that the level of technology for the period rises from θ_0 to θ_1. There are no preference shocks. In Figure 11.2, this corresponds to an increase in labor demand that shifts the labor demand schedule in the lower left panel to the right from $N^d(\theta_0)$ to $N^d(\theta_1)$. Because this productivity shock is permanent, it also increases the demand for capital by firms, which raises their financing requirements and is reflected in a rightward shift in the bond supply schedule from $(B/P)^s(\theta_0)$ to $(B/P)^s(\theta_1)$ as shown in the lower right panel. To identify the final equilibria in the money, bond, labor, and goods markets, we must examine the decisions made by the representative household and by the monetary authority.

11.2   LIQUIDITY-CONSTRAINED HOUSEHOLDS

In the model in Chapter 10, households made their labor/leisure, consumption/savings, and portfolio allocation decisions with full knowledge of the productivity shocks and of the decisions that were to be taken by firms and by the monetary authority. Refer to Figure 11.1. The same is true in the model examined in this chapter. However, households must hold precisely the nominal quantity of money that is supplied by the monetary authority, which limits the quantity of nominal consumption expenditures that households can make. The only way to increase the volume of nominal consumption expenditures for a given nominal money supply is to increase the velocity of circulation of money within the period. Because that is costly in the way described in Chapter 3, households cannot increase velocity with impunity. The costs are explicitly modeled here. Nonetheless, if prices are perfectly flexible, the volume of real consumption purchases is not constrained because households need not increase velocity. That is, a positive productivity shock induces a fall in the price level such that real money balances rise. Hence, households can raise their real consumption purchases without incurring additional transaction costs, even though nominal consumption expenditures may not change.

When prices are set in advance, however, as in the model examined in this chapter, the constraint on the nominal money supply imposed by the money authority also constrains real money balances and thus limits the volume of real consumption purchases. Attempts at increasing the velocity of money in circulation are curtailed by the rise in transaction costs that are borne by households. The transactions costs are modeled explicitly by requiring an allocation of the households' resource time to transacting.[4] Consequently, less time is available for production and leisure, which can alter the households' labor/leisure decisions and affect the equilibrium conditions in the labor market.

If prices were flexible, the improved technology would have caused the household to increase the value it placed on its leisure time such that the labor supply schedule in the lower left panel of Figure 11.2 would have shifted back

---

[4]This allocation of time corresponds to the "market time" in Chapter 1. It is consistent with the "shopping time" models of Wang and Yip (1992) and the multiple means of payment models of Marquis and Reffett (1994) and Schreft (1992).

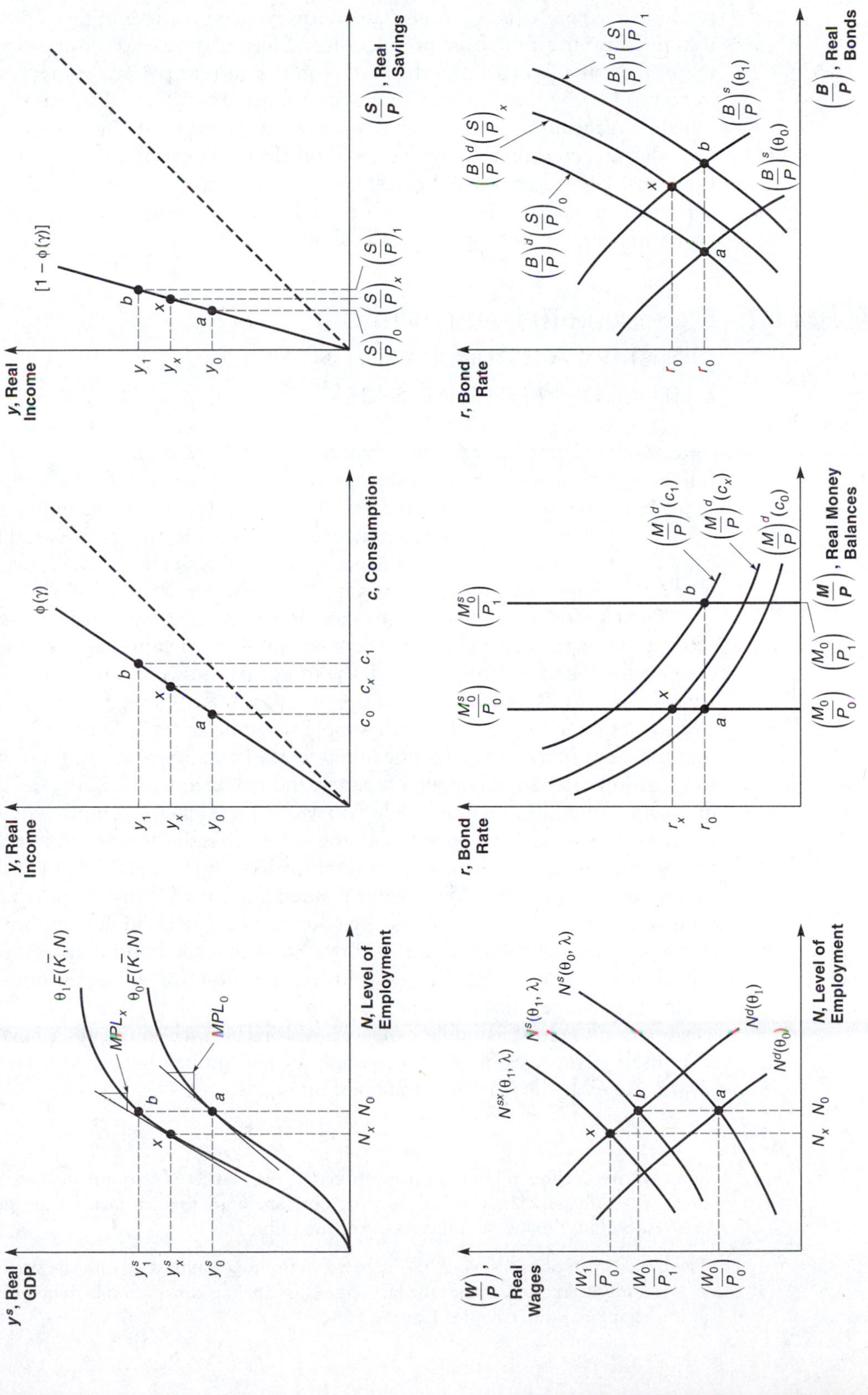

Figure 11.2   Analysis of the Economy's Response to a Positive Productivity Shock When Firms Set Prices in Advance in the Absence of Preference Shocks, and Without Monetary Accommodation

to the left from $N^s(\theta_0,\lambda)$ to $N^s(\theta_1,\lambda)$. However, with the liquidity constraint draining resource time from production and leisure, households further reduce their labor supply offered to the market in the current period,[5] as represented in Figure 11.2 by the shift back to the curve labeled $N^{sx}(\theta_1,\lambda)$. This labor supply schedule is included in the set of temporary decisions made by households on labor/leisure, consumption/savings, and portfolio allocation that combine with the firms' labor demand and investment decisions to produce the equilibrium described in section 11.3, in which the monetary authority does not alter its policy in response to the productivity shock.

11.3   EQUILIBRIUM RESPONSE WITHOUT MONETARY ACCOMMODATION IN THE ABSENCE OF PREFERENCE SHOCKS

Referring to Figure 11.2, suppose that at date $t = 0$ the economy is in the initial full-employment equilibrium characterized by the values with the subscript zero that are plotted at points denoted "a" on the graphs. At the beginning of the period, the economy is subjected only to a once-and-for-all positive total factor productivity shock. It receives no shocks in the next period, which begins at date $t = 1$. How does the economy adjust over the two periods?

When prices are not set in advance, the response is identical to that described in the preceding chapter. The final equilibrium values are portrayed in the graphs by points denoted "b." If the monetary authority fails to accommodate the shock, as shown in the lower left panel, the labor demand schedule shifts right to $N^d(\theta_1)$ and the labor supply schedule shifts to left to $N^s(\theta_1,\lambda)$ so that the labor market clears at the initial level of employment N_0. Output rises to y_1^s, as indicated in the upper left panel, and real income rises to y_1, as shown in the upper middle and upper right panels. The total factor productivity shock increases the demand for investment goods, which induces firms to issue more bonds and the supply schedule shifts right from $(B/P)^s(\theta_0)$ to $(B/P)^s(\theta_1)$ as shown in the lower right panel. The greater financing needs of firms are fully accommodated by an increase in savings by households. The bond demand schedule shifts right to $(B/P)^d(S/P)_1$ from $(B/P)^d(S/P)_0$ so that the bond market clears at the initial bond rate r_0.[6] The increase in consumption to c_1 raises the household demand for money and the money demand schedule shifts right to $(M/P)^d(c_1)$, as shown in the lower middle panel. To restore balance to the asset portfolios of households, prices fall and the supply of real money balances increases to (M_0/P_1) to clear the market at the bond rate r_0.

---

[5]Some of this decline in labor services offered to the market is also intended to replace the lost leisure associated with the greater cost of transacting. In fact, leisure time increases to offset the loss in utility from consumption.

[6]The breakdown of real savings $(S/P)_1$ between nominal savings, S, and the price level, P, is not important here, hence the labeling. This labeling convention is frequently used in this chapter and in Chapter 12.

However, when prices are fixed in advance and when there is no monetary accommodation, the labor supply schedule shifts to the curve labeled $N^{sx}(\theta_1,\lambda)$ as described above. The nominal wage rises from its initial level of W_0 to W_1 to clear the market. That occurs at an equilibrium denoted by "x" in the lower left panel of Figure 11.2, where employment is below the initial full-employment level N_0 and real wages are higher than they otherwise would have been. The higher real wages reflect the fact that the marginal product of labor has increased from MPL_0 to MPL_x as shown in the upper left panel, where the firm has shifted production to the improved technology that enables it to raise output to y_x^s even though employment has fallen. The higher level of output corresponds to an increase in real income to y_x. The question then is: What is happening in the goods market?

The positive total factor productivity shock has increased the firms' demand for investment goods and the additional financing requirements induce a rightward shift in the bond supply schedule to $(B/P)^s(\theta_1)$, as shown in the lower right panel of Figure 11.2. However, the liquidity constraint imposed on the household by the inflexibility of prices and the lack of monetary accommodation to the productivity shock diverts time away from production and ultimately reduces household income from what it otherwise would have been. Consumption rises to only c_x, as shown in the upper middle panel, and savings rise to only $(S/P)_x$, as shown in the upper right panel. The lesser increase in savings is reflected in a weaker increase in bond demand, such that the bond demand schedule shifts only to $(B/P)^d(S/P)_x$. At the initial bond rate r_0, there is an excess supply of bonds. Therefore, to clear the bond market, the bond rate must rise to r_x. The weaker increase in consumption to c_x coincides with a more modest increase in the demand for money by households. The money demand schedule shifts only to $(M/P)^d(c_x)$ so that equilibrium is restored at the higher bond rate r_x, given that the quantity of real cash balances is fixed at (M_0/P_0).

Eventually, firms will adjust prices to reflect the productivity shock that occurred at the beginning of the period just after date $t = 0$. This action is modeled by assuming that full adjustment takes place after one period. Therefore, at the beginning of the subsequent period following date $t = 1$, the price level is reset by firms to reflect all information that is available just prior to $t = 1$. Consequently, prices fall to a level given by P_1. We assume that no additional shocks occur at date $t = 2$. The price decline raises real money balances so that the additional liquidity shifts the money supply schedule to the right in the lower middle panel to the final position indicated by (M_0^s/P_1). Households are then able to increase their consumption to desired levels without incurring the additional transaction costs that require the use of their resource time. The labor supply schedule is therefore replaced by one that fully reflects the new technology, as labeled in the lower left panel of Figure 11.2 by $N^s(\theta_1,\lambda)$. The labor market clears at the lower real wage given by (W_0/P_1), which corresponds to full employment, N_0, and yields the full-employment levels of output, y_1^s, and income, y_1. Real money balances have risen to (M_0/P_1) so that the bond rate falls back to its initial position r_0.

The time paths for these variables are illustrated in Figure 11.3. Note that the economy shows some fluctuations that are undesirable in terms of the policy objectives of the monetary authority. In response to a positive productivity shock, output initially increases and employment falls. Therefore, output rises less than it would have if full employment had been maintained. Moreover, even after the period of weak output subsides and the economy adjusts back to full employment, prices do not remain stable. They fall to reflect the fact that the monetary authority failed to provide a sufficient quantity of money to the economy to meet its growing liquidity needs. Therefore, over the two periods when the economy is adjusting to the productivity shock, both of the monetary policy objectives are compromised.

Figure 11.3   Time Paths for the Macroeconomic Variables in Response to a Positive Productivity Shock in the Absence of a Preference Shock, When Firms Set Prices in Advance, and There is No Monetary Accommodation

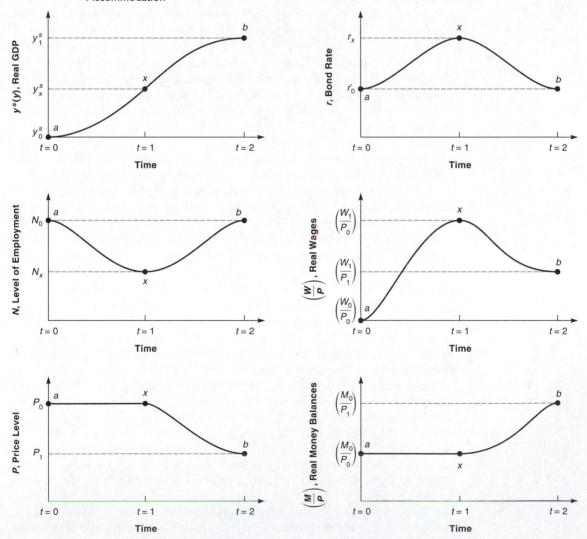

11.4 EQUILIBRIUM RESPONSE WITH MONETARY ACCOMMODATION IN THE ABSENCE OF PREFERENCE SOCKS

In the preceding example, the inability of prices to adjust downward to the positive productivity shock imposed a liquidity constraint on the purchase of consumption goods, inducing households to divert time away from production and into transactions. As a consequence, there is a temporary decline in employment, causing output to be lower than it otherwise would have been. Once prices are reset by firms to reflect the productivity shock, output increases to its full-employment level. The households' liquidity constraint could have been alleviated by the monetary authority had it chosen to increase the nominal money supply in response to the productivity shock. We can examine that effect with reference to Figure 11.4.

The initial equilibrium values have the subscript zero and are represented by points in the graphs denoted "a." At the beginning of the period, at date $t = 0$, firms set their product prices at P_0. The productivity shock is then observed by all agents in the economy. Firms respond by increasing their demand for labor and the demand schedule shifts to the right from $N^d(\theta_0)$ to $N^d(\theta_1)$ in the lower left panel of Figure 11.4. They also increase their demand for investment goods, which raises their financing needs and the bond supply schedule shifts to the right to $(B/P)^s(\theta_1)$ as shown in the lower right panel. Households want to take advantage of the productivity improvement by increasing leisure for any given real wage (which represents the opportunity cost of an additional unit of leisure), and by increasing consumption both today and tomorrow, where the latter requires additional savings. As a consequence, the labor supply schedule shown in the lower left panel shifts left from $N^s(\theta_0,\lambda)$ to $N^s(\theta_1,\lambda)$ and consumption and savings rise by the same percentage, as indicated in the upper middle and upper right panels.

However, for the household to implement those plans it must experience an increase in real money balances to raise its consumption purchases without sacrificing time for transacting that could otherwise go to production and thereby increase its real income. That is, the new equilibrium in the labor market must coincide with point "b" in the lower left panel. Suppose the monetary authority not only recognizes this need but is able to increase the nominal money supply by just the right quantity to keep the bond rate fixed at r_0. In that case, the real money supply would rise from (M_0/P_0) to (M_1/P_0) with the corresponding rightward shift in the money supply schedule to (M_1^s/P_0) as shown in the middle panel of Figure 11.4. Prices do not have to fall for real money balances to rise and thereby relax the liquidity constraint that households would otherwise experience. As shown by the time paths for the macroeconomic variables in Figure 11.5, the economy is able to absorb the positive productivity shock by increasing output while remaining at full employment without a change in the price level. Thus, the monetary authority is able to exactly achieve its policy objectives by accommodating the greater liquidity needs of the growing economy with an increase in the nominal money supply.

Figure 11.4   Analysis of the Economy's Response to a Positive Productivity Shock When Firms Set Prices in Advance, in the Absence of Preference Shocks, and With Monetary Accommodation

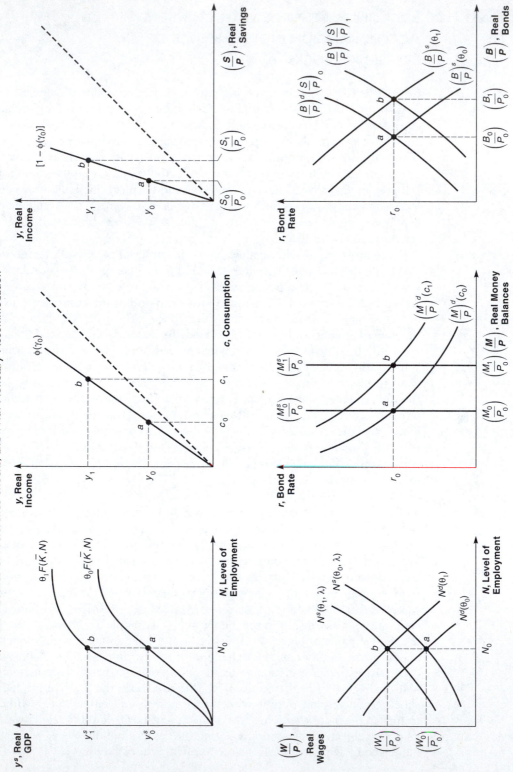

Figure 11.5   Time Paths for the Macroeconomic Variables in Response to a Positive Productivity Shock in the Absence of a Preference Shock, When Firms Set Prices in Advance, and There is a Monetary Accommodation

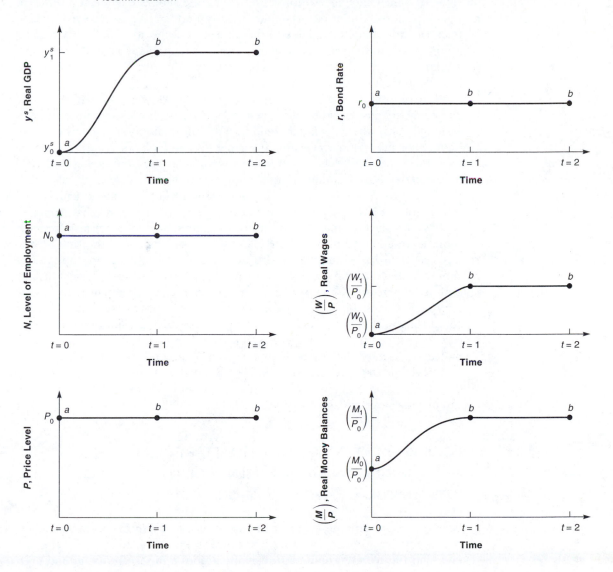

11.5   MONETARY POLICY AND THE SIGNAL EXTRACTION PROBLEM

In actual economies, when the monetary authority makes a policy decision, it is based on information collected from a variety of sources. The sources include surveys of households and firms and opinions of professional economists, as well as data from the financial markets and from the nonfinancial sectors of the economy. As the economy undergoes shocks, the economic significance of the shocks is reflected in the various sources of information. However, shocks have a variety of causes, some of which may call for a monetary policy response and some of which may not. Unfortunately, separate shocks that suggest different policy responses often occur simultaneously and cannot be resolved quickly from the information available to the monetary authority. The policy makers therefore form the best judgments of which they are capable and often must attempt to correct their mistakes as best they can *ex post*. The following examples illustrate how such problems can arise.

For the purpose of exposition, economic shocks were categorized in the preceding chapter as either permanent productivity shocks or transitory preference shocks, where the latter could be either intratemporal or intertemporal. Permanent shocks are irreversible and generally call for a policy response by the monetary authority, whereas transitory shocks are self-correcting and of a duration that is shorter than the time required for monetary policy to take effect on the economy. Consequently, the monetary authority wants to process the information it has on the economy in such a way that it can resolve economic shocks into their permanent and transitory components. It must address the signal extraction problem, whereby individual signals about the state of the economy can have multiple causes. In monetary policy, the appropriate response to that problem depends on the exact nature of the cause.[7] The monetary authority therefore has an incentive to try to identify the preference shock. One approach is to use history as a guide. For example, consumer sentiment surveys could suggest that households are anticipating greater consumption in the future. Is that finding random, perhaps due to the timing of the survey, or does it indicate a lasting change, perhaps reflecting expectations of higher income? Some evidence on that question could be obtained by analyzing the past history of survey responses. However, neither surveys nor other sources of information can provide a certain answer.

11.6   EQUILIBRIUM RESPONSE WITH MONETARY ACCOMMODATION IN THE PRESENCE OF AN INTRATEMPORAL PREFERENCE SHOCK

We now can reexamine the preceding example, in which the economy undergoes a positive productivity shock when firms set prices in advance, for the case in which the economy simultaneously undergoes a purely intratemporal preference shock that favors more consumption and less leisure. To recognize the transitory nature of the preference shock, the timing of events during the period is structured as shown in Figure 11.6. At the beginning of the period, date

---

[7]Lucas (1977) discusses the signal extraction problem in a slightly different context in which firms observe the "signals" they receive from the equilibrium product prices as indicators of demand, and then attempt to sort out how much is due to permanent versus transitory demand shocks and much is due to unexpected changes in monetary policy.

Figure 11.6

The Timing of New Information and Decisions with Price Setting in the Presence of Transitory Preference Shocks

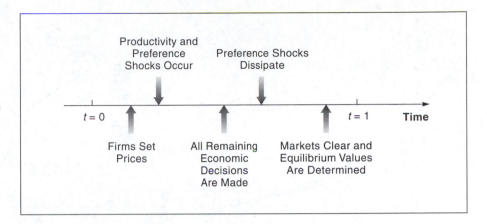

$t = 0$, firms set prices. The productivity and preference shocks occur, but their macroeconomic effects cannot be resolved individually by the monetary authority. Firms make their labor demand and investment decisions, households make their consumption/savings, labor/leisure, and portfolio allocation decisions, and the monetary authority chooses a policy that is known to both households and firms. The transitory preference shock then dissipates as households adjust their decisions, and markets clear as the economy moves to a new equilibrium at the end of the period, date $t = 1$. With that timing of information and decisions, the preference shock affects the final equilibrium only to the extent that monetary policy decisions are altered incorrectly. Because we want to indicate qualitatively how the lack of knowledge of preference shocks can lead to mistaken policies, we assume for simplicity that the monetary authority acts as though it believes no preference shock occurred.[8]

The analysis proceeds as follows. After the shocks occur and the decisions of households and firms are made, the new general equilibrium to which the economy would adjust if the preference shock were permanent is identified. The effects of the liquidity constraint on the households' decisions are portrayed graphically. Monetary policy is chosen to offset fully the effects of the liquidity constraint. After the policy action is taken, the preference shock dissipates and the economy establishes a new short-run general equilibrium. The consequences of the monetary authority's inability to solve the signal extraction problem completely are then analyzed.

In Figure 11.7, the initial equilibrium is again identified by variables with the subscript zero and their values are plotted on the graphs at points denoted "a." With prices set by firms at P_0, the productivity shock occurs. In isolation, the productivity shock causes firms to increase their demand for labor and investment goods. The labor demand schedule shifts right from $N^d(\theta_0)$ to $N^d(\theta_1)$ as shown in the lower left panel, and the bond supply schedule shifts right to $(B/P)^s(\theta_1)$ as shown in the lower right panel. Had prices remained flexible,

---

[8]The analysis is entirely general in this respect, as only the unanticipated change in preferences induces policy mistakes.

Figure 11.7   Analysis of the Economy's Response to a Positive Productivity Shock in the Presence of an Intratemporal Preference Shock

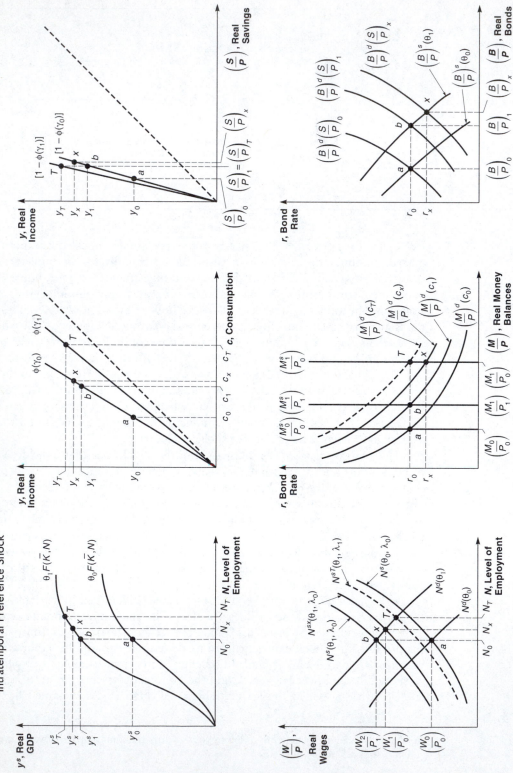

households would reduce their willingness to offer labor services to the market and the labor supply schedule would shift to the left to $N^s(\theta_1, \lambda_0)$ so that the labor market clears at N_0. At the improved level of technology, θ_1, output rises to y_1^s, which induces an increase in income to y_1, and consumption and savings rise to c_1 and $(S/P)_1$, respectively, as indicated in the upper panels.

However, with prices fixed, households experience a liquidity constraint on consumption purchases unless the monetary authority accommodates the productivity shock with an increase in the money supply. Therefore, as in a preceding example, as long as households remain liquidity constrained in their consumption purchases, the quantity of labor they supply to the market is reduced, and the economy reaches a short-run general equilibrium with employment and output below their full-employment levels. As before, the monetary authority wants to relax the liquidity constraint so that the economy fully absorbs the productivity shock and establishes a new general equilibrium corresponding to the values plotted on the graphs in Figure 11.7 as points "b."

The additional complication is the intratemporal preference shock that favors more consumption and less savings. In that case, the intensity of preference for consumption increases from γ_0 to γ_1, as shown in the upper middle panel, and the savings rate declines to $[1 - \phi(\gamma_1)]$ as shown in the upper right panel. At the same time, the intensity of preference for leisure falls to λ_1 from λ_0 and the labor supply schedule shifts right to $N^{sT}(\theta_1, \lambda_1)$ as shown in the lower left panel. Note that dashed lines indicate temporary shifts in household preferences. In the absence of liquidity constraints, the economy would tend toward a general equilibrium represented on the graphs in Figure 11.7 by the points labeled "T." The corresponding levels of employment, N_T, output, y_T^s, and income, y_T, exceed full-employment levels. At the higher level of real income, consumption would rise to c_T. However, the purely intratemporal preference shock has no net effect on savings, which then rises to $(S/P)_1$ as a response exclusively to the productivity shock. The increase in savings produces a greater demand for bonds, and the bond demand schedule in the lower right panel shifts to the right to $(B/P)^d(S/P)_1$ by an amount that just accommodates the increase in bond supply by firms so that the market clears at the original bond rate r_0.

In the money market, the heightened consumption raises households' demand for money, which is represented by a rightward shift in the money demand schedule to $(M/P)^d(c_T)$. Believing the shocks to be permanent, the monetary authority wants to accommodate the increase in money demand fully by raising real balances to (M_1/P_0) to prevent the households from becoming liquidity constrained in their consumption purchases. Therefore, the nominal money supply rises to M_1^s as the real money supply schedule shifts right to (M_1^s/P_0) in anticipation of money market equilibrium at the bond rate r_0. After the policy action is taken, the preference shock dissipates and households have excess liquidity. Less of their resource time is needed to conduct transactions and, as a consequence, they are more willing to supply labor to the market. The labor supply schedule does not shift all the way to $N^s(\theta_1, \lambda_0)$, which is the full unconstrained response to the productivity shock. Instead, it has a more modest leftward shift as illustrated by the new position labeled $N^{sx}(\theta_1, \lambda_0)$. Nominal wages rise to W_1 and the labor market clears at N_x, which exceeds full employment. Output, at y_x^s, and income, at y_x, are also above their full-employment levels as shown in the upper panels. The additional income in excess of the new full-employment level of y_1 is allocated between consumption and savings as equal percentage increases in their respective levels to c_x and $(S/P)_x$.

The higher level of savings corresponds to an increase in the demand for bonds, and the bond demand schedule shifts right to $(B/P)^d(S/P)_x$. The increase in bond demand precipitates a decline in the bond rate to r_x to clear the bond market. In the money market, the level of consumption c_x corresponds to a leftward shift in the money demand schedule from its temporary position indicated by $(M/P)^d(c_T)$ to its end-of-period, or date $t = 1$, position $(M/P)^d(c_x)$, and the money market clears at the lower bond rate r_x. As long as prices remain fixed at P_0, the economy will sustain the new general equilibrium reached at date $t = 1$, which is represented by the values labeled "x" on the graphs in Figure 11.7.

Eventually, firms will adjust their prices to reflect fully the permanent productivity shock. Assume that the price adjustments occur at the beginning of the next period, date $t = 1$, and are not followed by any additional productivity or preference shocks during that period. In that case, prices rise to, say P_1 to absorb the excess liquidity associated with the oversupply of money by the monetary authority. The labor supply schedule shifts to its unconstrained position $N^s(\theta_1, \lambda_0)$, which represents the labor/leisure decisions by households that fully reflect the greater value of their resource time inherent in the improved technology, measured by θ_1, given their intensity of preference for leisure, λ_0. Firms bid up the nominal wage to W_2, so that the labor market clears at the new real wage rate of (W_2/P_1) and at a level of employment that corresponds to full employment, N_0, as shown in the lower left panel of Figure 11.7. Output and income fall to their new respective full-employment levels of y_1^s and y_1 as indicated in the upper panels, and consumption and savings both decline. At the lower level of savings, $(S/P)_1$, the bond demand schedule shifts left to $(B/P)^d(S/P)_1$, as shown in the lower right panel, and the bond rate rises to r_0 to clear the bond market. The decline in consumption to c_1 reduces the demand for money and the money demand schedule shifts leftward to $(M/P)^d(c_1)$, as shown in the lower middle panel. For the money market to clear at the equilibrium bond rate r_0, prices must have risen sufficiently to reduce the level of real money balances to (M_1/P_1).

At the end of the second period after the shocks, or at date $t = 2$, the economy attains a new general equilibrium as depicted in Figure 11.7 by the points labeled "b" on the graphs. The general equilibrium is consistent with full-employment conditions in the economy under the improved level of technology resulting from the permanent productivity shock that occurred at date $t = 0$. The path the economy followed over the two periods that it took to absorb the shock is displayed in Figure 11.8. Note that neither of the policy objectives of full employment and stable prices have been fully achieved during the period. By treating the preference shock's transitory effects on the economy as though they were permanent, the monetary authority oversupplied money. The excess supply of money produced an unwanted short-run stimulus to the economy at date $t = 1$, as the bond rate fell and employment and output rose above their

Figure 11.8   Time Paths for the Macroeconomic Variables in Response to a Positive Productivity Shock in the Presence of an Intratemporal Preference Shock When Firms Set Prices in Advance

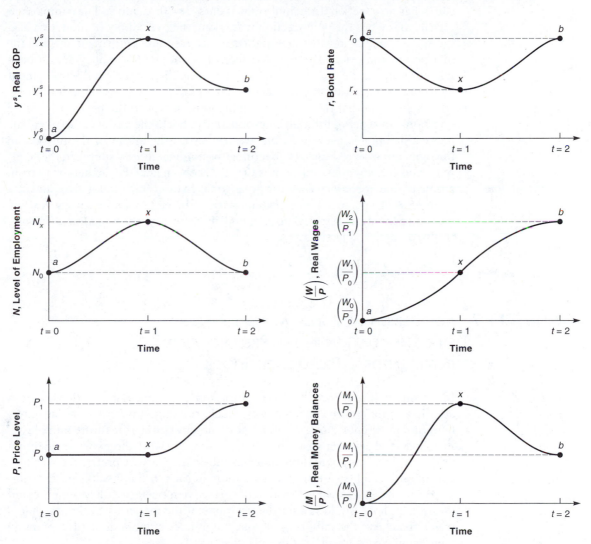

full-employment levels. In the second period after the productivity shock, the economy absorbed the excess supply of money with an increase in the money price of goods, such that the price level rose, as employment and output were restored to their full-employment levels.

As Figure 11.8 illustrates, the monetary authority failed to achieve its policy objectives precisely. However, was the policy action beneficial nonetheless? That is, did the policy action bring the performance of the economy more closely into line the policy objectives, or did it cause the economy to perform more poorly in terms of the policy objectives? Would the economy have been better off had no policy action been taken? To consider these questions, we can compare the time path of the economy in the presence of the policy action as shown in Figure 11.8 with the time path of the economy in the absence of monetary policy action as shown in Figure 11.3. Note that the transitory preference shock has no effect on the equilibrium at dates $t = 0, 1,$ and 2. The comparison reveals that when the policy action was taken, the oversupply of money caused output and employment to exceed their respective full-employment levels in the first period and prices to rise in the second period; had no policy action been taken, output and employment would have been below their full-employment levels in the first period and prices would have fallen in the second period. These results illustrate that there is no unambiguous answer to the previously posed questions. In general, for a given productivity shock, the stronger (weaker) the unidentified preference shock, the greater (lesser) the extent of the mistake in the monetary policy decisions governing the nominal money supply in the economy, and the more (less) likely it is that the economy will be farther away from a time path that characterizes the policy objectives of full employment and stable prices. The preceding exercise emphasizes the fact that an accurate reading on the economy is essential to a sound monetary policy aimed at achieving short-run policy objectives.

11.7 EQUILIBRIUM RESPONSE WITH MONETARY ACCOMMODATION IN THE PRESENCE OF AN INTERTEMPORAL PREFERENCE SHOCK

Intertemporal preference shocks can also cause policy mistakes. Suppose that in addition to the positive productivity shock, the economy undergoes an intertemporal preference shock such that households discount the future more heavily. That is, they want to receive more utility today at the expense of future utility. In this case, households increase their intensity of preference for both consumption and leisure and demand more of each. If the shock is purely transitory, in that it dissipates before any corrective monetary policy action could take effect, how would it alter the decisions of the monetary authority that is trying to achieve the stabilization policy objectives of maintaining full employment in an environment of stable prices?

This situation is represented graphically in Figure 11.9. The initial full-employment equilibrium values again have the subscript zero and are plotted on the graphs at points denoted "a." The positive productivity shock increases the firms' demand for labor, shifting the labor demand schedule to the right from $N^d(\theta_0)$ to $N^d(\theta_1)$ in the lower right panel, and the demand for investment goods, shifting the bond supply schedule from $(B/P)^s(\theta_0)$ to $(B/P)^s(\theta_1)$ in the lower right panel. Households reduce their willingness to supply labor in response to the productivity shock, which increases the value of the households' resource time. The labor supply schedule shifts to the left from $N^s(\theta_0,\lambda_0)$ to $N^s(\theta_1,\lambda_0)$, as shown in the lower right panel. If prices were flexible, or if the monetary authority exactly accommodated the increase in money demand associated with the increase in real income, the real economy would fully absorb

Figure 11.9   Analysis of the Economy's Response to a Positive Productivity Shock in the Presence of An Intertemporal Preference Shock

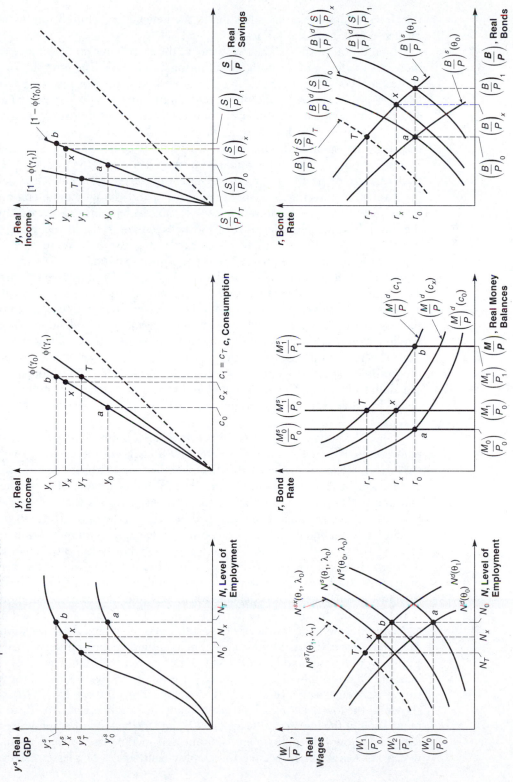

the shock in one period by adjusting to the new general equilibrium, which is plotted on the graphs as points "b."

In addition to the productivity shock, the intertemporal preference shock increases the demand for both consumption and leisure. The intensity of preference for consumption rises from γ_0 to γ_1 and the savings rate falls to $[1 - \phi(\gamma_1)]$ as shown in the upper middle and upper right panels of Figure 11.9. At the same time, the intensity of preference for leisure rises to λ_1 from λ_0 and the labor supply schedule shifts farther to the left to $N^{sT}(\theta_1,\lambda_1)$ as shown in the lower left panel. In the absence of any liquidity constraint, the labor market would clear at N_T and output and income would rise only to y_T^s and y_T, respectively. Given the strictly intertemporal nature of the preference shock as defined in Chapter 10, consumption would remain at c_1 and savings would temporarily fall to $(S/P)_T$. The decline in savings would cause a temporary leftward shift in the bond demand schedule to $(B/P)^d(S/P)_T$ as shown in the lower right panel, and the bond rate would tend to rise toward r_T to clear the bond market.

For the money market to clear at the equilibrium bond rate r_0, real balances would have to rise above their initial level (M_0/P_0). With prices fixed by firms at P_0, the increase in real balances could occur only if the monetary authority increased the nominal money supply. If it incorrectly attempted to accommodate the transitory preference shocks as well as the permanent productivity shock, it would raise the nominal money supply to M_1^s to prevent households' consumption purchases from being liquidity constrained. That policy is represented in the graphic model of Figure 11.9 by a rightward shift in the money supply schedule to (M_1^s/P_0). The economy would seek a new general equilibrium depicted by values for the macroeconomic variables plotted as points "T" on the graphs.

Once the policy is adopted and before its effects on the economy are fully realized, the preference shock dissipates and households increase their willingness to supply labor to the market. Employment tends to pick up and output and income begin to rise. However, the decline in the intensity of preference for consumption back to its original level, denoted γ_0, raises the savings rate to $[1 - \phi(\gamma_0)]$ and the bond demand schedule shifts to the right. The shift would precipitate a decline in the bond rate and the demand for money would begin to rise. Note that the increase in the demand for money is a movement along the demand curve labeled $(M/P)^d(c_1)$, which did not shift with the transitory preference shock that was strictly intertemporal. The decline in the bond rate therefore produces an excess demand for money that cannot be accommodated in the short run by an increase in real balances. That is, firms have fixed prices at P_0 and the monetary authority has established the nominal money supply at M_1^s. Consequently, households are once again liquidity constrained in their consumption purchases and become less willing to offer their labor services to the market. That response is represented by a weaker rightward shift of the labor supply schedule to $N^{sx}(\theta_1,\lambda_0)$ from its temporary position of $N^{sT}(\theta_1,\lambda_1)$ as shown in the lower left panel. Firms increase the nominal wage to W_1 to clear the market at the higher real wage (W_1/P_0) and at the level of employment N_x, which is below full employment. Output and income rise only to y_x^s and y_x, which are below the respective full-employment levels. The lesser increase in income reduces consumption to c_x and the money demand schedule shifts left to $(M/P)^d(c_x)$, which clears the money market at the bond rate r_x. Note that savings has a lesser increase to only $(S/P)_x$ and the bond demand schedule shifts to $(B/P)^d(S/P)_x$, thereby clearing the bond market at the new equilibrium bond rate of r_x.

By incorrectly attempting to accommodate the transitory preference shock, the monetary authority failed to supply the economy with enough money to prevent households from becoming liquidity constrained. In response, the economy reached a new general equilibrium depicted graphically by points labeled "x," at which employment and output are below their respective full-employment levels at the end of the first period after the shock, or at date $t = 1$.

At the end of the first period, firms adjust prices. If no additional shocks occur at date $t = 1$, prices will fall and relax the liquidity constraint. The labor supply schedule shifts right to $N^s(\theta_1, \lambda_0)$ as firms reduce the nominal wage to W_2 to clear the labor market at full employment, N_0. Output and income rise, leading to equal percentage increases in consumption and savings. The higher level of savings raises the demand for bonds, the bond demand schedule shifts to the right to $(B/P)^d(S/P)_1$, and the bond rate falls to r_0 to clear the bond market. The increase in consumption raises the demand for money, and the money demand schedule shifts to the right to $(M/P)^d(c_1)$. For the money market to clear at the equilibrium bond rate r_0, the price decline to P_1 was just sufficient to raise real balances to (M_1/P_1) as shown in the lower middle panels. The economy clears at the new full-employment general equilibrium at values corresponding to points labeled "b" on the graphs in Figure 11.9.

The time path the economy followed over the two periods that it took to absorb the productivity shock fully is shown in Figure 11.10. Again, the inappropriate policy response to the transitory preference shock caused the monetary authority to fail to accomplish fully either of its objectives of full employment and stable prices. It failed to supply a sufficient quantity of money in response to the positive productivity shock and the economy grew less rapidly than it otherwise would have during the first period, with employment falling below its full-employment level. A price decline followed during the second period. As was true in the example of an intratemporal preference shock, whether an active monetary policy designed to achieve short-run policy objectives can benefit the economy's actual performance in terms of the policy objectives depends on how well the monetary authority is able to distinguish the permanent from the transitory shocks to the economy.

11.8   SUMMARY

In the model examined in Chapter 10, the ability of agents to respond to new information is unimpaired. At the beginning of each period, the productivity shock is observed and households, firms, and the monetary authority make decisions with full knowledge of the other agents' objectives and constraints.

Figure 11.10 Time Paths for the Macroeconomic Variables in Response to a Positive Productivity Shock in the Presence of an Intertemporal Preference Shock When Firms Set Prices in Advance

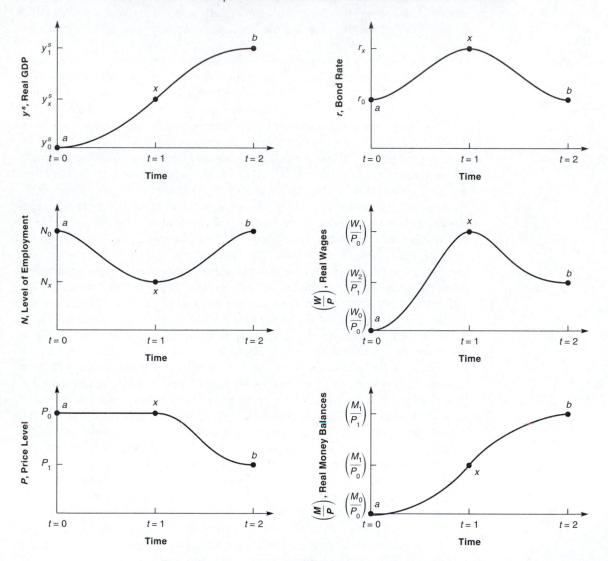

Consequently, the equilibrium the economy attains fully reflects all new information and, in the absence of additional shocks, the newly established prices and quantities would show no tendency to change in the future.

In this chapter, one alteration is made to that model. We assume that at the beginning of each period firms set the price of goods that are to be sold during that period prior to the realization of the productivity shock. Goods prices therefore reflect expectations of productivity for the period and the response that households, firms, and the monetary authority would have to that level of productivity. However, households are required to purchase consumption goods with money, the total supply of which is determined by the monetary authority. The quantity of money in circulation limits the nominal quantity of consumption purchases that households are able to make. When the productivity shock occurs, households and firms make their final decisions for the period that incorporate knowledge of the current period's monetary policy decision.

Two situations are examined initially. In the first, the monetary authority does not respond to a positive productivity shock. With the nominal money supply fixed and prices unchanged for the first period after the shock, real money balances are also fixed and households experience a liquidity constraint that limits their ability to expand their consumption purchases. To minimize the effect of the liquidity constraint on consumption, households increase the velocity of money by allocating more time to transacting, thereby reducing their willingness to offer labor services to the market. Consequently, the equilibrium levels of employment and output fall below their respective full-employment levels. In the second situation, the monetary authority takes an active role in accommodating the increase in the liquidity needs of the economy that result from the increase in output associated with the positive productivity shock. In this case, the monetary authority has an unimpeded view of the magnitude of the shock and is able to select a monetary policy that exactly achieves its policy objectives of maintaining full employment in an environment of stable prices.

The economic environment in which the monetary authority pursues these objectives is then altered by introducing a preference shock. Such shocks complicate the policy decisions in that, unlike the permanent productivity shocks that call for a policy response, they are transitory and dissipate before any policy action has time to take effect on the economy. Therefore, preference shocks serve only to confuse the policy makers by creating a so-called signal extraction problem. That is, the information or economic signals that the monetary authority receives on the state of the economy simultaneously reflect both the permanent productivity shocks and the transitory preference shocks. Because those two sources of changes in the economic signals require different policy responses, the monetary authority wants to resolve all signals into their component sources. However, such resolution is not possible *ex ante* and, as a consequence, policy mistakes are made. If the mistakes are large enough, the monetary authority's efforts to respond to short-run economic fluctuations, in comparison with a policy of ignoring such fluctuations, can actually worsen the economy's performance in terms of the policy objectives of allowing the economy to grow at its full-employment level while maintaining a stable price environment.

■ REVIEW QUESTIONS

1. The world oil supply shocks of 1973, 1979–1980, and 1990 preceded major recessions in the U.S. economy.
   (a) Assuming that these shocks were purely permanent negative productivity shocks, use the model developed in this chapter to illustrate how the economy would adjust to the shocks if firms set prices in advance and the monetary authority made no attempt to accommodate the shocks.

(b) What is the appropriate monetary policy response to this shock?

*(c) Did the Federal Reserve respond to the 1973 oil supply shock as you described in (b)? What was the consequence of its response? Show the consequence graphically.

2. Suppose a permanent negative oil supply shock occurs that is accompanied by a transitory shift in household preferences. If the monetary authority incorrectly perceives the preference shock to be permanent, illustrate graphically the policy mistakes that would be caused in the following cases.

(a) Households increase their intensity of preferences for leisure, but do not change their intensity of preference for consumption.

(b) Households increase their intensity of preference for consumption, but do not change their intensity of preference for leisure.

(c) The preference stock is purely intratemporal, favoring more consumption and less leisure time.

3. Suppose the economy undergoes a negative productivity shock accompanied by a transitory preference shock. Illustrate graphically the time path the economy would follow if the monetary authority mistakenly treats as permanent the following kinds of preference shocks.

(a) A purely intratemporal shock, with the households discounting the future more heavily.

(b) A shock identical to that in (a), with a slightly weaker intensity of preference for consumption.

(c) A shock identical to that in (a), with a slightly weaker intensity of preference for leisure.

*4. In the 1979–1980 world oil supply shock, the Organization for Petroleum Exporting Countries (OPEC) chose to restrict oil supplies in a way that would gradually increase oil prices over many months in accordance with a series of preannounced price targets.

(a) How should the "phasing-in" of higher oil prices affect the monetary authority's response to the shock?

(b) Does history suggest that the monetary authority responded as described in (a)? Explain.

*5. The history of cartels, such as OPEC, suggests that agreements to restrict supply artificially to achieve above-market prices tend to collapse over time, because members of the cartel always have an incentive to exceed their supply quotas and sell more of their output at the higher cartelized prices.

(a) Describe the policy the monetary authority would pursue if it believed a negative oil supply shock would last for only one year (one period) and would be completely reversed in the following year as the cartel's agreement collapsed. (Treat those events as two successive permanent productivity shocks.)

(b) Suppose the monetary authority pursues the policy described in the answer to (a), but the OPEC cartel manages to hold firm on the agreement in the second year. What would be the effects on the time path for the economy?

▨ REFERENCES

Cho, Jang-Ok, and Thomas F. Cooley. 1992. "The Business Cycle with Nominal Contracts." Unpublished manuscript, Queen's University (June).

Eden, Benjamin. 1994. "The Adjustment of Prices to Monetary Shocks When Trade Is Uncertain and Sequential." *Journal of Political Economy* 102 (June): 493–509.

Grandmont, Jean Michel, and Yves Younes. 1972. "On the Role of Money and the Existence of a Monetary Equilibrium." *Review of Economic Studies* 39 (July): 355–372.

Ireland, Peter N. 1994. "Monetary Policy with Nominal Price Rigidity." Unpublished manuscript, Federal Reserve Bank of Richmond (May).

King, Robert G. 1990. "Money and Business Cycles." Unpublished manuscript, University of Rochester (August).

Lucas, Robert E., Jr. 1977. "Understanding Business Cycles." *Carnegie-Rochester Conference Series on Public Policy, 5.*

Lucas, Robert E., Jr. and Woodford. 1993. "Real Effects of Monetary Policy Shocks in an Economy with Sequential Purchases." NBER Working Paper No. 4250 (January).

Marquis, Milton H., and Kevin L. Reffett. 1994. "New Technology Spillovers into the Payment System." *Economic Journal* 104 (September): 1123–1138.

Schreft, Stacey L. 1992. "Transactions Cost and the Use of Credit." *Economic Theory* 2(2): 283–296.

Wang, Ping, and Chang K. Y: 1992. "Alternative Approaches to Money and Growth." *Journal of Money, Credit and Banking* 24 (November): 553–562.

Yun, Tak. 1994. "Nominal Price Rigidity, Money Supply Endogeneity, and Business Cycles." Unpublished manuscript, University of Chicago (May).

CHAPTER 12

Stabilization Policy in the Presence of Long-term Nominal Wage Contracts

Chapter 11 examines an economy in which firms set prices in advance. When a positive productivity shock occurs, households are unable to raise their consumption to desired levels because of the lack of liquidity in their asset portfolios. That is, because of the inflexibility in prices, real money balances cannot rise unless the monetary authority intervenes with an increase in the nominal money supply. In the absence of such a policy response, the economy does not remain at full employment. However, when the monetary authority increases the nominal money supply, the liquidity constraint on consumption purchases is relaxed and the real economy expands, with output increasing toward its full-employment level where the productivity shock would be fully absorbed. In the terminology of Chapter 9, monetary policy is non-neutral, because the real economy is affected by the policy action. Preference shocks are transitory and assumed to dissipate more quickly than the time it takes for monetary policy actions to take effect. It is inappropriate for monetary policy to attempt to respond to them. Instead, the monetary authority must attempt to discern how much of the change in the economy's information signals is due to preference shocks versus productivity shocks and design a policy that would systematically respond to the latter while ignoring the former.

In this chapter, we examine an alternative view of modern economies, often associated with Keynesian economists, whereby monetary policy is both non-neutral and capable of achieving stabilization policy objectives to a limited extent. This view emphasizes long-lived, but ultimately transitory preference shocks that take place in an economy with rigidities in the labor market that prevent a rapid adjustment to full employment. Like the preference shocks examined in the preceding chapter, these preference shocks dissipate fully. However, unlike those in the preceding chapter, these shocks are viewed as having sufficient persistence (or duration) to possibly warrant a policy response. In addition, rather than assuming that firms fix prices in advance, which imposes a liquidity constraint on households' consumption purchases, firms and households (workers) are assumed to enter into long-term nominal wage contracts that essentially fix the nominal wage in advance.[1] The latter rigidity prevents the economy from rapidly absorbing the preference shock and provides a rationale for the monetary authority to pursue an active stabilization policy.

Advocates of this view tend to emphasize two features of the labor market. One is that the terms of employment for most households (workers) include a precommitment by the firm and the household to a fixed nominal wage. The other is limited mobility of labor in the short run that precludes households from moving from one sector of the economy to another. Therefore, when the economy undergoes, say, transitory shocks that cause temporary layoffs in one sector of the economy, households are not able to be quickly reemployed in another.[2] Those two features of the labor market are modeled by assuming that all workers are employed under the same labor contract, the terms of which are fully binding. The terms precommit both parties, the firm and the household, to a fixed nominal wage that lasts for one period in the model. As always, a period is defined as the time horizon necessary for monetary policy decisions to take effect on the economy and is assumed to be approximately one year. Given the nominal wage, households agree to supply whatever quantity of labor is demanded by the firms that employ them. Therefore, once the labor agreement is struck, the level of employment becomes completely demand determined. Firms choose the level of employment that sets real wages equal to the marginal product of labor, at which point they are maximizing profits. When preference shocks cause real wages to become, say, too high given the level of productivity, firms lay workers off (a movement along the labor demand schedule) and employment falls. The monetary authority then may be able to manufacture a price increase that reduces wages by raising the nominal quantity of money in circulation in the economy. As a result, firms increase employment and the economy's output rises.

---

[1]Examples of models that feature long-term labor contracts include those of Fischer (1977), Gray (1976), and Taylor (1980). Many Keynesian models also feature sticky prices. See, for example, Phelps and Taylor (1977), who examine stickiness in both prices and wages.

[2]The extent to which these "features" of the labor market are significant enough to warrant a monetary policy response is the subject of much debate. For example, alternative compensation schemes, such as overtime pay, bonuses, or COLAs, can introduce flexibility into nominal wages. Moreover, and perhaps even more important, limited short-run labor mobility for an individual worker does not necessarily restrict labor mobility for the aggregate economy. There is a very high turnover in the composition of workers who are temporarily unemployed and seeking work. A shock that causes layoffs in one industry may be beneficial to another. Therefore, the latter industry may raise its employment without having to hire the *same* workers who were layed off in the former industry.

The chapter begins by illustrating the effect of labor market rigidities on the ability of the monetary authority to achieve its policy objectives of full employment and price stability in response to a productivity shock. In the absence of a policy response, the shock has no adverse effect for the full-employment objective; however, the objective of stable prices is not automatically satisfied. This is expected given the results of Chapter 10, whereby an economy with neither sticky prices nor sticky nominal wages adjusts to a productivity shock by altering prices with no change to the nominal wage. Now, however, the monetary authority is unable to alter policy in an effort to achieve price stability without simultaneously compromising the objective of full employment.

Similar exercises are then conducted in the absence of productivity shocks, when the economy undergoes long-lived preference shocks that eventually dissipate. In these exercises, preference shocks are shown to cause the economy to deviate from full employment when the monetary authority fails to respond. However, policy makers are able to achieve the objectives of full employment and price stability simultaneously by adjusting the nominal money supply each period to offset the preference shock on the labor market. Those policy actions induce compositional changes in output between consumption and investment goods.

12.1   A KEYNESIAN LABOR MARKET

When nominal wages are set in advance by contractual agreements between firms and households, what is their effect on the monetary authority's ability to achieve the policy objectives of keeping the economy close to full employment while maintaining an environment of stable prices? To examine that question, we must modify the model of the labor market to represent the binding nature of the labor contracts. The timing of events is represented in Figure 12.1. At the beginning of a period, say, at time $t = 0$, a contract is negotiated between the representative firm and the representative household that takes effect immediately and remains in effect for one period. It is then renegotiated. The agreement is assumed to take place before the period's shocks are revealed. It therefore is

Figure 12.1
The Timing of Events When Nominal Wages are Set in Advance with a Binding Labor Contract Between Households and Firms

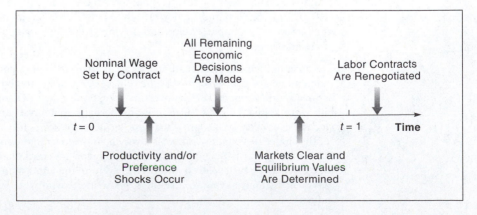

based on the long-run positions of the labor supply and demand schedules that reflect the level of technology at the beginning of the period, denoted θ_0. In Figure 12.2, the labor supply and demand schedules are labeled $N^s(\theta_0, \lambda)$ and $N^d(\theta_0)$, respectively. The nominal wage to which the firm and the household agree, denoted W_0, corresponds to a real wage of (W_0/P_0), at which the labor market initially clears at full employment, denoted N_0. Once the agreement is struck, the nominal wage remains fixed and labor becomes completely demand determined. This situation is represented by a post-agreement labor supply schedule, labeled $N^{sx}(\theta_0, \lambda)$, which is perfectly elastic at the prevailing real wage of (W_0/P_0). Therefore, in the absence of any shocks, the economy would remain at full employment.

To illustrate how the contract affects the short-run equilibrium level of employment, assume that, for whatever reason, prices rise from P_0 to P_x as a result

Figure 12.2
A Keynesian Labor Market with Long-Term Fixed Nominal Wage Contracts

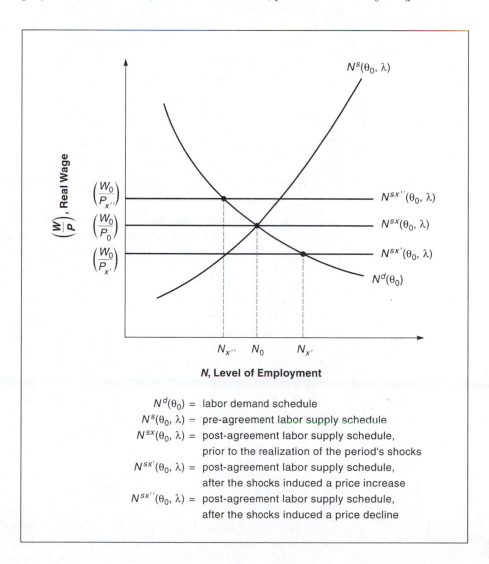

$$N^d(\theta_0) = \text{labor demand schedule}$$
$$N^s(\theta_0, \lambda) = \text{pre-agreement labor supply schedule}$$
$$N^{sx}(\theta_0, \lambda) = \text{post-agreement labor supply schedule,}$$
$$\text{prior to the realization of the period's shocks}$$
$$N^{sx'}(\theta_0, \lambda) = \text{post-agreement labor supply schedule,}$$
$$\text{after the shocks induced a price increase}$$
$$N^{sx''}(\theta_0, \lambda) = \text{post-agreement labor supply schedule,}$$
$$\text{after the shocks induced a price decline}$$

of shocks that are assumed, for simplicity, to leave the labor demand schedule unchanged. With the nominal wage fixed by the terms of the contract at W_0, the real wage falls to (W_0/P_x'). Because the household has agreed to supply whatever labor is demanded at the prevailing real wage, the labor supply schedule shifts down to $N^{sx'}(\theta_0,\lambda)$. The firm observes that its labor costs have fallen and increases its demand for labor, which is represented in Figure 12.2 by a movement along the labor demand schedule, and the labor market clears at a level of employment, $N_{x'}$, that exceeds full employment. What is the effect on the household? At the lower real wage, the opportunity cost of leisure time has fallen. Therefore, because the household is locked into the labor agreement, it is supplying too much labor and taking too little leisure. Note that the opposite occurs when prices fall. For example, suppose prices fall to, say, $P_{x''} < P_0$. Refer again to Figure 12.2. Real wages would rise to $(W_0/P_{x''})$, the labor supply schedule would shift up to $N^{sx''}(\theta_0,\lambda)$, and the equilibrium level of employment would be less than full employment, or $N_{x''} < N_0$. The opportunity cost of leisure time would increase and the household would be supplying too little labor and taking too much leisure as a result of the labor contract. "Too much leisure" is this model's characterization of involuntary unemployment.[3]

12.2   RESPONSE OF THE ECONOMY TO A POSITIVE PRODUCTIVITY SHOCK WHEN NOMINAL WAGES ARE SET IN ADVANCE AND THERE IS NO ATTEMPT AT MONETARY ACCOMMODATION

How does the labor contract under which nominal wages are set in advance affect the economy's ability to absorb, say a positive productivity shock? From the results of Chapter 10, we expect no effect, *provided* that the monetary authority does not attempt to accommodate the shock. With flexible prices, real wages are able to adjust fully to their long-run equilibrium level in the initial period of the shock without any need for nominal wages to change.[4] However, in terms of the objectives of monetary policy, prices do not remain stable, even though the economy remains at full employment.

The economy's equilibrium response to a positive productivity shock when nominal wages are fixed in advance by labor agreements and the monetary authority does not alter policy in response to the shock is shown in Figure 12.3. The economy is initially sketched at a general equilibrium coinciding with full employment as represented by points "a" on the graphs, where the macroeconomic variables assume values with the subscript zero. At time $t = 0$, firms and

---

[3]These implications of fixed nominal wage contracts illustrate another criticism of such models. Because the contracts are always suboptimal *ex post,* why do households willingly enter into them *ex ante?*

[4]As pointed out in Chapter 10 (see footnote 7), this is not precisely true for all mathematical representations of preferences and technology, but does hold for an important class of these models frequently studied in the theoretical literature.

Figure 12.3 Analysis of the Economy's Response to a Positive Productivity Shock When Nominal Wages are Set in Advance

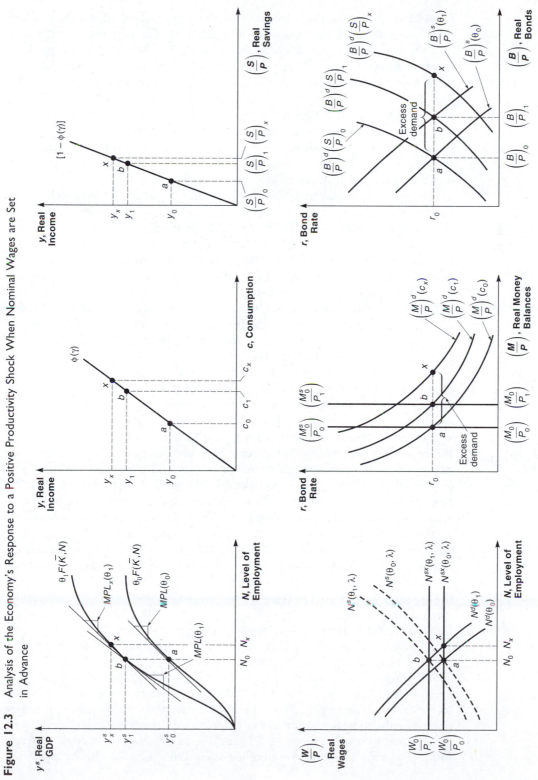

households enter into labor agreements with no prior knowledge of the productivity shock that will take place during the period. The negotiations that produce the labor contract therefore are based on the prevailing level of technology represented by θ_0. The relevant labor supply and labor demand schedules for the negotiations are given by $N^s(\theta_0, \lambda)$ and $N^d(\theta_0)$ in the lower left panel of Figure 12.3. Because both parties freely enter into the agreements, the established nominal wage that is to prevail for the one-period life of the contract is the one that clears the labor market at full employment if no shocks occur during the period. This nominal wage is given by W_0. Therefore, the post-agreement labor supply schedule, labeled $N^{sx}(\theta_0, \lambda)$, is completely elastic at the prevailing real wage, denoted (W_0/P_0), prior to the productivity shock.

The positive productivity shock then occurs, raising the level of technology from θ_0 to θ_1, and the short-run aggregate production function shifts up as shown in the upper left panel in Figure 12.3. Because it is a total factor productivity shock, the firm increases its demand for both labor and capital. The former is represented in the lower left panel by a rightward shift of the labor demand schedule to $N^d(\theta_1)$ and the latter is represented in the lower right panel by a rightward shift in the bond supply schedule from $(B/P)^s(\theta_0)$ to $(B/P)^s(\theta_1)$, reflecting the firms' greater financing requirements associated with their heightened demand for investment goods. To find the final equilibrium for the economy for this period, we first must establish the position of the labor supply schedule that clears the labor market.

Observe that if prices remain at P_0, the level of employment that would clear the market is N_x, which exceeds the initial full-employment level of N_0. It would imply higher levels of output at y_x^s and income at y_x, as illustrated in the upper panels of Figure 12.3. The increase in income would raise the households' consumption and savings to c_x and $(S/P)_x$, respectively. However, as shown in the lower middle and lower left panels, the increases in consumption and savings would raise the demand for money and bonds to $(M/P)^d(c_x)$ and $(B/P)^d(S/P)_x$, producing an excess demand in both markets. In this case, interest rates alone cannot adjust to clear the financial markets, because the bond rate would have to rise to clear the money market and fall to clear the bond market. Therefore, the adjustment that takes place is in the price level P, which must fall. As prices fall, real money balances, (M/P), begin to rise and the money supply schedule begins to shift to the right to absorb the excess demand for money. At the same time, a fall in the price level increases the real wage. Because the nominal wage is fixed by contract, the short-run labor supply schedule shifts up and the level of employment necessary to clear the labor market begins to fall. How far does the price level fall?

To clear the financial markets, the bond rate must return to its initial level r_0. That can occur only if the economy adjusts to a new general equilibrium consistent with full employment where employment, output, and income are equal to N_0, y_1^s, and y_1, respectively. Note that consumption and savings adjust to the levels c_1 and $(S/P)_1$. With the bond market in equilibrium, the money market will also be in equilibrium at r_0, provided that the price level falls to P_1 so that real balances rise to (M_0/P_1) and the money supply schedule shifts to (M_0^s/P_1) as shown in the lower middle panel. Referring to the lower left panel, we see that the price decline must have been just sufficient to shift the labor supply schedule up to $N^{sx}(\theta_1,\lambda)$, where the labor market clears at full employment, N_0, and the higher real wage rate (W_0/P_1), the latter reflecting the increase in labor productivity associated with the improved technology after the productivity shock.

At the end of the period, the labor contract is renegotiated. The implication is that the labor supply schedule is no longer perfectly elastic at the prevailing real wage rate (W_0/P_1), but is instead again free to represent fully the household's labor/leisure decision. In this case, however, prices adjusted over the period to reflect the total long-run change in productivity at the improved level of technology. Therefore, the households' underlying labor supply schedule, although no longer perfectly elastic, contains the equilibrium point "b" in the lower left panel of Figure 12.3. That is, at the current real wage (W_0/P_1), the optimal quantity of labor that households want to supply is given by the quantity N_0. This labor/leisure decision is represented by a leftward shift in the underlying labor supply schedule from $N^s(\theta_0,\lambda)$ to $N^s(\theta_1,\lambda)$. Therefore, once the labor contract expires, the labor supply schedule is seen graphically to pivot around point "b" in the lower panel from $N^{sx}(\theta_1,\lambda)$ to $N^s(\theta_1,\lambda)$. The labor contract that fixed the nominal wage at W_0 essentially had no effect on the economy's subsequent adjustment to the productivity shock. That is, the economy responded in precisely the same way as it did in Chapter 10 when nominal wages were fully flexible.

12.3 RESPONSE OF THE ECONOMY TO A POSITIVE PRODUCTIVITY SHOCK WHEN NOMINAL WAGES ARE SET IN ADVANCE AND THERE IS AN ATTEMPT AT MONETARY ACCOMMODATION

We saw in Chapter 10 that when nominal wages are flexible, there is a monetary policy response to a productivity shock that can also stabilize prices without compromising the full-employment objective. That is no longer the case when nominal wages are set in advance. Suppose that in the preceding example the monetary authority wanted to adjust policy to keep prices stable and simply ignored the full-employment objective. If it is successful in keeping the price level from falling, the real wage remains unchanged. Therefore, for the labor market to clear, a *quantity* adjustment is necessary. That is, under the improved technology, the real wage is too low and consequently employment rises above the full-employment level.

Refer to Figure 12.4. The economy is initially in equilibrium at full employment, where the variables have the subscript zero and their values are plotted at points "a" on the graphs. Before the contract negotiations, the labor supply and demand schedules on which the negotiations are based are denoted by $N^s(\theta_0,\lambda)$ and $N^d(\theta_0)$, as shown in the lower left panel. Households and firms agree to a nominal wage of W_0 and the post-agreement labor supply schedule becomes perfectly elastic at the real wage (W_0/P_0), which is denoted $N^{sx}(\theta_0,\lambda)$. At that

Figure 12.4   Analysis of the Economy's Response to a Positive Productivity Shock When Nominal Wages are Set in Advance and the Monetary Authority Chooses to Stabilize Prices

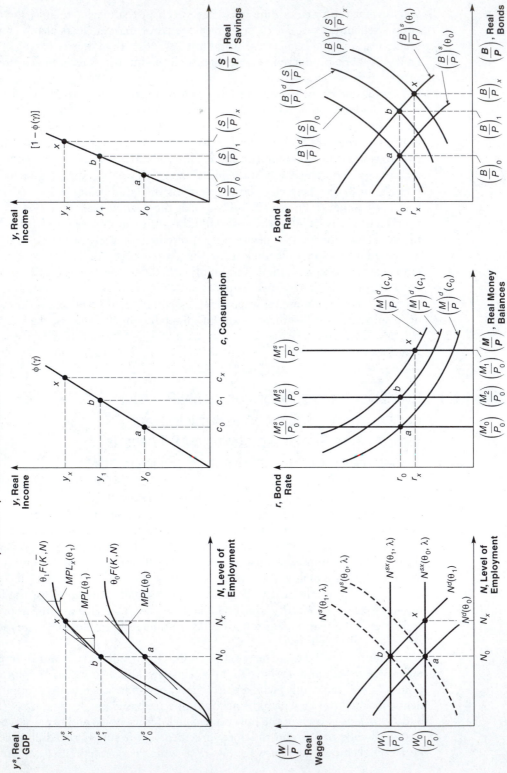

real wage, the labor market clears at N_0, and firms are maximizing profits with labor productivity under the beginning-of-period technology θ_0 represented by the marginal product of labor, $MPL(\theta_0)$, in the upper left panel.

With the labor agreement in place, the economy undergoes the positive productivity shock and the aggregate production function shifts up. The monetary authority recognizes that if no policy action is taken, prices will fall and real wages will rise to reflect the productivity improvement, which if the economy were to remain at full employment would rise from $MPL(\theta_0)$ to $MPL(\theta_1)$. It chooses to increase the money supply by an amount sufficient to prevent the price decline. If it is successful in achieving that objective, the price level remains fixed at P_0 and the real wage does not change. Consequently, the labor supply schedule also remains fixed at $N^{sx}(\theta_0,\lambda)$. However, the firm has increased its demand for labor due to the improved technology, which is represented by a rightward shift of the labor demand schedule from $N^d(\theta_0)$ to $N^d(\theta_1)$. Therefore, the labor market clears at the level of employment N_x that exceeds full employment. Note that because the real wage remains unchanged, productivity must also be unchanged even though the level of technology has improved. Therefore, $MPL(\theta_0) = MPL_x(\theta_1)$, as shown in the upper left panel, and output and income are seen to rise from y_0^s and y_0 to y_x^s and y_x, respectively.

What is happening in the goods market? Output has increased from y_0^s to y_x^s, but how is the additional output divided between consumption goods and investment goods? In relation to the decisions of firms, the total factor productivity shock has raised the productivity of capital as well as labor and firms respond by increasing their demand for capital. Financing requirements are increased by the greater volume of capital investment expenditures. The greater need for financing is reflected in the rightward shift of the bond supply schedule to $(B/P)^s(\theta_1)$ in the lower right panel of Figure 12.4. However, because of the labor agreement, households are temporarily oversupplying labor at the given real wage, (W_0/P_0), and are therefore taking too little leisure. Consequently, they incur a loss of utility in the current period. The utility loss is partially offset by the increase in current consumption to c_x and the increase in future consumption opportunities afforded by an increase in the level of current-period savings to $(S/P)_x$, as shown in the upper middle and upper right panels.[5]

With an increase in the level of savings to $(S/P)_x$, the demand for bonds by households rises and the bond demand schedule in the lower right panel shifts to $(B/P)^d(S/P)_x$. To clear the bond market, the bond rate declines to r_x. In the

---

[5] In this analysis we assume that the savings rate does not change even though the economy is above full employment. That assumption is made for convenience and does not affect the qualitative results the model is intended to demonstrate. However, in market-oriented economies, the savings rate generally tends to rise when the economy is producing above full employment and to fall when the economy is producing below full employment. The reason for such a response is that households generally want to "smooth" consumption over the business cycle and absorb the larger share of income shocks by saving. That behavior would be represented in the model with a slight decrease in the intensity of preference for consumption, γ, in response to a positive productivity shock.

money market, the money demand schedule shifts to $(M/P)^d(c_x)$ as shown in the lower middle panel. To keep the price level fixed at P_0, the monetary authority must raise the nominal money supply so that the money supply schedule shifts to (M_1^s/P_0), where the money market clears at r_x.

At the end of the period, or at date $t = 1$, the labor contract expires and must be renegotiated. The labor supply and demand schedules on which these negotiations are based are denoted $N^s(\theta_1, \lambda)$ and $N^d(\theta_1)$ in the lower left panel of Figure 12.4. As a result, the new labor agreement fixes the nominal wage so that, in the absence of any additional shocks, the labor market clears at the full-employment level of N_0. The nominal wage reflects the monetary authority's desire to maintain price stability. Therefore, the nominal wage in the new contract rises from W_0 to W_1, which in the absence of any price rise causes real wages to rise from (W_0/P_0) to (W_1/P_0), as shown in the lower left panel. The new labor agreement results in a new short-run labor supply schedule, denoted by $N^{sx}(\theta_1, \lambda)$ that is completely elastic at the higher real wage rate. The higher real wage rate reflects the higher level of productivity associated with full employment under the new technology, θ_1, as given by the marginal product of labor, $MPL(\theta_1)$. Output and income therefore fall to their new respective full-employment levels of y_1^s and y_1. Consumption and savings decline to c_1 and $(S/P)_1$, as shown in the upper middle and upper right panels. Those adjustments are accompanied by leftward shifts of the money demand and bond demand schedules to $(M/P)^d(c_1)$ and $(B/P)^d(S/P)_1$ as shown in the lower middle and lower right panels, respectively, and the financial markets clear at the original bond rate r_0. For the money market to attain this equilibrium without a price rise, the monetary authority would have had to reduce the nominal money supply to M_2^s as represented by the leftward shift of the money supply schedule to (M_2^s/P_0).

Time paths for the macroeconomic variables over the two periods of adjustment from date $t = 0$ to date $t = 2$ are shown in Figure 12.5 under the assumption that no additional shocks occur during the second period. From the lower left panel, we see that the monetary authority is successful in maintaining stable prices throughout the process of adjustment. However, its full-employment objective has been compromised, as seen in the upper and middle left panels. To summarize the sequence of events, the inability of either prices or wages to change in the short run has induced a quantity adjustment in the labor market in response to the positive productivity shock. At date $t = 1$, the firm takes advantage of the improved technology by increasing employment until the marginal product of labor falls to restore equality with the real wage. Output therefore rises above its full-employment level, with households over-supplying labor and taking too little leisure. They are partially compensated for the utility loss by an increase in current-period consumption and prospects for greater consumption opportunities in the future due to an increase in savings. The increase in savings raises the demand for bonds and drives down the equilibrium bond rate, as firms raise their demand for investment goods in response to a temporary reduction in their cost of funds. During this first period, the monetary authority accommodates the temporary increase in money demand associated with the greater liquidity needs of households, and real money bal-

Figure 12.5   Time Paths for the Macroeconomic Variables in Response to a Positive Productivity Shock When Nominal Wages are Set in Advance and the Monetary Authority Stabilizes Prices

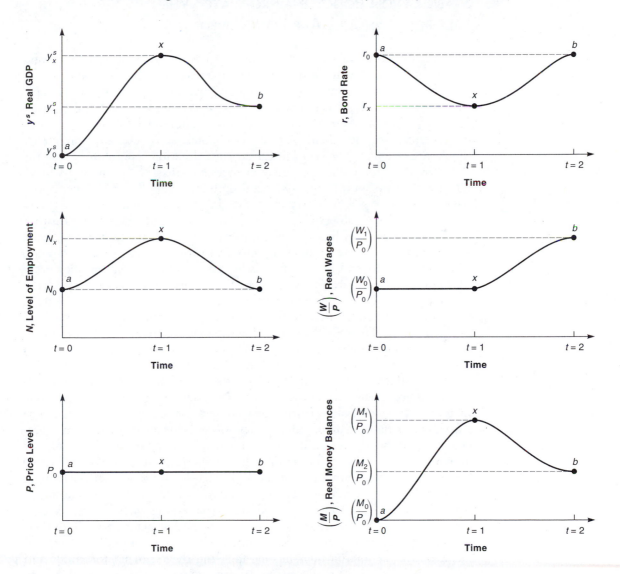

ances rise at date $t = 1$ as illustrated in the lower right panel. At the end of the period, or at date $t = 2$, nominal wages are free to adjust to restore full employment as illustrated in the middle right panel. At the lower level of employment, the household has more leisure time and reduces its demand for consumption goods, thus lowering its demand for money. The monetary authority therefore must reduce the nominal quantity of money in circulation to prevent prices from rising. This example illustrates that to achieve price stability after a productivity shock when nominal wages are fixed in advance, the monetary authority must sacrifice its full-employment objective.

12.4   Is the Full Employment Objective of Stabilization Policy Inappropriate When Preference Shocks Are Long Lived?

Productivity shocks have been described as permanent, in that once they occur they essentially remain for good. However, the effects of a positive shock in one period could be offset by the effects of a negative shock in the subsequent period. In contrast, preference shocks are viewed as transitory, in that they eventually dissipate and their effects die out without additional "offsetting" shocks in subsequent periods. In the preceding chapter, such transitory preference shocks are assumed to be very short lived, their duration being shorter than the time necessary for monetary policy changes to affect the economy. Consequently, they are not the proper object of stabilization policy. They simply create confusion for the monetary authority that is attempting to sort out how much of the change observed in economic data can be attributed to transitory preference shocks, to which it does not want to respond, and how much can be attributed to permanent productivity shocks, to which it may want to respond. In this chapter, we still view preference shocks as transitory in that they eventually die out. However, we assume that the duration of the shocks exceeds the length of time necessary for monetary policy to have an effect on the economy. The monetary authority may be able to offset the economic fluctuations caused by the shocks and therefore may question whether preference shocks are appropriate objects of stabilization policy.

The reason for focusing on this issue is to highlight the view of some economists, usually associated with Keynesian theories, that aggregate demand disturbances are a principal source of economic fluctuations in the business cycle that may have undesirable distributional consequences, and therefore should be placed within the domain of public policy concerns. As an example of an aggregate demand shock, suppose an individual member of a family chooses to give up work in favor of more leisure time (has an increased intensity of preference for leisure, λ). Now suppose that the additional leisure time includes looking after children, who previously had been in daycare, and doing chores at home, which had previously been contracted to a home services agency.[6] The daycare center and the home services agency both have a decline in the demand for their services and lay off workers. Those workers not only must find new employment, but in the interim their income falls and their demand for goods and services declines, which in turn affects the demand for goods of other producers, who must cut back, and so on. This "multiplier" effect resulting from the initial preference shock may lead to significant "churning" in the labor market that a policy maker may want to minimize, even though the effects are transitory.

---

[6]Some recent theoretical models (not of the Keynesian genre) treat leisure time as a factor input to a home production technology, the output of which provides utility to the household. See Greenwood and Hercowitz (1991) and Benhabib, Rogerson, and Wright (1991).

Such a perspective is taken in the following analysis, although the costs are not explicitly modeled.

It is important to recognize that the economic definition of "full employment" maintained throughout the text may be at variance with the "full-employment" objective associated with short-run stabilization policy in this context. Thus far, full employment has been identified with the economy's long-run adjustment to productivity shocks, and the full-employment objective of stabilization policy is to facilitate that adjustment when prices or wages are fixed in advance. When preference shocks dissipate quickly, the policy objective and the economic definition of full employment coincide. When preference shocks are long lived, however, the short-run economic definition of full employment differs from the long-run economic definition of full employment, because the former represents optimal resource allocations that take account of changing preferences as well as changing technology (but that abstract from distributional effects) whereas the latter represents only the changing technology. Therefore, an economic policy that is "successful" at smoothing out business cycles around the long-run level of full employment is essentially imposing the optimal *long-run* resource allocations on the economy in the *short-run*. Consequently, in terms of economic efficiency, the "successful" policy could actually be reducing the overall economic welfare of the economy rather than enhancing it.[7]

12.5   RESPONSE OF THE ECONOMY TO A LONG-LIVED INTRATEMPORAL PREFERENCE SHOCK WHEN NOMINAL WAGES ARE SET IN ADVANCE

In the example where the economy responds to a positive productivity shock with nominal wages fixed in advance, we see that no monetary policy action is necessary to keep the economy at full employment. The flexibility in prices is sufficient to enable real wage adjustments to clear the labor market at full employment. However, when the monetary authority seeks to maintain stable prices, the full-employment objective is compromised. Alternatively, when the economy is responding exclusively to preference shocks, those results do not obtain in terms of the long-run economic definition of full employment. That

---

[7]Economic welfare is not an easy concept to define in economies where households are heterogeneous. It is not sensible to simply add up utilities and take the total to be the measure of welfare. Such practices can lead to bizarre policy recommendations, such as giving all wealth to a small number of individuals while depriving others of *any* wealth. Models that assume a representative household, which are consistent with the model used in this text, cannot address the so-called equity issues associated with distributional effects. However, they do provide an internally consistent model for analyzing issues of economic efficiency.

is, if the policy objectives of the monetary authorities include the long-run definition of full employment, *which is assumed to be the case in the rest of this chapter*, the price mechanism will no longer cause either objective to be met automatically. Therefore, in the absence of a monetary policy response, the economy does not remain at full employment and prices do not remain stable. In the absence of productivity shocks, however, adopting a monetary policy that achieves the full-employment objective is not in conflict with the objective of maintaining stable prices.

In Figure 12.6, the economy is initially in a general equilibrium at full employment; the variables have the subscript zero and their values are plotted at points "a" on the graphs. The labor supply and demand schedules prior to the labor agreement are represented in the lower left panel by $N^s(\theta, \lambda_0)$ and $N^d(\theta)$, and the post-agreement labor supply schedule is represented by $N^{sx'}(\theta, \lambda_0)$. Once the labor agreement is in effect, an intratemporal preference shock occurs that favors more consumption and less leisure. That is, households increase their intensity of preference for consumption and reduce their intensity of preference for leisure. The shock affects their labor/leisure, consumption/savings, and portfolio allocation decisions.

In the labor market, the reduction in the intensity of preference for leisure corresponds to a decline in λ from λ_0 to λ_1, which is represented by a rightward shift of the underlying labor supply schedule to $N^s(\theta, \lambda_1)$. If the economy is to adjust with full accommodation of the preference shock, employment would rise to N_1 and output and income would increase to y_1^s and y_1, as shown in the upper panels of Figure 12.6. Because the shock is strictly intratemporal, the increase in the intensity of preference for consumption, represented by an increase in γ from γ_0 to γ_1, would be fully reflected in higher consumption, which would rise to c_1, whereas the level of savings would remain unchanged at $(S/P)_0$. With the level of savings unaffected, the bond demand schedule remains unchanged and the bond market would clear at the initial bond rate r_0. At the higher level of consumption, households increase their demand for money and the money demand schedule shifts to the right to $(M/P)^d(c_1)$ as shown in the lower middle panel.

By examining the labor market and the money market, we now can see that with nominal wages fixed at W_0, the price mechanism alone will not produce a general equilibrium in which the intratemporal preference shock is fully accommodated. Consider the conditions required to clear the labor market at the point plotted as "b" in the lower left panel. At the higher level of employment, N_1, firms must lower the real wage if they are to satisfy their hiring criterion that is consistent with profit maximization. Because the nominal wage is fixed, a decline in the real wage would require a rise in the price level to P_1. However, at the bond rate r_0, there was already an excess demand for money and it would be exacerbated by the higher price level. That is, real balances would fall and the money supply schedule would shift leftward to (M_0^s/P_1) as shown in the lower middle panel. Consequently, households are liquidity constrained in their efforts to acquire consumption goods in the quantity c_1.

In response to the liquidity constraint, households would prefer to shift some of their nonleisure time into activities that facilitate transactions, thereby increasing the velocity of money. The underlying labor supply schedule (not

Figure 12.6   Analysis of the Economy's Response to an Intratemporal Preference Shock Favoring More Consumption and Less Leisure in the Absence of a Monetary Policy Response

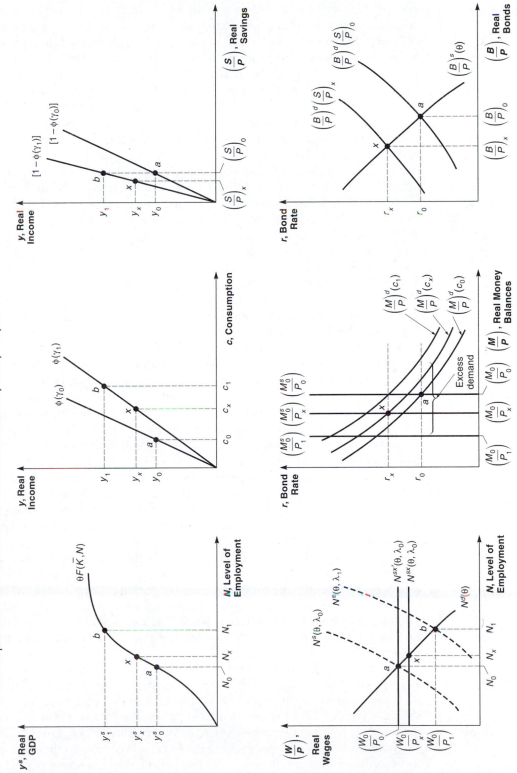

shown in Figure 12.6) would shift to the left, so that the effective labor supply schedule under the fixed nominal wage contract would shift upward to $N^{sx}(\theta, \lambda_1)$. In response, the level of employment that clears the labor market, as indicated in the lower left panel by N_x, would still be above the full-employment level, but below the level, N_1, that would have obtained if there had been no liquidity constraint and the intratemporal preference shock had been fully accommodated as the economy reached its new general equilibrium.

At the level of employment N_x, output and income rise only to y_x^s and y_x. As shown in the upper panels, this corresponds to a lesser increase in consumption to c_x and a decline in the level of savings to $(S/P)_x$. In the lower right panel, the reduction in savings reduces the demand for bonds and the bond demand schedule shifts left to $(B/P)^d(S/P)_x$. Consequently, the equilibrium bond rate rises to r_x. In the money market, the lesser increase in the price level to P_x causes the money supply schedule to shift leftward by a lesser extent to (M_0^s/P_x). The decline in money demand required to clear the market is brought about by two factors. One is the smaller increase consumption to c_x, as represented by the smaller rightward shift in the money demand schedule to $(M/P)^d(c_x)$. The second is that the higher bond rate, r_x, which cleared the bond market, raises the opportunity costs of holding money, thereby decreasing further demand for money, which is represented by a movement along the money demand schedule. Therefore, the financial markets clear at a higher bond rate and lower stocks of real money balances and real bonds.

In sum, the economy was initially in a general equilibrium at full employment. It was subjected to an intratemporal preference shock in which households wanted to increase their consumption and reduce their leisure. Households preferred to work more and use the additional labor income to increase current period consumption without affecting their level of savings. However, with nominal wages fixed by contract and with no improvements in technology that could otherwise have increased labor productivity, prices must rise so that real wages fall if employment is to increase. That is, real wages must reflect the lower level of labor productivity resulting from the diminishing marginal product of labor, which is an inherent feature of the technology. The higher price level reduces the real money supply and results in an excess demand for money.

To alleviate partially the liquidity constraint they face, households want to channel some of their resource time into transacting to raise the velocity of money. Consequently, the equilibrium level of output is lower than it otherwise would have been and households realize a lesser increase in current consumption than they would have preferred. They simultaneously borrow from the future by reducing savings, which somewhat restricts their future consumption opportunities.

At the beginning of the second period after the shock, or just after date $t = 1$, labor contracts are renegotiated. If the preference shock dissipates and no other shocks occur, the economy adjusts back to its long-run equilibrium as shown in Figure 12.6 by points plotted as "a" on the graphs. The time path for the economy over the two periods of adjustment is shown in Figure 12.7.

In terms of monetary policy, both the full employment and the price stability objectives are compromised. In the first period, the economy was producing

Figure 12.7   Time Paths for the Macroeconomic Variables in Response to an Intratemporal Preference Shock Favoring More Consumption and Less Leisure in the Absence of a Monetary Policy Response

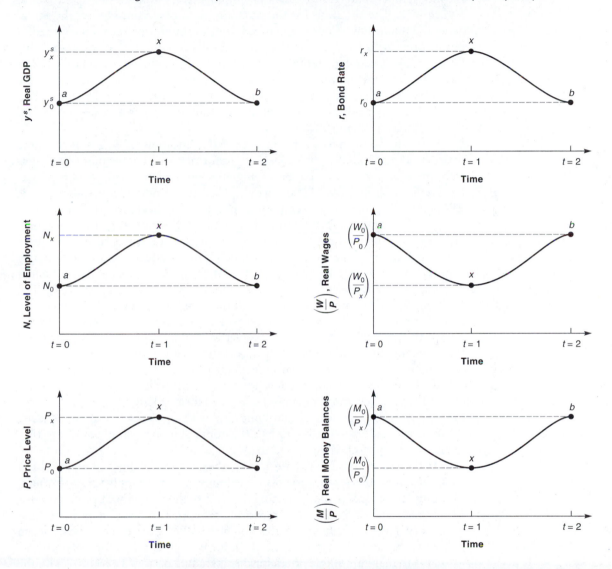

at a level that exceeded full employment, whereas prices rose in the first period and fell in the second period. To achieve the full-employment and stable-price objectives, the monetary authority must adopt a policy that would prevent the economy from picking up in the first period and then adjust the policy in the second period to prevent the economy from slowing as the preference shock dissipates. Note that such policy action, which is based on the long-run definition of full employment, attempts to offset the effects of preference shocks, which are transitory, on employment and output. It contrasts with the previous analysis in which the monetary authority attempted to accommodate fully productivity shocks, which are seen to be permanent.

To see how the monetary authority may be able to offset fully the effects of the intratemporal preference shock on employment, output, and prices, refer to Figure 12.8. The situation for the economy is as described before; the initial general equilibrium values are denoted with the subscript zero and plotted at points labeled "a" on the graphs. After the labor contract is negotiated, the labor supply schedule is represented in the lower left panel as $N^{sx'}(\theta, \lambda_0)$. The levels of employment, output, and income that would clear the market after the preference shock, if there were no liquidity constraint, are given by N_1, y_1^s, and y_1, respectively. In this case, consumption would rise to c_1 and savings would remain unchanged at $(S/P)_0$.

From the labor market, it is evident that with nominal wages fixed in the first period at W_0 and if the monetary authorities are able to maintain a constant price level at P_0, the economy will remain at full employment. In this case, both policy objectives would be achieved. However, from the previous exercise, it is also evident that prices tend to rise in the first period after the shock if no policy action is taken. Such response indicates that the monetary authority must reduce the nominal money supply in the first period if it is to prevent this price rise from occurring. To examine how much it must reduce the nominal money supply, refer to Figure 12.8 and assume that the policy is successful in the first period. That is, at the end of the first period, the price level is equal to P_0. The economy is at full employment, N_0, and the equilibrium level of income is y_0. From the upper middle and upper right panels, consumption is seen to rise to c_x while savings declines to $(S/P)_x$. The lower level of savings reduces the demand for bonds and the bond demand schedule shifts leftward to $(B/P)^d(S/P)_x$, thereby causing the bond market to clear at the higher bond rate, r_x. In the money market, the higher bond rate has reduced the demand for money, which is a movement along the new money demand schedule labeled $(M/P)^d(c_x)$. Therefore, for the money market to clear at that bond rate with no change in the price level, the monetary authority had to reduce the nominal money supply to M_1 so that the money supply schedule shifted to (M_1^s/P_0).

At the end of period 1, date $t = 1$, the preference shock dissipates and contracts come up for renegotiation. The long-run labor supply schedule therefore shifts back to $N^s(\theta, \lambda_0)$, reflecting the shift in the intensity of preference for leisure back to its original value represented by λ_0. Before the next period begins, a new labor agreement is struck and nominal wages are again fixed for the period. Included in the agreement is the information that the monetary authority wants to maintain stable prices for the upcoming period. Therefore, with the price level expected to be P_0, the nominal wage to which households (workers) and firms agree is W_0 and the new post-agreement labor supply schedule becomes $N^{sx'}(\theta, \lambda_0)$.

If the labor market clears at full employment in the second period, output and income will again equal y_0^s and y_0. However, as shown in the upper middle and upper right panels, as the preference shock dissipates, the intensity of preference for consumption falls back to its original value, which is represented by the decline in γ from γ_1 to γ_0. Consequently, consumption must fall back to its previous level c_0 and savings must rise to its previous level $(S/P)_0$. In the bond market, the increase in demand for bonds, represented by a shift in the bond demand schedule to $(B/P)^d(S/P)_0$, causes the market to clear at the lower bond

Figure 12.8 Analysis of the Economy's Response to an Intratemporal Preference Shock Favoring Consumption More and Leisure Less in the Presence of a Monetary Policy Response

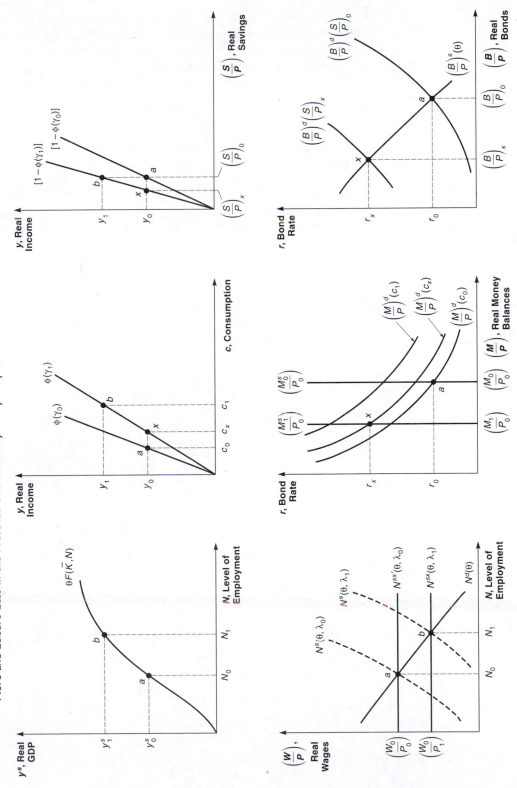

rate r_0. Despite a decline in the demand for money, as shown in the lower middle panel by a return of the money demand schedule to $(M/P)^d(c_0)$, an excess demand for money remains at the bond rate r_0. To absorb the excess demand, the monetary authority must increase the nominal money supply to its original level M_0 so that real money balances rise as the money supply schedule shifts right to (M_0^s/P_0).

The time path for the economy is represented in Figure 12.9. The monetary authority was able to achieve exactly both of its policy objectives, keeping the economy at full employment throughout the period of adjustment to the preference shock without volatility in prices. This outcome required an active

Figure 12.9   Time Paths for the Macroeconomic Variables in Response to an Intratemporal Preference Shock Favoring More Consumption and Less Leisure in the Presence of a Monetary Policy Response

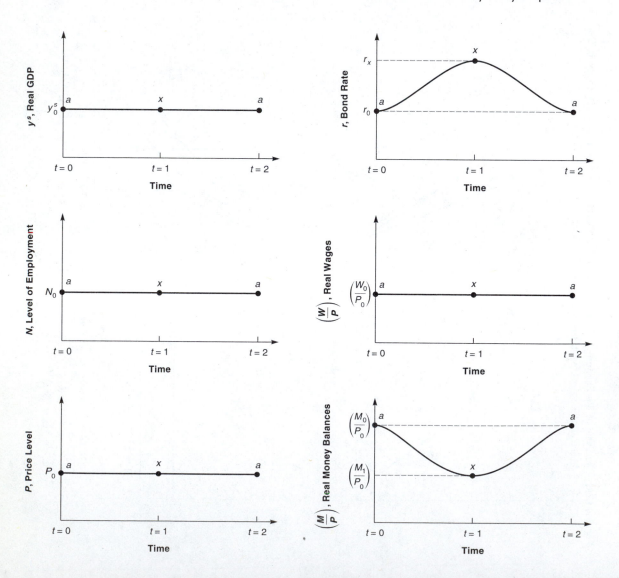

monetary policy whereby the nominal money supply was reduced in the initial period, which raised the bond rate, to prevent the economy from exceeding its full-employment level of production. However, to maintain that level of production, the composition of output goods changed. Consumption rose and the production of investment goods declined. In the second period, the money supply was increased, thereby lowering the bond rate to prevent households from becoming excessively liquidity constrained, which would have slowed the economy to a production point below full employment.

12.6   RESPONSE OF THE ECONOMY TO A LONG-LIVED INTERTEMPORAL PREFERENCE SHOCK WHEN NOMINAL WAGES ARE SET IN ADVANCE

When the economy undergoes a long-lived preference shock that is intertemporal, the monetary authority is able to achieve its full-employment and stable-price objectives simultaneously. To attain those policy goals, it must conduct an active monetary policy that offsets completely the impact of the shock on the labor market in each of the two periods that the preference shock takes to dissipate fully.

Refer to Figure 12.10. As in the preceding example, the economy is initially in a general equilibrium that coincides with full employment, where equilibrium values have the subscript zero and are plotted as points "a" on the graphs. The post–wage agreement labor supply schedule is denoted by $N^{sx'}(\theta, \lambda_0)$. After the labor agreement takes effect at date $t = 0$, the economy undergoes an intertemporal preference shock whereby households become more impatient to receive utility today at the expense of future consumption opportunities. Both the intensity of preference for consumption and the intensity of preference for leisure rise. The latter is represented in the lower left panel by an increase in λ from λ_0 to λ_1 such that the underlying labor supply schedule shifts leftward to $N^s(\theta, \lambda_1)$. If the shock were fully accommodated, the price level would have to decline to P_1, causing the real wage rate to rise to (W_0/P_1) and employment to fall to N_1. With no change in technology, output and income would have to decline to y_1^s and y_1, respectively, as shown in the upper panels. Because the preference shock is strictly intertemporal, the increase in the intensity of preference for consumption from γ_0 to γ_1 would have been sufficiently strong to leave consumption unchanged at c_0. The decline in the savings rate to $[1 - \phi(\gamma_1)]$, along with the decline in income, would result in a reduction in the level of savings from $(S/P)_0$ to $(S/P)_1$. As savings fall, the demand for bonds declines, with the bond demand schedule shifting to $(B/P)^d(S/P)_1$ as shown in the lower right panel, and the bond rate rises to r_1 to clear the bond market. However, the decline in the price level raises the real money supply, and the money supply schedule shifts right to (M_0^s/P_1) as shown in the lower middle panel. With the demand for money unchanged, there is an excess supply of money at r_1. Again, the price mechanism

Figure 12.10 Analysis of the Economy's Response to an Intertemporal Preference Shock Favoring Current Utility over Future Utility in the Absence of a Monetary Policy Response

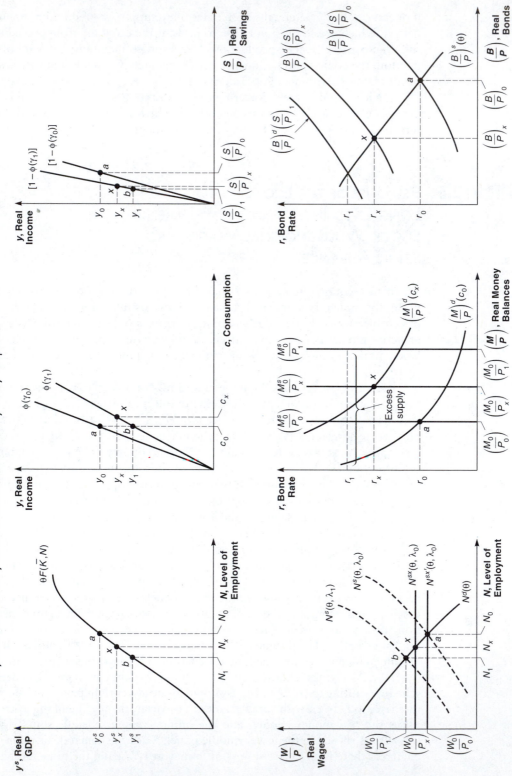

is unable to clear the money market so that the intertemporal preference shock is fully accommodated.

Households have excess liquidity that must be absorbed with additional consumption purchases. In equilibrium, the production of the additional output goods is achieved by channeling more of the households' resource time out of transaction activities (and perhaps leisure) and into production. The underlying labor supply schedule shifts right (not shown in Figure 12.10) and the effective labor supply schedule, for which nominal wages are fixed, shifts down to $N^{sx}(\theta,\lambda_1)$. Consequently, prices fall only from P_0 to P_x, which corresponds to a lesser rise in the real wage to (W_0/P_x) and a lesser decline in employment to N_x. Output and income also have modest declines to y_x^s and y_x, as shown in the upper panels. Therefore, consumption is higher at c_x and the decline in savings is mitigated somewhat to $(S/P)_x$. The latter results in a lesser decline in the demand for bonds, represented by the shift in the bond demand schedule to $(B/P)^d(S/P)_x$, and a lesser increase in the equilibrium bond rate to r_x.

The bond rate is now able to clear the money market, as shown in the lower middle panel, as a result of two factors. With a lesser fall in prices, real money balances did not rise as much, as indicated by the shift in the money supply schedule to (M_0^s/P_x). In addition, the increase in consumption raised the demand for money, which is represented by the rightward shift of the money demand schedule to $(M/P)^d(c_x)$. Therefore, the smaller increase in the money supply and the greater increase in money demand eliminated the excess supply of money, allowing the market to clear at r_x.

In general, with no monetary policy response to the intertemporal preference shock, in which households become more impatient to receive utility in the current period, output falls below the full-employment level and the price level declines. If no further shocks occur in the second period after the preference shock dissipates, full employment is restored. The time path for the economy over the two periods is shown in Figure 12.11. Once again, both of the policy objectives are compromised.

To prevent the economy from falling below its full-employment level of output, the monetary authority wants to increase output in the first period after the shock occurs. It can do so by providing more liquidity to the economy. Households continue to respond by raising consumption, which in equilibrium necessitates a greater allocation of resource time to production. Refer to Figure 12.12, where the post-agreement labor supply schedule after an indentical intertemporal preference shock (analyzed above) is represented by $N^{sx}(\theta,\lambda_0)$. If the monetary authority is able to gauge correctly the amount of monetary stimulus required, this response of households would continue until the underlying labor supply schedule coincides with its original position $N^s(\theta,\lambda_0)$, so that the effective labor supply schedule under the fixed nominal wage is perfectly elastic at the original real wage rate (W_0/P_0). In this case, the price level remains at P_0 and the equilibrium level of employment returns to the full employment level N_0.

As shown in the upper panels, at the full-employment level of income, y_0, consumption must rise further to c_x and savings increases to $(S/P)_x$. The latter increases the demand for bonds, which is represented in the lower right panel by a leftward shift in the bond demand schedule to $(B/P)^d(S/P)_x$, and the bond market clears at r_x. In the lower middle panel, the increase in consumption

Figure 12.11   Time Paths for the Macroeconomic Variables in Response to an Intertemporal Preference Shock Favoring Current Utility over Future Utility in the Absence of a Monetary Policy Response

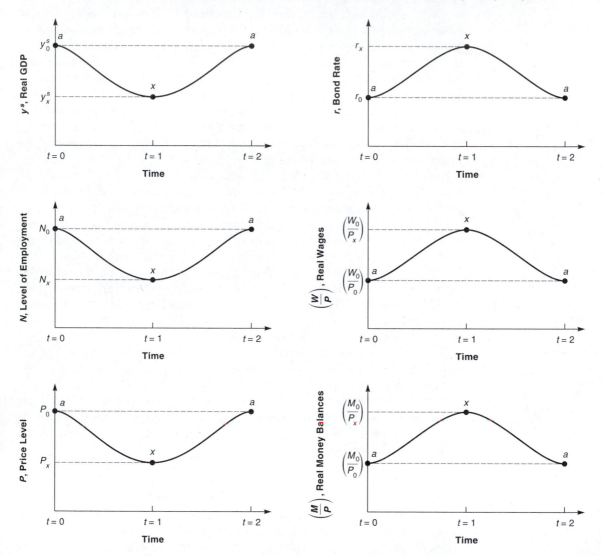

raises the demand for money, with a rightward shift of the money demand schedule to $(M/P)^d(c_x)$. Therefore, to clear the money market at r_x while maintaining a stable price level at P_0, the nominal money supply would have to be raised to M_1^s so that the money supply schedule shifts right to (M_1^s/P_0) as shown.

At the end of the first period, or just after date $t = 1$, the shock dissipates and the labor agreement is renegotiated. The labor negotiations incorporate the knowledge that the monetary authority wants to achieve full employment at the current price level, P_0. With the intensity of preference for leisure restored to λ_0, the post-agreement labor supply schedule once again appears as $N^{sx}(\theta,\lambda_0)$. If no further shocks occur in the second period, employment, output, and income remain at their full employment levels of N_0, y_0^s, and y_0. With the intensity of

Figure 12.12   Analysis of the Economy's Response to an Intertemporal Preference Shock Favoring Current Utility over Future Utility in the Presence of a Monetary Policy Response

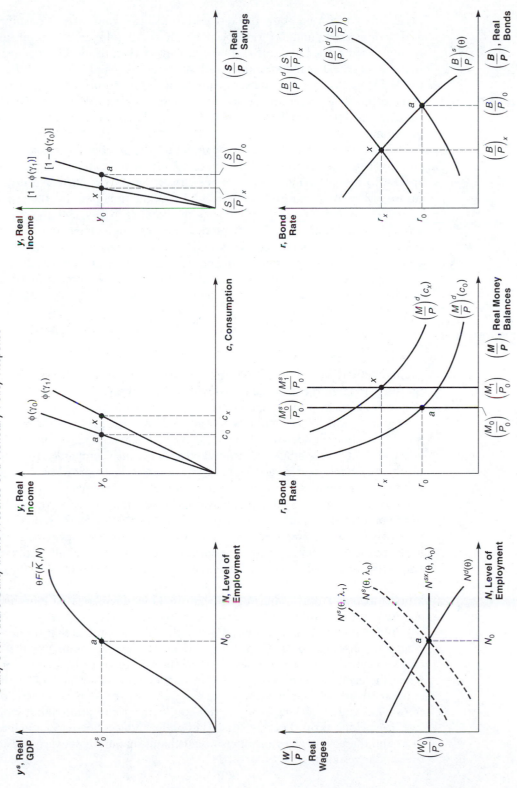

preference for consumption also restored to its prior value of γ_0, consumption and savings are c_0 and $(S/P)_0$, respectively. In the bond market, equilibrium is reestablished at the bond rate r_0. In the money market, the decline in consumption reduces the demand for money and the money demand schedule shifts back to $(M/P)^d(c_0)$. To prevent an excess supply of money from emerging, the monetary authority must reduce the nominal money supply to M_0^s so that the money supply schedule shifts back to (M_0^s/P_0), which coincides with its original position.

As previously stated, the monetary authority is able to achieve its full-employment and stable-price objectives simultaneously in each period in response to the intertemporal preference shock that favors current utility over future utility. As illustrated in Figure 12.13 by the time path for the economy over the two periods that the preference shock takes to dissipate, the monetary authority adds liquidity in the first period to boost employment and output and removes liquidity from the economy in the second period to avoid an overstimulation of the economy that would otherwise occur as the shock dissipates. Once again, the composition of output is affected. Consumption increases in the first period, while production of investment goods falls.

12.7   SUMMARY

In this chapter, we examine two features of the economy often stressed by economists who favor theories associated with J. M. Keynes. One is the presence of long-term labor contracts that fix the nominal wage for an extended period of time, during which labor mobility is limited. This feature is modeled by assuming that all households are employed under a single labor agreement and that labor mobility is prohibited. A productivity shock unaccompanied by a monetary policy response is demonstrated to be completely absorbed by a price adjustment that enables the economy to remain at full employment, without the need for a change in the nominal wage. However, in contrast to the economy of the preceding chapter in which prices were set in advance, the monetary authority is unable to simply accommodate the productivity shock with a change in the nominal money supply that would enable it to meet the full-employment and stable-price objectives simultaneously. It must make choices. For the economy to remain at full employment, prices must adjust, but achieving price stability forces quantity adjustments that include deviations of output and employment from their respective full-employment levels.

In the absence of productivity shocks, the labor contracts that set nominal wages in advance preclude an adjustment of the economy to the full-employment level in which prices remain stable. However, if a shock occurs when the economy is initially in equilibrium under a labor agreement that is consistent with full employment, a monetary policy exists that can exactly offset the shock while achieving both the full-employment and price-stability objectives for as long as the shock persists. That policy induces fluctuations in interest rates and thereby involves a compositional change in output between consumption and investment goods.

Figure 12.13   Time Paths for the Macroeconomic Variables in Response to an Intertemporal Preference Shock Favoring Current Utility over Future Utility in the Presence of a Monetary Policy Response

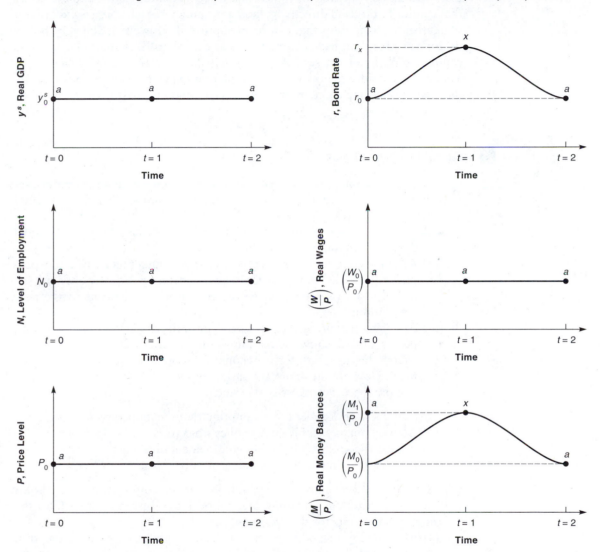

The short-run economic definition of full employment may include preference shocks. Because such shocks are transitory, the short-run economic definition of full employment may differ from the long-run economic definition of full employment, which ignores transitory shocks. Because the full-employment objective is based on the latter definition, there is some question as to whether or not it is an appropriate goal for policy. A case must be made that transitory preference shocks can induce a costly adjustment that may involve a certain amount of "churning" in the factor markets, particularly in the labor market. However, even if that were true, some degree of factor market churning is constructive in that it is accompanied by a reallocation of resources over time, which is a vitally important feature of any healthy, dynamic economy. To a large extent, comparisons of the costs and benefits are *microeconomic* issues that cannot be targeted directly by monetary policy, which consists exclusively of aggregate policy tools that can be manipulated. However, monetary policy decisions can and do have consequences at the micro level and policy makers cannot simply ignore these issues when they consider alternative policy goals. They must consider them when contemplating explicit policy actions that are directed at achieving a narrower set of macroeconomic goals.

■ REVIEW QUESTIONS

1. With the economy in equilibrium at full employment, assume that households and firms negotiate a one-period labor contract that fixes nominal wages for the upcoming period.
   (a) Sketch the initial equilibrium for the economy using the graphic model developed in this chapter.
   (b) After the contract takes effect, the economy undergoes a negative productivity shock. In the absence of any monetary policy response, use the model in part (a) to describe the economy's adjustment to the new equilibrium.
   (c) Assuming that no further shocks occur in the economy in the following period, describe how the economy adjusts in the second period.
   (d) Sketch the time path for the economy over the two periods of adjustment. How are the monetary authority's stabilization policy objectives compromised over these two periods?

2. Answer question 1 under the assumption that the monetary authority:
   (a) Actively pursues stabilization policy objectives.
   (b) Is concerned only with the full-employment objective.
   (c) Is concerned only with the stable-price objective.

3. With the economy initially in equilibrium at full employment, households and firms negotiate a binding one-period labor agreement that fixes the nominal wage rate for the upcoming period.
   (a) After the contract takes effect, the economy undergoes an intratemporal preference shock that favors leisure over consumption. Illustrate the equilibrium response of the economy in the absence of any response by the monetary authority.
   (b) How would that equilibrium differ if the monetary authority is actively pursuing short-run stabilization objectives?
   (c) Explain how households are frustrated in fulfilling their short-run objectives in the case described in (a). How are their short-run objectives frustrated in the case described in (b)?

*4. The timing of events is crucial in determining the equilibrium to which the economy adjusts in response to economic shocks. Describe the time path for the economy in each of the following instances, where the events described all occur at the beginning of "period 1."

(a) The economy is initially in equilibrium at full employment. Households and firms agree to a one-period labor contract that fixes the nominal wage for the upcoming period, after which the economy undergoes a positive productivity shock. The monetary authority responds in an effort to achieve short-run stabilization objectives.

(b) With the economy initially in equilibrium at full employment, the economy undergoes a positive productivity shock that is incorporated into the one-period labor contract that fixes the nominal wage for the upcoming period. Afterward, monetary policy is altered to achieve short-run stabilization objectives.

(c) With the economy in equilibrium at full employment, the economy undergoes a positive productivity shock. The monetary authority responds in pursuit of short-run stabilization objectives. Households and firms then enter into a one-period labor agreement that fixes the nominal wage for the upcoming period.

*5. The terms of the labor agreement may be very important to the monetary authority's ability to achieve its objectives. In each of the following scenarios, assume that the following events take place over a two-period time frame. At the beginning of period 1, a positive productivity shock occurs, followed by a change in monetary policy. At the beginning of period 2, an intertemporal preference shock that favors future utility over current utility occurs and monetary policy responds. In both periods, the monetary authority is pursuing short-run stabilization objectives.

(a) Before the productivity shock occurs in the first period, households and firms sign a two-period labor agreement that fixes the nominal wage over the life of the contract.

(b) After the productivity shock in the first period but before the monetary policy response, a two-period labor agreement is signed by households and firms that fixes the nominal wage over the life of the contract.

(c) After the productivity shock and the monetary policy response at the beginning of period 1, a two-period labor agreement is signed by households and firms that fixes the nominal wage over the life of the contract.

(d) In each of the three cases (a), (b), and (c), speculate on how the answers would change if only part of the workforce were bound by the labor agreement. How would the results change in this case if labor were mobile?

◼ REFERENCES

Benhabib, Jess, Richard Rogerson, and Randall Wright. 1991. "Homework in Macroeconomics: Household Production and Aggregate Fluctuations." *Journal of Political Economy* 99 (December): 1166–1187.

Fischer, Stanley. 1977. "Long-Term Contract, Rational Expectations, and the Optimal Money Supply Rule." *Journal of Political Economy* 85 (February): 191–206.

Gray, Jo Anna. 1976. "Wage Indexation: A Macroeconomic Approach," *Journal of Monetary Economics* 2 (April): 221–235.

Greenwood, Jeremy and Zvi Hercowitz. 1991. "The Allocations of Capital and Time over the Business Cycle." *Journal of Political Economy* 99 (6): 1188–1214.

Phelps, Edmund S. and John B. Taylor. 1977. "Stabilizing Powers of Monetary Policy under Rational Economics." *Journal of Political Economy* 85 (February): 163–190.

Taylor, John B. 1980. "Aggregate Dynamics and Staggered Contracts." *Journal of Political Economy* 88 (February): 1–23.

Descriptive Dynamics and Inflation

CHAPTER 13

A CRITIQUE OF STABILIZATION POLICY

Actual economies are continuously undergoing real shocks, such as new product development, OPEC oil supply decisions, and natural disasters, that collectively may affect aggregate employment, output, and prices. Shocks may cause an economy to move away from its long-run equilibrium position of full employment. Moreover, the economy may not quickly absorb the shocks, but may remain below or above full employment for an extended period of time. The slow adjustment could be due to price or nominal wage rigidities in the economy, such as those described in Chapters 11 and 12, or to the costly real-location of the economy's resources of capital and labor necessitated by the shock, that is, from an industry that is adversely affected by the shocks to another industry that is favorably affected.[1] The economy's slow adjustment to shocks suggests a possible role for the monetary authority with respect to the full-employment objective examined in the preceding chapters.

An active stabilization policy requires the monetary authority to monitor continuously the state of the economy, observe the shocks to which it is being subjected, forecast the consequences of those shocks if the economy were left unattended, and finally design and implement policies that would counteract any expected adverse affects of the shocks to keep the economy as close to full employment in the short run as possible. Obviously, such a policy is a complex undertaking that requires an extraordinary depth of knowledge of the economy. Do the policy makers have such knowledge? That is, is such a policy feasible?

The purpose of this chapter is to illustrate the difficulties inherent in stabilization policy. A critique of traditional stabilization policy is given, which is

---

[1]For empirical evidence on these adjustment costs, see Lilien (1982), Abraham and Katz (1986), Loungani, Rush, and Tave (1990), and Toledo and Marquis (1993).

consistent with the views of economists known as monetarists who are associ-ated with the economic theories of monetarism. Monetarists believe that, be-cause of a lack of knowledge, efforts by the monetary authority to smooth business cycles are more likely to fail than to succeed. As a consequence, the economy will become less rather than more stable under stabilization policies. The conclusion is that active stabilization policies should not be pursued. Chap-ter 14 examines the alternative policy prescriptions that have been proposed by the monetarists.

13.1   THE MONETARIST CRITIQUE OF STABILIZATION POLICY

No generally accepted list of principles collectively constitutes a doctrine called monetarism any more than one does for Keynesian or the more modern new classical theories.[2] No such cataloguing of principles is attempted here. Instead, a few overarching features of monetarism that distinguish it from the traditional Keynesian theories are revealed within the context of a critique of the type of active stabilization policy that would be favored by Keynesian economists.[3] Note that although the theoretical paradigm under which mod-ern macroeconomic research is conducted has shifted significantly in recent years, many of the distinctions drawn here are still at issue in contemporary policy debates.

A fundamental premise of monetarism is that market economies are inher-ently stable unless they are acted upon by erratic government policies. Business cycles are seen to be naturally occurring phenomena that represent part of the evolution of a healthy, dynamic economy. They arise from the need to reallo-cate resources in a more efficient way when the opportunities for making the most of those resources change as a result of technological progress or other real shocks to an economy.

From that perspective, it is unclear that the goal of stabilization policy, to smooth business cycles, is a proper one. First, if the economy can absorb shocks relatively quickly on its own, there is no need for government action to accel-erate or decelerate economic activity in the short run. That is particularly true if there is a long time lag between the implementation of policy and its ultimate effect on the economy. Second, the principal goal of stabilization policy is spec-ified in terms of full employment, that is, according to the economic definition of that term. How do policymakers identify full employment when they see it?

---

[2]Mayer (1978) attempted to compile such a list. Also, Stein (1982) attempted to evaluate some of the crucial differences between Keynesian, monetarist, and new classical theo-ries when the last were still at a very early stage of development. More recently, Hoover (1988) and Lucas (1987) have attempted to characterize new classical theories paradigmatically.

[3]The organizing principles of this critique are taken from Friedman (1953).

If they are unable to identify it, they do not have a clearly defined policy objective.[4]

Identifying full employment is a very practical problem for policy makers. In general, to monitor the progress of the economy through time, policy makers rely on government economic statistics, such as the civilian unemployment rate, GDP, and others. To have a clearly stated policy goal, they must be able to state the goal in terms of numerical values for one or more of those statistics. One way to approach the problem is to collect the statistics over a period of time and attempt to identify long-run trends or patterns in the data. A statistical procedure could then be used to approximate the full-employment time path for the statistics, which is assumed to be represented by the long-run trends. Current observations on the statistics may show them to be above or below the paths, which in combination could suggest that the economy is either below or above full employment and in need of a corrective policy action.

The problem with this approach is that the *operational definition* of full employment on which policy decisions *are* based is generally not the same as the *economic definition* of full employment on which policy decisions *should* be based. There are two general causes of the discrepancy. One is measurement error due to the inability of a statistic to portray accurately a phenomenon that it was designed to quantify. A particularly notorious example is the U.S. civilian unemployment rate. Ideally, a policy maker would like to have a number that reflects whether the economy is growing fast enough to keep pace with the long-run trend rate of growth in the labor force. When the number becomes "too high," the economy is below full employment and requires a stimulus; when the number becomes "too low," the economy is temporarily above full employment and requires a contractionary policy. Unfortunately, the civilian unemployment rate measures the percentage of the total labor force that is currently unemployed, *but actively seeking work*. The qualifier leads to unusual movements in the number. Often, for example, a large surge in employment raises expectations of securing a job among people out of work and they reenter the labor market. The measured unemployment rate then rises, not because more people are out of work, but because the economy strengthened!

A second problem in identifying the state of the economy that corresponds to the economic definition of full employment is that a dynamic, healthy economy is *always* undergoing some degree of fundamental structural change as better methods of using the economy's resources are sought. An extrapolation or projection of past trends into the future—even if those trends accurately portrayed full employment in the past—does not necessarily represent conditions that will be consistent with full employment in the future. Again, the U.S. civilian unemployment rate is a particularly egregious example of this problem. In the 1960s, the full-employment level (or natural rate) of unemployment was approximately three percent. However, the figure rose dramatically during the 1970s and early 1980s because of both demographic changes, with the post-

---

[4]This is also a problem, although to a lesser extent, for the monetarists' policy alternatives. The issue is taken up in the next chapter.

war baby boomers coming of age, and the changing attitudes of women toward work. Those factors caused the supply of labor to grow more rapidly than the economy was able to expand jobs. By the late 1980s, the full-employment level of unemployment appeared to have risen to more than six percent, or to have more than doubled![5] Policies based on the three percent figure would have been grossly in error.

Most economic data (at least for developed countries such as the United States) do not have the problems of measurement error and structural change to the same extent as the U.S. civilian unemployment rate, but they are not immune from those problems. Keynesian economists who favor an active stabilization policy would argue that the problems with measurement error and structural change, where the latter is assumed to occur slowly over time, can be minimized by not relying on a small set of statistics. Instead, the monetary authority should obtain information from a wide variety of sources that collectively provide a picture of the economy's long-run growth potential, thereby operationalizing the policy objective of full employment, as well as a picture of the economy's short-run performance. To the extent that those two pictures do not match, an appropriate set of policy actions can be undertaken.

However, that argument suggests that in setting an operational definition of full employment, the data are open to interpretation. Monetarists argue that the result is an ill-defined policy objective usually expressed in a vague statement of intent and subject to change and manipulation. It may become an important source of uncertainty in the economy that can have negative long-run consequences, as described more fully in the next chapter.

13.2 TIME LAGS AND MACROECONOMIC DYNAMICS

The policy analysis conducted in the chapters of Part III first identifies a sequence of equilibria through which the economy passes under a given monetary policy as it absorbs a particular set of shocks. The analysis is then repeated for an identical set of shocks, but under an alternative policy. The effects of the change in policy on the time path of the economy are determined by comparing the sequences of equilibria. In a dynamic context, however, the principal objective of stabilization policy can be stated as attempting to keep the economy *continuously* at or near full employment. Hence, in the design and implementation of policy, timing is everything. Because the equilibrium analysis ignores all of the intervening dynamics during the adjustment process between successive equilibria, it may provide an incomplete description of the effects of alternative policy choices and could result in misleading policy recommendations. That is particularly true if the dynamic adjustments of the economy to policy

---

[5]Recent empirical evidence suggests that this figure began to decline in the early 1990s, as the economy had largely absorbed the surge of new entrants to the workforce during the 1970s and early 1980s.

and/or non-policy-related shocks are less predictable and involve longer lags than the model suggests.

We can understand the importance of the time dimension for the success of stabilization policy by considering four kinds of time lags and the macroeconomic dynamics that characterize an economy. The recognition lag is the time it takes for the policy maker to recognize that the economy has moved significantly away from the policy goal of full employment and is in need of a corrective policy action. The policy design and implementation lag is the time it takes to formulate and put into place a corrective policy. Once the new policy action has been taken, a third time lag is associated with the dynamic adjustment of the economy to the policy change. That is, it takes time for the economy to absorb the policy shock completely. Finally, between the time the economy moves away from full employment and the time the corrective policy action takes effect, the state of the real economy is continuously changing. By the time a, say, stimulative policy is felt in the real economy, the underlying macrodynamics of the economy that are unrelated to the policy change may already have restored the economy to full employment.

13.3 RECOGNITION LAG

Policy makers must rely on data to assess the current state of the economy in terms of full employment. Unfortunately, with the exception of financial market data such as interest rates and stock and bond prices, the data cannot be monitored continuously because they are available only at monthly, or even quarterly, intervals. Hence, policy makers are *always* relying on "old data" that reflect what the state of the economy *was* in the recent past, and not what the state of the economy currently *is* at the time policy decisions are being taken. To compound this problem, the data are initially compiled into statistics, such as business fixed investment, and released for a given period, say, for the first quarter of the year, then subsequently revised as more information on the particular statistics become available. The magnitude of the revisions is often quite large. Consequently, a policy based on the initial figures (that is, before the revisions) is premised on an inaccurate picture of the state of the economy in the recent past and for that reason alone could be substantially in error.

One of the most important sets of statistics (perhaps the single most important) that characterizes the state of the U.S. economy is the National Income and Product Accounts (NIPAs). Among the data included in the NIPAs are Gross Domestic Product (GDP) and Gross National Product (GNP), which are measures of the total value of goods and service produced in the United States.[6] The numbers are compiled quarterly. The Commerce Department releases the GDP figures in three stages. The "preliminary" or "initial" release is made ap-

---

[6]GDP is defined as GNP less the value of goods and services produced by offshore plants owned by U.S. firms plus the value of goods and services produced by foreign-owned plants in the United States.

proximately three weeks after the quarter has ended. However, these numbers are based on samples and therefore are only estimates. Within a month, after more data become available, the Commerce Department releases what is called the "first revision," usually during the third week of the second month after the quarter has ended. Within the next few weeks, more data become available, particularly the international trade or current account data, and are incorporated into the so-called "final revision."[7] The revisions are often very large. It is not uncommon for revisions to growth rates to exceed 50 percent!

The magnitude of the revisions suggests that the monetary authority should not be too quick to alter policy as new economic data become available. The longer it waits to respond to the picture of the economy drawn from the economic statistics, the more accurate will be the picture of the actual state of the economy for that time period. This poses a dilemma for the monetary authority. Should it act quickly on, say, the preliminary figures with the understanding that its policy is based on an inaccurate view of the economy, or should it wait until better data become available, albeit from a more distant past? In the latter instance, it runs the risk that further unforeseen dynamic changes to the underlying state of the economy will have occurred that could render the policy ill-timed and perhaps inappropriate.

13.4   POLICY DESIGN AND IMPLEMENTATION LAGS

Once the monetary authority has identified a mismatch between its picture of the current state of the economy and the policy goal of full employment, it must formulate a corrective policy and have it put into place. Once again, the longer the lags, the greater the risk that the policy will be ill timed. However, for monetary policy, the lags can be made quite short. For example, in the United States, the decision-making arms of the Federal Reserve are the seven-member Board of Governors, which determines discount rate and reserve requirement policies, and the 12-member Federal Open Market Committee (FOMC), which determines open market operations policy. The governors of the Federal Reserve are in frequent contact with one another and could quickly alter the discount rate or reserve requirement policies, but such policy changes are not made frequently. One reason is that changes in the discount rate or in reserve requirements tend to have large or "gross" effects on the economy whereas the effects of open market operations tend to be "incremental." Such changes therefore require considerably more forethought about their long-run consequences. That is particularly true of reserve requirements, where monetary control (or the ability of the Federal Reserve to control the supply of money in the economy) may become an issue. Therefore, the effort to "fine tune" the economy through monetary policy is principally accomplished through open market operations.

---

[7]In fact, this set of numbers is also revised after periodic reviews of the NIPAs.

The FOMC holds regularly scheduled meetings eight times a year to review its open market operations policy and make decisions about policy changes. In preparation for the meetings, background material on various aspects of the economy are compiled by staff members at the Federal Reserve. The information is distributed to the members of the FOMC and incorporated into subsequent policy discussions. From the discussions, a strategy is formulated to guide policy until the next FOMC meeting. The decisions are condensed into a policy directive, a set of guidelines on how the policy is to be implemented. The policy directive is then sent to the desk manager at the Federal Reserve Bank of New York, who is responsible for the actual conduct of open market operations.

The process takes time. However, if policy makers believe economic conditions warrant an immediate policy response, an unscheduled FOMC meeting can be called and a new policy can be formulated. Moreover, such meetings are often structured as conference telephone calls to expedite the decision-making process. As a result, monetary policy design and implementation lags can be rendered relatively inconsequential in terms of aggravating the risk of adopting an ill-timed policy.

The same *cannot* be said of fiscal policy design and implementation lags, particularly if new legislation is required. Since the 1960s, there has been greater recognition of this shortcoming of fiscal policy in the United States, along with a greater appreciation of the significant impact monetary policy can have on the economy (in the post-Bretton Woods era). Consequently, the emphasis of stabilization policy has shifted in a fundamental way, away from principal reliance on fiscal policy measures and toward a dominant role for monetary policy.

13.5 THE DYNAMIC RESPONSE OF THE ECONOMY TO A CHANGE IN MONETARY POLICY

Once the decision to change policy has been made and a new policy has been selected and implemented, the economy will require some time to absorb the change in policy completely. The important question for the monetary authority is: How long will the adjustment process take and how predictable is the economy's dynamic response to the policy change during the period of adjustment? Answers differ widely among economists. Monetarists believe the economy's dynamic response to a monetary policy change involves long and variable lags. Keynesians counter that the short-run response is relatively predictable. More modern economic theories hold that the response depends on the way in which monetary policy is altered and the extent to which the new policy is anticipated.

Unfortunately, the data that could potentially resolve these important issues are simply not powerful enough to distinguish unambiguously between the competing theories. What can be said from the data is that, on average, changes in the money supply have historically preceded changes in output and changes in the price level, and that the changes have all been in the same direction. That is, increases in the money supply are more often than not followed by a pickup in economic activity[8] and a rise in prices. Although this observation cannot be taken as evidence that changes in the money supply *caused* (in a literal sense) changes in economic activity, theories of the role of money in the economy cannot be incompatible with those empirical regularities if they are to be believed.

In this chapter, the monetarists' views are presented to illustrate the importance of these dynamic issues for stabilization policy. For exposition, it is useful to characterize monetary policy changes fully by changes in the nominal money supply. Therefore, the lag between open market operations and changes in the money supply via the multiple deposit creation mechanism described in Chapter 7 is assumed to be relatively short and of little consequence. That assumption reflects the efficiency with which the federal funds market quickly absorbs any undesired changes in excess reserves (that is, undesired by the commercial banks) in the banking system induced by open market operations. Therefore, the dynamic response of the economy portrayed is to a change in the money supply brought about by a one-time change in monetary policy.

With that characterization, a one-time change in monetary policy can fit into one of two qualitatively different categories. One is a one-time change to the *level* or stock of the money supply, which is essentially the type of policy analyzed in Chapters 9 through 12. The other is a one-time change in the *growth rate* of the money supply. The latter type of policy change can induce a sustained increase in the rate of change of the price level, or the inflation rate, whereas the former cannot. Distinguishing between these two one-time changes in monetary policy is therefore important in the policy analysis because they can have fundamentally different effects on the real economy. In this chapter, the focus is on changes in monetary policy that can be characterized fully by a one-time change in the growth rate of the nominal money supply.

13.6   SLUGGISH PRICES

On one point, most Keynesians and monetarists agree: Once the monetary authority changes the nominal money supply, all other nominal variables in the economy take time to adjust. That is, there is a certain "stickiness" to nominal variables that causes fluctuations in real variables over the period of adjustment. In the two preceding chapters, the consequences of sticky prices and sticky nominal wages were examined in the context of equilibrium models in which households were making consumption/savings, labor/leisure, and portfolio allocation decisions to maximize utility and firms were making employment and capital investment decisions to maximize profits. This chapter proceeds by simply offering a description of a set of economic dynamics that characterizes the

---

[8]Because of this statistical property of money, a measure of the money supply (currently M2) is one of the statistics that make up the U.S. Commerce Department's "index of leading economic indicators." Changes in this index tend to foreshadow changes in economic activity.

adjustment process. The pattern of economic dynamics is premised on the assumption of sluggish prices and is simply taken as an "empirical fact."[9]

Although monetarists believe prices adjust slowly in response to a change in the money supply induced by a change in monetary policy, the "transmission mechanism" they envision operating in the economy is somewhat different from that described in Chapter 9.[10] Their views are based on a theory of the demand for money that emphasizes the store-of-value feature of money rather than its function as a medium of exchange. Households have a portfolio of assets that constitutes their wealth holdings. The portfolio includes bonds, equities, human capital, and consumption goods, as well as money. The demand for money is based on the household's determination of the optimal quantities of each of those assets to hold that will enable it to maintain a portfolio balance. Hence, the (risk-adjusted) rate of return must be the same for all assets, where rate of return includes not only pecuniary (or dollar) returns, but also nonpecuniary (nondollar) returns. The return on real money balances then includes any interest income received, as well as the liquidity services that monetary assets can provide.

When a shock to the economy occurs, households' wealth portfolios are thrown out of balance as the returns across assets are no longer equal. Households have excess supply of some assets and excess demand for others. The resulting disequilibria cause the prices of, and therefore the returns on, the assets to change until a new equilibrium is reached. This portfolio adjustment process in response to a monetary shock is what determines the monetary transmission mechanism. The mechanism begins with all household portfolios in balance. The monetary authority then conducts open market operations that increase the growth rate of the nominal supply of money in the economy. Initially, before any prices have had a chance to adjust, real money balances increase. As a consequence, households find that their wealth portfolios are no longer in balance. They have an excess supply of real money balances, because the return to money is too low in relation to the return on alternative assets. To reduce their money holdings, households exchange money for other assets. That is, they use money to purchase other assets. The implication in this example is that the excess supply of money coincides with an excess demand for *all* other assets. To equilibrate these markets, the prices of nonmonetary assets rise and their returns fall. One of the nonmonetary assets is goods. As goods prices rise, the quantity of real money balances falls, which in turn raises the return to real money balances. That process continues until the returns to all assets in the wealth portfolios are equalized. If there were no shock to the economy other than the increase in the monetary growth rate, the final equilibrium would consist of an increase in the rate of change of *all* nominal variables by the same percentage as the original increase in the growth rate of the nominal money

[9]See Lucas (1975) for an equilibrium model that is largely consistent with the set of dynamics described in the chapter.

[10]See Friedman (1956) for the classic statement of this viewpoint.

supply. If the proportions of all real assets in the household's portfolio, including real money balances, are the same as they were before the shock, the real sector is seen to be independent of the monetary sector. When that result holds for a one-time change in the *growth rate* of the nominal money supply, monetary policy is said to be *superneutral.*

Superneutrality is a long-run equilibrium condition that is not present in all macro models.[11] However, in this chapter, the analysis centers on the feasibility of short-run stabilization policy. Therefore, for expositional purposes, monetary policy is assumed to be superneutral in the long run but not in the short run. The question of interest then becomes: What is the dynamic adjustment process to a one-time change in the growth rate of the nominal money supply? In particular, how long does the process take and how predictable are the dynamics?

13.7   LONG AND VARIABLE LAGS

The dynamic response of the economy to a one-time, say, increase in the growth rate of the nominal money supply is seen by monetarists to follow a sequence of events whereby the growth rate of output (or real income) initially rises above its long-run equilibrium level and then subsequently falls below its long-run equilibrium level.[12] When superneutrality is assumed to hold in the long run, the equilibrium growth rate of output after all of the dynamics have settled out equals its equilibrium level prior to the policy change. The initial response of the economy during the period of higher output growth is termed the "nominal income effect," and the later response during the period of slower output growth is termed the "price effect." These effects represent *net additions* (both positive and negative) *to output* in relation to what it would have been in the absence of the change in monetary policy. The sequencing of these effects results from the sluggish adjustment of prices that slows the rate at which inflation rises to its new long-run equilibrium level. However, superneutrality requires that after all of the dynamics have settled out, the cumulative changes in nominal income must equal the cumulative changes in the price level, and the percentage increases in the equilibrium growth rates of all nominal variables must be identical. This ensures that real income growth is unaffected by monetary policy changes in the long run. Therefore, the issue is: What happens to real income (and output) during the period of adjustment?

Figure 13.1 portrays the economy's dynamic response to a one-time increase in monetary growth that occurs at date $t = 0$. In the upper panel are the time paths for the change in the growth rates of the nominal variables (money, nominal income, and the price level) caused by the new policy. At any point in time, monetary growth is increased by $\Delta M_t = M^*$, and the effects of that

---

[11]The real effects of inflation are discussed in Chapter 15.

[12]See Brunner and Meltzer (1972) for a discussion of why variability in the economy's dynamic response to a monetary policy change may occur.

Figure 13.1
Dynamic Response of
the Economy to a
One-Time Increase in
the Growth Rate of
the Nominal Money
Supply

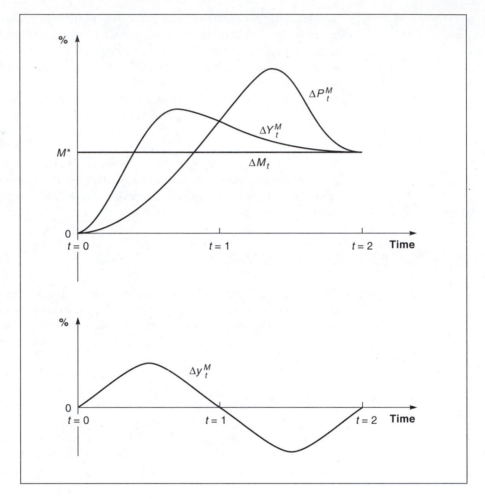

increase on nominal income growth and inflation are represented by ΔY_t^M and ΔP_t^M, respectively (the symbol "Δ" denotes "rate of change in"). One requirement imposed on these time paths by superneutrality is that all of the variables must have the same percentage increase in their long-run equilibrium growth rates, as is evident in the graph by date $t = 2$. The additional requirement that the cumulative effects on each nominal variable be the same implies that periods of slower than average growth in nominal income and prices must be offset by periods of faster than average growth during the adjustment period. In the early phase of adjustment, nominal income and prices are increasing more slowly than the nominal money supply. Consequently, if they are to catch up before date $t = 2$, there must be a period of time during which their growth rates overshoot their long-run equilibrium levels. Note that the sluggish adjustment of prices early in the adjustment period causes their overshooting to come later than that for nominal income and thus to be more pronounced (that is, there is more catching up to be done).

In the lower panel of Figure 13.1 is the time path for the additional effect of the more rapid money growth on real income (or output), denoted Δy_t^M , that is implied by the responses of nominal income and prices. Note that real income is defined as nominal income divided by the price level. Therefore, when the additional nominal income growth exceeds the increase in inflation, as in the time interval between dates $t = 0$ and $t = 1$, the monetary policy change is providing a stimulus to the economy, or $\Delta y_t^M > 0$. This is the nominal income effect. The reverse is true during the period from $t = 1$ to $t = 2$, when $\Delta y_t^M < 0$, which corresponds to the price effect. Over the entire time interval taken as a whole, the additional wealth created initially from the nominal income effect of the stimulative policy is offset by the lost wealth that follows from the price effect. Note that if this were not true, the monetary authority could create unlimited wealth by an ever-expanding or ever-contracting money supply.

Monetarists interpret the statistical evidence on the duration of the nominal income effect as suggesting that it ranges from three to nine months. Whether this period is three months or four months or nine months is unpredictable. Similarly, monetarists interpret the statistical evidence on the duration of the price effect as suggesting that it ranges from nine to 18 months. It is equally unpredictable. Simply taken together, the lengths of these periods suggest that a change in monetary policy could still have residual price effects on the economy for a full two years after the policy is implemented! Such duration far exceeds the normal maximum time horizon for stabilization policy objectives, which as stated in Chapter 9 is on the order of one year. The implication is that current monetary policy changes will introduce fluctuations into the economy that future monetary policy decisions will have to confront.

Why do the monetarists believe that the economy's dynamic response to a policy change involves such long and variable lags? Their view is that a healthy economy undergoes a continual (but stable) evolution as individuals actively seek better ways to utilize and expand their resources. Therefore, when the wealth portfolios of individuals are thrown out of balance by an increase in the money supply, it is not possible to predict the exact sequence of exchanges that would take place to restore the market equilibrium conditions necessary for portfolio balance because those exchanges are influenced by the ongoing underlying dynamics in the real economy. In fact, many sequences are possible. The uncertainty about the adjustment process prevents the monetary authority (or anyone else) from predicting movements of aggregate measures of real economic activity, such as real income or output, that are induced by changes in monetary policy.

The lower panel of Figure 13.1 portrays the general qualitative pattern of the economy's dynamic response to a one-time increase in monetary growth induced by a change in monetary policy. It illustrates how one necessary condition for an effective stabilization policy is met. A change in monetary policy today affects the real economy in the future. However, that condition is not sufficient for stabilization policy to be successful. The monetary authority must be able not only to affect output in the future, but also to predict the response *quantitatively*. That is, it must be able look to the future and determine how much additional stimulus would be created by a given change in the money supply today. The quantitative prediction has two dimensions, the *magnitude* of the response and the *timing* of the response. If the monetary authority is in error in either dimension of its prediction, a policy designed to smooth business cycles could have just the opposite effect.

To illustrate the quantitative prediction problems confronting the monetary authority, we can separate the two dimensions of magnitude and timing as in Figure 13.2. The heavy solid line represents an *expected* quantitative dynamic response of the economy associated with a given increase in monetary growth. This curve is the expected net addition to real income growth over the adjustment period, as described qualitatively in Figure 13.1, but here is labeled $E[\Delta y_t^M]$ to highlight the fact that this is an *expected* response. Note that the monetary authority is using the information it has at the time of policy formulation, or at $t = 0$, to predict what the net additions (both positive and negative) to real income will be in response to a given policy change. As suggested by Figure 13.1, the predictions are needed for the entire time path over which the economy is adjusting to the monetary stimulus.

Referring to Figure 13.2, we see that the simplest representation of an error in the prediction of the *magnitude* of the dynamic response of the aggregate economy to the monetary stimulus could be given by an actual time path such as $(\Delta y_t^M)_{mag}$. In this example, the *timing* predictions were correct. The economy was receiving both the positive and negative effects of the monetary stimulus when they were expected to be observed. However, both the positive and negative effects were stronger than anticipated. At time $t = a$, for example, the stimulus to the economy was greater than expected by an amount equal to $(\Delta y_a^M)_{mag} - E[\Delta y_a^M]$. Similarly, the simplest representation of a *timing* error in

Figure 13.2
Magnitude and Timing Errors in the Predictions of the Dynamic Response of the Economy to a One-Time Increase in the Monetary Growth Rate.

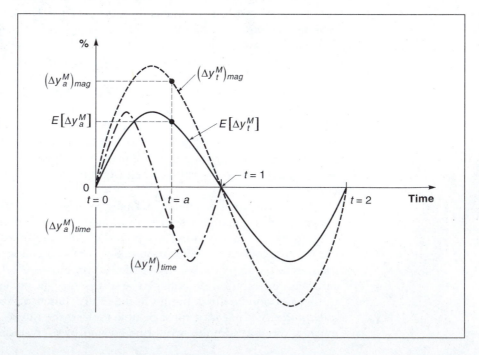

this policy is represented by an actual time path such as $(\Delta y_t^M)_{\text{time}}$. Here the magnitude of the effects of the stimulus is as anticipated, in that the amplitudes of the two curves $(\Delta y_t^M)_{\text{time}}$ and $E[\Delta y_t^M]$ (that is, their extreme positive and negative values) are identical. However, the economy actually absorbed the increase in the growth rate of the money supply by time $t = 1$ instead of $t = 2$. That is, the economy fully adjusted to the stimulative policy in exactly half of the time anticipated. In this case, the positive stimulus at date $t = a$ that was expected by the monetary authority when it designed policy, or $E[\Delta y_a^M] > 0$, was not realized. Instead, an adverse effect of the stimulus is observed, $(\Delta y_a^M)_{\text{time}} < 0$.

This discussion is intended to emphasize that the private decisions of households and firms in response to the government's monetary policy choices do not conform precisely to what the monetary authority expects them to be when it formulates policy. To the extent that the monetary authority is wrong, its policy selections will be in error and are likely to have unintended effects on the economy.

13.8   STABILIZATION POLICY IN PRACTICE

All of the issues in this chapter pertain directly to real world, practical problems that the monetary authority must confront. Policy mistakes can be caused by:

- the use of old data or an incomplete set of information,
- measurement errors and structural changes that could mislead the monetary authority into inaccurately portraying the future time path of the full-employment level of output,
- any future shocks to the real economy over the time horizon relevant to the policy decision, as well as lack of knowledge of the underlying dynamics at work in the economy at the time the decision is made, either of which could cause the forecast of future economic activity in the absence of a policy change to be in error,
- the time lag associated with the assessment of the state of the economy and the formulation and implementation of a corrective policy action, and
- unpredictability in the long and variable lagged response of the economy to a policy action.

Many economists, most notably the monetarists, believe these problems represent insurmountable obstacles to the successful conduct of an active stabilization policy. Attempts to smooth business cycles, they believe, will more often than not have the opposite effect. That is, efforts to stabilize the economy's output around its *true economic level of full employment* will actually be destabilizing, with business cycles becoming more frequent and more severe.

To appreciate this perspective, consider an extreme form of monetary policy activism that is designed to achieve short-run stabilization policy objectives. Whenever the economic data suggest that the economy has slowed unduely, monetary growth is accelerated and vice versa. In this case, the monetary authority is responding rapidly to "news." If subsequent information indicates that its prior policy actions were inappropriate because of an inaccurate forecast of economic activity, it simply adopts "corrective" policy actions to counteract any adverse effects that would otherwise ensue. Any additional errors created by the long and variable lagged responses to the corrective policies are addressed with future policy responses once their effects on the economy have been observed in the data.

A major problem with such a policy from a monetarist's point of view is that *each time* the monetary authority changes policy, it initiates and "locks into place" a set of future dynamics of the form Δy_t^M in Figure 13.1 that is uncertain in both the magnitude and the timing of its effects, but could still be operating on the economy for up to two full years after the policy was implemented. The result would be additional business cycle dynamics with which future policies would have to contend. Moreover, with frequent policy changes, the additional short-run dynamics would "pile up," adding greater uncertainty to future economic forecasts and thus causing additional policy errors to be made. Simply put, an erratic policy associated with continuous efforts to " fine tune" the economy elicits an erratic dynamic response of output that over time necessitates an even more erratic policy with an even more erratic response, and so on. As a consequence of this process, stabilization policy is rendered self-defeating.

Monetarists argue that in actual practice this process has resulted in a so-called "stop-and-go" monetary policy in the United States that has been destabilizing. Assume for example, that the economy enters a period of economic slowdown. If the monetary authority belatedly recognizes the situation and increases the money supply, the principal effect of the stimulus is not felt until the economy has largely recovered. At that point in time, the stimulus serves only to "overheat" the economy, causing the monetary authority to reduce the money supply, an action necessitated by its previous policy action. As with the stimulative policy, much of the effect of this contractionary policy occurs too late. The economy slips into a recession and the monetary authority must again attempt to add stimulus to the economy. At that point, the policy change sought by the monetary authority represents an effort to prevent its past policy decisions from creating a prolonged recession.

It is natural to ask whether the history of, say, the Federal Reserve's policy in the United States conforms to this "stop-and-go" policy during periods when it was ostensibly conducting an active stabilization policy. Unfortunately, the data that could potentially answer that question do not have the statistical power to discriminate between that view of history and an alternative view more favorable toward the use of an active stabilization policy. What can be said is that the issues raised in this chapter are indisputably of major concern. However, opinions differ as to whether policy makers' ignorance about the short-run state and dynamics of the economy is sufficient to rule out stabilization policy altogether, or merely to suggest that the monetary authority must be "appropriately" modest in the degree of activism it exercises in the actual conduct of monetary policy.

▌13.9   Summary

This chapter presents an argument against the monetary authority's pursuit of an active stabilization policy designed to smooth business cycles. Monetarists have long argued that evidence of inherent instabilities in the economy is insufficient to warrant the continual intervention in the financial markets by the central bank that such policy requires. Over the course of a normal business cycle, as the economy moves away from full employment, the episodes would not be severe enough in magnitude and duration to justify an attempt to damp them out. Moreover, such attempts by the monetary authority are more likely than not to exacerbate the severity of business cycle swings. That is, stabilization policy is simply not feasible. Monetarists point to several problems that they believe are collectively insurmountable. First, because the economic definition of full employment in a dynamic, growing economy is subject to change at any point in time, how does one measure it? There is no precise answer. Policy makers tend to examine a wide variety of data to arrive at a determination of what the current state of the economy would be if full-employment conditions prevailed. Consequently, the operational definition of full employment tends to change over time. For this reason, monetarists interpret full employment as an ill-defined policy objective that is subject to manipulation and simply creates confusion for the private sector, where long-term decisions must be made that can be rendered suboptimal by unanticipated actions by the central bank.

However, apart from not having a clearly defined objective, policy makers encounter many difficulties in attempting to achieve a *given* objective that resides in the real sector of the economy, such as attaining employment or output goals. Data relevant to the current state of the economy are unavoidably dated. Yet, using the old data, policy makers must project what the level of economic activity is likely to be in the near future. That task would be difficult even if they had accurate data on the current state of the economy. Events can unfold that would alter the future in such unpredictable ways that a policy deemed "best" before the events would only serve to worsen the state of economy in the future.

That possibility is particularly troublesome to monetarists, given their belief that actions taken today to alter the current growth rate of the money supply have effects on the real economy with long and variable lags due to the sluggish adjustment of prices. A stimulative policy first induces a nominal income effect, whereby output picks up with a lag of three to nine months. A price effect follows, during which inflation rises more rapidly than nominal income, and real income (and output) is thereby falling. The price effect could persist for an additional nine to 18 months. Therefore, a one-time increase in the monetary growth rate induces a set of dynamics into the economy that could last for as long as two years after the original policy action is taken, which far exceeds the time horizon of stabilization policy. The magnitude and timing of these two effects are unpredictable, and frequent adjustments of monetary growth in the short run therefore induce great instability in the economy as the dynamic effects tend to cumulate. The monetary authority then must alter policy in the short run in an effort to offset the effects of past policy decisions. It is these factors that monetarists believe have led the monetary authority to a "stop-and-go" policy—for example, stimulating the economy too late in the business cycle, thereby inducing inflationary pressures that necessitate a contractionary policy, which is often overdone and leads to a recession that would not otherwise have occurred and is also recognized too late, again eliciting a tardy stimulative policy, and so on. The economy is therefore made more volatile than it would have been had the monetary authority simply allowed the business cycle to run its normal course.

REVIEW QUESTIONS

1. Short-run stabilization policy must rely on accurate interpretation of changes in macroeconomic data. Describe the data problem that monetary policy makers face and how it could induce errors into policy decisions. Provide an example.

2. Describe the conditions necessary for an active short-run stabilization policy to be desirable. Given these necessary conditions, what additional conditions must be met for stabilization policy to be successful?

3. Suppose a national disaster occurred that caused households to be temporarily less optimistic about the future and to respond by reducing their planned consumption expenditures to increase their savings for the less opportune days ahead.
   (a) How would the monetary authority probably learn of the households' reaction?
   (b) What policy response might the reaction elicit?
   (c) Suppose households quickly reversed their pessimism. Describe the impact that the swing in consumer sentiment would be likely to have on the economy over time both in the absence of the policy response described in (b) and in the presence of the policy response.

*4. The Federal Reserve must maintain an ongoing forecast of economic activity if it is to conduct an active stabilization policy. The forecast includes the effects of past monetary policy decisions.
   (a) What is the current consensus forecast for employment, output, and inflation?
   (b) Describe what Federal Reserve policy has been over the past 12 months. Have there been any abrupt changes in that policy during the period?
   (c) What is the current consensus on the likely course of monetary policy in the near term? Relate it to your answers to (a) and (b).
   (d) If (c) is correct, what are the major risks the policy makers run in terms of their employment, output, and inflation objectives?

*5. Many economists have suggested that the Federal Reserve's monetary policy caused the Great Depression. Others believe that Federal Reserve policy merely precipitated the financial collapse that was imminent in any case.
   (a) What evidence is there of the Federal Reserve's role in this episode? (Hint: You may want to refer to Chapter 8.)

(b) Describe the state of the economy at the time the significant policy decisions relating to the evidence described in (a) were taken.

(c) In what ways are the policy choices that preceded the Great Depression inconsistent with what is thought of as stabilization policy today?

REFERENCES

Abraham, Katherine, and Lawrence Katz. 1986. "Cyclical Unemployment: Sectoral Shocks or Aggregate Disturbances?" *Journal of Political Economy* 94 (June, Part 1): 507–22.

Brunner, Karl, and Allan H. Meltzer. 1972. "Money, Debt, and Economic Activity." *Journal of Political Economy* 80 (September/October): 951–77.

Friedman, Milton. 1953. "The Effects of a Full-Employment Policy on Economic Stability: A Formal Analysis." In *Studies in the Quantity Theory of Money*, ed. M. Friedman. Chicago: The University of Chicago Press.

——————————. 1956. "The Quantity Theory of Money: A Restatement." Pp. 3–21. In *Studies in the Quantity Theory of Money*, ed. M. Friedman. Chicago: The University of Chicago Press.

Hoover, Kevin D. 1988. *The New Classical Macroeconomics: A Skeptical Inquiry*. Oxford and New York: Basil Blackwell.

Lilien, David M. 1982. "Sectoral Shifts and Cyclical Unemployment." *Journal of Political Economy* 90(4): 777–83.

Loungani, Prakash, Mark Rush, and William Tave. 1990. "Stock Market Dispersions and Unemployment." *Journal of Monetary Economics* 25 (June): 367–88.

Lucas, Robert E., Jr. 1975. "An Equilibrium Model of the Business Cycle." *Journal of Political Economy* 83 (6): 1113–44.

——————————. 1987. Models of Business Cycles. Oxford and New York: Basil Blackwell.

Mayer, Thomas. 1978. *The Structure of Monetarism*. New York: W. W. Norton.

Stein, Jerome L. 1982. *Monetarist, Keynesian, and New Classical Economics*. New York and London: New York University Press.

Toledo, Wilfredo and Milton H. Marquis. 1993. "Capital Allocative Disturbances and Economic Fluctuations." *Review of Economics and Statistics* 75 (May): 223–40.

CHAPTER 14

MONETARY RULES

The preceding chapter sets forth the monetarists' case against the monetary authority's pursuit of an active stabilization policy. The argument is that such policies are not needed, their objectives are not clearly defined, and they are simply not feasible. They require a depth of knowledge of the current state of the economy and of the short-run macroeconomic dynamics that no one could possibly possess. However, if that is true and if having no policy is not an option (apart from eliminating the central bank), what policy should the monetary authority adopt?

Monetarists offer an explicit policy prescription for the monetary authority. Their solution to the dilemma of policy makers who are attempting to alter the short-run course of the economy in a predetermined way when they do not have sufficient knowledge to do so is the so-called "constant growth rate" (of the money supply) or CGR rule. The design of this policy rule is based on certain *long-run* growth properties of the economy, about which monetarists believe economists *do* have sufficiently reliable information. However, this approach is also imperfect. In this chapter, the constant growth rate rule is described, its shortcomings are discussed, and some modifications to the rule that have been proposed to address partially the shortcomings are introduced. The chapter concludes with discussion (in the form of unresolved debates) about the potential long-run costs and benefits of conducting policy according to a monetary rule versus a discretionary policy of "fine tuning."

14.1 LONG-RUN POLICY OBJECTIVES

Monetarists believe monetary policy should be made transparent. The private sector should not have to guess continually about what public policy currently is and how it may change in the future. Moreover, for the reasons outlined in Chapter 13, monetarists do not believe short-run policy objectives are attainable. Hence, the monetary authority should focus only on the long run and on policy goals that are clearly stated. What long-run goal should it strive to achieve? The long-run neutrality of monetary policy indicates that a one-time, say, increase in the money supply has no long-run effects other than to raise prices. Therefore, monetary policy ought to be directed toward long-run price objectives. Defining the policy objective requires (1) a definition of "prices," (2) a clear statement of the time horizon of policy, or what is meant by the "long run," and (3) a description of the price behavior that the policy seeks to achieve.

The "prices" that are affected in the long-run by changes in the nominal money supply are the money prices of goods and services, that is, the number of currency units, which in the United States are dollars, needed to purchase, for example, an automobile or a haircut. The relative prices of automobiles and haircuts, which could be expressed as the number of haircuts that would have to be given up to purchase one automobile, can also change in the long run, but neutrality ensures that in the long-run these relative price changes are independent of their respective money prices. Relative price changes could be due to product innovations, such as automobiles becoming safer, more efficient, and less polluting but at a cost, or to changes in preferences, such as longer (shorter) men's hairstyles becoming fashionable and requiring less (more) frequent trips to the barbershop. Obviously, the monetary authority would want to choose a definition of prices that is insulated from long-run changes in relative prices. That is, it is interested in the general level of money prices of all goods and services in the economy. (Imagine what the consequences would have been if the Federal Reserve had chosen to keep the dollar price of a given computer system constant over the past decade!)

To obtain a measure of that price level, one could specify a basket of goods and services and use it to construct an index of prices. Such an index is simply a weighted average of the money prices of the items in the basket, where the weights are determined by the composition of the basket. Many choices of price level indices are available. Perhaps the two most relevant for monetary policy are the consumer price index (CPI) and the GDP implicit price deflator. There are two important differences between them. The obvious one is the composition of the baskets. The CPI is intended to measure the purchasing power of a unit of currency for the household. The basket used to construct the index is therefore intended to be representative of an average bundle of goods and services purchased by households in the economy, where the weights reflect household preferences or purchasing patterns. The GDP implicit price deflator is a much broader index that includes all goods and service produced in the economy, with weights given to the individual items in relation to their shares of GDP. The second major difference is the way the indices are constructed. The GDP implicit price deflator is calculated quarterly from actual national income and product accounts data, and is therefore subject to the same revisions as GDP described in the preceding chapter. The CPI is constructed from a monthly sample survey of consumer prices in retail stores and is *not* subject to revision.

Which of these price indices is preferred for the statement of the monetary policy objective? There is no unambiguous answer. The two indices do in fact behave somewhat differently over long time periods. In recent years, the CPI has tended to rise more rapidly than the GDP implicit price deflator (PGDP), as shown in Figure 14.1. If the monetary authority is using the index to monitor

Figure 14.1   CPI and GDP Implicit Price Deflator

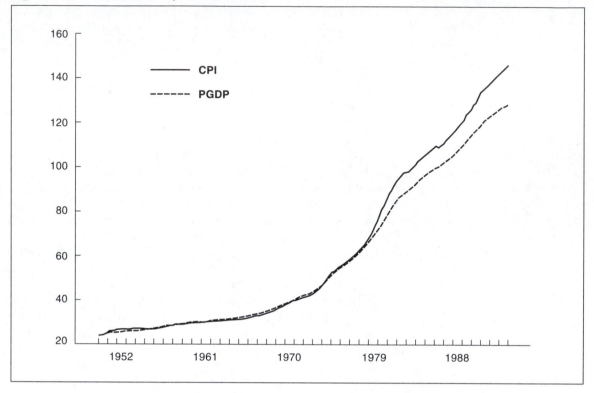

over time the purchasing power of the nominal wages of households, as re-flected in the value of the currency, the CPI may make more sense. However, purchasing patterns frequently change whereas the composition of the basket of goods and services used to construct the CPI is not often revised. To some extent, changes in purchasing patterns are automatically reflected in the GDP implicit price deflator, but that index includes many other items, such as busi-ness investment goods, that only indirectly affect the purchasing power of a household's nominal wages. Proponents of monetary rules have often stated that it is less important which price index the monetary authority chooses than it is to choose *one* index, incorporate it into the policy design, and stick with it. In this chapter, the price index is assumed to be the CPI. Its merits are discussed in more detail in the next chapter in the context of optimal inflation.

An empirical fact is that money prices fluctuate over the business cycle. Therefore, a policy addressing the long-run behavior of the price level must sys-tematically ignore the short-run fluctuations of prices associated with the business cycle. The maximum time horizon for stabilization policy of one year, described in preceding chapters, is clearly too short. The average length of business cycles in the United States economy since World War II is approximately seven and one-half years, which suggests that a minimum time horizon for a policy with long-run price objectives is seven to eight years. The policy objective therefore is stated in terms of the long-run average behavior of the price level over the business cycle.

In practice, the implication is that the relative success or failure of this monetary policy can be measured only in relation to the actual cycle-average behavior of the price level. That is, it must be compared with the stated objectives of the monetary authority. For reasons that are discussed more fully in the next chapter, a predictable long-run average price level is generally seen to be desirable. The monetarist policy objective can be stated as the attainment of long-run average price level stability. It amounts to picking a long-run average inflation rate of zero, such that on average the price level remains unchanged. The implication is that the purchasing power of the currency for the basket of goods used to define the price level remains constant (on average) over time.

14.2   Policy Design: The Constant Growth Rate (CGR) Rule

To achieve the price-level objective, the monetary authority must decide how fast to allow the money supply to grow. Excessive monetary growth leads to systematic inflation whereas insufficient monetary growth is deflationary. The growth rate is determined in part by the continual expansion of liquidity needs that naturally occurs as the result of economic growth. The first step in policy design is therefore to make a forecast of long-run economic growth, which is defined as the cycle average rate of growth of real GDP. That rate is denoted $\hat{y}^P$, where the "hat" designates percentage growth rates and the superscript "P" indicates that the long-run changes are permanent.

The monetary authority then must choose the measure of money whose supply it wants to control. The many potential choices generally include the monetary aggregates M1, M2, M3, and L that were defined in Chapter 3 and the reserve aggregates, such as total bank reserves, nonborrowed reserves, and the monetary base, that were defined in Chapter 7. The two basic criteria for this choice are: (1) How much control does the central bank have over the supply of the aggregate? and (2) How predictable is the demand for the aggregate? It is important to emphasize that the answers to these two questions should be based on different time horizons. The preceding chapter makes the case that *short-run* fluctuations in the *money supply* are a major source of instability in the economy. This suggests that a monetary policy designed to limit instability in the real economy that is attributable to monetary sources should be one that stabilizes the rate of expansion of the money supply over relatively short time periods. However, the time period ultimately chosen may depend on which of the monetary or reserve aggregates the central bank selects as the instrument of policy.[1] In general, the more narrowly defined the aggregate, the closer the control the central bank can exercise over its supply. For example, the central bank

---

[1]In this chapter, no distinction is made between policy instruments and intermediate targets. However, by definition, monetary rules such the CGR rule rely on reserve aggregates as the policy instrument and monetary aggregates as the intermediate target. The distinction between policy instruments and intermediate targets, along with the "optimality" of the choice, is discussed at length in Chapter 16.

can control the supply of any of the reserve aggregates through open market operations and through the administration of the discount window (where member banks can borrow reserves from the central bank on a short-term basis) within in a very narrow range on a week-by-week basis.[2] In contrast, the central bank has less short-run control over the monetary aggregates, as described in Chapter 7. Control declines as the definition of money becomes broader. For example, the monetary authority has better short-run control over M1 than over M2 and better short-run control over M2 than over M3. The role of bank decisions about excess reserves and the structure of their liabilities and the role of household decisions on the composition of their liquid asset portfolios become more significant as the aggregate becomes more encompassing of a larger set of assets. The monetary authority can exercise relatively good control over the supply of any one of those aggregates over a several-week period. However, the money supply cannot be kept within as narrow a range as would be possible for reserve aggregates. In terms of controllability, therefore, reserve aggregates are preferred to monetary aggregates and narrow measures of money are preferred to broad measures.

For policy design purposes, the interest in the predictability of the demand for the monetary or reserve aggregate derives from the need to identify the long-run equilibrium relationship between the nominal supply of the aggregate, real income or output (real GDP), denoted y, and the price level, P. Recall from Chapter 3 that, for a monetary aggregate, this relationship is summarized by the long-run trend in velocity, V, which is defined as the ratio of nominal income or nominal GDP, denoted Y and equal to the product y(times)P, to the nominal money supply, M. A similar velocity measure could be constructed for a reserve aggregate by replacing M with the nominal supply of reserves. An empirical fact that is that *all* velocity measures are procyclical. This once again suggests that attention should be focused on the long-run trend, or cycle average, behavior of velocity when selecting the monetary or reserve aggregate according to criterion 2 above.

To illustrate the implications for the selection of the policy instrument, recall from Chapter 3 the discussion of the behavior of the velocity measures in the United States. Prior to the implementation of the Depository Institutions Deregulation and Monetary Control Act of 1980, M1 velocity was very stable in the short run and had a very predictable long-run trend of approximately three percent a year. It therefore could have been a good instrument through which to conduct this particular monetary policy that has long-run objectives. After 1980, that was no longer the case. The long-run trend became difficult to identify. In contrast, M2 velocity was relatively unchanged after 1980, particularly in its long-run average trend, which has remained virtually constant at a zero annual growth rate since 1960.[3] On the basis of criterion 2, M2 has become a clear choice over M1 since the early 1980s. Moreover, in terms of the

---

[2]The administration of the discount window is discussed in more detail in Chapter 16.

[3]However, as noted in Chapter 3, M2 velocity has shown anomalous behavior in the early 1990s, with an unusually sharp rise due in part to the growing use by households of stock and bond funds in their overall investment portfolio planning.

long-run average trend rate of growth of velocity, M2 has historically had the most predictable pattern of all of the monetary and reserve aggregates that are traditionally monitored.

What this example suggests is that the selection of the monetary or reserve aggregate for policy purposes would differ under the two criteria. Short-run controllability favors a reserve aggregate, whereas the predictability of the long-run average demand for the aggregate favors M2. Among the economists who advocate the monetary policy under discussion, opinions differ on what this choice should be, although today most favor either the monetary base or M2. As with the choice of definition of the price level to be used in the design of the policy rule, monetarists argue that which of the aggregates the monetary authority chooses is less important than choosing *one* and sticking with it.

The next step in the design of monetary policy according to a CGR rule is to determine how rapidly the selected monetary or reserve aggregate, denoted *A*, should be allowed to grow. The growth rate must be sufficient to accommodate the expanding needs of a growing economy without inducing systematic money price inflation. Precisely what this rate of growth should be is determined by the long-run average demand for money. This demand for money can be expressed in terms of the behavior of the selected monetary or reserve aggregate as a velocity measure, denoted V_A^P:

$$V_A^P = y^P P^P / A$$

where the superscript "*P*" indicates, as before, permanent changes or trend behavior over the business cycle. Converting this expression into growth rates and solving for the growth rate of *A*, or $\hat{A}$, yields

$$\hat{A} = \hat{y}^P + \hat{P}^P - \hat{V}_A^P .$$

Therefore, to determine how the aggregate should be allowed to expand, we need (1) the forecast of the long-run average rate of economic growth, $\hat{y}^P$, (2) a prediction of the trend rate of growth of velocity, $\hat{V}_A^P$, and (3) the selection of an inflation objective, $\hat{P}^P$.

As an example, suppose the monetary authority in the United States, the Federal Reserve, sought to achieve an inflation objective of price-level stability in the CPI by controlling the growth rate of M2. Assume that it has made a forecast of the long-run average annual growth rate of GDP of $\hat{y}^P = 3$ percent. From Chapter 3, we know that $\hat{V}_A^P$ is essentially zero. Then, the zero long-run average inflation objective, or $\hat{P}^P = 0$ percent, dictates an expansion in the growth rate of M2 of $\hat{A} = 3$ percent per year.

Once this growth rate is determined, the monetary authority should attempt to maintain it as closely as possible within the short run, as discussed above. That is, no effort should be made to fine tune the economy to offset swings in the business cycle. Moreover, because monetarists believe monetary (and fiscal) policy should be made as explicit and understandable as possible, the CGR rule that is being followed should be announced publicly. The announcement expresses a formal commitment by the monetary authority that enables the private sector, particularly firms that are contemplating investment decisions, to form firm expectations of future monetary policy actions and to monitor whether the monetary authority is remaining in compliance with the stated policy.

14.3   LONG-RUN STRUCTURAL CHANGES AND THE CGR RULE

Just as the monetarists are critical of the traditional stabilization policy, non-monetarists are critical of the CGR rule. It is appropriate to ask: If the monetary authority were to pursue strictly a CGR rule, what could go wrong? To answer this question, we first must look at the information used in formulating policy. It includes the forecast of long-run average economic growth, $\hat{y}^P$, and the prediction of trend movements in velocity, $\hat{V}_A^P$. If errors are made in either, policy errors will be introduced that would be systematic, permanent, and irreversible. Overprediction of $\hat{y}^P$ and/or underprediction of $\hat{V}_A^P$ would result in a systematic oversupply of money (and reserves) and lead to systematic inflation. Underprediction of $\hat{y}^P$ and/or overprediction of $\hat{V}_A^P$ would lead to a systematic deflation. Either of those mistakes may involve costs that the monetary authority would like to avoid.

Those two long-run trends are in fact unobservable. They can only be estimated and they are not invariant over time.[4] Changes in the trends represent fundamental structural changes in the economy similar to that discussed in Chapter 13. If the long-run average rate of productivity growth for the economy were to, say, increase because of a more rapid rate of technological advance or an increase in the rate of human capital accumulation, the long-run average rate of economic growth would rise. If the increase were unforeseen, monetary growth would be too slow to accommodate the more rapidly growing liquidity needs of the economy. The effect would be deflationary and could restrain growth for an extended period of time in relation to what would otherwise have been achieved.

Similarly, fundamental structural changes in the financial markets could induce permanent changes in the demand for money. As described in Chapter 3, the rate of change at which efficiency gains in the U.S. payments system were being realized after 1973 led to an increase in the trend rate of growth of M1 velocity. Failure to accommodate the improvements in the payments system by monetary policy would lead to a systematic oversupply of money. Sustained inflation would result.

Although such problems cannot be fully circumvented unless the monetary authority is able to perfectly predict the structural changes and accommodate them as they take effect, their impact can be mitigated without abandoning a monetary rule to govern policy decisions.[5] Rather than picking a single once-and-for-all number for $\hat{y}^P$ and another for $\hat{V}_A^P$ to be used as inputs to the CGR rule, the monetary authority could update those numbers *systematically* as new information becomes available. For example, $\hat{y}^P$ and $\hat{V}_A^P$ could be calculated as weighted moving averages of quarterly growth rates for the past seven or eight

---

[4]In fact, neither of the trends is independent of policy. Issues pertaining to the long-run effects of inflation taxes are addressed in Chapter 16.

[5]This rule was first proposed by Meltzer (1987). Also, see McCallum (1988).

years, a time horizon that corresponds to the average length of the business cycle or

$$\hat{y}^P(t) = \sum_{i=1}^{n} \omega_i \, \hat{y}(t - i)$$

$$\hat{V}_A^P(t) = \sum_{i=1}^{n} \omega_i \, \hat{V}_A(t - i)$$

where t is the date of the forecast, n is number of quarters over the seven- or eight-year period, and ω_i is the weight attached to the growth rate i periods in the past that is used in forecasting. Note that the weights must sum to one, or $\sum_{i=1}^{n} \omega_i = 1$. The choice of the weights can be structured to attach more significance to the most recent observations. The differences are illustrated in Figure 14.2. As the top panel of Figure 14.2 illustrates, if there were a slowdown in economic growth, as occurred over the late 1980s, it would be missed in the formulation of the CGR rule (FORE1), but taken into account in the modified CGR rules (FORE2 and FORE3). Similarly, the bottom panel of Figure 14.2 suggests that a dip in M2 velocity, as occurred in the early 1980s, followed by a subsequent rise, as in the late 1980s and early 1990s, would be missed in the CGR rule (FORE4), and partially accounted for in the modified CGR rules (FORE5 and FORE6).

These modifications enable the monetary rule to incorporate structural changes in productivity growth and in the financial markets systematically, albeit with a lag, into policy design while maintaining the principal features of the CGR rule. Those features are (1) long-run average price stability as the policy objective, as opposed to real output or employment objectives, (2) a focus on the long run in conducting monetary policy, rather short-run stabilization, and (3) the absence of uncertainty about policy decisions, which are conducted according to a *simple* rule that can be announced publicly, enabling the private sector to monitor the monetary authority's compliance.

14.4 FINANCIAL INSTABILITY AND THE CGR RULE

Many Keynesian economists would argue that these modification to the CGR rule are simply inadequate to cope with what they perceive to be fundamental instabilities inherent in the economy, particularly in the financial sector. Obviously, they favor an active stabilization policy that incorporates a role for the monetary authority similar to that described in Chapter 12. Their claim is that unless policy actions are taken to offset shocks quickly, and not in the systematic passive way just described, the result will be large swings in real economic activity away from full-employment levels. Up to this point, the analysis of Keynesian policy prescriptions (in preceding chapters) has focused primarily on shocks that originate in the real sector, but it applies equally to the financial markets.

To illustrate the Keynesians' concern about financial market instability, assume that the monetary authority is conducting policy according to a CGR rule,

Figure 14.2   Example of Predictions for GDP Growth and M2 Velocity (V2) Growth, post-1979, with Alternative Weights, ω_i

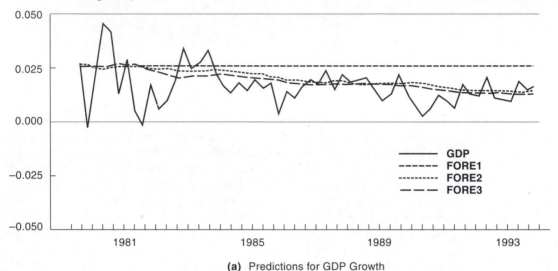

(a) Predictions for GDP Growth

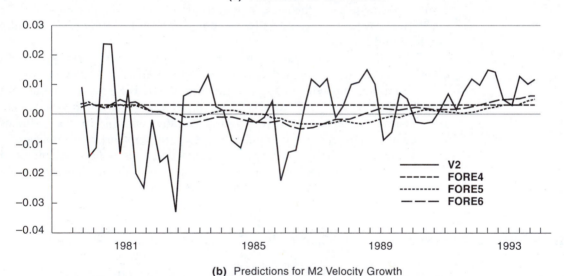

(b) Predictions for M2 Velocity Growth

Prediction 1
Once-and-for-all predictions based on average quarterly growth rates for GDP and V2 from 1973:1 to 1979:4, shown as FORE1 and FORE4.

Prediction 2
Predictions based on a moving average of the previous 30 quarters with identical weights, $\omega_i = 1/30$, shown as FORE2 and FORE5.

Prediction 3
Predictions based on a moving average of the previous 30 quarters with declining weights according to the SYD (sum of years digits) formula, $\omega_i = (n + 1 - i)/(n(n + 1)/2)$, with $n = 30$ and shown as FORE3 and FORE6.

Note: This formula produces the following sequence of weights:
$\omega_1 = 30/465$; $\omega_2 = 29/465$; $\omega_3 = 28/465$; etc..., where $\sum_{i=1}^{n} \omega_i = 1$.

where $\hat{A}$ has been determined with a once-and-for-all forecast of $\hat{y}^P$ and a one-time prediction of $\hat{V}_A^P$. What happens to output when the economy undergoes shocks to the financial markets that alter the demand for money relationships in the short run? Such shocks, denoted ε, can be characterized as deviations of actual velocity growth, $\hat{V}_A$, from $\hat{V}_A^P$, or $\hat{V}_A = \hat{V}_A^P + \varepsilon$. From the velocity relationship, actual output growth, $\hat{y}$, is given by

$$\hat{y} = (\hat{V}_A^P + \varepsilon) + \hat{A} - \hat{P} .$$

For the purpose of exposition, assume there are no shocks originating in the real sector. In that case, when $\varepsilon = 0$, $\hat{y} = \hat{y}^P$ and $\hat{P} = \hat{P}^P$. However, if ε is positive (negative), output must rise (fall) to absorb the shock unless either prices rise (fall) to reflect fully the reduction (increase) in money demand, or the money supply decreases (rises) as reflected in $\hat{A}$. Under a CGR rule, the latter cannot occur. Therefore, if prices are perceived to adjust slowly, as both Keynesians and monetarists believe, some of the financial market shock must be absorbed by output. If one further believes that the financial markets are a major source of instability in the economy, that is, the variance of ε is large, following a CGR rule allows the shocks to be transmitted directly to the real sector, leading to large swings in output and employment.[6] From that perspective, the CGR rule appears naïve. Instead, the proper role of monetary policy is to be ever vigilant in identifying disturbances in the financial markets as they arise and to respond by adjusting the money supply so that the policy actions buffer the real sector of the economy from financial market instability.

14.5 LONG-RUN CONSEQUENCES OF AN ACTIVE STABILIZATION POLICY

The principal goal of traditional stabilization policy is to attempt to regulate economic activity to keep the economy as close to full employment as possible in the short run. Stated another way, the policy attempts to smooth business cycles, thereby reducing the overall level of volatility in the real economy. That has been assumed to be a desirable goal in and of itself.[7] A question that has not been addressed is: Does an active stabilization policy have any consequences for long-run economic growth? To answer that question, we must identify the fundamental determinants of long-run economic growth and examine which if any of them could be affected by such policy. Note that inflation taxes have the potential to affect long-run growth. However, it is conceivable that

---

[6]For a statement of this position, see Blinder (1981). Note that it may be tempting to relate ε to the difference between V2 and FORE4 in the lower panel of Figure 14.2, and interpret that as evidence against the CGR rule. However, this would not be a sensible comparison, since the actual time path of V2 was influenced by a monetary policy that was *not* following a CGR rule. One can only conjecture as to what the actual path of V2, and for that matter GDP, would have been had such a policy been followed.

[7]However, see the qualifications to this view in Chapter 12, where the distinction is made between the short-run and long-run definitions of full employment.

stabilization policy can be conducted without an inflationary bias; that is, an active stabilization policy could be pursued while maintaining *any* cycle-average inflation rate, including zero. The discussion in this chapter therefore abstracts from the important issue of inflation taxes, the consequences of which are discussed in Chapter 15.

The fundamental determinants of long-run economic growth are the rates of physical and human capital accumulation. In other words, how rapidly are the factors of production growing?[8] In this chapter, we consider the rate of physical capital accumulation as determined by investment in new plant and equipment by firms. The premise is that long-run economic growth, denoted $\hat{y}^P$, is a positive function of the cycle-average level of investment, denoted in $\bar{i}^d$, or $\hat{y}^P = f(\overset{(+)}{\bar{i}^d})$. An essential determinant of investment is the interest rate, denoted r, which is now more fully specified as the expected risk-adjusted real rate of return. That interest rate represents the real cost of borrowing to firms. As it rises, any projects firms might adopt become more costly and fewer potential projects would be expected to be profitable, or $\bar{i}^d = \overset{(-)}{g(r)}$. Therefore, higher risk-adjusted real interest rates lower the rate of investment in new plant and equipment and retard long-run economic growth. Mathematically, $\hat{y}^P = f(g(r)) = \overset{(-)}{h(r)}$.

What determines the cycle-average level of the risk-adjusted real interest rate that a firm must pay to borrow from investors? Ultimately, that interest rate must reflect the rate of return associated with projects the firm undertakes. Consider what an investor "buys" upon acquiring a share of a firm's stock. Figure 14.3 is a firm's abbreviated income statement. The first entry in the income statement is sales. It is a flow variable and represents the gross revenues for the firm over a given period, such as one month or one quarter. As we move down the income statement, the various expenses the firm incurs are subtracted, including cost of goods sold, operating expenses, interest, and taxes. At the bottom of the income statement is the firm's earnings or net income for the period. As a shareholder, the investor is purchasing claims to a fraction, say $1/N$, of that net income, where N represents the number of shares outstanding. The shareholder receives the income either in the form of dividends or in the form of capital gains associated with the portion of net income that the firm has chosen to reinvest.[9] The risk-adjusted rate of return associated with the investment in the firm is therefore equal to the expected (present) value of the income stream to the shareholder divided by the share price. The higher the discounted income stream is expected to be, the higher is the price at which the firm can sell new shares of its stock. However, because investors are risk averse, the more uncertain the income stream becomes, the lower will be the price at which the

---

[8]Investment in R&D ultimately affects the rate of human capital accumulation and alters the rate of physical capital accumulation. An example of a growth model that focuses primarily on R&D investment is given by Romer (1990).

[9]These capital gains represent the expected present value of the higher future earnings associated with the new investment.

Figure 14.3
Entries on a Firm's
Income Statement

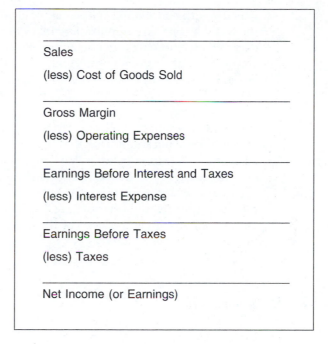

Sales

(less) Cost of Goods Sold

Gross Margin

(less) Operating Expenses

Earnings Before Interest and Taxes

(less) Interest Expense

Earnings Before Taxes

(less) Taxes

Net Income (or Earnings)

firm can sell new shares. This uncertainty, denoted σ, raises the risk-adjusted real interest rates that firms must pay to attract investors and thereby raises the costs of new projects and reduces the level of new investment in plant and equipment, or $\overset{(+)}{r(\sigma)}$. Therefore, higher uncertainty reduces long-run economic growth, or $\hat{y}^P = h(\overset{(-)}{r(\sigma)}) = F(\sigma)$.

The relevant question is: How does an active stabilization policy affect the level of uncertainty, σ? The answer depends largely on whether the stabilization policy is successful. A successful stabilization policy is one that reduces volatility in the overall level of economic activity. It would in general reduce the volatility in a firm's sales and, as we read down the income statement, we see that it would also reduce the level of volatility in net income. Therefore, the discounted stream of returns over which an individual investor is forming expectations when contemplating an investment is more predictable, and the level of uncertainty, σ, is reduced. Consequently, the investor demands a lower expected return on the investment, thereby reducing the cost of borrowing to firms. The reduction in the firms' cost of capital stimulates the rate of capital formation and the rate of long-run economic growth. From a Keynesian perspective, then, an active stabilization policy has the positive effect of stimulating the long-run growth potential of the economy.

Monetarists, of course, believe just the opposite. For the reasons outlined in the preceding chapter, they believe efforts to smooth business cycles will fail more often than not and exacerbate the volatility in the economy. The greater volatility increases the uncertainty investors face and curtails new investment, which in turn retards long-run economic growth. In addition, monetarists stress the fact that an active stabilization policy *requires* that the monetary authority exercise discretion in the conduct of monetary policy. For investors, policy discretion translates into policy uncertainty. For example, in the United States, the Federal Reserve could unexpectedly sell U.S. government bonds in the open market. The sale could depress bond prices, raise interest rates, and reduce the value of outstanding securities. Investors thus must confront an additional source of uncertainty, policy uncertainty, when making investment decisions. The additional uncertainty has the effect of deterring investment. Therefore, for an active stabilization policy to have a *net* positive effect on long-run economic growth requires more than simply being "successful" in reducing the amplitude of business cycle fluctuations. The reduction in investors' uncertainty about returns associated with business cycle fluctuations must more than offset the additional uncertainty introduced by the exercise of discretion in the timing and magnitude of policy interventions in the open market that is required of such policy.[10]

14.6   SUMMARY

What is the alternative to stabilization policy? If short-term goals set for the real economy, such as employment and output, are not achievable, the monetary authority should focus instead on long-term objectives. However, monetary policy neutrality suggests that the only reasonable long-run objective is to stabilize the average money price level of goods. Monetarists believe that is the sole objective the central bank should pursue. Moreover, they believe monetary policy itself should be announced publicly and designed in such a way that the public can easily monitor compliance by the central bank. One such policy is the constant growth rate (CGR) rule for a measure of the nominal money supply.

The basis for designing the CGR rule is a stable long-run relationship between money and nominal income, or velocity. Using this relationship, the monetary authority must forecast the long-run average growth rate for the economy, which can then be used to determine how rapidly the money supply needs to be expanded on average to maintain zero inflation on average over the business cycle. Once that growth rate is determined, the monetary authority should announce it and should attempt to achieve it in the short run while making no effort to offset normal business cycle fluctuations systematically as they occur.

As described, such policy is completely inflexible and does not allow for important structural changes in the real economy that could alter the long-run growth potential of the economy or in the financial markets that could alter the demand for money. One approach that addresses those problems systematically, while preserving the principal features of the CGR rule, is to modify the

---

[10]See Mascaro and Meltzer (1983) for an effort to document this effect.

rule governing the rate of monetary growth such that it is based on a weighted average of past changes in output growth and past changes in the growth rate of velocity, both of which encompass the most recent full business cycle, such as over the previous seven to eight years. The weights attached to the growth rates could be adjusted to give more significance to recent events, thus enabling the rule to incorporate structural changes more quickly as they occur in the economy. Under this rule, monetary policy is still focusing on long-term average price stability as its objective. The policy rule is simple enough that the weights could be announced, and the public could easily determine how closely the monetary authority is adhering to the rule.

Finally, short-run stabilization policy can affect long-run growth to the extent that it alters individuals' willingness to make long-term commitments, such as capital investment. Many Keynesian economists argue that monetary policy is largely successful and consequently the returns to investment are made more predictable. The stability reduces real interest rates by lowering the risk premium that is imbedded in them. Firms are able to borrow at lower cost and thereby increase their level of planned investment, which stimulates long-term growth. However, as described in the preceding chapter, monetarists argue that stabilization is largely unsuccessful and consequently investments are riskier than they would be otherwise, which slows capital investment and retards growth. Moreover, stabilization policy requires frequent unpredictable policy changes to fine tune the economy. The result is an atmosphere of policy uncertainty that introduces additional risk for investors and further slows capital investment, thus adversely affecting long-run economic growth. The latter outcome can be avoided when monetary policy is conducted according to a simple monetary rule.

◼ REVIEW QUESTIONS

1. Suppose the Federal Reserve wants to conduct monetary policy according to a monetary (CGR) rule.
   (a) List the steps it would follow in designing the rule. What information is required at each step? Be specific.
   (b) Under what conditions would the CGR rule outperform an active stabilization policy in terms of an inflation or stable-price objective?
   (c) Under what conditions would the CGR rule outperform an active stabilization policy in terms of an employment or output objective?

2. As with an active stabilization policy, measurement error can cause significant policy mistakes under a CGR rule.
   (a) Suppose the Federal Reserve's policy objective is to maintain a long-run average inflation rate of zero. What are the possible sets of prices that the Federal Reserve could choose to stabilize? For each set, how would you define the price level? What is being "averaged?"
   (b) Some economists have argued that the CPI overstates inflation by not accounting for the improvements in product quality over time. (Compare the computer that can be purchased for $4000 today with the

computer that could have been purchased for $4000 in 1990.) If that were true and if the Federal Reserve failed to factor in the bias in the CPI, what would be the likely consequences for the economy?

3. Long-term secular changes in the economy are not always easy to identify and could have significant detrimental effects on the economy if the Federal Reserve pursued a monetary (CGR) rule and failed to adjust to them.
   (a) If the pace of financial innovations that increased the efficiency of the payment system accelerated unexpectedly, what would happen to velocity?
   (b) What adjustments should the Federal Reserve make to its CGR policy rule in responding to (a)?
   (c) What would be likely to occur if no policy adjustments were made in response to (a)?

*4. In 1973, the Organization of Petroleum Exporting Countries (OPEC) sharply curtailed oil production and world prices, measured in U.S. dollars, tripled.
   (a) If the Federal Reserve had chosen not to respond to that event, what would the likely consequences have been for the traditional stabilization policy objectives of employment, output, and prices?
   (b) If the Federal Reserve had been conducting an active stabilization policy when the oil supply shock occurred, what would the likely response have been?
   (c) Given the lagged effects of policy changes on the economy that were described in the preceding chapter, what would the consequences of the policy described in (b) have been for inflation?
   (d) Answer (b) and (c) if the Federal Reserve had been pursuing a CGR rule.

*5. During the 1980s, many firms in the United States underwent dramatic restructuring designed in part to raise the productivity of their employees.
   (a) During the period when the accelerated restructuring was taking place, what effect should the restructuring have had on the inflation rate?
   (b) Restructuring is always taking place in a healthy, dynamic economy. However, the pace of restructuring can change over time, as occurred in the 1980s. Suppose the pace of restructuring were to accelerate for three years, level off for two years, and then decline to a rate that represents a long-run average. Describe how monetary policy might attempt to respond to such an environment.
   (c) If the response to monetary policy involves long and variable lags as described in the preceding chapter, what are the difficulties for the policy described in (b)?

▨ REFERENCES

Blinder, Alan S. 1981. "Monetarism is Obsolete." *Challenge* 24 (September–October): 35–41.

Mascaro, Angelo, and Allan H. Meltzer. 1983. "Long- and Short-Term Interest Rates in a Risky World." *Journal of Monetary Economics* 12 (November): 485–518.

McCallum, Bennett T. 1988. "Robustness Properties of a Rule for Monetary Policy." *Carnegie-Rochester Conference Series on Public Policy* 29 (Autumn): 173–203.

Meltzer, Allan H. 1987. "Limits on Short-Run Stabilization Policy." *Economic Inquiry* 25 (February): 1–14.

Romer, Paul. 1990. "Endogenous Technological Change." *Journal of Political Economy* 98 (October, part 2) S71–S102.

CHAPTER 15

INFLATION AND SEIGNIORAGE: WHAT IS OPTIMAL?

Opinions on the "optimal" long-run cycle-average rate of inflation differ markedly among economists. Some economists would cite numbers ranging from -3 to $+6$ percent and others would say that there is no specific number or that the issue is irrelevant. The purpose of this chapter is to provide an overview of the arguments that summarize the various perspectives. The variety of viewpoints illustrates just how complex the question of optimal inflation really is. The issue has been much discussed and much researched and yet remains largely unresolved. Its prominence in public policy debates suggests the importance that many attach to maintaining *some* desired level of inflation to support a smoothly functioning economy.

15.1   INFLATION TAXES IN THE ISLAND ECONOMY

In the island economy of Chapter 1, certain transactions had become monetary. In particular, the household would produce perishable goods at home, take them to the market, and sell them for fiat money. The money was then held for one production/trading period, after which it was taken to the market to buy perishable market goods that had been produced by other households at distant locations on the island. However, there was no mechanism to ensure that the supply of fiat money by the Walrasian auctioneer did not become excessive or insufficient. In fact, the Walrasian auctioneer, acting as the central bank for the economy, could produce any positive or negative growth rate for the money supply, provided only that households would continue to hold money willingly. That is, each household had to believe others would be willing to exchange money for goods and goods for money. Money had to continue to serve as a common medium of exchange and as a store of value.

Suppose the Walrasian auctioneer is able to construct a price index that reflects the money price of a representative market basket of all perishable goods traded on the island. He then uses the index to gauge how fast he should allow the money supply to expand. Initially, he is able to maintain a constant money price of the basket of goods, so that the inflation rate in the economy is zero. Is this optimal? Remember how the benefits of the gradual elimination of the trading frictions in the economy were measured; "optimality" was defined in terms of the most efficient allocation of the economy's resources. Such allocation produces the highest level of per capita utility or welfare. Anything that inhibits the optimal allocation of resources causes welfare losses. When trade is conducted with commodity money versus fiat money, where the common medium of exchange is corn rather than paper money, one of the clear costs of trading is the requirement that individuals must hold corn from one period to the next to conduct trades. Because corn has value in consumption, the one-period holding time for corn raises the costs of trading and the number of trades is reduced. Corn is assumed not to increase in value over the period to compensate the household for postponing consumption.

An analogous cost is incurred by the household in a fiat money economy in a zero-inflation environment (although without the direct resource costs). To acquire market goods with money, households first must produce goods at home and take them to the market to sell, that is, to trade for money. They hold the money one period before using it to buy market goods that can then be consumed. Therefore, households must produce goods today to acquire market goods for consumption tomorrow. Over the intervening period, they hold their wealth in the form of money that does not increase in value, leaving them uncompensated for having postponed consumption for one period. Households therefore have an incentive to reduce their "idle" money balances. However, because money is the sole medium of exchange in the economy, it is needed for the purchase of market goods.[1] A reduction in the stock of intertemporal money holdings is accompanied by a reduction in the volume of monetary transactions. Hence, the volume of trade in the economy declines. Households reduce their respective consumption of market goods to suboptimal levels and the welfare, or per capita utility level, of the economy declines.[2]

How important are such costs to the household? The greater it perceives them to be, the greater will be the magnitude of its response. Suppose a

---

[1]This description coincides with the "cash-in-advance" view of money demand that emphasizes the medium-of-exchange property as a singular feature of "money." See Clower (1967), Grandmont and Younes (1972), and Lucas (1980) for early formalizations of these models in a general equilibrium context.

[2]These decisions are accompanied by a reallocation of capital and labor resources. Exactly how much the welfare level declines and how the resources are reallocated as a result of the "economic distortion" is determined by the options available to the households that could mitigate these costs. That is, they depend on the margins along which households are able to adjust when making their decisions. For example, households could reduce consumption and increase leisure in a manner consistent with an intratemporal preference shock as examined in Chapters 10 through 12.

household has one unit of the economy's fiat money, call it a dollar, which it takes to market. With that dollar it is able to purchase, say, 10 pounds of flour. The household knows that prices are stable, so that if it were to refrain from spending the dollar for one period, it could return to the market at that time and acquire the same 10 pounds of flour. However, given the choice between acquiring the 10 pounds of flour today or acquiring the same 10 pounds of flour tomorrow, the household would choose to buy the flour today. It always prefers consumption today over consumption tomorrow.

Suppose the household encounters a peculiar seller of flour, who makes the following offer (which as a profit maximizer he would never do!). He takes the dollar bill that the household is about to give him in exchange for the 10 pounds of flour, places an identifying mark on the bill (perhaps his signature), and hands it back to the household. He then tells the household that if it brings the marked dollar bill back next period, he will exchange it not for 10 pounds of flour, but for 10.01 pounds of flour. Would the household agree? The household is likely to say no. The seller responds by raising the offer to 10.02 pounds and asks again. That process continues with higher offers until eventually a point is reached at which the household agrees to the terms.[3] Suppose agreement is reached at an offer of 10.1 pounds. What does this say about the household's time rate of preference for consumption? Essentially, the implication is that the household is indifferent between consuming 10 pounds of flour today and 10.1 pounds of flour next period. The household therefore discounts the future at a rate of 1 percent per period. Clearly, the higher this personal discount rate, the greater the costs of monetary transactions to the household, because it must postpone consumption without compensation by holding money that is just maintaining a constant purchasing power over time.

Could the Walrasian auctioneer, who controls the money supply, reduce or even eliminate this cost to the household? The answer is yes. In the hypothetical situation just described, the household has a marked dollar bill that is more valuable in the second period than in the first. It would buy 1 percent more goods in the second period. Holding the marked bill therefore provides a positive rate of return in an amount of 1 percent per period. Suppose the discount rate determined above is representative of preferences for all households in the economy. What the Walrasian auctioneer must do is adjust the expansion of the money supply so that each dollar bill performs just as the marked dollar bill does. That is, the bills must increase in value by 1 percent each period. Relative scarcity is what produces economic value, so for money to increase in value over time it must be becoming more scarce in relation to the supply of goods. Therefore, on a per capita basis, the Walrasian auctioneer must *reduce* the money supply over time. To completely eliminate the cost of holding money intertemporally, the rate of reduction of the money supply must be sufficient to reduce the money price of goods by 1 percent per period. In this case, households are

---

[3]Assume no strategies are available to the households that could enable it to withhold a truthful revelation of its preferences.

no longer penalized for holding money intertemporally, because the money is gaining in value at exactly the rate at which they are discounting the future.

Suppose the money supply were contracted at a more rapid rate than the rate of discount. In this case, money is becoming too scarce. Households would want to hoard money rather than trade it for goods, and the fiat money equilibrium would collapse. The economy would return to barter or to some other form of trade. Therefore, there is a limit on the minimum rate of growth of the money supply that the Walrasian auctioneer is permitted. Any growth rate (whether it is positive, zero, or negative) that is above the minimum imposes costs on households because they are no longer fully compensated for holding money intertemporally. Such costs are known as "inflation taxes" because they are imposed on all monetary transactions.[4]

In this context, the optimal rate of inflation is therefore determined by preferences. It corresponds to one version of Milton Friedman's *optimal deflation rule:* In the absence of other distortions in the monetary economy, the rate of deflation that restores Pareto optimal allocations of resources, thus rendering the highest per capita utility or welfare level possible, is equal to the rate at which households discount the future.[5]

15.2   PRICE LEVEL STABILITY

An alternative view shared by many economists is that the optimal rate of inflation is zero. That is, they place a premium on price-level stability. The argument is based on the empirical fact that relative prices become more volatile as the inflation rate increases.[6] Examples of relative prices (as described in Chapters 1 and 13) include the fish price of corn, the haircut price of automobiles, and so on. Changes in relative prices therefore reflect changes in the market valuations of goods, such that the supply and demand factors in one goods market have been affected differently from the supply and demand factors in another market. Inflation refers to the rate of change of the money price of a market basket of goods such as the CPI. By regulating the supply of money, the monetary authority is able to determine the average rate of inflation over a time interval corresponding to, say, the average length of the business cycle. What the preceding empirical fact suggests is that the closer this rate of inflation can be brought to zero, the more stable *relative* prices will be. The question then becomes: Is greater stability in relative prices desirable?

---

[4]Inflation taxes can be positive even in a deflationary environment.

[5]See Friedman (1969). This also corresponds to a zero nominal interest rate, which makes households indifferent between holding money and holding other forms of wealth.

[6]See Cukierman (1983).

Consider an economic environment in which the general price level is stable. That is, the long-run average rate of inflation is zero. However, the economy is being subjected continuously to real shocks. They take the form of supply and demand disturbances that are either specific to individual markets or aggregate shocks that differentially affect various markets. In response to the shocks, relative prices change. In such an environment, an individual firm may realize (larger than expected) productivity gains in its production process, perhaps because of improved technology or better worker training. The gains would lower the market price of the firm's product in relation to other goods. Alternatively, households may (unexpectedly) shift their preferences toward the firm's product and away from its competitors' products, possibly because of a successful marketing campaign or some random change in consumer tastes. In this case, the relative market price of the firm's product would rise.

In each of those examples, important information is contained in the changes in the relative market price of the firm's product that the firm would like to have when making its production and investment decisions. However, its task is to understand *why* the price change occurred.[7] There are obviously many possible causes for any single price change, and the firm's response to the various shocks might be different if it were certain of the source. The firm has a so-called *signal extraction problem* similar to that described in Chapter 11. In this case, the firm has one price signal that has many potential causes, and can only imperfectly resolve the price change into its ultimate source(s). As a result, the firm will inevitably make mistakes in its production and investment decisions.

The mistakes are ultimately reflected in the value of the firm, and hence in the return to its shareholders' investments. The larger the mistakes, the lower the return. Consequently, households would require a higher real interest rate (or risk premium) to compensate them for undertaking risk, which raises the cost of borrowing to the firm, which in turn reduces its long-run average level of investment in new plant and equipment. In sum, there are costs associated with a high degree of variability in relative prices.

The complete elimination of relative price changes is neither possible nor desirable. The production and investment decisions firms make in response to relative price changes represent the way in which the economy's resources are reallocated toward their most highly valued use. The fact that the price signals on which those decisions depend are imperfect predictors of future supply and demand conditions is unavoidable and represents an essential degree of risk that a healthy economy must incur. However, what is the significance of the empirical fact stated above? It suggests that as inflation rises, the signal extraction problem becomes more difficult for firms to resolve. Mistakes are amplified and the level of risk incurred by households when making investments in the firms rises. The mistakes lead to a misallocation of the economy's resources. From an economywide perspective, correcting the mistakes is costly as capital and labor

---

[7]This description follows Lucas (1977).

must be redeployed in the economy.[8] Moreover, firms invest less in new plant and equipment, which reduces the rate of expansion of productive capacity in the economy, thus retarding growth. Price-level stability, or zero inflation, thereby reduces the unnecessary "noise" in relative price changes and minimizes the attendant adverse consequences for investment, growth, and welfare.

15.3 LABOR MARKET RIGIDITIES AND MODERATE INFLATION

Households offer labor services to firms in exchange for labor income. In general, labor supply and demand decisions are based on the level of the real wage. However, many (Keynesian) economists believe that nominal wages are not flexible in the short run. The presence of long-term labor contracts is one reason frequently given for nominal wage rigidity, as described in Chapter 12. As indicated by the analysis in that chapter, when the price level is flexible and nominal wages are not, shocks to the economy that alter the price level may induce changes in real wages that require employment levels to adjust if the labor market is to clear at full employment. However, contractual arrangements may preclude such adjustment from taking place over the duration of the contract.

To the extent that nominal wage rigidity is an important factor influencing macroeconomic fluctuations, it is relevant to ask what impact a moderate rate of inflation would have on the economy when nominal wages adjust slowly. Begin with another empirical fact: the general price level, measured for example by the CPI, becomes more volatile as the inflation rate rises.[9] Hence, at higher rates of inflation, real wages become more volatile but also more flexible. Is this good or bad? On the negative side, the purchasing power of nominal wages becomes less predictable. Households therefore are incurring a greater degree of risk associated with the return they receive for labor services. To incur that risk, households would require a higher nominal wage, which would raise labor costs to firms and would lead to a suboptimal level of employment through both a substitution of capital for labor and a reduction in output.[10] Moreover, to the extent that the volatility in the general price level does not reflect the industry-specific changes in productivity, the greater flexibility in real wages achieved by a moderate inflation is actually detrimental to the efficient allocation of labor resources.

---

[8]See Lilien (1982), Davis (1987), Abraham and Katz (1986), Loungani, Rush, and Tave (1990), and Toledo and Marquis (1993) for some evidence on the macroeconomic consequences of this misallocation of resources and the costs of adjustment.

[9]Again, see Cukierman (1983).

[10]Casual empirical evidence suggests that the demand for cost of living adjustment clauses (COLAs) in formal labor contracts increases during periods of high inflation. This finding is consistent with the desire to reduce the risk to workers associated with the return to their labor services.

Some economists believe the inflexibility in nominal wages is asymmetric. When contracts are renegotiated, nominal wages can rise, but there is resistence to an outright decline in nominal wages.[11] Reasons given for the asymmetry include ignorance of the general level of prices on the part of the worker, often referred to as "money illusion," and a perception of "fairness." That is, the employer has no control over the general price level and therefore can do nothing about the inflation rate, but does have direct control over the nominal wage paid to employees. A cut in nominal wages may therefore be seen as less "fair" than an increase in the inflation rate, even though the effect is the same: real wages decline. If asymmetry in the degree of flexibility of nominal wages were present and significant, a moderate amount of inflation, of say 2 to 5 percent, could enable firms to lower their real wages more easily in the event that productivity declined. Thus labor could be allocated more efficiently across the economy and welfare would be improved.

15.4   SEIGNIORAGE

In general, national (or federal) governments must raise revenues to fund government expenditures. To raise revenues, the government must either impose taxes or issue debt. If it issues debt, it incurs a stream of liabilities associated with repayment. The liabilities can be met by dedicating future tax revenues to repayment or the debt can be *monetized*. In the latter case, the revenues are essentially funded by inflation taxes. The inflation taxes arise from the government's monopoly control over the money supply, and the revenues they generate are termed *seigniorage*.

The act of raising revenues through seigniorage or inflation taxes is often referred to colloquially as raising revenues by "printing money." For example, suppose the U.S. government wants to purchase a new bomber for $1 billion, but does not want to raise taxes to cover the expenditure. Instead, the Treasury Department issues 30-year government bonds. The Treasury Department must pay the owners of the bonds semiannual coupon payments of a fixed nominal value on each bond for the life of the bond and then return the face value of the bond to the owner upon maturity. If the purchaser of the bond is a private citizen, the government is indebted to the private citizen. Suppose, however, that the bond is purchased by the Federal Reserve. Is there a difference?

As described in Chapter 7, when the Federal Reserve receives revenues from its stock of U.S. government debt, the revenues are simply turned back to the Treasury Department after the Federal Reserve has paid its operating expenses and its dividends to member banks. In the example above, the Treasury Department receives the bomber that it purchased from the sale of the bonds, and in addition has the coupon payments it pays to the Federal Reserve returned to

---

[11]However, recent evidence from micro data indicate that nominal wages are as flexible downward as they are upward and, in fact, there is surprisingly little nominal wage rigidity overall. See McLaughlin (1994).

it. In this case, the cost of the plane to the Treasury Department appears to be zero. That is, taxes did not have to be raised to fund the expenditure.

Of course, the plane was not free. Ultimately, it had to be paid for by households. To clarify how the payment was made, recognize that the bond purchase by the Federal Reserve was simply an open market operation. As described in detail in Chapter 7, it would cause an increase in bank reserves, and the money supply (however it is measured) would rise. If the excess reserves to total bank reserves ratio and the currency deposit ratio were relatively stable, the open market operation would correspond to an increase in the demand for currency in the economy. With the Federal Reserve's monopoly over the supply of currency (which is "legal tender"), the Federal Reserve would meet this increase in demand by literally "printing money." The costs are borne by everyone who engages in monetary transactions as discussed above. That is, money has become less scarce and hence is less valued in relation to goods, whose money prices, in turn, rise. Consequently, the inflation taxes were imposed on monetary transactions and the collection of those inflation taxes or seigniorage from households financed the purchase of the bomber.

Viewed from the perspective of the public finance of federal government expenditures, the question of determining an optimal rate of inflation is couched within the context of where the incidence of inflation versus alternative forms of taxation falls. Do the distortions in private decisions that inflation creates have a greater or lesser effect on welfare than, for example, capital or labor income taxes or a consumption tax? The answers to those questions are not completely clear. The full general equilibrium effects of any tax are difficult to identify, much less to quantify. Moreover, inflation taxes are even more elusive than others.

When inflation taxes impinge only on the monetary transactions associated with the purchase of consumption goods, as in the island economy, the welfare losses of moderate inflation may not be as large as those associated with capital or labor income taxes that are sufficiently high to raise the same amount of government revenue.[12] However, as the inflation tax rises and becomes ever more persistent, households respond by allocating resources toward devising alternative nonmonetary means of payment. An increasing share of the economy's resources may be diverted into unproductive activities in the financial services industry and away from the production of goods, from which households derive utility directly, and away from research and development activities, which produce improved technology, or away from formal training, which is a source of enhanced worker productivity, and the long-run growth potential of the economy declines.[13] As a result, output falls, the economy is placed on a slower growth path, and welfare may be substantially reduced.

---

[12]See Cooley and Hansen (1991) for evidence that the efficiency losses are significant, but less than those associated with income taxes.

[13]See Marquis and Reffett (1994) for evidence that inflation taxes have the potential to produce large welfare losses by draining resources from production and R&D.

As described in Chapter 3, households may also hold money for precautionary reasons. That is, they want to smooth their levels of consumption over time, but their income stream may be volatile.[14] To insure against unexpected declines in income that would otherwise force a reduction in consumption, households hold a reserve stock of money. To the extent that the precautionary motive for holding money is significant, high and volatile inflation rates induce larger precautionary balances to be held. This increases the welfare costs of inflation taxes to the point where they could exceed the costs of a tax on labor income that is sufficient to raise the same amount of government revenue.[15]

The determination of the long-run inflation rate is a matter of government policy. When we examine the empirical evidence on inflation from countries around the world, we see that sharply different policy choices have been made. Some economies have undergone sustained periods of hyperinflation that have lasted for decades. Argentina and Chile, for example, had triple-digit inflation until the recently enacted monetary reforms took effect. Other economies, such as Israel and Germany, had shorter bouts with hyperinflation before regaining control over their money supplies. Still others, such as the United States, have been able to sustain relatively low to moderate inflation, say, below 20 percent, for many years. Why is such a widely divergent set of policy choices observed?

Some economists have attributed the choice of high inflation regimes to inefficient tax collection systems that foster tax evasion and high collection costs.[16] The high costs tilt governments increasingly toward seigniorage as a principal source of revenue. For example, evidence shows many less developed economies to be characterized by the combination of inefficient tax collection systems and high inflation. That correlation is found even among developed countries. As an example, inflation in the United States, where voluntary tax compliance is very high, has historically been below that of Italy, where tax evasion is widespread.[17] Other economists have suggested that political instability could frustrate the governmental decision-making process when legislative action is required to raise tax revenues. The government then turns to inflation taxes by default.[18] Of course, political instability could foster or simply reflect an environment in which tax evasion is pervasive and the cost of collecting taxes is high.

---

[14]This characterization of money demand is modeled by Imrohoroglu (1989).

[15]These conclusions are reached by Imrohoroglu and Prescott (1991) under various regulatory regimes for deposit rates and reserve requirements.

[16]Cukierman, Edwards, and Tabellini (1992) provide some empirical evidence to support this belief.

[17]The connection between tax evasion and seigniorage is made by Roubini and Sala-i-Martin (1994).

[18]Alesina and Drazen (1991) describe the incentives that bias the government toward inflationary finance.

15.5   SUMMARY

From a general equilibrium perspective, to eliminate inflation taxes completely the monetary authority would have to follow Friedman's rule, which produces a deflation equal to the personal rate of discount (or equal to the real, risk-adjusted interest rate on capital). Any faster monetary growth would penalize persons who hold money intertemporally and who, in their effort to avoid the tax, would alter their decisions in ways that lead to a misallocation of the economy's resources and to a reduction in welfare. An alternative perspective on inflation emphasizes the value of price stability in reducing the risk investors face when trying to assess the value of alternative investments. Empirical evidence suggests that higher inflation rates coincide with more variability in relative prices and therefore more uncertainty for firms in making their production and investment decisions, and consequently result in larger mistakes being made in those decisions. Here, a zero-inflation environment becomes the desired goal. It removes a deterrent to investment and stimulates long-term growth and raises economic welfare. Still another view centers on a perceived advantage associated with moderate inflation in allowing real wages to become more flexible downward in the event that nominal wages are relatively inflexible downward. Such flexibility may allow labor resources to be reallocated more efficiently in the economy in response to real shocks that differentially affect sectors. Again, the efficiency gains would lead to welfare improvements. Finally, some economists view inflation from the perspective of public finance. Seigniorage collection by the federal government associated with inflation taxes is perceived to be a substitute for revenues collected from other forms of taxation. The relative costs and benefits of relying on this source of revenues must therefore be evaluated and may in fact vary across countries.

Viewed in isolation, each of the arguments has merit. When they are taken together, however, the extent to which economies are penalized by some moderate levels of inflation is unclear.[19] Opinions among government leaders as to what the optimal level of inflation is for their own economies differ even more widely than the views of private economists. Moreover, in economies where a current inflation rate is perceived to exceed the optimal inflation rate, the question remains as to whether the present value of the costs of reducing inflation to a predetermined level that is seen to be optimal exceeds the present value of the benefits. If not, what is the "optimal" rate at which inflation should be reduced to achieve that goal? These important issues are certain to receive more attention from researchers and government policy makers alike.

---

[19]Peter Ireland (1994) has attempted to evaluate the relative merits of the Friedman rule, price-level stability, and moderate inflation in a single general equilibrium model with sticky prices. He concludes that on balance a negative inflation rate is optimal in the long run and the present value of the costs of quick adjustment from a higher level to the optimal level is lower than that of a slow adjustment.

■ REVIEW QUESTIONS

1. In the island economy of Chapter 1, inflation taxes reduce welfare by causing a misallocation of the economy's resources.
   (a) Describe the misallocation of resources when all purchases of perishable consumption goods are monetary transactions involving fiat money.
   (b) Answer (a) when the purchases of durable investment goods are also monetary transactions involving fiat money. What is the likely effect on economic growth?
   (c) Suppose households were able to use some of their resource time to conduct transactions by making individual credit arrangements with their suppliers rather than relying on monetary transactions. Describe how the availability of this alternative means of payment would affect the allocation of resources in environment (a) as the inflation tax rises.

2. Suppose you have $5000 in an MMDA account at a bank and are considering investing it in stock.
   (a) Pick an individual firm and describe the conditions under which you would be willing to make the investment.
   (b) Suppose your expectations of future inflation coincide with those of the market. If those expectations incorporated a doubling of the current inflation rate, what would be the effect on your decision?
   (c) How would the scenario in (b) affect the firm's ability to raise capital? Assuming other firms are in a similar situation, what effect would the higher inflation expectations have on economic growth?
   (d) Suppose your expectations of future inflation were above those of the market. How would they effect your investment decision?

3. Suppose you are in the job market and find your services in sufficient demand that you can bargain for terms of employment, including the pay structure.
   (a) If you and your prospective employer decided on a one-year contract that would fix your nominal wages for the year, how would inflation expectations enter into the contract? Distinguish between the level and variability of inflation.
   (b) Under what conditions would the variability of inflation be desirable from the employer's standpoint? Under what conditions would variable inflation be undesirable?

*4. It is often observed that countries such as Argentina that have had a long period of high inflation have developed very sophisticated payments systems.
   (a) Explain why that is a logical development.
   (b) Is an economy with a high inflation/sophisticated payments system likely to be a healthier economy than one with a low inflation/less developed payments system, such as in the United States?
   (c) Speculate on how the payments system in the United States would be likely to change if the Federal Reserve were to alter policy and raise the average inflation rate to 20 percent over a several-year period.

*5. In many countries around the world, governments have difficulty collecting taxes paid directly on labor and capital income and on individual transactions, such as a sales tax. Those countries often turn to seigniorage as a means of raising revenues.

(a) Give specific examples of this phenomenon.

(b) When a country turns more to inflation taxes, describe how the marginal revenues raised from seigniorage change with successive increases in the inflation rate.

(c) Would there ever be a case in which higher inflation taxes *reduce* the total collection of seigniorage?

▒ REFERENCES

Abraham, Katherine, and Lawrence Katz. 1986. "Cyclical Unemployment: Sectoral Shifts or Aggregate Disturbances?" *Journal of Political Economy* 94 (June, Part 1): 507–22.

Alesina, Alberto, and Allan Drazen. 1991. "Why Are Stabilizations Delayed?" *American Economic Review* 81 (December): 1170–88.

Clower, Robert. 1967. "A Reconsideration of the Microfoundations of Monetary Theory." *Western Economic Journal* 6 (December): 1–8.

Cooley, Thomas F., and Gary D. Hansen. 1991. "The Welfare Costs of Moderate Inflations." *Journal of Money, Credit and Banking* 23 (3), Part 2: 483–503.

Cukierman, Alex. 1983. "Relative Price Variability and Inflation: A Survey and Further Results." *Carnegie-Rochester Conference Series on Public Policy, 19.*

_____ , Sebastian Edwards, and Guido Tabellini. 1992. "Seigniorage and Political Instability." *American Economic Review* 82 (June): 537–55.

Davis, Steven J. 1987. "Allocative Disturbances and Specific Capital in Real Business Cycle Theories." *American Economic Review,* Association Papers and Proceedings, 77 (2): 326–32.

Friedman, Milton. 1969. "The Optimal Quantity of Money." Pp. 1–50 in *The Optimal Quantity of Money and Other Essays.* Chicago: Aldine.

Grandmont, Jean-Michel, and Yves Younes. 1972. "On the Role of Money and the Existence of a Monetary Equilibrium." *Review of Economic Studies* 39 (July): 355–72.

Imrohoroglu, Ayse. 1989. "Cost of Business Cycles with Indivisibilities and Liquidity Constraints." *Journal of Political Economy* 97: 1364–83.

_____ , and Edward C. Prescott. 1991. "Seigniorage as a Tax: A Quantitative Evaluation." *Journal of Money, Credit and Banking* 23(3), Part 2: 462–75.

Ireland, Peter. 1994. "Optimal Disinflationary Paths." *Journal of Economic Dynamics and Control* (forthcoming).

Lilien, David M. 1982. "Sectoral Shifts and Cyclical Unemployment." *Journal of Political Economy* 90(4): 777–83.

Loungani, Prakash, Mark Rush, and William Tave. 1990. "Stock Market Dispersion and Unemployment." *Journal of Monetary Economics* 25 (June): 367–88.

Lucas, Robert E., Jr. 1977. "Understanding Business Cycles." *Carnegie-Rochester Conference Series on Public Policy, 5.*

_____ . 1980. "Equilibrium in a Pure Currency Economy." *Economic Inquiry* 18 (April): 203–20.

Marquis, Milton H., and Kevin L. Reffett. 1994. "New Technology Spillovers into the Payment System." *Economic Journal* 104 (September): 1123–38.

McLaughlin, Kenneth J. 1994. "Rigid Wages?" *Journal of Monetary Economics* 34 (December): 383–414.

Roubini, Nouriel, and Xavier Sala-i-Martin. 1994. "A Growth Model of Inflation, Tax Evasion, and Financial Repression." Unpublished manuscript (July).

Toledo, Wilfredo, and Milton H. Marquis. 1993. "Capital Allocative Disturbances and Economic Fluctuations." *Review of Economics and Statistics* 75 (May): 223–40.

THE MECHANICS OF POLICY AND POLICY-MAKING

CHAPTER 16

OPTIMAL TARGETING AND THE RESPONSE OF THE FINANCIAL MARKETS

In Parts III and IV of the text, the consequences of changes in the nominal money supply induced by decisions taken by the monetary authority are examined in several contexts. Monetary policy is assumed to bring about the money supply changes without significant error. However, as described in Chapter 7, the monetary authority does not control the money supply directly, regardless of how "money" is defined. Instead, it has certain "policy tools" that it can freely manipulate to achieve its overall policy goals. In the United States, the policy tools are reserve requirements on certain bank deposits, the discount rate charged member banks on borrowings from the Federal Reserve, and open market operations that determine the rate of expansion of bank reserves.

Policy goals are not as clearly defined. Historically, they have taken many forms, but most often involve macroeconomic objectives associated with output, employment, and prices. Therefore, in practice, the monetary authority cannot conclude its policy analysis by relating changes in the money supply to ultimate changes in the macroeconomic variables in which its policy objectives are stated, but rather must relate quantitative changes in the policy tools to the macroeconomic objectives. Knowing, for example, how rapidly M2 must grow to achieve a certain rate of output growth or long-run rate of inflation is not enough. Instead, the monetary authority must know, for example, how rapidly to expand the central bank's portfolio of government securities holdings (through open market operations) to bring about those macroeconomic changes.

A principal purpose of this chapter is to describe the mechanism that links changes in policy tools to changes in the macroeconomic variables in which the policy goals are defined.[1] The monetary authority is limited in its selection of

---

[1]For a treatment of "tools, instruments, targets, and goals," see B. Friedman (1975).

policies by the fact that its policy tools are not independent of one another. That is, in practice, the three policy tools work together to form a single *effective policy tool*. The scope of monetary policy is thus restricted to addressing only one policy objective at a time or, at best, a tradeoff between competing policy objectives, such as short-run economic growth and inflation. The mechanism that links policy tools to the policy objectives includes both the money supply process described in Chapter 7 and the behavioral relationships that ultimately establish the macroeconomic relationships between money and the real economy that are the focus of Parts III and IV of the text. Important in this linkage are the very practical problems due to lags in the economy's response to policy changes, as described in Chapter 13. The lags give rise to the use of "intermediate targets" in the short-run conduct of monetary policy, whereby the policy objectives are translated into a value for the growth rate of a selected monetary aggregate or a level of a market interest rate. That value is then treated in the short run as though it were the policy goal itself.

The optimal selection of a policy target also is described in this chapter. That is, under what conditions is a monetary target versus an interest rate target optimal? Because the choice of a target and the numerical values selected for the target are premised on assumptions about behavioral and institutional relationships that affect money demand, the monetary authority needs to identify changes in those relationships that could affect its ability to achieve the policy objectives. To assist in identifying such changes, the monetary authority monitors a host of "information variables," often drawn from the financial markets, which historically have presaged some important changes in the macroeconomic variables that constitute its policy objectives.

Monetary policy has a very strong influence on the financial markets in the shot run. Consequently, participants in the financial markets devote a significant amount of resources to anticipating policy decisions long before they are actually implemented. Whenever information arrives in the financial markets that alters the expectations of future monetary policy, asset trading occurs that incorporates the new information into asset prices and interest rates. Such trading can lead to a seemingly perverse reaction of financial markets, a selloff on "good news" or a rally on "bad news." The viewing of the news events in the context of a likely monetary policy response is what precipitates such reactions.

16.1   STABILIZATION POLICY AND THE CHOICE OF AN INTERMEDIATE TARGET[2]

The objectives of monetary policy are stated in terms of numerical values for macroeconomic variables such as output, employment, and prices. Those numerical values become the goals of policy. The policy goals are related to numerical values of monetary aggregates and interest rates by a complex set of

---

[2]This discussion is based on the seminal work of Poole (1970).

behavioral and institutional relationships that effectively determine the aggregate demand for money. To the extent that the relationships are stable and predictable, explicit policy goals can be translated into desired numerical values of selected monetary aggregates or interest rates. Refer to the schematic drawing in Figure 16.1. Suppose, for example, a 3 percent growth rate of M2 is consistent with a long-run average inflation rate of 1 percent. If the latter is the policy goal, the monetary authority would be able to achieve it by focusing exclusively on the growth rate of M2 in the short run. In that case, the monetary authority is said to be "targeting M2 (or the money supply)" and its "target" or "intermediate target" is the numerical value of 3 percent growth in M2. Alternatively, the demand for money may be characterized by the value of a market interest rate, such as the federal funds rate, that is consistent with the policy goals. For example, the monetary authority may believe a 4 percent federal funds rate would lead to a long-run average rate of inflation of 2 percent. In that case, the monetary authority is said to be "targeting the federal funds rate (or a market interest rate)," and the explicit target is the numerical value of a 4 percent federal funds rate. The operational issue for the Federal Reserve is: Under what conditions is a monetary aggregate target preferable to a market interest rate target?

The choice of an intermediate target may be influenced by the choice of policy objectives and whether those objectives are short term or long term. For example, if the Federal Reserve wanted to achieve a given long-run inflation rate of, say, 1 percent that was the average over the business cycle, it may prefer to choose a monetary aggregate as the intermediate target, provided the long-run money demand relationship is perceived to be stable. In that case, a nominal target is used to achieve a nominal objective. If the long-run demand for money is not seen to be predictable, an interest rate target may be preferred.

Figure 16.1   Policy Tools, Instruments, Targets, and Goals

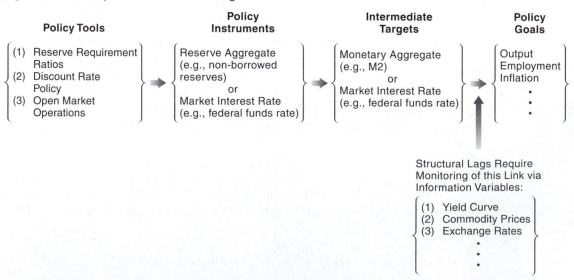

However, short-run concerns may also play a role in the selection of an intermediate target. That is, while pursuing long-run objectives, the monetary authority may give some weight to the effect that the selection of a target could have on short-term volatility in output and employment. Moreover, the policy objectives themselves may be short term, as in a traditional stabilization policy. Those objectives are defined as attempting to keep the economy as close as possible to full employment while maintaining stable prices.

In the preceding chapter, the economy's response to two generic macroeconomic shocks was examined. One was a productivity shock reflecting a change in the technology used in producing goods. Given that such shocks are permanent, the appropriate policy response is to accommodate them fully. The second was a preference shock, which could either be intratemporal or intertemporal. Because preference shocks are transitory, the appropriate policy response is to ignore them if they dissipate quickly (as in Chapter 11) or to offset them if they persist beyond the time horizon for which policy is being designed (as in Chapter 12). For shocks that dissipate quickly, the short-term effect on the economy is to produce fluctuations in employment and output around their respective full-employment levels. A principal question addressed in this chapter is whether the choice of an intermediate target by the monetary authority can minimize those fluctuations.

To examine that issue, we can consider the economic environment of a sluggish price adjustment described in Chapter 11. Refer to Figure 16.2. As before, the initial equilibrium values have the subscript zero and are plotted in the graphs as points "a." Suppose the economy undergoes an intratemporal preference shock that favors more current consumption and less leisure, such that if it were fully accommodated the level of savings would be unchanged. The labor supply schedule would shift to $N^s(\theta, \lambda_1)$, as shown in the lower left panel. If unconstrained, employment would rise to N_1 and output and income would increase to y_1^s and y_1, respectively. There is an increase in the intensity of preference for consumption, indicated by a rise in γ to γ_1, and a decline in the savings rate to $[1 - \phi(\gamma_1)]$ as shown in the upper middle and upper right panels. The additional income would be absorbed fully in the current period by an increase in consumption to c_1. With savings unchanged, the bond market clears at the original bond rate r_0, as shown in the lower right panel. However, the money market shown in the lower middle panel is now out of equilibrium, with an excess demand for money, as the money demand schedule has shifted to $(M/P)^d(c_1)$ in response to the higher level of consumption. How this market clears depends on the targeting procedure employed by the monetary authority.

If the monetary authority chooses to target the nominal money supply, it would attempt to fix the money supply at M_0, which corresponds to the stock of money that would keep the economy at full employment in the absence of the preference shock. In that case, the real money supply is also fixed at (M_0/P_0) and households are liquidity constrained in their effort to acquire the additional consumption goods. In response, households must reduce the volume of consumption for the period, which implies that labor services are withdrawn from the market in order to facilitate transactions as the labor supply schedule shifts to the left, say to $N^{sx}(\theta, \lambda_1)$. In the upper panels, that shift is seen to reduce

Figure 16.2   Response of the Economy to a Transitory Intratemporal Preference Shock under Money Supply versus Interest Rate Targeting

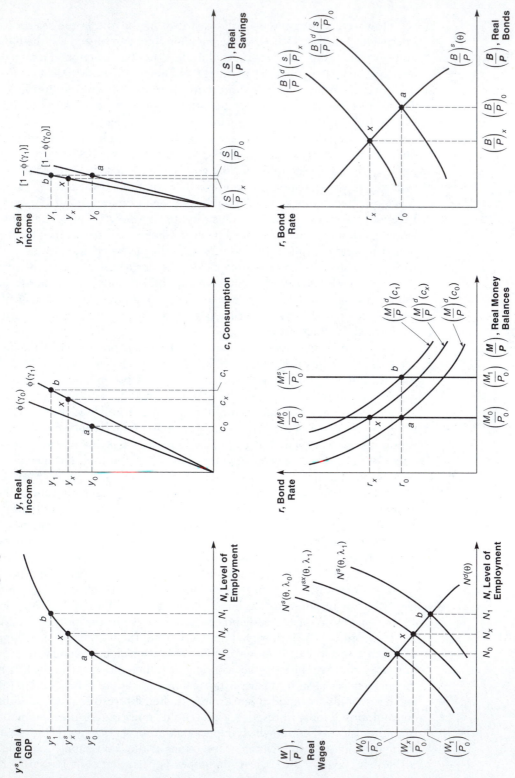

output and income to y_x^s and y_x. The lower level of income reduces consumption to c_x and savings to $(S/P)_x$. The effect of the lower savings is to increase the equilibrium bond rate to r_x and the effect of the lower consumption is to reduce the demand for money, as indicated by the leftward shift of the money demand schedule to $(M/P)^d(c_x)$. The excess demand for money is eliminated by the combination of lower opportunity costs and lower transactions requirements. However, the economy is now in a short-run general equilibrium, represented by points labeled "x" in the graphs, at levels of employment and output that exceed full employment.

How would the economy have adjusted if the monetary authority had chosen to target interest rates rather than the nominal money supply? In the example, the money supply schedule would be allowed to shift endogenously to (M_1^s/P_0), as indicated in the lower middle panel, in order to peg the interest rate at a level consistent with full employment in the absence of the preference shock, that is, at r_0. That targeting procedure accommodates fully the intratemporal preference shock and the economy clears at points labeled "b" in the graphs. The short-run general equilibrium to which the economy adjusts is characterized by employment and output levels that are even farther from full-employment conditions. Therefore, without alteration of the long-run policy goals, the economy would have remained closer to full employment in the short run for the duration of the intratemporal preference shock had the monetary authority chosen to target the nominal money supply rather than the market interest rate.[3] A similar outcome results from intertemporal preference shocks. (This is left as a review question at the end of the chapter.)

Suppose the monetary authority must cope with a third type of generic shock that reflects the unexpected changes in the rate at which new technology in the payment system is adopted by households. Such changes can be described in the model as transitory shifts in the money demand schedule, which would become manifest in the economy as velocity shocks of the type described in Chapters 3 and 14. Refer to Figure 16.3, where the economy is initially in a general equilibrium characterized by full employment. The initial values of the variables have the subscript zero and are plotted on the graphs as points "a." A velocity shock occurs whereby households make more effective use of their money holdings in conducting transactions without having to devote additional resources to transacting. For the same level of consumption, c_0, the money demand schedule shifts left, say to the curve labeled $(M/P)^{dv}(c_0)$. At the initial bond rate r_0, there is now an excess supply of money. If the monetary authority were targeting the nominal money supply, it would conduct policy to bring about a nominal money supply of M_0^s that would correspond to a general equilibrium consistent with full employment had no transitory velocity shock occurred. However, in this case, households have excess liquidity that must be absorbed with additional consumption purchases. In equilibrium, this situation induces a shift of resource time from transaction activities (and possibly leisure)

---

[3]This outcome is consistent with Poole's (1970) results whereby money supply targeting is preferred to interest rate targeting when the uncertainty the monetary authority faces is from transitory shocks to the "goods market."

Figure 16.3   Response of the Economy to a Transitory Velocity Shock under Money Supply versus Interest Rate Targeting

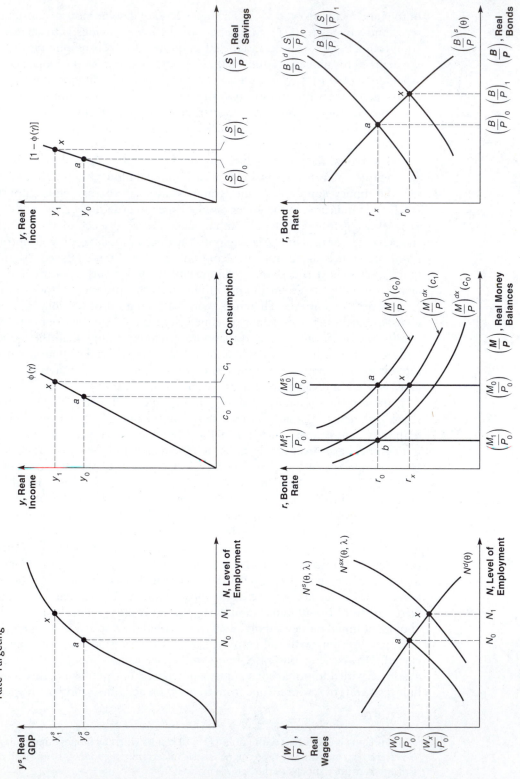

into production. The labor supply schedule shifts right to $N^{sx}(\theta,\lambda)$, as shown in the lower left panel, and the labor market clears at the higher level of employment, denoted N_1. Output and income rise to levels y_1^s and y_1 as shown in the upper panels. With no change in the intensity of preference for current consumption, both consumption and savings increase to the levels denoted c_1 and $(S/P)_1$. At the higher level of savings, the bond demand schedule shifts right to $(B/P)^d(S/P)_1$, as shown in the lower right panel, and the bond rate falls to r_x to clear the bond market. The money market is also able to clear at the lower bond rate because of both the increase in money demand associated with the higher level of consumption, as indicated by the rightward shift of the money demand schedule to $(M/P)^{dx}(c_1)$ in the lower middle panel, and to the drop in the opportunity cost of holding money associated with the decline in the bond rate. The economy attains a new short-run general equilibrium at levels of employment and output that exceed full employment.

   Now examine what happens when the monetary authority targets interest rates. The money supply would be adjusted endogenously to peg the interest rate at r_0, which would coincide with full employment in the absence of the velocity shock. The excess supply of money would be absorbed by a reduction in the nominal money supply such that the velocity shock would be fully accommodated. As no reallocation of resource time would be required, the labor market would be unaffected. With the labor supply schedule at $N^s(\theta,\lambda)$, the labor market clears at N_0, restoring the economy to full employment. These results suggest that without altering the long-run policy goals, the monetary authority is able to keep the economy closer to full employment in the short run for the duration of the transitory velocity shock by targeting interest rates rather than the nominal money supply.[4]

   In sum, if the monetary authority believes there is less stability in the goods (and labor) markets associated with transitory preference shocks[5] than in the money market due to transitory velocity (or money demand) shocks, the nominal money supply is the optimal intermediate target that minimizes the magnitude of short-term employment and output fluctuations about their full-employment levels. Conversely, if the velocity shocks induce less instability into the money market than preference shocks induce in the goods market, interest rates are the optimal target.

16.2   POLICY INSTRUMENTS AND POLICY TOOLS

Once an intermediate target is chosen, the monetary authority must take into account the money supply process described in Chapter 7 when attempting to hit its target. This is partly represented in Figure 16.1 as the choice of a policy instrument between a reserve aggregate, such as nonborrowed reserves, and a

---

[4]This outcome is consistent with Poole's (1970) results whereby interest rate targeting is preferred to money supply targeting when the uncertainty the monetary authority faces is from transitory velocity shocks.

[5]This conclusion also applies to transitory productivity shocks.

market interest rate, such as the federal funds rate. The policy instrument is to the intermediate target as the intermediate target is to the policy goal. For example, if the target is a 3 percent growth rate for M2, the monetary authority may choose to achieve that monetary target as an average over a several-week time period by either regulating the average growth rate of nonborrowed reserves over a very short duration by, say, allowing nonborrowed reserves to expand over a two-week period at an average rate of 3 percent, or alternatively by maintaining a stable federal funds rate of, say, 4 percent over the same time period. The monetary authority is able to observe the behavior of the alternative policy instruments closely by monitoring the activities in the very active market for bank reserves known as the federal funds market. The implementation of policy can be focused narrowly on achieving numerical values for the policy instruments in a timely way. However, those numerical values are usually subordinated to the intermediate targets. That is, there is a continual feedback of information on whether the targets are being met. If they are not, numerical values for the policy instruments are likely to be adjusted accordingly.

As described in Chapter 7 and discussed in some detail in Chapter 17, the monetary authority in the United States does not perfectly control the volume of nonborrowed reserves in the banking system or the value placed on reserves in the market, which is the federal funds rate. However, it can determine those numerical values very closely on average over a relatively short period of time. It does so by manipulating its policy tools. It can alter the demand for reserves by changing the reserve requirement ratios or the discount rate, which is the rate charged member banks that borrow directly from the Federal Reserve at the discount window. Alternatively, the Federal Reserve can alter the supply of reserves by conducting open market operations. However, there are limits on what those policy tools can accomplish. They are all essentially operating in a single market, the market for bank reserves. Therefore, the choices made for the three policy tools must be coordinated. A discount rate policy cannot be independent of the policy governing open market operations. The three policy tools must work together toward achieving the same end. Consequently, in practice the Federal Reserve has only ONE *effective policy tool* at its disposal. This point is important because it implies that at any given time the Federal Reserve can focus on only ONE policy goal. It cannot attempt to achieve both high employment and low inflation (in the short run) at the same time. Therefore, as illustrated in preceding chapters, the Federal Reserve is often forced to choose between conflicting policy goals.

16.3   THE FEDERAL FUNDS MARKET

The federal funds market is an interbank market for bank reserves. In the United States, a bank's total reserves are the sum of its vault cash and the deposits that it maintains with the Federal Reserve. Neither of those assets is interest bearing. Moreover, they are the *only* non-interest-bearing assets of the bank (apart from buildings and equipment). Banks therefore do not want to hold reserves beyond the amount required for normal operating activities resulting from currency demand by their customers and from check clearing, much of which is done through their Federal Reserve accounts. Banks would like to channel any additional reserves toward "working assets" that generate interest income. However, for approximately one-third of the roughly 11,000 banks in the United States (which represent more than three-quarters of total assets in the banking system), the demand for reserves associated with normal bank operations is below the quantity of reserves they are required by the Federal Reserve to maintain, as described in Chapter 6. For that reason, those banks tend to manage their reserves closely by attempting to maintain a sufficient quantity to meet reserve requirements (or required reserves) while minimizing the quantity held in excess of requirements (or excess reserves).

An important consideration in the bank's management of reserves is the volatility imparted to its reserves holdings by unexpected net withdrawal demands by the public. Such a positive net withdrawal can reduce the bank's reserves position to a point where it is no longer meeting reserve requirements. Prior to 1960, the principal methods of addressing that problem were to hold a large quantity of highly liquid (and therefore low yielding) assets, such as U.S. Treasury securities, which could be liquidated on short notice to raise reserves, and/or to hold additional (non-interest-bearing) excess reserves as a precaution against an unusually high volume of net withdrawals. However, the correlation of the net withdrawals *across* banks is far below unity. That is, on any given day, some banks may have positive net withdrawals and run short of reserves whereas others may have negative net withdrawals and unwanted buildups of excess reserves. Therefore, in principle, the banking system as a whole may have enough reserves to meet every bank's requirements if only those reserves were distributed properly among the banks. Allocating reserves across the banking system is precisely the role of the federal funds market and it performs that function very efficiently. The growth of the federal funds market was extraordinary after 1960 and has today become the principal avenue by which reserve-deficient banks can reliably meet reserve requirements. Consequently, excess reserves and banks' holdings of U.S. government securities have fallen substantially as a percentage of total assets in the banking system.[6]

What enables the federal funds market to operate so efficiently is that the transactions are conducted over Fedwire, which is part of the electronic payment system operated by the Federal Reserve. It is described in more detail in Chapter 17. Records of the participating banks' deposit balances with the Federal Reserve are maintained on the system. Each bank's deposit balance is added to its vault cash to determine total reserve holdings. Therefore, reserves can "move" from one bank to another very quickly, very cheaply, and in large volume simply by having the Federal Reserve debit and credit the respective deposit accounts.

Because the federal funds market plays such a central role in the day-to-day implementation of U.S. monetary policy, it is worthwhile to examine a federal

---

[6]In the late 1980s, many banks once again raised their government securities holdings, principally to improve asset quality after the problems of the banking industry during the mid-1980s that culminated in a large number of bank (and thrift) failures.

funds transaction with T-accounts. Three parties are involved: the reserve-deficient bank, bank A; the bank with excess reserves to lend, bank B; and the Federal Reserve. Refer to Figure 16.4. Suppose bank A needs to borrow $1 million in reserves and bank B has the reserves to lend. The two banks must first come to terms on the loan. That is, they must agree on the duration of the loan, which could be anywhere from overnight to several days, and on the "price" of the loan, the interest rate. The interest rate is called the federal funds rate and, as the example suggests, is determined by supply and demand conditions in the federal funds market where banks "buy and sell" reserves among themselves.[7]

Once they agree on the terms, the two banks notify the Federal Reserve, which is then authorized to debit bank B's deposit account by $1 million and credit bank A's deposit account by $1 million. Because both deposit accounts are liabilities to the Federal Reserve, it simply exchanges one liability for another and the overall size of its balance sheet is unaffected. The Federal Reserve's action reduces bank B's reserve asset, deposits at the Federal Reserve, by $1 million and raises bank A's by $1 million. The offsetting entries for the banks represent the obligation that bank A has incurred to repay the loan from bank B: a liability to bank A termed "federal funds bought" and an asset to bank B termed "federal funds sold." Note that bank A has now acquired the additional reserves that it needed and, in so doing, its balance sheet has expanded. That is, total assets have increased. Bank B has exchanged an idle non-interest-bearing asset, deposits at the Federal Reserve, for a working asset, federal funds sold.

At times when the reserves market is particularly slack, when there are more banks with reserves to lend than banks that are reserve deficient, the supply and demand conditions in the market cause the federal funds rate to decline. Conversely, when the banking system as a whole is short of reserves, the relative scarcity of reserves tends to elevate the federal funds rate. When banks are managing reserves very closely, their ability to extend credit may be limited by their reserves position and the federal funds rate becomes a very sensitive indicator

Figure 16.4
A Federal Funds
Market Transaction

Bank A (borrowing)		Federal Reserve		Bank B (lending)	
Assets	Liabilities	Assets	Liabilities	Assets	Liabilities
+$1M (Deposits at Federal Reserve)	+$1M (Federal Funds Bought)		+$1M (Deposits of Bank A)	−$1M (Deposits at Federal Reserve)	
			−$1M (Deposits of Bank B)	+$1M (Federal Funds Sold)	

[7]The federal funds rate that is the principal focus of monetary policy, when it is selected as the policy instrument and/or as the intermediate target, is a sample average of rates charged on overnight loans, which is called the "effective" federal funds rate.

of the economy's overall credit conditions. In that case, the Federal Reserve is able to have a significant influence in the credit markets by altering the supply of and/or demand for bank reserves through manipulation of its three policy tools: open market operations, reserve requirements, and the discount rate.

Open market operations alter the supply of reserves in the banking system as described in detail in Chapter 7. Essentially, when the Federal Reserve buys Treasury securities in the open market, it (ultimately) pays for them by crediting the deposit account(s) that a commercial bank(s) holds with it, thus increasing that bank's reserves by the total amount of the purchase. The resultant increase in the supply of reserves in the banking system induces a decline in the federal funds rate and tends to ease credit conditions. A cut in the reserve requirement ratio has similar effects on the federal funds rate and the credit markets by reducing the demand for bank reserves, because less are needed to meet reserve requirements. The effect of a cut in the discount rate is less straightforward.

16.4 DISCOUNT RATE POLICY

When a bank is short of reserves, one of its options is to purchase federal funds from banks that have surpluses of excess reserves to lend. Another is to borrow funds directly from the Federal Reserve at the discount window. The tighter the federal funds market, the higher the federal funds rate and the more likely the bank will be to turn to discount window borrowings. However, the attractiveness of borrowing at the discount window can be altered by the Federal Reserve when it determines its discount rate policy.

The Federal Reserve has been established as the "lender of last resort," and as such stands ready to make short-term "adjustment credit" loans to banks that are unexpectedly short of reserves. Such loans are not intended to be a permanent source of funding for banks. In fact, the duration of the loans is generally overnight, and almost never for more than a few days, the latter being restricted to certain loans extended to small banks.[8] Therefore, in practice, the Federal Reserve discourages excessive borrowing by individual banks and attempts to regulate the total volume of borrowing for the banking system as a whole. It relies on two aspects of its discount rate policy to achieve its borrowing objectives. One is the discount rate it sets, which is the rate at which eligible banks can borrow from the Federal Reserve.[9] Obviously, the higher the

---

[8]A category of longer term loans labeled "extended credit" consists of Federal Reserve loans to troubled banks that are undergoing a restructuring of their assets. Such loans are made only in unusual circumstances and the total volume is generally small. In addition, the Federal Reserve provides so-called "seasonal credit" to banks to support the seasonal fluctuations in credit demand arising principally from agricultural production needs, such as planting and harvesting.

[9]Each of the Federal Reserve District Banks operates a discount window for banks in its district. However, the discount rates across the Federal Reserve Banks are determined by the Board of Governors and are nearly always uniform across districts.

discount rate, the lower the demand for discount window borrowings. None-theless, if the federal funds rate were to spike upward, banks would have a greater incentive to borrow from the Federal Reserve. What matters to the banks is not simply the level of the discount rate, but the spread of the federal funds rate over the discount rate. The spread is the second aspect of discount rate policy used by the Federal Reserve to achieve its borrowing objectives.

As illustrated in Figure 16.5, the spread is generally positive. In equilibrium, however, banks must perceive the marginal (or per dollar) cost of raising funds in the federal funds market to be identical to the marginal cost of borrowing at the discount window. The discrepancy between those two rates is due to the fact that banks that overutilize the discount window may become the subject of additional regulatory oversight or regulatory pressure. That is, in its regulatory function, the Federal Reserve is vested with the authority to micromanage the bank (including the authority to dismiss the managers for incompetence) if it deems the bank's actions to be inconsistent with "safety and soundness" crite-ria. In practice, the Federal Reserve seldom resorts to such extreme measures. One early signal of a problem bank is excessive reliance on adjustment credit loans. Therefore, in a preemptive way, the Federal Reserve voices its displeasure with banks that return to the discount window week after week and thus tries to discourage borrowing at the discount window in the expectation that the

Figure 16.5   Federal Funds Rate and the Discount Rate

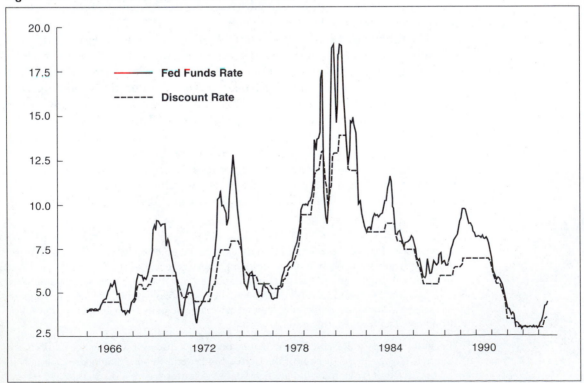

banks will be encouraged to address the root causes of their chronic reserve deficiencies.

The extent to which the Federal Reserve applies such "regulatory pressure" is a matter of policy. At the micro level it is intended to preclude individual banks from adopting policies that could threaten the viability of the bank's continued operations. At the macro level, tolerance for discount window borrowings is often used as a signal of monetary policy itself and whether the Federal Reserve is leaning more or less toward, say, easing credit conditions. The signals are often subtle changes that take place over an extended period and culminate in, say, a discount rate cut. Conversely, at times the signals sent by the Board of Governors (and/or the FOMC) that are associated with discount rate policy have been abrupt, resulting in an unexpected change in the discount rate. However, as is evident in Figure 16.5, those changes normally accompany changes in open market operations, which are in turn reflected in the federal funds rate.

16.5   MONETARY TARGET CONES AND "BASE DRIFT"

Since the mid-1970s, the Federal Reserve has been providing Congress with "targets" for selected monetary and credit aggregates. The targets currently consist of upper and lower bounds on the growth rates for M2 and M3 and a monitoring range for total private domestic nonfinancial debt, which produce "target cones" within which the nominal value of the aggregate is expected to remain. Such ranges are illustrated in Figure 16.6. Since 1978, the Federal Reserve has been required to include the target ranges in its semiannual reports to Congress. The purpose of the reporting is to establish some degree of accountability for monetary policy decisions. To that end, the selection of the targets is intended to reflect the Federal Reserve's forecasts for monetary growth that are consistent with its policy goals. The policy goals reflect the Federal Reserve's general view of the current state of the macroeconomy and are incorporated into its forecast of economic growth and inflation, which is also contained in its report to Congress. That forecast is, of course, contingent on future monetary policy decisions. Therefore, the target cones represent the Federal Reserve's best guess of the monetary growth rates that will support its contingent forecast for economic growth and inflation. Consequently, monetary growth above the upper bound is expected to be too inflationary, whereas growth below the lower bound is expected to slow the economy unduely as a result of excessively tight credit conditions.

The Federal Reserve is not obliged to keep the aggregates within their respective target cones. If economic conditions appear to change so that the target cones are no longer consistent with policy goals, the monetary targets can be abandoned. When such a disconnection between monetary policy decisions and the target cones occurs with regularity, the target cones themselves have no meaning. They provide neither the information for congressional oversight nor the discipline for Federal Reserve policy decisions, which are always susceptible to myopic overreaction to short-term transitory events.

Figure 16.6
The Federal Reserve's
Target Cones for the
Monetary Aggregates

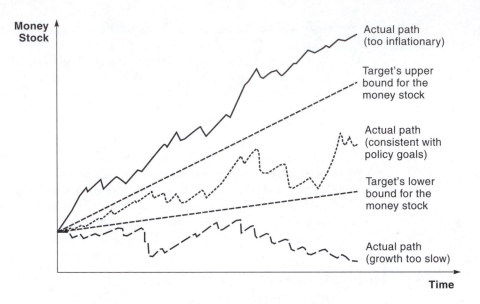

One example of that problem is the monetary policy of the 1970s that produced the high inflation in the United States toward the end of that decade. The policy decisions are illustrated in Figure 16.7 in terms of the Federal Reserve's target cones. During that period, the Federal Reserve would report target cones to Congress and subsequently ignore them. In retrospect, it is obvious that the Federal Reserve misjudged the impact of the macroeconomic shocks that affected the economy during the period and systematically oversupplied money.[10] Therefore, when the Federal Reserve returned to Congress to report on monetary policy, monetary growth was consistently above the target cones. The response was simply to ignore the old target cone by repositioning the apex of the new target cone at the current level of the money stock (as shown). That approach was repeated throughout the late 1970s, during which time the target cones were rendered essentially meaningless. The practice of letting "bygones be bygones," whereby new target cones are always selected to accommodate fully the past movements of the monetary aggregates regardless of the extent to which they may have drifted beyond the old target ranges, has come to be known as "base drift." [11] During the 1970s, when the short-term pressures on the Federal Reserve were toward policy "ease," the practice of base drift coin-

---

[10]The shocks included restrictions on world oil supplies by the OPEC cartel and the labor supply shocks associated with demographic changes and the changing attitudes toward work as more women entered the workforce. Those factors caused the Federal Reserve to bias its policy toward excessive money creation.

[11]For discussions of the various consequences of the practice of "base drift," see Poole (1976), Broaddus and Goodfriend (1984), Walsh (1986), Goodfriend (1987), Van-Hoose (1989), and Marquis (1992).

Figure 16.7
The Phenomenon of "Base Drift"

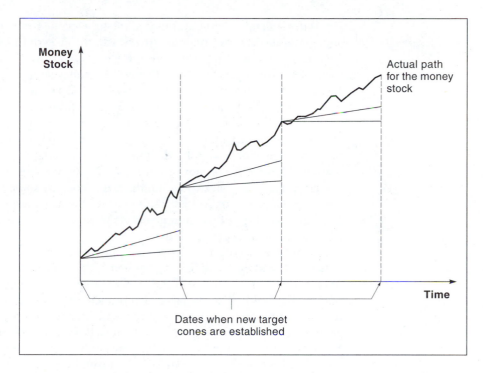

Money Stock

Actual path for the money stock

Time

Dates when new target cones are established

cided with a practice of systematically oversupplying money, with the subsequent runup in inflation.

16.6   MONETARY AGGREGATE TARGETING AND THE RESPONSE OF THE FINANCIAL MARKETS TO THE WEEKLY MONEY SUPPLY ANNOUNCEMENTS

By 1979, inflation in the United States had reached double digits, and many short-term market interest rates exceeded 20 percent. In response, the Federal Reserve abruptly changed policy. Its principal objective became reducing inflation. To achieve that goal, it chose to switch from targeting an interest rate (the federal funds rate) to explicitly targeting the money supply, with particular focus on the monetary aggregate M1. The implication was that the target cones it had been announcing to Congress were now to become meaningful indicators of future monetary policy. That information was not lost on the financial markets, which began to scrutinize closely the aggregate money supply figures released by the Federal Reserve each week.

To see how the "news" contained in the weekly money supply figures affected trading in the financial markets, refer to Figure 16.8.[12] Suppose at date

---

[12]For empirical evidence of this type of response, see Roley (1987).

$t = 0$ the Federal Reserve announced the target cone for its principal monetary aggregate, say M1, to Congress. Afterward, the growth rate of M1 brought the aggregate above the upper bound of the target cone as shown. On date $t = 1$, the Federal Reserve is to release the weekly money supply figures to the public. Just prior to the release, the financial markets form expectations about what the money stock will be as represented in Figure 16.8 by the conditional expectation $E[M1_1|\Omega_1]$, where Ω_1 is the set of information available to the financial markets just prior to the announcement. In addition, if the announced monetary policy as represented by the target cone has credibility with the financial markets, they form expectations of the future monetary growth in M1 that will bring the aggregate back to within the target cone by some future date, such as date $t = 2$. Therefore, M1 is expected to follow an average time path, such as $E[g_1|\Omega_1]$, the slope of which represents the expected average rate of growth of M1 over the intervening period.

Now suppose the actual money supply figures are released to the public at date $t = 1$, and the stock of M1, denoted $M1_1$, exceeds market expectations, or $M1_1 > E[M1_1|\Omega_1]$. How will the markets respond? If they continue to believe that the Federal Reserve is just as determined as before to restore M1 to within its projected target range, the markets will alter their view of future monetary growth as indicated by the time path labeled with the conditional expectation $E[g_1|\Omega_1 + \text{money supply announcement}]$, where the money supply announcement has been added to the markets' information set. That is, the time frame for returning M1 to within target is unchanged; however, the M1 money stock is farther from target than the markets (and the Federal Reserve) had expected and, as a consequence, future monetary growth is expected to slow. The re-

Figure 16.8

Response of the Financial Markets to the Weekly Money Supply Announcements

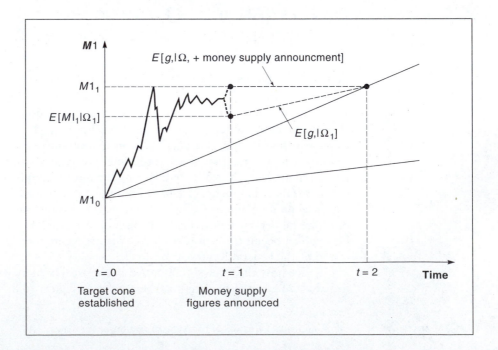

duced growth rate is represented by the lesser slope of the future expected time path of the money supply just after the announcement relative to the corresponding slope of the expected time path of M1 just prior to the announcement. Therefore, the markets take the new information as suggesting a tighter monetary policy in the near future. The expected slowdown in the growth of money and credit implies higher market interest rates and therefore lower stock and bond prices. This discussion suggests that when the Federal Reserve is following a credible policy whereby it is explicitly targeting a monetary aggregate, the weekly money supply figures contain important information relevant to future monetary policy decisions. When the money supply turns out to be higher than expected, the financial markets are likely to lower their expectations of future monetary growth, which results in a selloff in the stock and bond markets. If the money supply figures are lower than expected, the markets are likely to revise their expectations of future monetary growth upward, and bond prices and stock prices rise on the news.

16.7 LESS THAN COMPLETE MONETARY AGGREGATE TARGETING AND THE RESPONSE OF THE FINANCIAL MARKETS TO OTHER MACROECONOMIC NEWS THAT COULD ALTER MONETARY POLICY

By 1983, the Federal Reserve had begun to lose confidence in the macroeconomic relationship between M1, income, and interest rates. After passage of the Depository Institutions Deregulation and Monetary Control Act of 1980, the stability of the demand for M1 was called into question as discussed at length in Chapters 2 and 3. The Federal Reserve could no longer formulate meaningful targets for M1 that reflected its ultimate policy goals of price stability and sustained economic growth. Consequently, the Federal Reserve began to move away from M1 targeting, and the weekly money supply announcement gradually became a less important event on Wall Street because the information content of the announcement was waning.

The weakening in the feedback from the intermediate target of M1 growth to the policy instrument, which at the time was nonborrowed reserves, increased the direct sensitivity of monetary policy to other macroeconomic news events. That is, those events did not necessarily have to show up in M1 growth (the target) for nonborrowed reserves (the instrument) to be affected by open market operations. (The same was true of the subsequent policy regime of M2 targeting with a borrowed reserves instrument as discussed more fully in section 16.8.) In response, the financial markets began to adjust their trading activities increasingly to reflect their expectations of how the Federal Reserve would react to various macroeconomic shocks. This response is illustrated in Figure 16.9 with reference to the Federal Reserve's target cone.

Suppose the monthly employment data are to be released at date $t = 1$. Just prior to the release, M1 is above the target cone, which previously had been

Figure 16.9
Response of the
Financial Markets to
Macroeconomic News
That Could Affect
Monetary
Policy Decisions

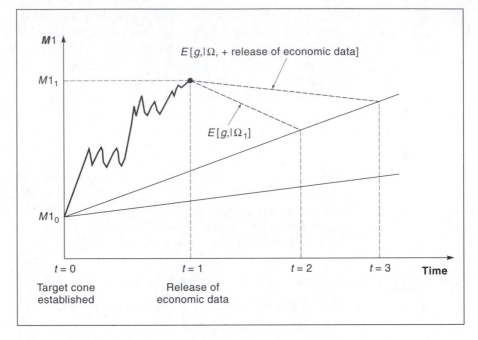

established at date $t = 0$. The financial markets form expectations of future monetary policy, which incorporate market expectations of what the employment data will show and of how the Federal Reserve will respond to that information. The market expectations are summarized in Figure 16.9 by M1 growth that is anticipated to follow a time path such as $E[g_1|\Omega_1]$, which would return M1 to the upper bound of the target cone by date $t = 2$. Suppose that when released the employment data indicate weaker job growth than had previously been expected. How would the financial markets respond to that "bad news?"

In the absence of any monetary policy response, if the weaker than expected economic performance is believed likely to persist into the future, stock prices would decline, reflecting the weaker anticipated future earnings for firms. Conversely, bond prices may rise if the weakness is expected to reduce credit demand and thereby lower interest rates. However, if the markets perceive the Federal Reserve's policy goals to include stronger growth as well as lower inflation, they are likely to expect a policy response designed to offset somewhat the unexpected weakness in the economy suggested by the data, which would further compromise their monetary targets. In that case, the financial markets will revise their expectations of future monetary growth upward, as represented in Figure 16.9 by the time path for M1 labeled by the conditional expectation $E[M_1|\Omega_1 + \text{release of economic data}]$. A faster expansion of money and credit is expected to reduce interest rates further. The expected additional short-run stimulus to the economy could be sufficient to bolster stock prices, and bond prices may rise even more. "Bad news" on the economy therefore translates into good news on Wall Street, but *only* because the markets expect the Federal Reserve to alter its monetary policy in light of the news.

The sketch in Figure 16.9 would also characterize the response of the financial markets' expectations of the monetary policy response to better than expected news on inflation. For example, if the news released at date $t = 1$ is that the producer price index (PPI) had risen less than expected in the previous month, the markets are likely to expect the Federal Reserve to relax somewhat its effort to reduce inflation and to focus more on stimulating economic growth. In that case, the time frame for restoring M1 to within its target range is again lengthened and the markets anticipate a more rapid expansion of money and credit than they had expected prior to the release of the good economic data on the PPI. Once again, the change in the expectation of future monetary policy would tend to support higher stock prices, which may otherwise have fallen if the lower PPI numbers were interpreted as indicative of a weaker economy. Bond prices are also likely to rise on the expectations of lower interest rates.

16.8 THE TRANSITION BACK TO FEDERAL FUNDS RATE TARGETING

Between 1983 and 1989, the Federal Reserve moved increasingly away from explicit targeting of the money supply. The behavior of M1 had become so erratic during the phase-out of interest rate ceilings on deposit accounts (as described in Chapters 2 and 3) that it was abandoned altogether and the Federal Reserve discontinued its reporting of an M1 target cone to Congress. The principal monetary aggregate became M2. However, as discussed in Chapter 3, M2 velocity is more volatile than M1 velocity has been historically, that is, prior to 1980. The Federal Reserve therefore continued to lessen its reliance on the monetary targets and to increase its reliance on projecting growth in reserves more directly. Such practice became so pronounced that many economists have claimed that the Federal Reserve was actually targeting reserves during the period, and ignoring the monetary aggregates altogether.[13]

The policy instrument was switched from nonborrowed to borrowed reserves. The reason for the switch was that the interest elasticity of M2 is substantially lower than that of M1. Consequently, when M2 velocity (or money demand/supply) shocks occurred that the Federal Reserve wanted to offset to meet its target, larger changes in total reserves were required. Under a nonborrowed reserves instrument, those shocks would have to be absorbed by changes in borrowed reserves, which are only a small fraction of bank reserves. To avoid erratic swings in discount window borrowing, the Federal Reserve chose to switch to a borrowed reserves target, thereby fixing the desired level of borrowings. Under that procedure, the velocity shocks were fully accommodated by open market operations and thereby absorbed with changes in nonborrowed reserves.

---

[13]For a lucid discussion of these issues, see Miller and VanHoose (1993). Also see Cosimano and Jansen (1988) for an empirical study on the change in operating procedures that occurred in 1979.

A second aspect of the switch to an M2 target is that short-term interest rates became much more volatile, which translated into greater volatility in the spread between the federal funds rate and the discount rate. However, for a given discount rate, the Federal Reserve's open market operations policy could be used to determine the federal funds rate and, hence, the spread between the two interest rates. Over time, the desire to reduce short-run interest rate volatility began to play an increasingly prominent role in the policy decisions themselves, as the role of the monetary aggregates diminished. When the short-run relationship between M2, interest rates, and output also began to deteriorate in 1989, the Federal Reserve felt it could no longer rely on the demand for M2 to guide monetary policy decisions. Money supply targeting was abandoned and the Federal Reserve returned to its pre-1979 operating procedures of explicitly targeting the federal funds rate.[14]

It is worth reemphasizing that the experience with interest rate targeting between 1973 and 1979 was not good. In retrospect, we see that the Federal Reserve attempted to depress short-term interest rates artificially in an effort to stimulate the economy. Consequently, it systematically oversupplied money. The result was double-digit inflation by the end of the decade. That episode has led many economists to question whether the Federal Reserve has the information necessary to choose interest rate targets wisely. That is, has the Federal Reserve learned from the experiences of the past, or is it destined to repeat the policy errors of the 1970s?

16.9   SUMMARY

To implement monetary policy, the Federal Reserve must first decide on its policy goals for the macroeconomy. How it chooses to conduct policy may depend in part on the choice of objectives and the time frame over which its goals are defined. A long-run objective of price stability (or an inflation goal) may be achieved with either a monetary aggregate or an interest rate target. However, the choice can have consequences for the extent to which, in the short run, output and employment fluctuate about their long-run equilibrium levels. Moreover, minimizing those fluctuations is often taken as the policy goal itself, that is, when the monetary authority chooses the short-run goals of a traditional stabilization policy. In the event that transitory (or productivity) preference shocks introduce greater volatility in the goods market equilibrium conditions than velocity shocks introduce into the money market equilibrium conditions, a money supply target is preferred. Conversely, when velocity shocks introduce more volatility into the money market than preference shocks introduce into the goods market, pegging a market interest rate is preferable.

---

[14]The operating procedure is to use borrowed reserves as the policy instrument by estimating the "reserves need" associated with a given federal funds rate and accommodating that "need" with nonborrowed reserves on a biweekly basis, which is the length of the reserves maintenance period.

Because the ultimate policy goals for inflation, output, and employment respond to monetary policy with a considerable lag, the monetary authority selects values for the intermediate target that it believes to be consistent with those goals. Once the values are chosen, they are treated as though they were the ultimate goal. That is, the conduct of monetary policy is designed to hit the target exactly, with the understanding that doing so maximizes the chances of eventually achieving the ultimate policy goals. However, in the day-to-day operations of monetary policy, the Federal Reserve does not control the intermediate target directly. Rather, it manipulates the policy tools of open market operations, reserve requirements, and the discount rate to achieve the target. Those policy tools all operate on a single market, which is the market for bank reserves, the federal funds market. Therefore, the monetary authority must coordinate the use of the tools to affect the equilibrium in that single market. In essence, the monetary authority has only a single effective policy tool, which limits its policy to focusing on one objective at a time.

When the Federal Reserve shifted its focus to disinflation in October 1979, it chose to target M1 while relying on nonborrowed reserves as the instrument that linked its policy tools to its intermediate target. The financial markets responded to the policy shift by increasing their scrutiny of the weekly money supply announcements, which then contained significant policy information. Whenever the money supply was above target, an unexpectedly high number implied that the monetary authority would have to tighten policy even more rapidly than expected to return the aggregate to within target, which implied a tighter monetary policy and higher interest rates in the future. The markets would sell off on the news and interest rates would rise immediately. The converse was also true.

By 1983, the demand for M1 was seen to be very unstable after the DIDMCA of 1980, and the Federal Reserve shifted its intermediate target to M2. At about the same time, the lesser interest elasticity of M2 caused a switch in the choice of a policy instrument from nonborrowed reserves to borrowed reserves. In addition, short-term market interest rates became more volatile. Over time, heightened concern about the additional short-term interest rate volatility caused the Federal Reserve to lessen its reliance on the intermediate monetary target. The weekly money supply announcements became less informative to the financial markets about future monetary policy. The focus shifted to other macroeconomic news to which the Federal Reserve was likely to respond. Whenever such news suggested an easier policy, perhaps to offset some negative news on economic growth or perhaps to relax the restriction on monetary expansion in response to positive news on inflation, the markets would generally have a "good" day and vice versa.

By 1989, the demand for M2 had begun to behave unpredictably. The Federal Reserve then switched its target back to the federal funds rate, which it had employed prior to October 1979. To implement a federal funds rate targeting procedure, the Federal Reserves first estimates the volume of nonborrowed reserves that it believes to be consistent with federal funds trading in the neighborhood of its target value for the federal funds rate, given a predetermined level of borrowed reserves. It then supplies reserves in that amount through its open market operations. When market conditions change, the Federal Reserve adjusts the quantity of nonborrowed reserves that is expected to restore the federal funds rate to target. The next chapter describes such desk operations in more detail.

■ REVIEW QUESTIONS

1. The optimal choice of money versus interest rate targeting depends on the relative stability in the labor and goods markets versus the money market. Use the graphic model developed in the text, when prices are fixed in the short run, to answer the following questions.
   (a) Suppose the economy undergoes an intertemporal preference shock that favors savings over current consumption. Illustrate how the economy adjusts to the shock when the monetary authority targets the interest rate versus how it responds when the monetary authority targets the money supply.
   (b) Answer question (a) when the shock is a velocity shock whereby the rate of adoption of new payment system technology by households temporarily slows.
   (c) If all transitory shocks in the economy are of the types examined in (a) and (b), describe the conditions under which interest rate targeting is preferred to money supply targeting and vice versa.

2. As the lender of last resort, the Federal Reserve stands ready to supply reserves to banks in need on a weekly basis. The funds are borrowed by the banks at the Federal Reserve's discount window.
   (a) What alternatives to the discount window does a bank have when it is short of reserves at the end of reserve maintenance period and must comply with reserve requirements?
   (b) Differentiate between borrowed reserves, total reserves, net free reserves, nonborrowed reserves, excess reserves, and required reserves.
   (c) Is a "tight" reserves market likely to show up in the spread between the federal funds rate and the discount rate, the volume of borrowed reserves, and/or net free reserves?

3. Suppose the Federal Reserve has previously announced its monetary targets to Congress and the range for M2 is zero to 5 percent per year. Since the announcement, M2 has grown below its target. Answer the following questions with reference to the monetary target cones.
   (a) On Thursday afternoon, the Federal Reserve announces a growth rate for M2 for the week that exceeds the market's expectations. How would the bond market be likely to respond to this news if it believes the Federal Reserve is serious about meeting its money targets?
   (b) Suppose additional information about the economy suggests that the inflation rate was less than expected during the previous month. How would the markets be likely to respond to this news if they believe the Federal Reserve is concerned only with maintaining a balance between inflation and employment growth over the short run and would largely ignore its money targets?

*4. Suppose the economy undergoes positive productivity shocks that are transitory in that they last one period and then dissipate fully.
   (a) If the monetary authority wants to offset those shocks in an environment where prices are "sticky" as in Chapter 11, illustrate whether it would achieve its short-run stabilization of objectives for employment and output better with an interest rate or money target.
   (b) If prices were fully flexible, in which of the two targeting regimes described in (a) are prices more stable in the short run?

*5. The financial markets expend significant effort attempting to second-guess monetary policy decisions, but the Federal Reserve also looks to the financial markets for important information that could portend future changes in goal variables, such as the inflation rate. Describe what interpretation the Federal Reserve may give to each of the following developments in the financial markets. (Hint: This information is published daily in *The Wall Street Journal*.)
   (a) Changes in an index of raw commodity prices, such as the Commodity Research Bureau's (CRB) index over the past week.
   (b) Changes in the value of the U.S. dollar in relation to the currencies of the United States' major trading partners over the past month.
   (c) Changes over the past four weeks in the slope of the Treasury yield curve. (Hint: You may want to reread the relevant sections of Chapter 4.)

REFERENCES

Broaddus, Alfred, and Marvin Goodfriend. 1984. "Base Drift and the Longer Run Growth of M1: Experience from a Decade of Monetary Targeting." Federal Reserve Bank of Richmond *Economic Review* 70 (November/December): 3–14.

Cosimano, Thomas F., and Dennis W. Jansen. 1988. "Federal Reserve Policy, 1975–1985: An Empirical Analysis." *Journal of Macroeconomics* 10 (Winter): 27–47.

Friedman, Benjamin. 1975. "Targets, Instruments, and Indicators of Monetary Policy." *Journal of Monetary Economics* 1 (October): 443–73.

Goodfriend, Marvin. 1987. "Interest Rate Smoothing and Price Level Trend-Stationarity." *Journal of Monetary Economics* 19 (May): 335–48.

Marquis, Milton H. 1992. "Capital Accumulation, Price Stability, and Base Drift." *Journal of Macroeconomics* 14 (Spring): 321–35.

Miller, Roger LeRoy, and David D. VanHoose. 1993. *Modern Money and Banking*, 3rd edition. New York: McGraw-Hill, Inc.

Poole, William. 1970. "Optimal Choice of Monetary Policy Instruments in a Simple Stochastic Macro Model." *Quarterly Journal of Economics* 84 (May): 197–216.

—————————. 1976. "Interpreting the Fed's Monetary Targets." *Brookings Papers on Economic Activity* 1: 247–59.

Roley, V. Vance. 1987. "The Effects of Money Announcements under Alternative Monetary Control Procedures." *Journal of Money, Credit and Banking* 19 (August): 292–307.

VanHoose, David D. 1989. "Monetary Targeting and Price Level Non-Trend-Stationarity." *Journal of Money, Credit and Banking* (May): 232–39.

Walsh, Carl. 1986. "In Defense of Base Drift." *American Economic Review* 76 (September): 692–700.

CHAPTER 17

DESK OPERATIONS AND THE REPO MARKET FOR TREASURIES

On weekdays at about 11:30 A.M. (EST), the trading desk at the Federal Reserve Bank of New York conducts its daily open market operation (if any) to alter the supply of bank reserves in a manner consistent with the Federal Open Market Committee's (FOMC) policy objectives.[1] Those operations determine the rate at which the central bank's portfolio of government securities is allowed to expand, as described in Chapter 7. However, the vast majority of daily open market operations do not consist of outright purchases and sales of government securities. Instead, the Federal Reserve relies extensively on temporary holdings of claims on government securities, known as repurchase agreements, repos, or RPs. Under such an agreement, the Federal Reserve acquires a claim on a Treasury bill, for example, for a duration as short as overnight to as long as 15 days. In exchange for the claim, the Federal Reserve creates so-called base money, that is, it adds to the monetary base by increasing reserves to the banking system. When the repurchase agreement expires, the Federal Reserve returns the Treasury security to its counterparty, thus extinguishing the claim on the T-bill and effectively "erasing" the base money liability that it had created. Bank reserves are thus returned to their former levels. The Federal Reserve can also construct a set of financial transactions that resemble entering into a repurchase agreement on the opposite side. Such transactions are termed matched sale-purchases or MSPs and are used when the Federal Reserve wants to drain reserves from the banking system temporarily. Only when the Federal Reserve wants to add permanently to its portfolio of government securities does it engage in an outright purchase of Treasury securities. In the long run, outright purchases are necessary to provide sufficient reserves for the banking system to meet the growing liquidity needs of the economy.

---

[1] The Federal Reserve is not restricted to a single intervention per day, but in recent years that has become the standard practice anticipated by the markets.

This chapter first describes in some detail an RP contract and the extent of the repo market. For the Federal Reserve to rely on the repo market as the principal vehicle for implementing its monetary policy decisions on a daily basis, the market must be highly liquid. That is, the repo market must fulfill an economic need that is independent of the Federal Reserve's open market operations. That need is created on one side of the market by large investors, such as mutual funds and commercial banks, that are seeking very liquid investments, and on the other side by government securities dealers and some commercial banks that are seeking financing for their inventories of government securities. In the past two decades, the repo market has grown to the point where even unusually large open market operations by the Federal Reserve of, say, $10 billion constitute only a small fraction of the estimated total quantity of the more than $500 billion in trading that takes place in the market each day.[2] The various types of interventions by the Federal Reserve are described in this chapter and an explanation is given for the Federal Reserve's selection of the overall mix of RPs, MSPs, and outright purchases over time.

17.1   THE REPURCHASE AGREEMENT[3]

A repurchase agreement can be described either as a short-term collateralized loan or as a short-term investment.[4] The issuer of the RP generally owns a security and must raise funds, which it does by selling a claim to the security to a second party that has funds to invest. What makes the RP agreement distinctive is that coincident with the sale, an agreement is made that the original owner of the security will repurchase the claim at a future date and at a predetermined price. The price at which it originally sells the claim is below the price at which it subsequently buys it back. The difference represents the interest income to the second party for the use of the funds. Therefore, an overnight RP between, say, a government securities dealer and a money market mutual fund would involve the two transactions depicted in Figure 17.1. The government securities dealer would issue the RP and "send" securities, often referred to as the collateral, to the money market mutual fund. The mutual fund is then said to be "doing a

---

[2]See Stigum (1989, p. 8).

[3]The books by Stigum (1988, 1989) are excellent sources of information on the many facets of the repo market. Also, see Stigum (1983), which has become a standard reference for institutional details on the money markets more generally.

[4]Legally, there is a "neither fish nor fowl" aspect to RPs, in that which party actually owns the security in the case of bankruptcy by the issuer of the RP has not been clearly established. If the RP is seen to be a collateralized loan, the lending party may not receive full compensation for the "loan" because that party becomes one of many claimants to the assets of the bankrupt firm. However, if ownership of the security is transferred under the terms of the RP, in which case the RP is more like a typical investment, the second party retains the full rights of ownership of the security.

Figure 17.1
The Two Transactions
of an RP

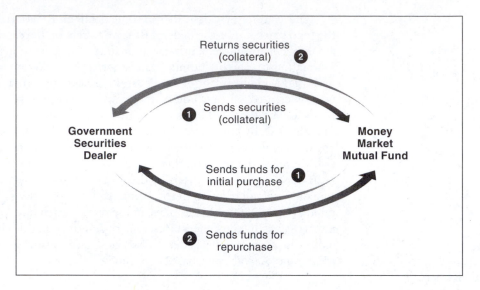

reverse RP," that is, it is sending funds to the government securities dealer and "reversing in" securities, which become assets of the mutual fund. The following day, the RP expires and the mutual fund returns the collateral, whereas the government securities dealer sends the funds, including the interest payment, to the mutual fund.

Such a financing arrangement may appear to be unduly cumbersome, seeming to involve high transactions costs that would limit its use to unusual circumstances requiring urgent short-term financing; however, that is *not* the case. Transactions costs are in fact very low because of the automation of the process. Moreover, repurchase agreements (especially those involving Treasury securities) provide a safe, liquid, short-term asset to large institutional investors, which therefore sustain a demand for that form of investment. On the opposite side of the market are government securities dealers, who often buy securities outright and immediately "put them out on repo" while maintaining an interest rate spread that is sufficient to yield them an adequate return after accounting for the interest payment to the institutional investor. For the most part, government securities dealers are "market makers" for government securities, which means that they stand ready to buy or sell the securities at preannounced prices. However, they must finance their inventories of government securities at all times and a principal source of the financing is the RP market.

17.2   THE FEDERAL RESERVE'S BOOK ENTRY SYSTEM FOR TREASURY SECURITIES

Over the past 20 years, the U.S. Treasury Department—in conjunction with its fiscal agent, the Federal Reserve—has been phasing-in a paperless system to support trading in Treasury securities. Today all U.S. Treasury bills (Treasury securities with maturity of one year or less, which are sold on a discount basis) are paperless securities, and progress has been made toward increasing the volume of Treasury notes and bonds (which have coupons attached and therefore are not sold on a discount basis) that are being traded as paperless securities. The system works as follows. Each Treasury bill, for example, is identified on a central computer at the Federal Reserve. Associated with its entry is an owner(s) or an agent(s) for the ultimate owner(s). The agent must be qualified to maintain an account with the Federal Reserve, a requirement that restricts that role to depository institutions and the Treasury.[5] Therefore, a private citizen who purchases a Treasury bill does not receive the security itself, but instead receives acknowledgment of ownership through a commercial bank or the Treasury, which in turn acts as the individual's agent and establishes ownership on the books at the Federal Reserve.

To examine the details of this transaction by way of example, we can include an additional intermediary in the form of a mutual fund. Suppose the Treasury Department issues a $10,000 T-bill as part of its weekly multibillion-dollar refinancing program (that is, "rolling over" maturing debt). At the same time, a household deposits $10,000 in a mutual fund that invests exclusively in Treasury securities. Assume the mutual fund buys $10,000 of the new issue at the weekly auction. How does the Treasury receive payment and the mutual fund receive a claim to the T-bill? Because the mutual fund does not have an account with the Federal Reserve, it must find a commercial bank to serve as its agent.[6] The mutual fund must identify its agent to the Federal Reserve. In turn, the mutual fund manages the investment portfolio, against which the household has a claim. The household sends $10,000 to the mutual fund, which deposits that sum at its bank with instructions to purchase the T-bill.[7] The bank notifies the Federal Reserve of its desire to purchase the T-bill and the Federal Reserve transfers ownership of the new security to the bank, debits its account by $10,000, and credits the Treasury Department's account with the Federal Reserve by $10,000.

How have the balance sheets of the various parties to the transaction been affected? Refer to Figure 17.2. The Treasury Department's balance sheet expands, with an increase in its outstanding liabilities of $10,000, the T-bill, and an offsetting increase in assets of $10,000 in its Federal Reserve account. The commercial bank's account at the Federal Reserve falls by $10,000, but that amount is exactly offset by the $10,000 received from the mutual fund. The claim on the T-bill is simply transferred between accounts at the Federal Reserve. On net, the mutual fund has expanded its balance sheet by acquiring an additional asset, the T-bill, while incurring an additional liability, the $10,000 increase in the account of the household. The household has simply

---

[5]In addition to those of the Treasury Department, accounts of some federal agencies, such as the Federal Home Loan Banks, and a number of foreign official accounts are maintained at the Federal Reserve.

[6]Such mutual fund "custodial" business is highly concentrated within the banking industry. State Street Bank in Boston holds the large share of the market.

[7]There is a time delay in this transaction if the purchase is made at a Treasury auction. In that case, the mutual fund must first submit a tender to the Treasury for the security. A few days later it receives the bill on the so-called settlement date.

Figure 17.2
T-accounts for the
Completed
Transaction of a
Household's Purchase
of a Newly
Issued Treasury Bill

Treasury Department			Commercial Bank		
Assets	Liabilities		Assets	Liabilities	
+$10,000 (Deposits at Federal Reserve)	+$10,000 (T-Bill)		+$10,000 (Cash from Mutual Fund) −$10,000 (Deposits at Federal Reserve)		

Mutual Fund			Household		
Assets	Liabilities		Assets	Liabilities	
+$10,000 (T-Bill)	+$10,000 (Household Account)		−$10,000 (Cash) +$10,000 (Account at Mutual Fund)		

exchanged one asset, the $10,000, for another, the shares in the mutual fund in which it wanted to invest.

When primary government securities dealers want to purchase Treasury securities, the story is similar. In effect, the dealers are purchasing securities to add to their own investment portfolios and they must use a commercial bank as their agent with the Federal Reserve.[8] However, government securities dealers are also financial intermediaries. That is, they are not the ultimate source of the funds they are investing. Where do those funds originate?

17.3   DEALER FINANCING IN THE RP MARKET AND DVP TRANSFERS ON THE SECURITIES WIRE

On any given day, a large fraction of the inventory of the government securities that primary government securities dealers hold is financed in the repo market. Such strategy implies that each day maturing repurchase agreements are replaced with new RPs and a daily pattern of trading over the Federal Reserve's book entry system is created. An important characteristic of the trading is that the timing of the individual transactions is governed by their so-called

---

[8]This business is also highly concentrated in the banking industry, with the two major "clearing banks," Chase Manhattan Bank and Chemical Bank, having the largest share of the market.

"delivery-versus-payment," or DVP, feature. For example, suppose a commercial bank is acting as an agent for a mutual fund that wants to invest in government securities through a repurchase agreement with a dealer. The mutual fund and the dealer would agree to terms and both would notify their respective agents of the impending transaction. The transaction does not take place until the securities are sent to the RP lender's bank, a process that can be initiated only by the owner of the securities as registered on the books of the Federal Reserve. Therefore, the government securities dealer, through its agent, controls the timing of the *initial* transaction. The mutual fund's commercial bank sends authorization to the Federal Reserve to transfer funds from its account into the account of the dealer's commercial bank upon receipt of the securities. Once the dealer's bank sends instructions to the Federal Reserve to send the securities to the mutual fund's commercial bank and to accept payment into its account, the Federal Reserve effects the transaction. That is, claims on the securities are transferred to the account of the mutual fund's bank and, at the same moment, that bank's deposit balance is debited by the size of the purchase and the account of the dealer's bank is credited.

A large volume of such transactions take place each morning shortly after the Federal Reserve's so-called "securities wire" open at about 8:30 A.M. The dealers are securing financing for the day for their inventories of government securities. The following morning, the RP is unwound and the Federal Reserve reverses the transaction of the previous day, with allowance for the interest payment to the account of the mutual fund's commercial bank. That transaction is also on a DVP basis, the timing of which is now controlled by the mutual fund's bank, which is sending the securities or returning the collateral. Acting as an agent for the mutual fund, the commercial bank has an incentive to return the collateral as quickly as is permissible under the terms of the RP contract because it receives "good funds" that it may choose to reinvest. Consequently, each morning just after the Federal Reserve's securities wire opens there is a rush to unwind overnight RPs. The unwinding of the repurchase agreements involves debits to the accounts at the Federal Reserve of primary securities dealers' banks, and that process generally places them in an overdraft position. Because banks are not permitted to run overnight overdrafts on their Federal Reserve accounts, the overdrafts must be eliminated by the time the securities wire closes for the day, which officially is 2:30 P.M. but is usually extended to around 4 P.M. Dealers must therefore secure financing of the securities that were returned to them in the morning before that deadline.[9] Hence, throughout the day, new overnight RPs are extended to investors such as mutual funds, which hold them overnight, and the daily cycle is completed each morning when the collateral from the previous day's repurchase agreements is returned.

---

[9]Beginning in April 1994, the Federal Reserve began charging an intraday overdraft fee. The fee has created an additional incentive for dealers to complete their inventory financing early in the day and has increased the volume of transactions that take place before the Federal Reserve's traditional "intervention time" of 11:30 A.M. As a consequence, the market is somewhat thinner when the Federal Reserve enters, but has remained sufficiently liquid to support open market operations.

17.4   RPs with the Federal Reserve and Their Connection with the Federal Funds Market

In addition to the securities wire, the Federal Reserve operates an electronic system for federal funds transactions known as the Fedwire funds transfer service.[10] The funds wire is used by commercial banks as a vehicle for electronic payments. One use is check clearing, when one bank receives a deposit in the form of a check drawn on another bank. The check may be cleared over Fedwire by debiting the account of the bank against which the check is drawn and crediting the account of the bank that receives the check as a deposit. Because bank deposits at the Federal Reserve constitute a major portion of bank reserves, the reserves of the former bank are reduced and the reserves of the latter bank are increased by the amount of the check, so the overall reserves in the banking system are unaffected. A second use of the funds wire is the transfer of federal funds from a bank that has excess reserves to lend to a bank that is reserve deficient. That type of transaction is described in detail in the preceding chapter. Of interest here is how trading in the federal funds market is affected by activities of the Federal Reserve in the repo market.

Some confusing terminology is commonly used to refer to the Federal Reserve's participation in the repo market. As defined above, a firm that owns securities and puts them out on repo is said to be issuing an RP; the firm that is temporarily acquiring the securities is said to be doing a reverse RP. When the Federal Reserve is involved in the transaction, it is said to be "doing an RP" when it *acquires* the securities. Legally, the Federal Reserve is prohibited from borrowing from the private sector. However, it can buy securities and sell securities from its portfolio. Therefore, if it wants to enter into an RP transaction on the opposite side, where it temporarily gives up ownership of securities, it consummates two permanent transactions. In one it sells a Treasury security from its portfolio and in the second it repurchases the same security for delivery at a future date. Such transactions are therefore called matched sale-purchases or MSPs. They are simply another way of negotiating a (reverse) repurchase agreement in which the Federal Reserve temporarily reduces its portfolio holdings of government securities.[11]

---

[10]Fedwire opens earlier in the day and remains open later in the day than the securities wire. Recently, the Federal Reserve has pursued a policy of gradually extending the number of hours per day Fedwire is open. It reflects, in part, the greater perceived need for interbank transactions associated with a greater interconnectedness of global financial markets.

[11]There are some technical differences between an MSP and a reverse RP. The pricing mechanism is modified for the MSP because it requires two separate transactions and hence two separate prices, whereas a reverse requires only one price or interest rate. In addition, many of the Federal Reserve's term repos have withdrawal provisions that permit the counterparty to terminate the agreement early, which it may want to do in the event of unfavorable interest rate movements. No such provisions are attached to the MSP because such transactions are outright purchases and sales of securities.

In RP transactions such as the one described between the government securities dealer and the mutual fund, commercial banks operate strictly as intermediaries and do not have any net changes in their balance sheets. Moreover, although bank reserves in the form of deposits with the Federal Reserve may flow from one bank to another, there is no net change in the total volume of reserves in the banking system as a result of the transactions. That is *not* the case when the repurchase agreement involves the Federal Reserve on one side or the other of the transaction. When the Federal Reserve does an RP with the market, that is, when it enters into a repurchase agreement in which it temporarily acquires securities, it makes payment by creating base money in the form of bank reserves. Those reserves are then traded in the federal funds market.

For example, suppose the Federal Reserve decides to engage in an open market operation in which it does an RP for $1 billion with a primary government securities dealer. The dealer notifies its bank of the impending transaction and the bank sends the securities over Fedwire to the Federal Reserve, which adds them to its list of assets while simultaneously debiting the commercial bank's account by the amount of the purchase. Note that in this case the bank continues to act solely as the financial intermediary in the transaction with no net change in its assets. However, its reserves in the form of deposits with the Federal Reserve have risen, and there is no corresponding decline of reserves elsewhere in the banking system as a result of the transaction. Consequently, there is an increase in the supply of total bank reserves. Banks that are reserve deficient do not have to compete as aggressively for the funds, which are now more readily available, and the federal funds rate declines, as described in the preceding chapter.

When the Federal Reserve participates in the RP market (for government securities), the federal funds market is directly affected. Unlike the relatively small direct effect that the Federal Reserve has on the RP market, where its transactions are only a small portion of the trading that takes place each day, its effect on the federal funds market can be very pronounced. When the Federal Reserve does an RP, it temporarily adds reserves to the banking system and the federal funds rate falls. An MSP has the opposite effect. Reserves are drained from the banking system and the greater scarcity of bank reserves causes the federal funds rate to rise.

17.5   ARBITRAGE OF THE RP RATE AND THE FEDERAL FUNDS RATE

The relationship between the federal funds rate and the RP rate is very close. The principal reason is that commercial banks are in a position to arbitrage any unusual spread that may open up between them. In general, federal funds sold are viewed as unsecured loans, albeit with very little risk because they are loans of very short maturity and the lender is a commercial bank. Reversing in securities under RP is viewed as even less risky, because the loan is collateralized by the government securities that are put up to acquire the loan. Therefore, the RP rate is more often than not a few basis points below the federal funds rate.

Suppose, for example, that the relationship goes awry and the federal funds rate suddenly rises to five or six basis points above the RP rate. How would the banks respond? Commercial banks that are in a position to do so would have an incentive to put more of their government securities out on repo at the lower rate and lend the funds in the federal funds market at the higher rate. That process would increase the supply of federal funds and thereby lower the equilibrium federal funds rate until the opportunity was eliminated. Not all banks are in a position to take advantage of such an opportunity because the trading requires unpledged collateral. Moreover, there may be unusual conditions in the repo market, when dealers are having difficulty placing their securities. One service that many commercial banks offer is to be the residual lender to dealers, who must finance their inventories by day's end. In that event, the commercial banks are reversing in securities that they themselves must fund, often in the federal funds market. Such service also has the affect of reducing the spread between the two rates, because the banks will pass along the higher costs to the dealers, which effectively raises the RP rate. The opposite arbitrage condition is available when the RP rate becomes high in relation to the federal funds rate. Commercial banks can simply borrow in the federal funds market and do reverse RPs with the dealers. Such activity would tend to increase the demand for federal funds, causing that rate to rise, while increasing the demand for RPs, causing the RP rate to fall.

17.6   THE MIX OF OUTRIGHT PURCHASES, RPS, AND MSPS[12]

Over time, the liquidity needs of a growing economy expand. To meet those needs while maintaining a stable average money price of goods over the business cycle, the Federal Reserve must expand bank reserves. If reserves expand too slowly, prices will fall; if they expand too rapidly, the economy will undergo systematic inflation. To provide for the long-run average rate of growth of bank reserves, the Federal Reserve must expand its asset base. To do so, it relies almost exclusively on purchases of government securities, which are called the System portfolio.[13]

One way of expanding the System portfolio is simply to buy securities in the open market. Such outright purchases, or "outrights," represent permanent

---

[12]An excellent reference for this material from the Federal Reserve's perspective is Meulendyke (1989).

[13]The Federal Reserve also acts as an agent for foreign governments that want to participate in the U.S. government securities market. It may acquire securities for them, which are purchased from accounts they maintain with the Federal Reserve. Repurchase agreements acquired on behalf of foreign governments are called customer RPs. They have little effect on the overall implementation of monetary policy through open market operations, because their effect on the reserves market can always be offset by trading from the System portfolio. However, they are sometimes used to signal to the market the Federal Reserve's view of current conditions in the federal funds market.

additions to the portfolio. They can subsequently be resold, but are permanent in the sense that at the time of their purchase no plans are made to remove them from the portfolio at a future date. Hence, they contrast with RPs and MSPs, which are explicitly temporary adjustments to the size of the System portfolio.

Outright purchases of securities are relatively infrequent, with perhaps four to eight such operations per year. Consequently, temporary transactions are necessary to bring the System portfolio into balance with the perceived reserve need as illustrated in Figure 17.3. In the upper panel, the solid line represents the long-run secular growth in the System portfolio. The dashed line represents the permanent contributions of outright purchases. They take the form of a step function, where each step represents a single operation. In this example, with each outright purchase, the System portfolio is just meeting the reserve need and no temporary transactions are necessary. Afterward, however, the reserve need continues to grow and temporary transactions become necessary. In that case, the Federal Reserve will do RPs in an amount sufficient to meet the additional reserve need, which is represented in the figure by the vertical distance between the solid line and the dashed line. Note that over time, the quantity of RPs that the desk is required to arrange continues to grow, until at some point a decision is made that the daily operation has simply become too large. At that point, such as date $t = 1$, the Federal Reserve makes a new outright purchase of securities that is just sufficient to eliminate the need for any immediate temporary transactions and the process repeats.

The middle panel shows an alternative combination of permanent and temporary transactions that could be used to meet the secular growth in the reserve need. The outright purchase done at date $t = 0$ exceeds the amount of the securities that would meet the reserve need. The desk therefore engages in temporary transactions that reduce the size of the System portfolio in the amount indicated in the figure by the distance from the dashed line to the solid line. That temporary MSP operation drains reserves from the banking system. Over time, as the reserve need grows, the size of the MSP operations declines until a point is reached, such as date $t = 1$, when temporary operations are no longer needed. However, as time passes, the permanent portion of the System portfolio is insufficient to meet the reserve need and the desk arranges RPs. They continue to grow in size until such time, as at date $t = 2$, another outright is deemed appropriate.

If the reserve need were as deterministic as indicated in the upper and middle panels of Figure 17.3, temporary operations would not be necessary. The desk could simply adopt a schedule of systematic outright purchases that would add to the System portfolio in just the right quantities to meet the reserve need. However, the real world is not so simple. Factors other than desk operations that affect reserve availability induce substantial swings in the reserve need on a week-to-week, or even day-to-day basis. To maintain enough flexibility in its operations to meet unpredictable events, the desk engages in frequent temporary operations. Refer to the lower panel of Figure 17.3. The reserve need that the Federal Reserve wants to meet is shown as the solid line, which now reflects the random fluctuations. The pattern of outright purchases is again represented by the dashed line. In this more realistic case, there are times, such as date

Figure 17.3
Selecting the Mix of
Temporary and
Permanent Open-
Market Operations

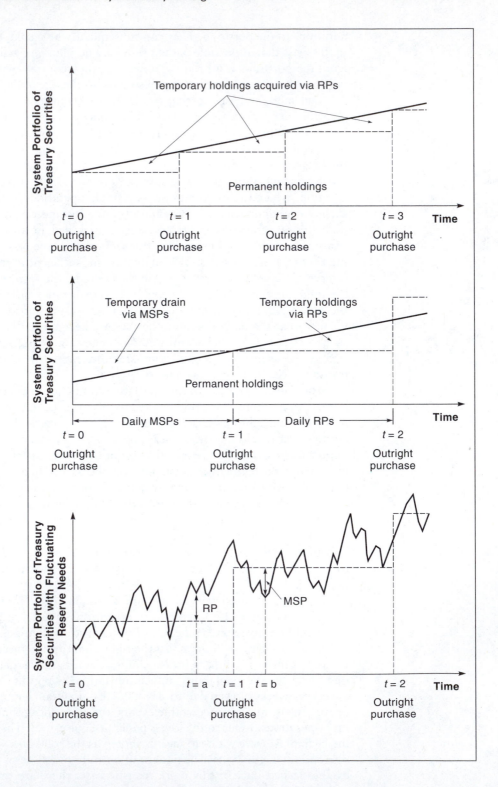

t = a, when the desk is called upon to add reserves by doing RPs with the market; at other times, such as date t = b, the desk must drain reserves through MSPs to meet its reserve objective. When reserve needs fluctuate to the extent suggested in the figure, temporary transactions are preferred to a series of outrights, which are technically more difficult to arrange. Therefore, the bulk of open market operations conducted by the desk at the Federal Reserve Bank of New York are temporary operations in the RP market involving either repurchase agreements when there is a temporary need to add reserves or matched sale-purchases when there is a temporary need to drain reserves from the banking system.

17.6 SUMMARY

As the economy expands, its liquidity needs grow. If the banking system is to provide the additional liquidity, there must be secular growth in bank reserves. That requires an expansion of the Federal Reserve's balance sheet. The Federal Reserve expands its balance sheet by increasing its holdings of Treasury securities through outright purchases in accordance with the policy directive it receives from the Federal Open Market Committee. However, on a day-to-day basis, the policy directive allows some latitude in the actual implementation of policy. Latitude is necessary to respond to transitory events or shocks to the reserves market. To maintain enough flexibility to respond to such events, the Federal Reserve relies on temporary open market operations in the RP market.

The RP market is a large, highly liquid market for government securities in which transactions estimated to total more than $500 billion per day are conducted. Many of the transactions are conducted through the electronic systems for book entry securities and funds transfer that are operated by the Federal Reserve. Those highly efficient systems keep transactions costs to a minimum. As market makers in the Treasury security market, government securities dealers hold large inventories of government securities that must be continually financed. The RP market is a principal vehicle for dealer financing. On the other side of the market are the large institutional investors, such as money market mutual funds, that demand short-term investments with high liquidity and low risk.

The commercial banks play an important role in the RP market, not only as intermediaries in the transactions, but also as issuers of RPs and as residual sources of dealer financing. Their ability to arbitrage rates between the RP market and the federal funds market ensures that open market operations, which are relatively small in proportion to the total volume of RP transactions each day, can nonetheless have a significant impact on the RP market. That is one important channel through which changes in monetary policy are transmitted to the economy.

REVIEW QUESTIONS

1. Most of the Federal Reserve's open market operations are conducted under temporary repurchase agreements rather than through permanent outright purchases and sales of securities.

   (a) Describe the details of an overnight repurchase agreement in which the Federal Reserve acquires temporary claims on U.S. Treasury securities.
   (b) What is the advantage to the Federal Reserve of relying on RPs versus outright purchases?
   (c) How does a matched sale-purchase differ from a repurchase agreement that is arranged by the Federal Reserve with the primary government securities dealers?

2. More than $500 billion in transactions are conducted in the RP market for U.S. Treasury securities each day, but the Federal Reserve seldom acquires more than $10 billion in securities on a given day. How is the Federal Reserve able to have such an important influence on interest rates when it appears to be such a small player in the RP market for Treasury securities, in which most open market operations are conducted?

3. Using T-accounts, answer the following questions.
   (a) How can an individual household "loan" money to the government with a mutual fund acting as the intermediary?
   (b) What is the role of the overnight RP market for government securities in the financing of inventories of securities by primary government securities dealers? Describe the transactions associated with the inventory financing that take place throughout a typical day.
   (c) How is a matched sale-purchase arranged by the Federal Reserve with primary government securities dealers?

*4. The Federal Reserve has been accused of excessive "churning" of its portfolio of government securities, that is, doing too much buying and selling, which could contribute unnecessarily to the transaction costs of its operations.
   (a) Suggest ways in which the Federal Reserve could minimize churning.
   (b) What are the economic conditions that contribute to churning?
   (c) Would it be possible to completely eliminate churning? (Hint: Remember the distinction between defensive operations and those related to strict implementation of policy.)

*5. Recent developments in the RP market for government securities include more extensive use of continuing contracts and tri-party arrangements. (Hint: Consult the references listed at the end of the chapter.)
   (a) In the former contract, overnight RP contracts can be renewed automatically each day, but at the new RP rate, until one of the two parties terminates the agreement. What are the advantages of this arrangement? Under what conditions would you expect such contracts to become increasingly prominent?
   (b) In the latter arrangement, a third party, such as a commercial bank, could intermediate the trade between two government securities dealers or between a government securities dealer and a mutual fund. The commercial bank "holds" the collateral and effects the trade by debiting and crediting accounts that the two parties maintain at the bank. What

are the advantages of this arrangement? Under what conditions would you expect such arrangements to become increasingly prominent?

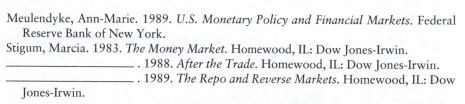

REFERENCES

Meulendyke, Ann-Marie. 1989. *U.S. Monetary Policy and Financial Markets.* Federal Reserve Bank of New York.

Stigum, Marcia. 1983. *The Money Market.* Homewood, IL: Dow Jones-Irwin.

——————————— . 1988. *After the Trade.* Homewood, IL: Dow Jones-Irwin.

——————————— . 1989. *The Repo and Reverse Markets.* Homewood, IL: Dow Jones-Irwin.

CHAPTER **18**

TIME INCONSISTENCY AND THE CREDIBILITY OF MONETARY POLICY

Government policies are part of the economic environment in which households and firms make decisions on how best to allocate their resources to achieve their objectives of maximizing utility and profits. When the government changes a policy or adopts a new policy, the economic environment also changes and prior decisions of households and firms may no longer be optimal. For that reason, resource allocation decisions must be forward-looking, and households and firms must attempt to evaluate the credibility of any new government policy. Before committing resources to a particular course of action, they must ask: Will the government stick to the new policy, or is the policy decision likely to be modified or even abandoned in the future? If the new policy is not lasting, what will replace it?

To answer those questions, households and firms evaluate the incentives that government policy makers face when they select one policy option over others. For example, if policy makers are believed to be resolute in their pursuit of a specific policy objective, the totality of their incentives may be captured by their desire to achieve that objective. If so, a particularly troublesome question arises. If the economic environment were to change in the future in such a way that the original policy is no longer the best policy option for achieving the objective, would the government feel free or even duty bound to change its policy? Such a policy reversal is likely to render the resource allocation decisions to which households and firms have previously committed less than optimal. Recognizing that possibility, households and firms are less likely to make any such initial commitment of resources.

The process of private-sector decision making may make the selection of any so-called optimal policy problematic if the government retains the ability to alter policy in the future. For example, suppose the government policy objective is to find a cure for AIDS or skin cancer and to make the treatment available to the largest number of people in need as possible. To achieve that objective, the government grants extended patent protection for up to 25 years (versus the normal 17 years), which essentially grants monopoly rights to the discoverer of the treatment. As the sole supplier, the discoverer would adopt the monopoly solution to its profit-maximizing production decision, which would yield lower output and higher prices than would exist in a competitive industry. In the absence of other inducements, such "monopoly rents" are necessary if a firm is to channel more of its resources into research aimed at finding the cure. The rents represent just rewards for having undertaken a very risky investment. The issue the government may face is that if its patent extension policy is successful in accelerating the process of discovering a cure, the treatment will not be disseminated to the public as widely as would be socially desirable. Consequently, the government has the incentive to renege on its policy and allow free entry into the market to move the production point to the competitive solution (or even beyond with subsidies). Therefore, the success of the original policy in altering resource allocations in the economy is *itself* responsible for altering the economic environment in such a fundamental way that continuation of the policy is no longer optimal and even appears socially irresponsible!

This example illustrates the phenomenon known as the time inconsistency of optimal policy design, which can alter the response of the private sector to the policy. Obviously, in the example, any firm that considers whether to commit a higher percentage of its resources to finding the desired cure would recognize that the government could not possibly commit to such a policy. The policy therefore lacks the credibility necessary to entice firms into making the investment. That is, if the government cannot credibly commit to a policy, the firm will not commit its resources to the desired course of action that the policy is intended to elicit. The time-inconsistency dilemma potentially affects the design of all discretionary public policies, including monetary policy, that are intended to achieve a specific policy objective, and it provides a basis for favoring the conduct of policy according to visible rules.

The purpose of this chapter is to describe how the dilemma plays out within the context of monetary policy in which the short-run objectives of full employment and price stability are pursued. The inability of the central bank to commit to a specific policy when it maintains discretion to respond to macroeconomic shocks may preclude *any* such short-run policy decisions from having desirable effects on the economy. That conclusion holds even when the policy makers and the public agree on the objectives of the policy. In addition, in the presence of other economic distortions such as capital income taxes that reduce the full-employment levels of employment and output, the pursuit of the short-run policy objectives of full employment and price stability may introduce an inflation bias into monetary policy that would not otherwise be present. The chapter closes with a discussion of how the incentives of policy makers can be exploited to reduce the inflation bias. One option is the use of performance-based incentives in a contract to which each central banker must agree, where performance is measured by comparing the actual inflation rate with a publicly announced inflation target. Such a contract may allow some constructive use of stabilization policy without the attendant inflationary bias.

18.1   TIME INCONSISTENCY IN MONETARY POLICY[1]

In actual economies, policy makers may attempt to choose an optimal policy according to criteria that coincide with maximizing social welfare. In the preceding chapters, such criteria were often represented by a policy objective of keeping the economy as close to full employment (according to the economic definition of that term) as possible while maintaining stable prices. Let us assume that households and firms, the private sector, agree to that policy objective. Nonetheless, they must continue to make their own microeconomic decisions involving the future commitment of resources. In making those decisions, because the future economic environment is uncertain, households and firms must form expectations of what the economic environment will bring, which includes the likely course of monetary policy. However, the selection of an optimal monetary policy depends on those expectations.

To illustrate the dilemma that this situation creates for selecting an optimal monetary policy, consider an economy in which the future commitment made by the private sector consists of adhering to the terms of a binding nominal wage contract as in Chapter 12 while the monetary authority pursues its full-employment and stable-price objectives. For expositional purposes, the terms of the contract and the timing of events are modified slightly. Refer to Figure 18.1. At the beginning of the first period, or at date $t = 0$, the shocks for the period occur $(\theta_0, \lambda_0, \gamma_0)$. The monetary authority chooses a policy, M_0, and the households and firms enter into a labor agreement consisting of a *two-period* contract that determines the nominal wage in each period, (W_0, W_1). The contract commits resources in the second period of its life by fixing the nominal

Figure 18.1
Timing of
Macroeconomic
Shocks, Policy
Decisions, and Labor
Agreements

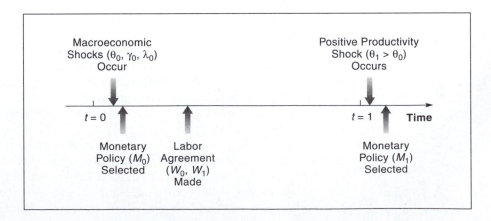

[1]The seminal articles on the topic are by Kydland and Prescott (1977) and Calvo (1978).

wage rate at W_1, which encompasses an economic environment that is uncertain at the time the agreement is made. In arriving at the labor agreement, households and firms must predict the future state of the economy, which includes a projection of the likely course of monetary policy. That projection is summarized by their joint expectations of the money supply in the second period, which is denoted $E[M_1]$. They then choose an optimal contract that maximizes the households' utility and the firms' profits, given their expectations of the future. Denote the contract by the optimal choices for the nominal wage in each period as $\{W_0^*(M_0^*), W_1^*(E[M_1])\}$. The notation highlights the fact that the nominal wage in the first period is based on knowledge of monetary policy during that period, but the nominal wage in the second is based on the expectations of monetary policy that are made by the households and firms.

With the monetary authority pursuing a short-run stabilization policy of minimizing deviations of employment and output around their full-employment levels while simultaneously stabilizing prices, it must use its discretion each period to alter policy as the economy undergoes shocks. Therefore, it will choose the money supply that is consistent with its objective on a period-by-period basis. In period 1, it chooses M_0^*. That choice is observed by households and firms and is incorporated into the nominal wage for that period, $W_0(M_0^*)$ and is shown in Figure 18.2, the labor market clears at "a" with the economy at full employment, N_0. Now suppose that at date $t = 1$ the economy undergoes a positive productivity shock such that $\theta_1 > \theta_0$. When the monetary authority does not respond by altering policy in an unanticipated way, $E[M_1]$

Figure 18.2
An Illustration of the Time Inconsistency of Optimal Policy: A Positive Productivity Shock and Long-term Nominal Wage Contract

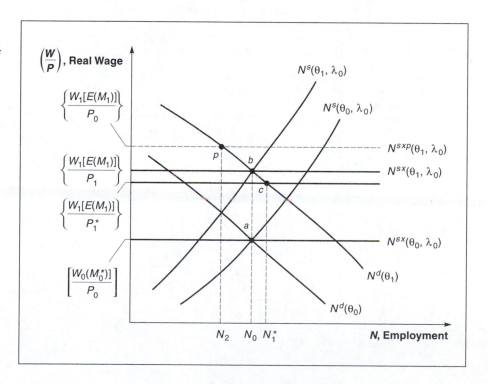

$= M_1$, implying that the actual monetary policy is fully incorporated into the nominal wage during the second period. This permits prices to fall to P_1 to accommodate the shock fully as described in Chapter 12, and the labor market clears at "b." The time paths for the macroeconomic variables that are the subject of policy, employment and prices, are shown in Figure 18.3. Note that the economy remains at full employment, N_0, throughout, but at the cost of instability in prices.

Because the monetary authority is concerned about stability in *both* employment and prices, the outcome described is not optimal in the second period. At date $t = 1$, the monetary authority has an incentive to alter policy. It would be willing to compromise on the full-employment objective to achieve greater stability in prices. As shown in Figure 18.2, this would coincide with a new equilibrium in the labor market plotted as point "c," where the optimal level of employment for the second period is above full employment, or $N_1^* > N_0$, and the optimal deflation for the second period yields a higher price level than would otherwise have been the case, or $P_1 < P_1^* < P_0$.

To achieve that preferred outcome in the second period, the monetary authority must increase the money supply beyond what is anticipated in the first period, or $M_1^* > E[M_1]$. That change in policy reduces the real wage rate to $W_1[E(M_1)]/P_1$ and invalidates the optimality of the labor contract, hence the dilemma. The condition that optimal monetary policy be consistent over time means that the optimal policy selected in the second period must be the same policy that was chosen in the first period on which resource allocation decisions were based, or $M_1^* = E[M_1]$. However, in an uncertain world, that is not likely to be the case. The conclusion is that an "optimal" policy is time inconsistent,

Figure 18.3
Time Path of
Employment and
Prices in Response to
a Positive Productivity
Shock

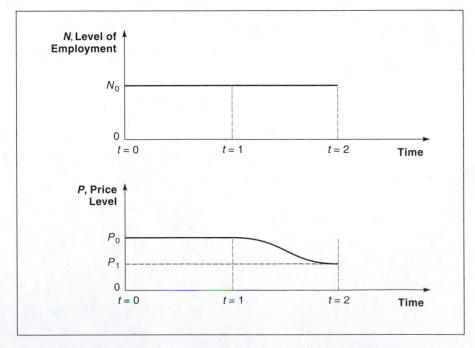

because a policy that is optimal today affects private-sector decisions, in this case the nominal wage in the second period, that in turn render the policy sub-optimal in the future. Conversely, a "consistent" policy, one that pursues a short-run objective such as the stabilization policy described above, is subopti-mal, because each period it necessarily alters the economic environment on which past private-sector commitments were based.

18.2   RULES VERSUS DISCRETION

When the monetary authority pursues consistent policies whereby it seeks to achieve full-employment and stable-price objectives simultaneously, *no* pro-nouncement that it can make today about future policy can be fully credible. That is, the private sector realizes that the monetary authority will not continue a policy that is inconsistent with its short-run stabilization objectives and that such a policy will be abandoned. The exercise of discretion can lead to a long-term inflationary bias in the policy that could be eliminated if the monetary authority conducted policy according to a hard-and-fast rule that preserves price stability over a longer time horizon.

For illustration, we can modify the economic environment by assuming the level of employment that enters into the determination of the policy makers' short-run objective exceeds the underlying economic definition of full employ-ment.[2] Policy makers may pursue that objective if they have not fully incorporated the detrimental effects that other distortionary policies, such as capital gains taxes, would have in reducing the underlying level of full employ-ment that can be sustained in the economy. Alternatively, there may be a so-called agency problem (discussed in a different context in Chapter 5), whereby political pressure could induce policy makers to pursue a policy aimed at achieving a higher level of employment than is economically feasible over time.[3] In either case, the level of employment that is deemed to be socially optimal would be above full employment.

That level of employment is denoted N^* in Figure 18.4. The policy objec-tive becomes one of minimizing short-run fluctuations of employment around N^* while maintaining stable prices. Ideally, the monetary authority would like to pursue a policy over the two periods described above that would set employ-ment equal to N^* in each period while holding the price level at P_0 over both periods. Again, because of the uncertain future, any policy deemed optimal to-day would be inconsistent over time, making it impossible for policy makers to commit credibly to a future policy. Because the private sector understands the

---

[2]That is the assumption made by Barro and Gordon (1983) and virtually all other au-thors who have subsequently pursued this line of research, whose articles are cited else-where in this chapter.

[3]See Canzoneri (1985) and Cukierman (1992) for fuller discussions of why policy mak-ers may use discretionary policies to pursue an unsustainable level of employment and output.

Figure 18.4
Illustration of the
Inflation Bias in
Monetary Policy

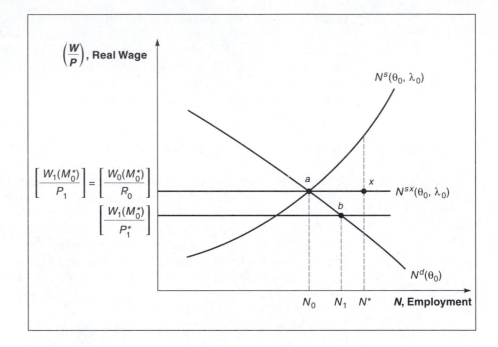

dilemma faced by the policy makers, the nature of the contracts the private sector would be willing to write also changes. That is, the contracts entail private-sector commitments that affect the future allocation of resources by households and firms, and their optimality is affected by future policy decisions.

Over time the economy undergoes many productivity and preference shocks that cause short-run economic fluctuations of employment and prices. On average, the shocks would have no effect on employment because the economy is always adjusting back to full employment. However, the effect of the shocks on prices is determined by monetary policy decisions. If the money supply grows too rapidly over time, the economy will have systematic inflation; if it grows too slowly, prices will fall. Therefore, a discretionary monetary policy that responds to shocks in the short-run with adjustments in the nominal money supply will induce a systematic inflation if the cumulative policy responses result in excessive monetary growth.

To illustrate how the unattainable employment objective N^* can induce systematic inflation, consider how the monetary authority responds on average to shocks in the economy by considering the average set of period shocks, which correspond to a period in which there are no unanticipated changes in technology or preferences. In Figure 18.4, technology and preference shocks at the beginning of the first period are given by $(\theta_0, \lambda_0, \gamma_0)$. The private sector settles on a two-period contract that sets wages at $\{W_0(M_0^*), W_1(E[M_1])\}$. The monetary authority chooses a policy for the initial period that sets the nominal money supply at M_0^*. Assume the policy was either announced or observed by households at date $t = 0$ and was included in the labor contract. The question is: How will the private sector set the nominal wage in the second period?

To arrive at a nominal wage for the second period that maximizes expected utility and profits, the private sector forms expectations of what technology and preferences are likely to be for that period. For exposition, assume they correctly predict that there will be no changes in either technology or preferences. In that case, they would like to design a contract that will clear at full employment, which is plotted as point "a" in the graph. However, monetary policy will determine the price level in the next period, P_1^*, and that will determine what the appropriate nominal wage should be for the labor market to clear at N_0.

If the monetary authority were pursuing a stabilization policy with full employment, N_0, as its employment objective, the appropriate policy for the second period would be to maintain the same money supply as in the first period, or $M_1 = M_0^*$. If the private sector understood that to be the policy, wages in the second period would be set such that $E[M_1] = M_0^*$, or $W_1(E[M_1]) = W_1(M_0^*) = W_0(M_0^*)$. The real wage remains unchanged at $W_1(E[M_1])/P_0 = W_0(M_0^*)/P_0$ and the economy clears at full employment, N_0. Both of the policy objectives are fully achieved.

Now suppose the monetary authority instead pursues the perceived socially optimal level of employment N^* as part of its short-run stabilization objectives. In that case, it would have an incentive to supply more money to the economy on average than is consistent with full employment. Reconsider the preceding exercise, but with the modification to the short-run policy objective. Obviously, the monetary policy that was chosen fully achieved the stable price objective, but fell short of the employment objective. If both are important to the policy makers, they would prefer instead to sacrifice the stable price objective somewhat in the second period to move somewhat closer to the employment objective.

In Figure 18.4, the ideal state of the economy in the second period relative to the policy objective would be a level of employment N^* and price level P_0, plotted as point "x" in the graph. However, that is not an equilibrium. When the monetary authority achieved price stability, the private sector adopted a contract that caused the market to clear at full employment. Therefore, the monetary authority would have to surprise the private sector with a money supply increase to raise the price level, reduce the real wage, and thereby increase output above the full-employment level. For example, if the monetary authority were believed to have chosen a monetary policy for the two periods of (M_0^*, M_0^*), the nominal wage contract for the two periods would consist of $[W_0(M_0^*), W_1(M_0^*)]$. However, instead of attempting to achieve the outcome consistent with the labor market equilibrium plotted as point "a," the monetary authority instead optimally picks an equilibrium such as "b," where the level of employment moves closer to N^* at the expense of some price instability. In that case, it would increase the nominal money supply, say, to $M_1^* > M_0^*$, which would cause prices to rise unexpectedly in the second period to P_1^*. However, because the nominal wage is unchanged, the real wage rate falls to $[W_1(M_0^*)/P_1^*]$ and the market clears at N_1.

Obviously, the unexpected change in policy has rendered the labor agreement between the households and firms less than optimal. That is, because $E[M_1] < M_1$, the wage agreement that was based on $E[M_1]$ would not have been chosen had the true policy for the second period been known at the time the contract was negotiated. The problem the policy makers face in implementing such a policy over time is that they cannot fool the private sector *systematically*. The private sector knows that on average the monetary authority will be attempting to achieve the level of employment N^* with monetary injections, and will simply incorporate that expectation into wage contracts so that, for example, $E[M_1] = M_1^* > M_0^*$. The long-run effect is that the higher money growth is reflected not only in higher prices, but also equally in higher nominal wages. That is, the nominal wage contract would consist of $[W_0(M_0^*), W_1(M_1^*)]$ such that the price level could rise from P_0 in the first period to P_1 in the second period without affecting the real wage, or $[W_0(M_0^*)/P_0] = [W_1(M_1^*)/P_1]$. Consequently, the economy clears at full employment in the second period, but at a higher price level. The conclusion is that over a long time period, the pursuit of short-run policy objectives causes the monetary authority to introduce an inflation bias into its policy as prices rise each period while the average level of employment remains unaffected. Note that if the monetary authority chose to surprise the public by setting the money supply in the second period at $M_1 < E[M_1^*]$, prices may remain constant at P_0, but the economy would slow as real wages would be too high to be consistent with full employment.

The undesirable outcome is the result of the monetary authority's inability to commit credibly to a policy because the private sector understands the time inconsistency of the monetary policy. Any policy deemed optimal today will not be optimal tomorrow, and the monetary authority therefore will have an incentive to alter policy in the future in pursuit of short-run goals. Recognizing the lack of commitment, the private sector will alter its future commitments (which are in the form of a nominal wage contract in the preceding example) to reflect the tendency of policy makers to achieve the stated socially optimal goals. Once the inflation bias is incorporated into the private sector's expectations, the best the monetary authority can do is to fulfill those expectations. Figure 18.2 illustrates this phenomenon in the presence of a positive productivity shock. Assume the nominal wage contract reflects the expectations of the inflation bias as before, so that expected real wages rise to $\{W_1[E(M_1)]/P_1\}$ to reflect the higher productivity. Suppose the monetary authority chooses not to fulfill those expectations, but rather to opt for price stability in the second period such that the price level remains at P_0. That policy surprise would cause real wages to rise to $\{W_1[E(M_1)]/P_0\}$, the labor supply schedule would shift up to $N^{sxp}(\theta_1, \lambda_0)$, and economic activity would slow, with the labor market clearing at "p" and employment falling to N_2. Once again, failure to fulfill the private sector's expectations that incorporate the inflation bias causes the economy to fall below its full employment levels of output and employment.

Clearly, a mechanism is needed that would force policy makers to commit to a specific policy that would achieve a more desirable long-run outcome—in particular, a policy that would eliminate the inflation bias without having a less desirable outcome for employment. One such policy would be to require the monetary authority to abandon its short-run goals and conduct policy according to a hard-and-fast, publicly announced rule. One such rule is a monetary rule described in Chapter 14, whereby the rate of monetary growth is consistent with an average inflation rate of zero. In that case, optimal labor contracts could be written that are premised correctly on an average inflation rate of zero. However, by definition, a policy conducted according to a rule eliminates policy makers' discretion in decisions. The switch in policy regimes may have an important consequence: unless a rule could be written that contains contingencies for all possible future events, short-run stabilization policy must essentially be abandoned.

18.3 REPUTATION-BUILDING AND DISCRETIONARY POLICY

Many economists have argued that conducting monetary policy according to a publicly announced rule, such as the constant growth rate rule or the gold standard, may not be desirable or even politically feasible. For example, the monetary authority may have private information about velocity shocks which, as described in Chapter 16, should be accommodated fully by changes in the money supply to avoid undesirable fluctuations in output and employment that would otherwise result.[4] In that context, one may reasonably ask whether institutional arrangements or other mechanisms could be structured to cope with the time inconsistency problem. Is it possible to allow policy makers some discretion in their pursuit of short-run policy objectives while eliminating the inflation bias?

In search of an answer to that question, means have been sought to "punish" policy makers in some sense when they lean too much toward their inflation bias. Under the supposition that the policy makers have some private information that could be exploited to the public's benefit, one inherent method of punishment is to limit the degree of credibility that the private information gives to the policies chosen.[5] That is, the private sector would respond to policy pronouncements as warranted by past policy decisions. If inflation were to begin to rise, the private sector may believe that the monetary authority is leaning more toward its inflationary policies and not using its private information to the public's benefit. In that case, the reputation of the policy makers would be

---

[4]See Rogoff (1985) and Lohmann (1992) for related discussions of this issues. Garfinkel and Oh (1993) stress the limitations of private information, as it requires interpretation by the monetary authority that must translate into accurate forecasts. Therefore, even in the presence of private information, giving the monetary authority discretion to act on the information still may not lead to superior outcomes relative to conducting policy by rule. VanHoose (1992) describes how relatively small costs of establishing policy can amplify the policy errors under alternative operating procedures.

[5]This issue is examined in detail by Canzoneri (1985) and Cukierman (1992). Also, Cukierman and Meltzer (1986) and Stein (1989) examine strategic practices of the Federal Reserve in its use of private information that may enable it to maximize the credibility private information affords it.

damaged and subsequent policy pronouncements would lose credibility with the public.

Consider the private sector's response to a monetary policy designed to accommodate a positive velocity shock, as was analyzed in Chapter 16. If households increase their demand for money because of a slowdown in the rate at which new payment system technology is being adopted, the monetary authority may have information on the macroeconomic consequences of the velocity shock before the general public. In that case, there would be a reduction in labor supply as more resource time than previously anticipated is being channeled into transacting. This adjustment is illustrated in Figure 18.5 by a shift in the labor supply schedule to $N^{sx}(\theta,\lambda)$. If the monetary authority chose not to respond, the equilibrium employment level would fall to N_1 as prices fall to P_1 (point "b"). However, the monetary authority could offset the shock's effect by increasing the money supply sufficiently to accommodate the increase in demand. Suppose it announces an increase in the money supply to M_1^*. Labor agreements could then be struck that would set the nominal wage at $W_1(M_1^*)$. If the private sector believed the increase in the money supply from M_0^* to M_1^* was due solely to an aggregate velocity shock that the monetary authority was accommodating, the nominal wage, denoted $W_1(M_1^*)^c$ where the superscript "c" indicates that the policy is credible, would be identical to the nominal wage it would have set in the absence of a velocity shock and the attendant monetary accommodation, or $W_1(M_1^*)^c = W_0(M_0^*)$. That is, the increase in the money

Figure 18.5
Reputational Effects in the Response of Monetary Policy to a Velocity Shock

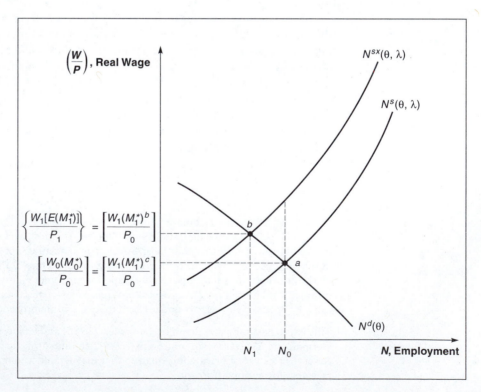

supply would have been just sufficient to prevent the price level from declining, and the labor market would clear at its full-employment level, N_0, plotted as point "a" in the graph.

Now suppose the monetary authority has no credibility with the private sector. The increase in the money supply to M_1^* would be viewed as a continuation of the inflation-biased policy. The nominal wage that the private sector would incorporate into its contract, denoted $W_1^*(M_1^*)^b$ where the superscript "b" indicates that the policy is believed to represent an inflation bias, would be inflated. The increase in the nominal money supply could prevent the price level from falling, but would nonetheless fail to prevent the real wage from rising. The economy would slow as employment and output fall below their full-employment levels. Note that in the two examples, the monetary authority responded in precisely the same way to the same velocity shock. When its policy was credible, the economy remained at full employment and prices remained stable. When the monetary authority failed to achieve a reputation as an inflation fighter, the economy dipped below full employment as prices fell. The potential loss of reputation is one incentive for the monetary authority to limit the inflation bias in its policy decisions. Once it loses its reputation as an inflation fighter, the loss of credibility weakens the effectiveness of monetary policy. In turn, the loss of effectiveness makes it even more difficult for the monetary authority to regain its former reputation and credibility.

18.4   IS THERE AN OPTIMAL CONTRACT FOR THE POLICY MAKER?

The incentive of maintaining the credibility associated with a strong reputation as an inflation fighter may not be enough to reduce the inflation bias significantly. In that case, could institutional arrangements be employed that essentially increase the punishment the policy makers experience for an excessively inflationary policy? One possibility is to appoint conservative central bankers who have a stronger aversion to inflation than society at large. The incentives provided by their own personal preferences would lessen the inflationary bias.[6] However, that solution lacks enforcement provisions to ensure that a professed "conservative" appointed as a central banker would remain conservative after the appointment.

More specific provisions that would complement the personal preference incentives of a conservative central banker could be established by a formal contract. For example, the New Zealand government contemplated tying

---

[6]Rogoff (1985) analyzes the potential benefits that such an appointment could bring. Waller (1992) provides a scenario under which labor market heterogeneity may reduce the social benefits of the appointment of a conservative central banker, if the increased output variability associated with lower inflation disproportionately affects the sector of the economy operating under a nominal wage contract versus a sector in which nominal wages are perfectly flexible.

central bankers' salary to the actual inflation rate in relation to a publicly announced inflation target. The closer the inflation rate was to the target, the
higher would be the central bankers' salary. That provision was not ultimately
adopted in the final legislation, but is clearly a viable option.[7] A contract between the government and a central banker could have terms that provide an
incentive for the central banker to reduce the inflation bias. Importantly, the
contract could contain a criterion for evaluating the central banker's performance that is readily observed and easily enforced. Therefore, the central banker's compliance with the terms of the contract, as well as the enforcement of the
contract by the government, could be easily monitored by the private sector.
Under those conditions, if the penalty for noncompliance were sufficiently strin-
gent and its enforcement provisions were credible, the private sector could make
commitments that affect future allocations of resources on the presumption that
the inflation bias would be reduced, or at least that the actual inflation rate
would not substantially exceed the inflation target.

Such a contract eliminates some of the disadvantage of a purely discretionary regime by reducing the inflation bias, and retains some of the potential advantage of allowing the central bankers to operate with enough discretion to
pursue short-run stabilization objectives. However, an optimal contract is one
that simultaneously achieves its stabilization objectives, optimally weighing the
short-run volatility in output and employment against price instability, while
eliminating its long-run inflation bias. In principle, "punishment" of the central
bankers that is based solely on the inflation target could produce an optimal
contract. However, it requires precise knowledge of each central banker's inflation bias and the value of the personal disutility of the "punishment" that the
enforcement provisions carry. Neither is likely to be known with sufficient ac-
curacy to make the optimal contract realistic. Nonetheless, contracts with
performance-based incentives have the potential to reduce the problems of
inflation bias and suboptimality associated with the time inconsistency and
credibility problems inherent in monetary policy design.

18.5   SUMMARY

When households and firms make long-term commitments, the future allocations of their resources are affected. Current decisions therefore must be
forward-looking. Optimal plans for the deployment of resources are premised
on expectations of what the future economic environment is likely to be. Government policy is a part of that economic environment. When the government
alters its policy in the future, the past decisions made in the private sector are
no longer optimal. That is, had the households and firms known that the

---

[7]In the final version of the legislation, the central banker was required to sign a contract
with the government to maintain the inflation rate within a specified target range. If
that inflation target was not met, the central banker could be dismissed. See Walsh
(1995).

government would adopt a new policy, their previous decisions would have reflected that information about the future economic environment and they would have made different resource allocations. Only when the government commits to a future policy are optimal plans not disrupted. Hence, policy makers seeking short-run policy objectives in an uncertain world face a dilemma.

In the context of monetary policy, the short-run policy objectives can be stated as minimizing employment and output fluctuations while maintaining stable prices. When the monetary authority fails to take fully into account the adverse affects of other government distortions, such as taxes on capital income, that could lower the actual full-employment levels of output and employment, or if it complies with political pressure to achieve on average a higher level of employment than is economically feasible, its policy will have an inflation bias. The private sector recognizes the inflation bias and incorporates it into its future plans. In that case, the best the monetary authority can do is to fulfill the private sector's expectations. Otherwise, it will introduce policy shocks to the economy that induce undesired fluctuations in output and employment.

To eliminate inflation bias, monetary policy could be conducted according to a hard-and-fast, publicly announced rule, such as a monetary growth rate rule or the gold standard. However, because a rule could not be written that would cover all future contingencies, discretion would be necessary if short-run policy objectives are to be pursued. If the monetary authority has private information about the shocks the economy is undergoing, the potential gains that a discretionary policy could bring to the economy cannot be realized under a policy regime that essentially eliminates all discretion.

In the absence of a monetary policy governed entirely according to a rule, some reduction in the inflation bias could be achieved by the knowledge that high inflation policies entail a loss of reputation of the central bankers as inflation fighters. Such a loss in reputation reduces the credibility of policy pronouncements, which in turn, reduces the effectiveness of monetary policy. In recognition of that fact, policy makers must avoid high inflation policies over an extended period of time to establish the credibility necessary to conduct an effective policy. The reduction in the inflation bias of monetary policy could be enhanced by the appointment of conservative central bankers whose personal preferences represent a greater aversion to inflation than the public's.

Further inducement to reduce the inflation bias of discretionary monetary policies could be achieved by introducing performance-based incentive clauses in contracts to which central bankers would be required to agree. Performance could be measured by comparing the actual inflation rate with a preannounced target range. Performance-based incentives would constitute an optimal contract if they enabled the monetary authority to exploit its private information on the economy by pursuing short-run stabilization objectives from which society may benefit without simultaneously incurring the inflation bias that is normally created by its lack of credibility. It is not likely that such an optimal contract could be designed, as it would require knowledge of each central banker's inflation bias and personal preferences in relation to the incentives built into the contract. Nonetheless, central banker contracts may provide an intermediate solution to the policy dilemma created by the time inconsistency problem, allowing some policy discretion without causing a private-sector expectation of a substantial inflation bias that the monetary authority would be obliged to fulfill.

■ REVIEW QUESTIONS

1. Time-consistent policies are generally not optimal.
   (a) Define an optimal policy.
   (b) Define a time-consistent policy.
   (c) Explain why optimal policies are generally time inconsistent.

2. The credibility of monetary policy plays an essential role in how effective the policy is likely to be.
   (a) Why do optimal monetary policies that have short-run stabilization objectives inherently lack credibility?
   (b) Why might the pursuit of an output or employment objective that exceeds the full-employment level be perceived by both the monetary authority and the public to be an optimal part of the monetary authority's stabilization objectives?
   (c) When the monetary authority attempts to achieve an optimal policy with output objectives as described in (b), what are the likely macroeconomic consequences?

3. Various proposals have been put forth to cope with the perceived inflation bias in discretionary monetary policy.
   (a) Explain how policy rules could alleviate that problem.
   (b) What provisions are necessary in an optimal contract under which the central bankers could conduct a discretionary policy that did not have an inflation bias?
   (c) Discuss alternative feasible contracting provisions that could reduce the inflation bias. Are any of them optimal?

*4. Empirical evidence links an economy's rate of inflation to the central bank's degree of independence in its conduct of monetary policy from the nation's political bodies, such as the executive and legislative branches of government in the United States. That is, the more independence the central bank has in determining monetary policy, the lower is the inflation rate. [Hint: See Alesina and Summers (1993).]
   (a) Explain why that might be true.
   (b) Give examples of countries that conform to the empirical finding. Can you think of any countries that do not?

*5. Until very recently, Argentina had triple-digit inflation for many years. It attempted monetary reforms that involved issuing new currencies, along with a series of other measures such as capital controls that it announced would be followed to reduce inflation.
   (a) Common wisdom holds that economies undergoing rapid disinflation are likely to suffer severe side effects in the form of high unemployment

and low income growth during the early years of the transition. Explain why that perception complicated the attempts at monetary reform introduced by the Argentine government.

(b) One feature of the most recent monetary reform was the pegging of the new Argentine currency to the U.S. dollar at a fixed exchange rate. Discuss how that is likely to have contributed to the success of the policy, which has brought the inflation rate down from triple digits to single digits, when other reforms had failed.

(c) Speculate on the likely response to the most recent monetary reform, both immediately and over time, in the private sector and in the international financial markets.

REFERENCES

Alesina, Alberto, and Lawrence H. Summers. 1993. "Central Bank Independence and Macroeconomic Performance." *Journal of Money, Credit and Banking* 25 (May): 151–62.

Barro, Robert J., and David B. Gordon. 1983. "A Positive Theory of Monetary Policy in a Natural Rate Model." *Journal of Political Economy* 91 (August): 589–610.

Calvo, Guillermo A. 1978. "On the Time Consistency of Optimal Policy in a Monetary Economy." *Econometrica* 46 (6): 1411–28.

Canzoneri, Matthew B. 1985. "Monetary Policy Games and the Role of Private Information." *American Economic Review* 75 (December): 1056–70.

Cukierman, Alex. 1992. *Central Bank Strategy, Credibility, and Independence: Theory and Evidence.* Cambridge, MA: MIT Press.

————————, and Allan H. Meltzer. 1986. "A Theory of Ambiguity, Credibility, and Inflation under Discretion and Asymmetric Information." *Econometrica* 54 (September): 1099–128.

Garfinkel, Michelle R., and Seonghwan Oh. 1993. "Strategic Discipline in Monetary Policy with Private Information: Optimal Targeting Horizons." *American Economic Review* 83 (March): 99–117.

Kydland, Finn E., and Edward C. Prescott. 1977. "Rules Rather than Discretion: The Inconsistency of Optimal Plans." *Journal of Political Economy* 85 (3): 471–91.

Lohmann, Susanne. 1992. "Optimal Commitment in Monetary Policy: Credibility Versus Flexibility." *American Economic Review* 82 (March): 273–80.

Rogoff, Kenneth. 1985. "The Optimal Degree of Commitment to an Intermediate Monetary Target." *Quarterly Journal of Economics* 100 (November): 1169–89.

Stein, Jeremy C. 1989. "Cheap Talk and the Fed: A Theory of Imprecise Policy Announcements." *American Economic Review* 79 (March): 32–42.

VanHoose, David D. 1992. "Optimal Choice of Monetary Policy Instruments When Policymaking Is Costly." *Journal of Economics and Business* (forthcoming).

Waller, Christopher J. 1992. "The Choice of a Conservative Central Banker in a Multisector Economy." *American Economic Review* 82 (September): 1006–12.

Walsh, Carl E. 1995. "Optimal Contracts for Central Bankers." *American Economic Review* 85 (March): 150–67.

Author Index

Abraham, Katherine, 276fn1, 315fn8
Alesina, Alberto, 318fn18, 376

Barro, Robert J., 170fn1, 367fn2
Baumol, William, 46fn4
Benhabib, Jess, 256fn8
Bernanke, Ben, 95fn6, 153fn18
Bernhardt, Dan, 97fn7
Black, Fischer, 18fn19, 123fn1
Blinder, Alan S., 303fn6
Boyd, John H., 124fn3
Broaddus, Alfred, 338fn11
Brunner, Karl, 14fn12, 153fn19, 285fn12

Calvo, Guillermo A., 364fn1
Canzoneri, Matthew B., 367fn3, 371fn5
Cargill, Thomas F., 148fn10
Cho, Jang-Ok, 220fn2
Clower, Robert, 3fn1, 311fn1
Cooley, Thomas F., 220fn2, 317fn12
Cosimano, Thomas F., 343fn13
Cukierman, Alex, 313fn6, 315fn9,
    318fn16, 367fn3, 371fn5
Cunningham, Steven R., 51fn10

Davis, Steven J., 2315fn8
Diamond, Douglas W., 90fn2, 95fn6,
    110fn4, 124fn3
Drazen, Allan, 318fn18
Dybvig, Phillip, 110fn4

Eden, Benjamin, 220fn2
Edwards, Sebastian, 318fn16
Eichenbaum, Barry, 153fn18

Fama, Eugene, 123fn1
Feinman, Joshua, 126fn4
Fischer, Stanley, 245fn1
Fisher, Irving, 75fn1
Friedman, Benjamin, 324fn1
Friedman, Milton, 19fn21, 45fn3,
    116fn13, 145fn1, 145fn3, 153fn19,
    153fn20, 277fn3, 284fn10, 311fn5

Garcia, Gillian G., 148fn10
Garfinkel, Michelle R., 371fn4
Gertler, Mark, 95fn6
Goldenweiser, Emmanuel Alexandrovich,
    145fn1
Goodfriend, Marvin, 163fn41, 338fn11
Gordon, David B., 367fn2
Grandmont, Jean Michel, 219fn1, 311fn1
Gray, Jo Anna, 245fn1
Green, Jerry, 175fn6
Greenwood, Jeremy, 256fn6

Hamburger, Michael J., 75fn1
Hansen, Gary D., 317fn12
Hercowitz, Zvi, 256fn6
Hester, Donald, 58fn18
Hoover, Kevin D., 16fn17, 199fn1,
    277fn2
Horvath, Michael T. K., 199fn2

Imrohoroglu, Ayse, 318fn14, 318fn15
Ireland, Peter N., 18fn19, 51fn10,
    58fn18, 220fn2, 318fn19

James, H., 153fn18
James, John A., 145fn1, 145fn3, 146fn5,
    147fn7, 148fn10
Jansen, Dennis W., 343fn13

Katz, Lawrence, 276fn1, 315fn8
Keynes, John M., 155
King, Robert G., 18fn19, 140fn17,
    203fn5, 220fn2
Kiyotaki, Nobuhiro, 15fn14
Kydland, Finn E., 170fn1, 199fn1,
    364fn1

Lacker, Jeffrey M., 95fn6
Leeper, Eric M., 210fn9
Lilien, David M., 276fn1, 315fn8
Lohmann, Susanne, 371fn4
Long, John B., 199fn1, 206fn7
Loungani, Prakash, 276fn1, 315fn8

Subject Index